The Light of Other Days

Denis Rogers

Clachan
Publishing

3 Drumavoley Park, Ballycastle, BT54 6PE,
Glens of Antrim.

Clachan Publishing
3 Drumavoley Park, Ballycastle, BT54 6PE,
Glens of Antrim.

Email: info@clachanpublishing.com
Website: http://clachanpublishing-com.

This edition published 2017
Available at clachanpublishing.com

ISBN - 978-1-909906-42-6

Copyright © Denis Rogers & Clachan Puplishing 2017

This book is sold under the condition that it is not sold, by way of trade or otherwise, be lent, resold, hired out or in otherwise circulated without the publisher's prior consent in any form of binding or cover other than that in which it is published and without similar condition, including this condition, being imposed on the subsequent purchaser.

Table of Contents

About the author iii
Map of Ireland iv
PROLOGUE v
CHAPTER 1 - Returning to Doe Castle 1
CHAPTER 2 - The Hill of Aileach 18
CHAPTER 3 - A banquet in Enniskillen castle 29
CHAPTER 4 - The Falls of Assaroe 44
CHAPTER 5 - *Brookeborough Raid* 60
CHAPTER 6 - A Gallowglass captain 65
CHAPTER 7 - Maguire expels England's Sheriff 79
CHAPTER 8 - Maeve O'Rourke 92
CHAPTER 9 - Ambush at the Ford of Belleek 103
CHAPTER 10 - Red Hugh returns to Donegal 118
CHAPTER 11 - Story of a Daring escape 123
CHAPTER 12
    Red Hugh is elected O'Donnell Chieftain   129
CHAPTER 13 - Battle of Atha Culainn 139
CHAPTER 14 - *Enniskillen* 143
CHAPTER 15 - Dunvegan in Skye 154
CHAPTER 16 - The Spanish Armada 166
CHAPTER 17 - Plotting rebellion 180
CHAPTER 18
    Desecration of Rathmullen and Tory monasteries 186
CHAPTER 19 - Battle of the Yellow Ford 194
CHAPTER 20 - *Bloody Sunday* 205
CHAPTER 21 - Capture 214
CHAPTER 22 - The O'Reilly fortress 225
CHAPTER 23 - Battle of the Curlews 240
CHAPTER 24 - *The Orange and the Green* 254
CHAPTER 25 - Death of Maguire 282
CHAPTER 26 - A Birth 289
CHAPTER 27 - A Hostage 296
CHAPTER 28 - A Betrayal 303
CHAPTER 29 - *A Peace Proposal* 315
CHAPTER 30
    1798 Rebellion. "Who fears to speak of '98 318

CHAPTER 31 - A devastated land 328
CHAPTER 32 - A Spanish army in Ireland 335
CHAPTER 33 - March to the final battle 342
CHAPTER 34 - Nial Garve's revenge..................................... 347
CHAPTER 35 - *Famine* 353
CHAPTER 36 - Preparation for battle 372
CHAPTER 37 - *A new life in Old Quebec*................................ 376
CHAPTER 38 - Kinsale and the Final Battle 392
EPILOGUE 396

About the author

Denis Rogers is a native of Belleek, Co Fermanagh, Northern Ireland. He left Ireland in the late 1950s and served as a navigator for six years in the Royal Canadian Air Force. After returning to Ireland he attended Galway University and qualified as a Doctor. He then went back to Canada and settled eventually in Sechelt, British Columbia, where he has practised as a GP for over forty years. His wife, Agatha, is a native of Co. Galway, and he has three sons – David, Michael and John.

Denis's love for his native land shines through every page of *The Light of Other Days*. He writes about an area in West Fermanagh, South Donegal, Leitrim, Cavan and Sligo with which he would have had intimate knowledge as a young boy and teenager growing up in the area. His knowledge of Irish History is unsurpassed and his prose has a lovely lyrical quality not frequently encountered in a first-time novelist. He tells a great story and his dialogue has a humour, an authenticity and a ring of truth that makes the narrative entirely credible.

Front cover is a modified image courtesy of Barry Kieran.

Map of Ireland

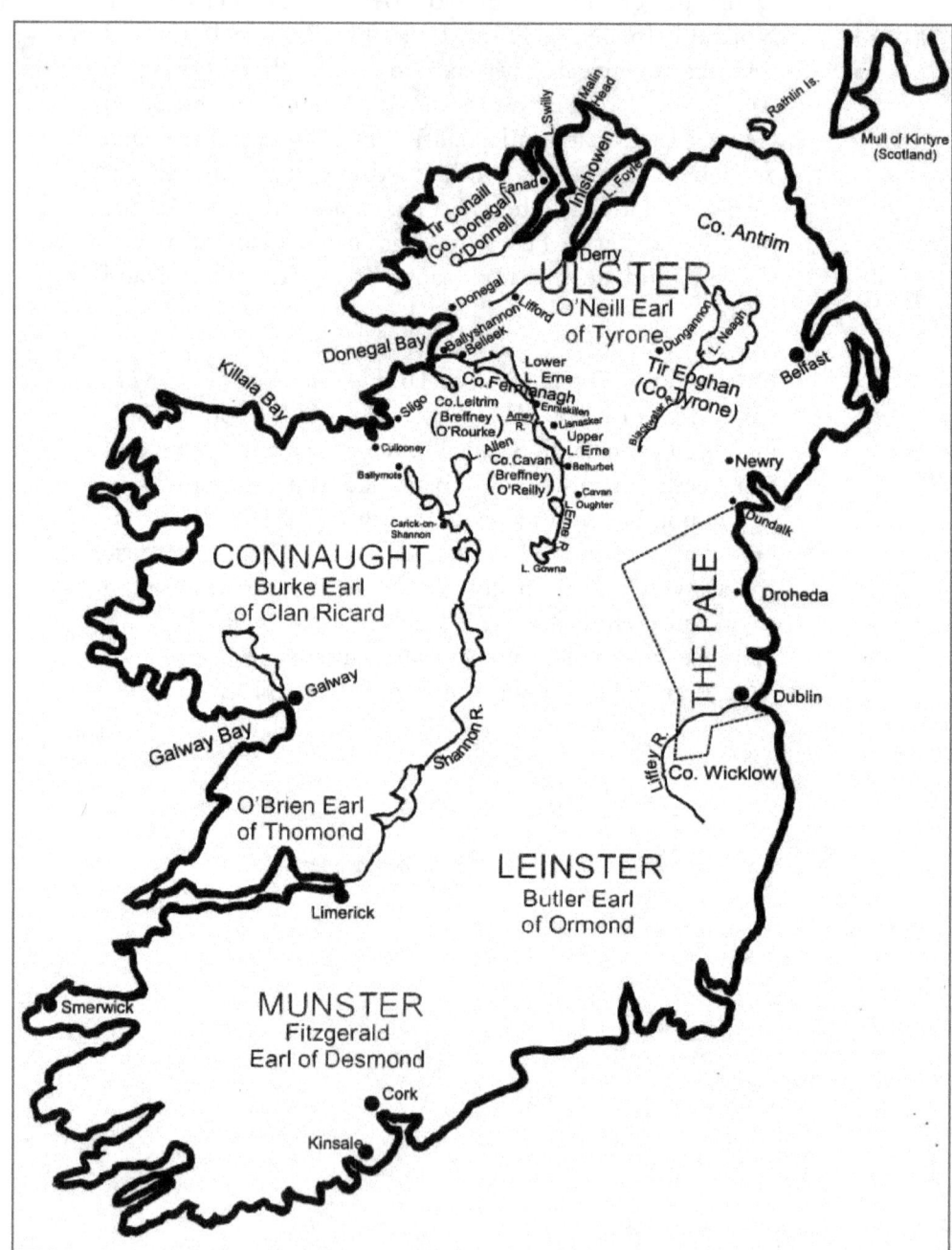

PROLOGUE

Oft in the stilly night, ere slumber's chains have bound me,
Fond memory brings the light of other days around me.

Thomas Moore

"*Memento homo quia pulvis es, et in pulverem reverteris.*" - "Remember man that thou art dust and unto dust thou shalt return." The doleful peal of the bell punctuated the sonorous voice of the Cardinal of Spain who spoke the mournful words.

In the coffin the earthly remains of Red Hugh O'Donnell. The noble dust of a Tir Conaill[1] prince, whose family traced its ancestry back to an Iberian king, had returned to the dust of Spain. The tolling bell sounded a requiem for the last of Ireland's great Gaelic chieftains, prince leaders of their clan, warriors, and poets, brave and brutal in battle, generous and courteous in council, wily and rapacious, cultured, noble and refined, personal courage an expected attribute and seldom lacking. The final peal of the bell was the last farewell to a way of life stretching back into the mists of memory.

Much departed with that lifeless body. Much was lost. With him departed a way of life that was wild, glorious, and free; gone the bright spirit; gone the hope of a people; gone the dream of a nation; the leader, resourceful and brave, now dust in his coffin; the voice, uplifting in battle, silenced forever; for the captain, no victory; for the soldier, no brave death in battle; for the patriot, no tomb midst his fathers; he, who would never accept defeat, vanquished and dead – but to live for ever in Ireland's memory.

If the sightless eyes could see down the future, would they weep to see how much had really been lost in that last battle, how much was yet to be lost? Would the soul of *Tir Conaill's* prince, in ceaseless sorrow, return to sigh an eternal moaning dirge on the wild Atlantic winds of Inishowen?

---

[1] *Tir Conaill*, (Irish) "Country of Conaill", present-day Donegal.

The gallowglass[1], Turlough MacRory, stood bareheaded and weaponless. His face was that of a soldier. A scar ran diagonally across his forehead up into his black hair. From the hairline, the thin linear streak of white hair that extended to the top of his head betrayed the full length of the scar. His nerveless right arm hung at his side.

The survivor of many an O'Donnell battle, his scars, and hardships were written on his face; his cloak hid those on his body. Weary sadness dulled his eyes. Twelve years of unceasing warfare in Ireland had marked him with the mien of a man who had seen too much horror. He was thirty years of age, the same age as O'Donnell. As a gallowglass, he had stood many times in the *bearna baoil* – the gap of danger – protecting his chieftain.

Gall Óglaig! Neither his name nor his race was foreign to the country in which he had fought. O'Donnell was not his lawful chieftain, but no assassin could have reached O'Donnell unless he had first killed his gallowglass.

"*In nomine patris* ..." With the thumb of his left hand he imitated the Cardinal, and inscribed a small cross on his forehead, "... *et filii* ..." on his lips, "... *et spiritus santi*" on his chest.

An assassin had, however, reached Red Hugh. The *Sassenach's*[2] weapon had reached out and found him in exile. Hugh Roe O'Donnell, Prince of *Tír Conaill*, last of Ireland's Gaelic chieftains, had died of poison.

A brown-robed Franciscan stood beside the Spanish cardinal. A vague guilt gnawed and mingled with his grief, though neither emotion reached his composed ascetic features. At forty-two years of age, Father O'Mulconry was many things – a scholar, a patriot, a confidante of the Spanish Church Hierarchy, an emissary of Pope Clement VIII sent to aid the Catholic Irish in their rebellion against Protestant England. A native of Galway, and educated on the continent, he was the Provincial of the Franciscans in Ireland. Fourteen years earlier in 1588, he had sailed with the Spanish Armada on their disastrous expedition to conquer England. His

---

[1] Gallowglass; in Irish, Gall Óglaig, "Foreign warrior".
[2] *Sassenach*, "English" or "Saxon".

friendship with O'Donnell spanned most of the dead man's short life.

There had been rumours that an English agent, James Blake, operated in Spain with the intent of neutralizing O'Donnell's influence there. The thought tortured Father O'Mulconry's mind. Could he have been more vigilant? The manner of O'Donnell's death suggested that he should have been. He, too, had accompanied O'Donnell in his exile and would accompany his earthly remains to their final resting-place at the Franciscan monastery in Valladolid.

CHAPTER 1

Returning to Doe Castle

The Isle of Skye, dim in the mist and the twilight, fell low on the horizon astern. A veil of evening cloud to seaward parted briefly and the last rays of a winter sun slanted a wan light across the bleak slopes of Barra to starboard. The cloud stole back to shroud the dying sun, and once again sea, land, and sky merged in the muted shades of the gathering dusk.

The boat left the channel between the Inner and Outer Hebrides heading south. A following wind, carrying the chill bite of the northern seas, pressed the small craft into the grey heaving swells of the Atlantic. The high-raking prow of the boat, a clinker-built Hebridean birlinn, cleaved the waves with the same haughty ease of her precursor, the Viking long ship. Seven hundred years earlier, the ominous silhouette would have set watch-fires blazing from Tiree to Mull to Islay to Kintyre – the fires on Kintyre, about sixteen miles from Rathlin off the Irish Coast, to warn the Celtic kin there that the Norse marauders were on the sea. Or perhaps some chieftain in Kintyre, having formed a new alliance with a Viking Jarl, would have stayed the hand that reached to set the watch fire on the headland, and in the early dawn, the monks on Rathlin would be dealt red death by the merciless sparth-axe of the Norse, never knowing of their kinsman's treachery.

The boat had been modified with a small deck forward and another aft. Beneath the forward deck was a small cabin. The boat was steered with a tiller from the aft deck and was powered by sail and oars, fifteen oars to each side and two men to each oar. Now with a following wind the oars were stowed inboard and the oarsmen mingled with others of the crew. Banks of seats for the oarsmen lined both sides of the inner hull.

One man flanked by two boys stood on the forward deck. The man stared upward, following the flight of a wedge of Northern geese that had come up from the sky behind and passed overhead, their mournful calls drifting back across the darkening sky.

MacSweeney stood impervious to cold, feet braced against the motion of the boat, squinting to keep in focus the small brown specks as they disappeared toward the south. He spoke enviously to the sky.

"What freedom! That same wind that drives us through these clinging waves speeds them effortlessly on. They follow their paths in the sky, charted by the ghosts of their past generations."

He dropped his gaze to the open water ahead in the direction of the North Irish coast. Home and his castle of Doe were still a night's sailing away.

"O'Doherty, there!"

The boy on MacSweeney's left flinched at the sudden bellow. MacSweeney's powerful voice carried aft to the master standing by the helmsman.

"Keep sail on her throughout the night and with this wind we'll be off Malin Head at dawn."

O'Doherty waved an acknowledgement and shouted something back, but his voice was carried away in the wind.

On Eoghan MacSweeney's election to the chieftainship of the MacSweeneys of Doe, neighbouring septs in *Tir Conaill* had jostled each other to test the young chieftain whom they considered more poet than warrior. In MacSweeney's lifetime they would not repeat the error. Nor would it have been of much consolation to those rash neighbours, still smarting from the swift vehemence of MacSweeney's retribution, to know that the warrior heart that beat beneath the breastplate bearing the MacSweeney crest of two crossed battleaxes, was indeed the heart of a poet.

To the right of MacSweeney stood a boy of ten years or so. His happy face was pushed forward into the spray and wind. When the ship's bow plunged into a wave and a sheet of drenching spray lashed across the deck on which he stood, he laughed in defiance. The cold seawater did nothing to dampen his animation. His long red hair lifting from his shoulders was carried out like a banner on the wind. His cloak, too, fluttered like an unsheeted sail, affording him little protection from the elements, but he did not seem to care greatly. This cloak – velvet lined and richly embroidered, pinned on the right shoulder with a Celtic clasp of intricate design – seemed strangely out of place compared with the clothing of the others, not however, out of place on the boy who wore it. The son of Hugh

Duv O'Donnell, Lord of *Tir Conaill*, this boy, Red Hugh, was born to lead and was already a born leader.

At the foot of a gangway which led to the forward deck, stood about twenty men, distinguishable from the crew by their large size and by their dress. These men were gallowglass, elite mercenary soldiers from Scotland's western isles, and there was the hint of a shared characteristic of feature between them and the other boy on MacSweeney's left. Their blood was Gall/Gael, a mixture of the original Gaelic inhabitants of the isles intermingled with the Norse. They were renowned for a warrior ethos and ferocity in battle. Each gallowglass wore a conical steel helmet and chain-mail armour over a padded woollen garment that reached to his knees. Below the knees his legs were bare. His feet were shod in leather sandals. Each was armed with a claymore, a large broadsword slung in a sheath across his back, the hilt projecting above the shoulder. When not in battle this heavy weapon would be carried by an accompanying servant but MacSweeney insisted that whenever the heir to The O'Donnell was present his escort of gallowglass be armed at all times wearing helmet, chain mail, and sword. The claymore, when wielded with the expertise of the gallowglass, was a fearsome weapon that inflicted a fearsome wound. In battle they sometimes carried a targe, a small circular shield of wood covered with tough oxide and with a central metal boss. The targe was attached to the forearm.

A greater number of men stood apart from the gallowglass. These men wore no protective armour. They were clothed in *leine*, *inar*, and *brat*. The *leine* was a linen shirt-like garment that reached to below the knee; the *inar* was a woollen jacket reaching to the hips and the *brat* a simple unadorned cloak. Their legs and feet were bare. In battle these servants or kerns, usually two to each gallowglass, would carry any extra weapons for their masters and procure and cook his food. Thirty oarsmen, their appearance and dress indistinguishable from that of the kerns, completed the crew.

MacSweeney, too, carried a weapon – not the claymore, but a short-handled version of that feared weapon of his Norse forebears, the sparth axe. This he carried attached at his waist to a broad leather belt. His prowess with this, his favourite weapon, was legendary. "MacSweeney of the Battleaxe" he was called. It was said that he preferred this short-handled modification as he wished to be close enough to see into the eyes of his enemy. MacSweeney gestured toward the west where the dying sun, in a last paroxysm of splendour, pierced the darkening sky with shafts of golden light and burnished a flaming arc across the rim of the ocean.

"Look there, Hugh. Is that not a glorious sight? A golden sky reaching down to a golden ocean. Is it any wonder that we are always drawn to the West as the land of our dreams? In the sixth century Saint Brendan voyaged far beyond that horizon and discovered new lands. The Norse, in their sagas, speak of discovering, four centuries later, a land out there, which they called Vinland the Good. It may have been the same land that a man called Cabot found nearly a hundred years ago now. Do you think, Hugh," MacSweeney's chuckle welled up from deep in his chest, "that they may have found *Tir na nÓg*, the 'Land of Eternal Youth'?"

O'Donnell's eyes glistened as he looked up at MacSweeney.

"Wouldn't it be the greatest thing to sail into the west and discover a new land?" The elation trailed off to be replaced with a note of rueful reproach as he continued to look up at MacSweeney. "If there's any left to find. Of course, I myself have never been allowed farther west than Tory Island."

"Not for the want of trying. You were five years old when the *Shanachie*[1] first told you the story of how Ossian was wafted on his steed across the ocean to *Tir na nÓg*. A few days later we found you urging your pony toward Horn Head and the land of eternal youth! Your steed, however, wasn't as eager to make that leap of faith as was its rider. But the *Shanachie* had already taken you there.

"*Tir na nÓg* is a realm of the mind. We lose something, Hugh, something that is lost forever, when somewhere along life's journey we stop seeing with the eyes of a child. Would that we could walk through our lives looking out on the world as we did in our childhood; our souls, forged in heaven, still bright from the furnace; our spirits aglow; our hearts aflame. Where is the glory that can ever replace those lost shining years? Only cold ashes of memory remain. I, too, remember how the *Shanachie* breathed life into the story of Ossian[2].

---

[1] Shanachie, (Irish) "Storyteller", "guardian of lineage".
[2] Ossian, mythical Irish hero.

"I wandered heart-thrilled with Ossian through *Tir Na nÓg*, and eventually after three hundred years, I too shared with him the longing to again revisit *Éireann*. Like him, I solemnly nodded my understanding that my foot must not touch the soil of *Éireann* or I would immediately become an old, old man and suffer death. I was behind Ossian on his white horse when he reached down to help some men of *Éireann* who struggled to move a mighty boulder, an easy task for Ossian! When his saddle girth broke, I gasped and reached – too late – to prevent him from falling to the ground. I stared in horror as his flesh shrivelled away before my eyes."

Red Hugh peered around MacSweeney's bulk to address the other boy.

"In the Isles you have the same legends of *Tir na nÓg*, do you not, MacRory?"

Not only was there none of the animation of his companion in this boy's appearance but there was a dejected stillness that suggested the silent endurance of a hurt animal. He had been staring back toward the Hebrides, turned and in answer merely nodded his head. His shoulder-length, black hair blew around his face. He shivered, either from the cold or from his thoughts, and Red Hugh felt ashamed that he himself felt so elated while this boy suffered his memories.

In a gesture totally in keeping with his nature, Red Hugh unfastened the silver and gold Celtic brooch that pinned his cloak at his shoulder, and with a nod toward the boy, handed the cloak to MacSweeney. MacSweeney hesitated, but only briefly, before draping the cloak around the other boy's shoulders. By the custom of fosterage, MacSweeney was father and mentor to Red Hugh, with a father's authority, but already the will of the young chieftain was not readily brooked. The gesture of kindness was met with a brief look of gratitude from the boy's blue eyes, before they turned away again to look at the Hebrides. The act of kindness offered to one in such a deep, emotional abyss resonated in the boy at some subconscious level. A small kindness, but for a young man, heir to a powerful chieftain, to give his cloak to an orphan boy might not be regarded as any small gesture. Perhaps here was the beginning of the bond that would last a lifetime for each.

The lingering twilight faded to darkness. The Hebrides sank on the horizon astern to finally merge with the blackness of the sea. MacSweeney turned to Red Hugh. "Do you wish to go below,

Hugh? O'Doherty can probably keep the ship pointing at Ireland whether we're on deck or not."

He turned to the other boy.

"There's a fire in the cabin below, MacRory. At this time of year the north wind blows bitter at night, and there's little warmth in that linen clothing you're wearing."

"Do you mind if I remain on deck for another while?" The question was addressed to O'Donnell.

The language each spoke was readily intelligible to the other. Red Hugh, speaking Irish, was quite familiar with the Scots Gaelic the boy spoke. There were dialectic differences, with which Red Hugh, through frequent contact with MacSweeney's gallowglass, was familiar.

One thousand years had passed since the Irish Dalriada had left Ireland to form a kingdom in the Western Isles and west coast of Scotland. It was from these Irish, whom the Romans called *Scoti*, that Scotland got its name. North-East Ulster was still closer to western Scotland in sentiment and distance than it was to Dublin.

MacSweeney, too, was familiar with both Irish and Scots Gaelic. Nearly three hundred years earlier a MacSweeney ancestor, Murchadh Mear[1], had left Castle Sween in Scotland and sailed into Lough Swilly. Initially gallowglass to the O'Donnells, the MacSweeneys were now chieftains in *Tir Conaill* with land grants from the O'Donnells, and two other branches of the family had castles at Fanad and Banagh. The warrior blood of his ancestors flowed in the veins of Eoghan MacSweeney, who now ruled at Doe, in the manner of those ancestors; making war on his enemies and hosting his guests, yesterday's bitter enemy, often today's honoured guest.

His mission to the Hebrides had been to Rory MacRory of North Uist to recruit gallowglass to serve with the O'Donnells and MacSweeneys in Ireland. But Rory MacRory and two of his sons had died at the hand of a MacDonald one week before MacSweeney and Red Hugh's arrival; the boy on deck, Turlough MacRory, was the only surviving member of that family. He returned with

---

[1] (Irish) "Mad Martin".

MacSweeney to Ireland caring not where, nor indeed whether, he lived.

Below, warming himself before a small fire, MacSweeney, speaking quietly to Red Hugh so as not to be heard by the boy above their heads, told some of the history of the MacRorys.

"They were of the MacDonalds or the MacDonalds were of them. The MacRorys trace their ancestry back to Sorley, Lord of the Isles, and back beyond that to Ulster and the mists of legend.

"When the Norse raiders broke on Ireland and Scotland six hundred years ago, these war-like invaders, after a century of warfare, overran the Hebrides, making themselves masters of the Western Isles. These isles became known as *Inse Gall*, the islands of the Norse or foreigner. The MacRorys of the Isles were one of the clans whose blood mingled, first in battle and later in lineage, with the Norse invaders.

"The blood of that boy up there is as much *Gall*[1] as Gael, which should make him useful with the sword. When Sorley, himself part Norse, finally defeated the Norse in the 1100s, he became King of Argyle and the Islands. The MacRorys of the Isles, once a powerful clan, destroyed themselves in constant feuding. Pride! They lie proud in the grave. They say the proud man's grave is as cold as the humble man's. Is there a lesson in that somewhere, Hugh?"

The reply came without hesitation. "While the blood runs warm in your veins, live proud, and die with your wounds in front, for the grave chills the blood of all men."

MacSweeney, whose question had been rhetorical, gave his young protégé a sidelong glance. "Certainly one way of looking at it, but perhaps not what I had in mind, Hugh. In any event, with centuries of warfare, first against the Norse and later among each other, they breed good fighters. A MacRory fought alongside Robert the Bruce at Bannockburn and a MacRory died with Edward Bruce, brother of Robert, at Faughart in Ireland. The boy's great-great grandfather, Alain MacRory, ran afoul of his king and was executed in the king's presence.

---

[1] (Irish) "Foreigner"

As you are aware, many of the name are gallowglass for Maguire in Ireland, some also for O'Donnell and O'Rourke.

The boy's life was in danger in the Isles and I owed it to his father to help. He has MacRory kin with Maguire's gallowglass in Ireland."

Dark night had fallen on a black sea. Dark memories, unwanted and unbidden, flitted through the mind of the boy on deck, memories that kept stealing back like grim ghosts of a nightmare. Often in the past week he had been forced to relive the memories, each time raw and searing as before. Unbidden, the flames kept leaping up in his mind. The smells returned to his nostrils. The smell of smoke had awakened him and brought him outside the barn, where he slept to care for a sick horse, into the arms of his family's murderers. The smell of burning flesh – the flesh of his father and brothers.

Screams from the house mingled with the obscene jeering of the men who held him in the light of the flames and forced him to watch. The flames dancing on the hard demonic faces – the flames that consumed his family – he saw again through tightly closed eyes. He heard the crackling flames, heard again the screams and jeers as the roaring pile of thatched roof collapsed inward and the flames leaped higher accompanied by a shower of sparks. The enemy had prepared carefully, piling hay at each door and window, and setting it alight.

When he heard the screams come closer, he had opened his eyes. His father had burst from the house like a burning pyre to be dispatched with a jeering sword thrust by Alistair MacDonald. His father was the luckiest of the family, luckier than his two sons who continued to scream, luckier than the son thrown aside with a contemptuous kick as his family's killers mounted and rode off.

Alistair had reined in his horse to call back to him.

"We'll let you live for a while yet till you're old enough to be worth killing."

Perhaps they thought he would suffer more by being left alive. Alistair MacDonald knew about such things. No thought of revenge came to the boy's mind. The enormity of the crime seemed such as to be left to God.

From his earliest years he had been exposed to the endless feuds that were a way of life on the islands. He had heard tales of the savagery of these feuds, but his mind recoiled in horror from the savagery that now visited his own family. He knew of the feuding between his family and the MacDonalds. His father had killed Ranald MacDonald, brother of Alistair, both men meeting with swords. His own mother had been a MacDonald, and although close kin to Alistair MacDonald, she was also as far removed from him as heaven from hell. She had died a year earlier, and from heaven would watch with sorrow as her brutish kinsman forged his unerring path to hell.

It was said that he, Turlough, took after his mother. Thoughts of her seemed to soothe his torment and he tried to think back to her. He tried to dwell on her gentleness and serenity in the hope that it would ease his torment.

In the Western Isles the cult of the fighting man, the result of centuries of strife, was all-pervasive. He had instinctively gravitated toward his mother, and she had sensed and seen a gentler nature in her youngest son. But with a certain sadness she had also seen in him something else. Some part of him was different and unreachable, living in another world. He walked alone, and from infancy had met his challenges alone. She ached to enter that world, to walk beside him, to share, to console, and to tell him that he was not alone in his alien world. As a child, he never cried and when hurt; he did not seek solace from others, but retired to lick his wounds in solitude. His eyes, and her instinct, told her of his love but he could neither articulate nor otherwise express it. He had an unusual affinity with animals, and seemed to relate more to them than to humans.

She tried to protect him from the harsh and brutal life on those islands – a life his older brothers and his father cheerfully embraced. Turlough still grieved her death of nearly a year ago, but he solaced his grief by visiting her in his mind. There would be no such haven where he could revisit his father and brothers, no memories of the gruff, protective love of his father, nor the chiding, competitive life with his unruly brothers. Any memories of them would always be those last memories. It would be some years before he finally succeeded in banishing his father and brothers from him.

The Hebrides and his home were hidden in the darkness astern and all around only the dark, impartial, heaving sea. He found himself shivering, this time from the night cold. He noticed some of the gallowglass sheltering beneath the forward deck peering curiously through the gloom at him. He clutched the rich cloak more tightly around himself and quietly descended to the warm cabin.

Voices above his head awoke MacRory. He emerged from the cabin and found MacSweeney, on deck staring at a low shoreline ahead and perhaps five miles off to larboard. The boat pitched and rolled in huge white capped swells as during the night the wind had risen to gale force. MacSweeney, distaining the steps that led down from the forward deck, leaped into the waist of the boat and lurched toward the aft deck, his broad bulk careening into a gallowglass who was slow in getting out of his way. He frowned at the man as he passed and growled,

"Where's your sword?"

The man muttered something as he reached under the aft deck, retrieving his sword from where it lay and sheathed the sword left-handed.

"What's wrong here, O'Doherty?" MacSweeney demanded of the ship's master on the aft deck. "You've sailed these waters all your life. Are we off course?"

"Aye, we are. That island up there shouldn't be there. It's too big to be Inishtrahull and if it's Rathlin we're way off course to the east. It can't be Tory for I know Tory well. The compass must be off." The master's voice was gruff with embarrassment. He glared at the instrument that had tarnished his reputation. "I got one brief glimpse of the twins [*stars- Castor and Pollux*] when the clouds parted during the night and I did indeed think that they were too far to the right for that time of night. I should have paid more attention and not trusted this damn newfangled gadget. Now that it's daylight and we don't need the cursed thing, of course, to shame me, it's reading right".

As the dawn lightened further and as they sailed closer to the coast of Ireland, the unmistakable shape of Rathlin Island became apparent removing all doubt as to their position. They must be at least fifty miles to the east of their course, as Rathlin was some forty miles from Malin Head, their proposed landfall and Sheephaven a further twenty miles to the west of Malin. During the darkness they had sailed away to the east of their course toward the North Antrim coast, away from O'Donnell lands and toward the territory of Sorley Boy MacDonnell.

"Perhaps Sorley Boy will invite us to a banquet," MacSweeney grunted as he looked at the young O'Donnell who had joined him on the deck.

Shane, son of Conn O'Neill, first Earl of Tyrone and uncle of the present Hugh O'Neill, second Earl of Tyrone, fled from the O'Donnells whose territory he had rashly invaded and sought sanctuary with his erstwhile enemies, the MacDonnells. At a banquet near Cushendun, perhaps remembering Shane's earlier slaughter of their family in remote Glenshesk, perhaps as the result of a regrettable word – which he did not long live to regret – perhaps by prior design, the MacDonnells murdered him. Shane had been in rebellion against the English of the Pale and his pickled head was later presented to Dublin. For months afterward the skull, impaled over the city's North gate, grinned a macabre rictus of death as the empty eye sockets stared sightlessly back towards Ulster. The incident made McDonnell hospitality a byword. "To banquet with Sorley Boy" became synonymous with living dangerously indeed.

Ahead, the rising sun's rays slanted on the rock-bound northern coast of Ireland and on a distant castle. The castle, perched on a cliff high above the sea and gilded by the rising sun, presented a surreal appearance. This, Dunluce Castle, had been built centuries earlier by the Norman knight, De Burgh, and was now held by the English. Not only was the castle perilously close to a sheer cliff, it was perilously close to Sorley Boy MacDonnell, the restless and acquisitive chieftain of the MacDonnell Scots of North Antrim.

While those aboard stared shoreward at the castle, Red Hugh O'Donnell glanced to the left and put a hand on MacSweeney's arm. A large, two-masted ship had materialized from Rathlin Island and was bearing toward them. MacSweeney stared for some minutes in its direction before speaking to the ship's master. The crew, urged on by curses from an unhappy O'Doherty, hauled on lines, and set the ship surging on a broad reach toward Malin Head and O'Donnell country. MacSweeney remained staring astern as the two ships sailed along the inhospitable, cliff-bound North Irish Coast. The coast was indented by two large sea loughs, Lough Foyle, and farther to the west, Lough Swilly.

In a rising sea they sailed past the basalt columns of the Giant's Causeway, past the eerily imposing bastion of Dunluce Castle. They sailed off a coast rich in history and legend. Robert the Bruce had sheltered in a cave on Rathlin Island after his defeat by the English King Edward in 1307. It was in this cave that he reputedly learned the lesson of patience while watching a spider laboriously weave its web.

Eight years ago in 1574 Walter Devereux, the first Earl of Essex, had sent a raiding party under Sir John Norris and the pirate Drake to Rathlin where Sorley Boy had sent the old, the sick, the women, and the children of the MacDonnells for safety. Drake and Norris butchered all on the island. Essex in a dispatch to his queen, Elizabeth, described in detail how his soldiers had sought out "the pretty little ones and their dam." It was said that Sorley Boy raved like a madman on the mainland as he heard their screams across the intervening water, but was impotent to help; if so, the screams must have been loud indeed, and the wind southerly, to carry across the six miles separating Rathlin from the mainland. For this and other similar actions in Ireland, Queen Elizabeth had warmly commended Essex, describing him as "a great ornament of our nobility" and praising him for his vigour in introducing Irish chieftains to English customs.

This body of water separating Scotland from Ireland was the Sea of Moyle, celebrated in Irish legend as the place where King Lir's three daughters, having been turned into swans by a jealous stepmother, were banished for three hundred years. Dunluce Castle itself was a lodestone for Celtic superstition – ghosts were as plentiful and commonplace as living residents. Banshees[1] abounded, and old men frightened young children with stories of their unearthly cries, which were always a harbinger of death. *Silkies* and *Murrughachs*[2] were said to dwell in the sea caverns in the cliff

---

[1] Irish "Fairy Women".
[2] Mermaid-like creatures.

beneath the castle. On nights when the wind from the Moyle drove ghostly veils of cloud across the moon, the long-dead Norman Earl, de Burgh, could be seen patrolling his battlements.

To the east of the castle rose the distant blue-grey hills of Antrim, and beyond, the peaceful land that had never known peace – the ancient land of ancient memories. It was among those hills that a friendless, barefooted slave boy had tended sheep and with gnawing hunger in his belly and an aching loneliness in his heart, had looked eastward across the sea toward his home in Britain. The boy was remembered forever with love as the Apostle of Ireland, while his proud master, Miliuc, was remembered only because Patrick had been his slave. Among those hills Sorley Boy and his McDonnells had murdered Shane O'Neill.

During the night the wind had veered to the north east and now blowing with gale force was bringing huge rolling seas in to smash on the inhospitable shore to larboard. The wind should have favoured the larger, two-masted ship astern, if it was her intention to overhaul them. However, she did not seem to be closing, although both ships maintained the same heading.

As Lough Foyle opened up a few miles ahead, MacSweeney seemed ill at ease. He continued to stare back toward the other ship three to four miles astern. She was certainly not coming closer and might even be falling back. He considered entering the Foyle. The ship astern worried him. The Foyle separated O'Donnell country on the west from Sorley Boy's territory to the east. At the head of the sea lough the territory of the O'Neills stretched southward. The Foyle could be a hazardous haven in the ever-changing sept alliances of sixteenth-century Ireland. He made his decision not to enter the Foyle, but to continue on to the assured safety of his castle in Sheephaven Bay. Perhaps the ship holding astern was a Spaniard, a small carrack or a *nao* on a trading mission to Sorley Boy MacDonnell. She had seemed to materialize from Rathlin, which was presently held by that quarrelsome Scot.

Having committed themselves by crossing the mouth of the Foyle, they sailed along the bleak, sea-scoured coast of the Inishowen Peninsula, a desolate and weary land, battered and seared by millennia of Atlantic waves and wind. Today, too, that shore was storm-tossed and forbidding. Inishowen, although separated by the deep-sea lough of the Swilly from the remainder of O'Donnell country to the west, was held by the O'Dohertys for the

O'Donnells. The powerful O'Donnell sept claimed as their territory all of the northwest and had also at various times over the centuries laid claim to that part of North Connacht known as Breffney-O'Rourke, and even further south into the land of the Clanwilliam Burkes.

MacSweeney closely watching the ship astern, now uttered a hoarse curse. The ship was not only overhauling them, but doing so rapidly. He had no doubt they were in danger and cursed himself for having been duped. He had been cunningly herded beyond any possible safety in the Foyle, herded with the solicitous care of a wolf herding a sheep! With the larger ship astern closing rapidly, it was obvious they would be overhauled long before reaching the safety of either his kinsman's castle at Fanad in the Swilly or his own farther along the coast in Sheephaven.

As the distance between the ships closed steadily, the ship's master, O'Doherty, conferred with MacSweeney. He then took the helm himself and altered course to starboard. They had been steering a course to closely round Malin Head while still keeping clear of the Garvan reefs, but now he steered farther out to sea on a course that would take them further from the headland and seemed to do nothing to lessen their danger.

MacSweeney gestured to his gallowglass, who moved protectively around O'Donnell. He chose one gallowglass, the left-handed one who had previously drawn down his displeasure for being unarmed, to go forward in the bow to keep a look-out. Both ships, heeled over on a broad reach, ploughed through heavy seas, the larger now only a mile or so astern.

The man on the bow shouted back, pointing to something ahead. Off the bow was a small island and even at this distance, a white line of breaking waves was discernable. The ship astern was now so close that they could see armed men, some with swords drawn, lining the rails. The two boys stood together on the aft deck surrounded by gallowglass, watching the larger ship steadily come on astern. O'Donnell had again an animated look of excitement on his face and seemed to enjoy the chase, and MacRory, caught up in the drama, was mercifully freed from his demons.

As the beam wind drove them on toward the island of Inishtrahull, an ominous roar of breaking surf became louder. The boat steered to round the western end of the island. O'Doherty heaved on the helm to bring her dangerously close to the breakers, which foamed, rolling in and retreating on a rock-studded shore. Spray sheeted back from the bow, drenching those aboard. The gallowglass in the bow clung desperately to a stay rope as the *birlinn's* high prow plunged into the breaking seas and he disappeared in the white foam. He reappeared like a Neptune arising from the sea long hair plastered to his face and clinging desperately to the stay. Hundreds of sea birds shrilled an indignant cacophony as this new, grey-winged intruder ploughed through the waves close by their cliff-side perches. A green wall of froth-topped water swept aboard. The wave rolled aft, flooding the open waist of the boat. In a tumult of roaring, breaking waves, they ploughed through the heavy seas under a cliff into calmer seas in the lee of the island.

At a curt word from the master, the sail flapped loosely against the mast and the boat lost way. She lay rolling heavily in the swell, the stout, wooden mast scribing an arc across the morning sky, knee-deep seawater swilling back and forth in the bilge. A raucous cheer rose above the noise of the breaking surf as the pursuing ship surged in on its prey. Their quarry, useless sail flapping, lay waiting to be taken like a dove before a hawk.

The ship astern seemed to shudder and then above the roar of the surf, and drowning out the cheers, came the awful sound of rending timbers as the larger ship disembowelled herself on the reef.

MacSweeney and the master examined the compass, which was again off by thirty degrees, as they sailed down the sheltered waters of Sheephaven Bay within sight of MacSweeney's castle at Doe.

"It's an adventure sailing with you, O'Doherty. First you nearly run us into Rathlin Island in the dark, and then you try to gut us on Inishtrahaul's rocks in broad daylight." MacSweeny placed a hand on O'Doherty's shoulder.

"You knew your way around Inishtrahull well enough when you led that ship onto the reef?"

"Aye,. I know these waters well enough. In another hour with the ebbing tide not even the *birlinn* would have crossed that reef. She has the design of the Viking galley, with a shallow draft for use in the inlets and loughs, but with her broad beam and flexibility, she's also a boat for the open sea."

"You have done old Hugh a favour today, me, and Red Hugh, too. If they had taken him, I'd sooner sup with Sorley Boy than have to face Red Hugh's mother, Ineen Duive[1]."

"Were they Sorley Boy's men then?"

"No they were English, although we'll never prove it, as it's unlikely any man of them survived in that maelstrom. If any did and managed to stagger ashore on Inishowen he wouldn't live long there once your O'Dohertys found out what he'd been up to. They were after Red Hugh. Held hostage in Dublin, the boy would be certain surety for old Hugh's good behaviour. Sorley Boy MacDonnell is capable of many things, but he would not deliver Red Hugh to the English. The boy's mother is a MacDonnell and kin to Sorley Boy. Forty years ago, when the English became alarmed at the increasing power of the Antrim MacDonnells, Sorley Boy himself was held hostage in Dublin Castle, and the English sent a fleet under the command of a James Croft to capture his brother, Colla MacDonnell, on Rathlin. However, it was Colla who captured Croft and held him for ransom to secure Sorley Boy's release. These English of the Pale are becoming bold to again venture so close to O'Donnell lands."

MacSweeney's hand unconsciously strayed to his side, but his battle-axe for once was not there. He leaped down the gangway and retrieved the weapon from where he had placed it beneath the aft deck. His face grim and thoughtful, he joined the two boys.

The gallowglass still clustered around Red Hugh, even though the danger was over and they were safe ashore at Doe. MacSweeney had finally relieved the man from his position at the bow and accompanied him ashore.

"You were without your sword back there."

The words were spoken softly, but the gallowglass knew he was in serious trouble. With the next words he knew he was in mortal danger.

"Was your sword placed beneath the compass by accident or design?" The voice was still soft.

---

[1] (Irish) "Dark daughter".

With a frightening suddenness, the tones and postures changed. MacSweeney stood wide-legged in front of the man, who raised both hands, palms outward, as if pleading for reason.

"MacSweeney, you cannot ..."

Everything about the man's posture gave MacSweeney his answer. Eoghan MacSweeney was a soldier, who had defended himself in many a fray, a man to whom body language was as intelligible as the spoken word. He was especially wary of any man who, protesting his innocence, moved his hand closer to his sword hilt.

In one fluid movement, the man's hands reached over his right shoulder to the haft of his broadsword, the manoeuvre perfected by years of practice, to unsheathe and cleave in one motion. MacSweeney's battle-axe was still on his belt at his waist and to those watching, he was already a dead man.

MacSweeney seemed to move almost leisurely, but as his cupped left hand came up, it struck the other's left elbow with a violence that not only rammed the partially drawn sword back into its sheath, but also lifted the man bodily backward. At the same time MacSweeney's right hand moved downward and backward, returning in a gleaming arc. The gallowglass staggered back, his hands still on his sheathed sword hilt, eyes staring up at the fearsome blade of the sparth axe poised above his face. MacSweeney stared into the man's eyes as he spoke. "You're a brave man to attempt to kill me in the midst of my own gallowglass, for you must have known that your own death would swiftly follow. You'll need all your courage if you fail to answer some questions that I have for you."

MacSweeney ordered the captain of his gallowglass to secure the man before turning away and commenting to Red Hugh. "Unusual for a gallowglass to play false, but then you'll remember from your Latin that there's something sinister about a left handed man."

CHAPTER 2

The Hill of Aileach

The coast of Donegal was indented by many inlets offering varying degrees of shelter from the wild Atlantic without. One such refuge, Sheephaven Bay, was a funnel-shaped inlet in the remote north west of the country. In the farther reaches of the inlet was Doe Castle, built on a promontory that was almost completely surrounded by the sea. In this stark grey-stoned fortress, in this lonely corner of a remote land, in this fitting and spartan aerie for an eaglet, Red Hugh O'Donnell spent his early years, and for five of those years Turlough MacRory was his constant companion. The two boys swam among the seals and otters in the frigid waters of the bay. On horseback and on foot they explored the silent hills, came on hidden dark loughs in the moorland, the secluded haunt of coot, moorhen, teal, loon and mallard. They hunted the wild boar and the wolves in the woods and led their wolf-hounds to mist-veiled mountain glens to hunt the red stag. They drank from the streams that fell down through lichened rocks from pristine upland tarns. They stood on bleak and windswept headlands and stared up with envy at the eagles and hawks that soared above. In the drowsy warmth of August's sun they lay in the scented heather and feasted on handfuls of bilberries. Braving December's chill they tested their predator skills by following the tracks of wolves that followed the tracks of deer through snow-covered mountain passes. They slept at night on straw-filled mattresses in an airy stone vaulted garret, and awoke each morning to the screeching wail of the gulls.

MacRory was allowed no time for his hurt to feed on itself, for morbid rumination to gnaw in the marrow of his soul, for life in MacSweeney's castle was too busy and vital for much introspection. The life of rough companionship, of ready acceptance into a surrogate family, of vigorous and often dangerous endeavour restored him.

Red Hugh's generous spirit reached out in empathy to assuage the aching grief of his new companion. Soon after his arrival at Doe, MacSweeney had decided to send MacRory to his kin who were gallowglass of the Maguires in Fermanagh. But Red Hugh, a force in Sheephaven equal to MacSweeney himself, suggested that MacRory remain at Doe. One, who took exception to this arrangement, was Niall Garve O'Donnell, a cousin of Red Hugh and a sometimes visitor to Doe. On one such visit, and in MacRory's presence, he voiced his opinion.

"This nameless orphan, not noble by birth, has no place among us. He belongs in the gallowglass barracks."

Red Hugh remained silent for some moments, containing his anger. When he replied his carefully worded answer bespoke all that the future chieftain of the O'Donnells was, and all that his cousin was not.

"Many of noble birth are not noble, as is often demonstrated by their manners. Turlough is my friend and my comrade and will remain here in Donegal. His name is MacRory, a name in the Isles as noble as your own, and his manners bring no dishonour on that name." The two young O'Donnells stared at each other, Neil Grave wondering if he had just been insulted, and Red Hugh wondering how his cousin could doubt it.

Thereafter, MacRory, as a friend of Red Hugh, was treated as a member of the MacSweeney household, accorded the same training and education as his well-born companion. He instinctively absorbed the values and conduct of his companions. The spark of friendship and comradeship kindled between the two boys gradually lifted MacRory out of his grief. Initially, looking to Red Hugh as a beacon of light in his night of darkness, MacRory responded later with a fierce and loyal devotion. When the red-haired boy became the O'Donnell chieftain, many were similarly drawn to him.

There could well have been a gulf between the heir to The O'Donnell and the orphan from the Hebrides. O'Donnell's destiny was to rule *Tir Conaill*, as had his family for three centuries before him, absolute in power. O'Donnell's destiny was to send his people to war when he choose, to send his gallowglass, bonnaghts[1], and kerns[2] to their deaths if need be. O'Donnell's destiny was to stand as an equal with the chieftains of the north – the O'Neills, the

---

[1] Native Irish mercenary soldiers.
[2] Irish serfs.

Maguires, the O'Reillys, the O'Rourkes, and the MacMahons. Yet it would still have been unlikely that the princely O'Donnell would have become the friend and companion of MacRory had he not seen in him some of his own well-born manners.

From earliest childhood O'Donnell had listened to the *shanachie's* recitation of lineage. It was an essential part of his education. The *shanachie* was an important personage, the jealous custodian of lineage. He was entrusted, before the widespread use of the written record, with memorizing, not only the lineage of his own chieftain, but also that of others as all the noble families were intertwined through the centuries. The *shanachie* of the O'Donnells could go back one hundred generations. O'Donnell himself would have been aware also of MacRory's lineage, the family originally from Ireland and later Lords in the Western Isles.

Lineage had also to be recognized by the manners that accompanied it. O'Donnell could have shown politeness and kindness to one of his kerns, but could never have related as a companion in the way he did to MacRory. Despite MacRory's destitute situation, he was recognizable to O'Donnell by his manners. These Gaelic chieftains were quite punctilious in the matter of manners. They might insult by design, and by design they often did, but it was considered ill-bred to give insult by accident. In a society of proud people, each prouder than the other, and all armed, manners were a matter of some importance.

MacSweeney's duty was to protect his people and his lands. His duty entailed both pre-emptive and retaliatory raids on neighbouring septs. In sixteenth-century Ireland, foray against one's neighbour was both a duty and a sport. Eoghan MacSweeney, as sportive as any of his neighbours, did his duty with zest, and was a favourable model to his foster son.

The old Gaelic custom of fosterage cemented alliances between noble families. Perhaps it was an evolution and refinement of the still more ancient custom of hostage taking, although that ancient custom was also still practiced. To the one fostered, the foster family became, at least, as close as his own blood family. The MacSweeneys, chieftains under the O'Donnells, had become a powerful force in their own right. The bond of fosterage between the families was not only an honour and recognition of service, but also an important formal binding of alliance between the two families.

MacSweeney ruled at his castle at Doe in the same manner as had three generations of his ancestors. His bard composed poetry and sang creative songs immortalizing his chieftain's exploits in battle and his munificence in the hall. His *shanachie* recited his lineage. His physician had the dangerous task of accompanying him into battle and treating his wounds, as well as administering to his household during the occasional peaceful interludes. His priest ministered to his spiritual well being and periodically gave him absolution for his sins against neighbouring septs, and thus absolved he felt free to sin again with a Gaelic vengeance.

He ruled according to the precepts of Irish Brehon Law. Brehon Law was a huge compendium of custom and precedent codified into law over the centuries, and a class of hereditary judges, called Brehons, interpreted this code of law. The penalty for murder, the relationship of the chieftain to the sept, the responsibilities of fosterage, the treatment of pledges were all dealt with in detail. It dealt also with each and every mundane issue, the issue of one man's goat eating an apple from another man's tree and the issue of one man killing another man's goat. Any man, from prince to the lowest kern, could sue for justice and demand a judgement from the Brehons.

MacSweeny endowed lands to the church – the church that would at his death inter him in his family's vault with all due ceremony. His heir would continue the tradition, strong-holding the territory and trying through war, wile, or shrewd alliance to add to it. A weak successor could expect incursions from all sides. It was usually a priest who educated the young nobles of the household. Among other things they were taught poetry, Latin, English, and some Spanish. They were instructed in the Brehon Law. Celtic myth and legend they absorbed without formal teaching. Other essentials of their education were horsemanship and the use of the sword. At Doe, horsemanship and the use of the two-handed claymore were taught by MacSweeney. Swordsmanship with the new lighter "espada ropera" or "dress sword" was taught by a Spaniard at nearby Fanad, to which Red Hugh and MacRory were frequent visitors. With these chieftains, the past was very much a part of the present – lineage, past alliances, old glories, old defeats and old enmities. Even when they looked to the future, it was with a backward glance to wonder how future generations would regard them. They spoke the Irish language of their forebears.

MacSweeney, as did all of the northern chieftains, maintained a standing army of gallowglass.

The MacSweeneys themselves first came to Ireland as gallowglass from Castle Sween in Argyllshire. They were of Gaelic/Norse origin. Other gallowglass families were the MacDougalls, the MacRorys, the McCabes, and the MacDonnells.

The sixteenth century in Ireland was turbulent, as had been all centuries before. Ireland had long since assimilated the Norman invaders of the twelfth century, and they became Irish in custom and sentiment. They intermarried with the Irish, adopted Irish customs – including the custom of fosterage – and chose to govern by the precepts of Brehon Law. They spoke the Irish language. They became more Irish than the Irish themselves. Only a thin wedge of land around Dublin, known as "The Pale," was English. Beyond the Pale ruled the Gaelic and Norman/Gaelic warlords. Now, to an already volatile fermenting brew were added two new yeasty ingredients – religion and Tudor rule.

The Reformation, first vehemently denounced by, and then advantageously embraced by Henry VIII of England, found little acceptance in Ireland. Henry, and his later successor, Elizabeth, were determined to make Ireland Protestant and to reinforce the waning English influence in Ireland. These English were not a new force, having probed the island for centuries. New was the concerted effort of this determined, able, and united foe.

Each chieftain now eagerly sought how best to position himself in this new swirling dance of changing alliances: O'Donnell against O'Neill, O'Neill allied with the English against O'Donnell, O'Neill, and O'Donnell against the English. Every chieftain gleefully and spiritedly joined in the dance, each adding his own grace steps to the cotillion. There were endless possibilities and each was exploited. The dance had always been exciting, the music rousing. However, both the music and the dance had changed.

MacSweeney, looking out from his stronghold in remote Sheephaven, ruled to the best of his ability, as had his equally capable forefathers. He could not know that he was among the last of his brave breed.

"Here on the hill of Aileach, Turlough, you have the view of a falcon. Off to the north beyond Malin Head are the Atlantic and your Western Isles and Highlands of Scotland. South are the plains of Tir Eoghan, the land of the O'Neills. East and west of Lough Swilly are O'Donnell lands ruled by my father, and beyond Lough Foyle to the east is the land of the MacDonnells, my mother's people.

Over there, six or seven miles away on the far shore of Lough Swilly beyond Inch Island, is Fanad and the Carmelite Priory at Rathmullan. MacSweeney of Fanad brought me here years ago. He told me that if you listen, you will hear the ghosts of the people of Danaan[1] whisper on the wind."

MacRory, standing beside Red Hugh on the ruins of a cashel[2] wall, shouted, "If this howling wind is some ghost's idea of a whisper, they must think we're deaf."

"They probably have to yell to be heard down the centuries. A pre-Celtic people built the original earthen fort fifteen hundred years before Christ was born, and the Celts built the ruined stone fort on which we stand five hundred years after Christ was born. This place is known as *Grianan of Aileach*[3]. In pre-Christian times the druids used it as a place of worship, and for seven hundred years, until Murtough O'Brien destroyed it around 1100, the emblem of the Red Hand flew from its walls."

"The Red Hand?"

"The Red Hand of Tir Eoghan. A severed red hand, the emblem of the O'Neills, although the O'Reillys of Breffney also have a Red Hand on their *bratach*[4]."

"Did the O'Neills rule Ulster for seven hundred years?"

"For much longer than that. The O'Neill lineage is the oldest of any ruling family in Europe. King Niall brought Saint Patrick to Ireland as a slave at the beginning of the 5th century. Niall's kingdom in the North was divided between two descendants, Eoghan and Conaill, into what are now *Tir*[5] *Eoghan* and *Tir Conaill*. The O'Neills still rule *Tir Eoghan*, and the O'Donnells, descendants of Conaill, have ruled *Tir Conaill* since the twelfth century. When I

---

[1] Semi-mythical inhabitants of Ireland, before the coming of the Celts.
[2] An ancient circular stone fortification.
[3] "The Stone fort of the sun".
[4] (Irish)" banner".
[5] (Irish) "The country of".

am given the white wand as chieftain at *Carraig an Dun¹*, I will be the twenty-fourth chieftain of my name. The white wand reminds the new chieftain that he must rule with fairness and purity of purpose."

Red Hugh smiled. "If Gerald Cambrensis, the Norman monk who accompanied the first Norman invaders could be present at that inauguration, I'm afraid he'd be disappointed. The strange practises of which he wrote and that supposedly accompanied the inauguration of an O'Donnell chieftain existed only in his depraved mind. Those early Normans, Turlough, used pen, and sword as weapons against us. They were as ready to malign us with the pen as are their successors, the Tudors. MacSweeney says the conqueror always seeks to blacken the character of the vanquished before the world."

MacRory's education for the past two years at Fanad had included Brehon Law and he knew that while Red Hugh was the most likely candidate to succeed his father, his election to chieftain was not automatic. However he was not going to point this out to his friend.

"Surely Turlough MacSweeney doesn't believe in ghosts!"

"Don't you? The ghosts of those who have gone before us are all around us, especially here at Grianan of Aileach. Perhaps even the ghost of Dagda.

"There's many legends about the people who built this fort. The people of the goddess Dana ruled Ireland before the arrival of the Celts, and one legend says Dagda, the god of the people of the Danaan, built it. The legend says that Corgenn, the king of Connacht, visited Dagda and his son, Hugh, at Tara². When the young Hugh seemed to take too much of an interest in Corgenn's young wife, the old man took offence and slew Hugh.

"It seems that even the son of a god could lust after mortal women, and that even the son of a god could die at the hand of a mortal man! Dagda, in revenge for the death of his son, cast a *geis*³ on Corgenn. It would be his fate to wander all over Ireland carrying the dead Hugh until he found a stone the exact size to cover him.

---

[1] (Irish) "The Rock of Doon".
[2] The ancient seat of Irish Kings.
[3] (Irish) "A spell," "a curse".

Then he was to take the body to the nearest hill and there bury it, covering it with the stone. Corgenn wandered around Ireland carrying the dead Hugh in his arms until at length he found the stone he sought down there on the shores of Lough Foyle. On the hill on which we stand he dug Hugh's grave and carried the stone up this hill. But the exertion was too much for the old man and his heart burst. Dagda built the original earthen fort around the grave of his son here on the Hill of Aileach.

"Dagda was the good god of Ireland's pre-Celtic people, but Crom Cruach was their evil and terrible god. Crom Cruach they worshiped with human sacrifice on the Plain of Magh Slecht south of here, until Saint Patrick destroyed the pagan idol. Crom Cruach may have been worshipped here, too, at Grianan of Aileach. Here, Turlough, you can mingle with the ghosts of the pagan gods or the ghosts of the Celtic druids or the more earthly ghost of an O'Neill king. Since it's too late to get back to Fanad today, we'll spend the night here and you can tell me in the morning which ghost you found to be the most entertaining."

No ghosts seemed to disturb Red Hugh's sleep, but MacRory slept fitfully, sheltered from the moaning wind beneath the ruined walls. Like mists drifting through the valleys, disjointed fragments of dreams stole through his sleep. An O'Neill king marched up the hill with a white wand in one hand and a huge rock balanced in the other. Red Hugh stood pointing out the land of the O'Donnells to a white-robed druid, and then the two searched among the pebbles on the shore of the Foyle.

Suddenly the fragmented dreaming changed, and in sharp, ghastly focus, Crom Cruach, a monstrous, fiery, wickerwork skeleton enclosed MacRory's father and brothers. As they burned within the belly of the god they held their hands out in supplication. He tried to reach out to them, but he could not lift his right arm and Alistair MacDonald held his left. A man, who was his father, yet not his father, came up from the ocean and with slashing sword severed MacDonald's hand at the wrist. MacRory saw himself reach out with his freed left hand, but a widening gulf separated him from his father and brothers, who screamed and burned within the fiery god. Despite the gulf he heard their screams with terrible clarity and he heard the echo of their screams in the ruins of Grianan of Aileach. He heard his own answering screams.

"Turlough, wake up, wake up, Turlough." Red Hugh shook him.

He awoke with pounding heart.

"You were screaming in your sleep. Did you have a bad dream?"

He shook his head as if to rid himself of the dream. He steadied his voice to reply. "Aye, Hugh. Aye, I did."

Red Hugh suspected the nature of his friend's nightmare and felt it better not to ask about it. Unlike many a dream that fades on awakening, the vivid details seared in MacRory's mind and the hand he raised to his forehead trembled. Red Hugh, himself shaken by the soul-depth of horror in those quavering screams, put his arm around his friend's shoulder. "MacSweeney's priest says that when the maw of hell opens before us on earth, we need the help of heaven. Kneel with me and we'll pray together, Turlough."

The two boys knelt in the dark ruins and prayed to the god that Saint Patrick had brought to their ancestors. They prayed to their Christian God in this place where others before them had prayed to other gods.

Red Hugh rose from his knees and put his hand on his friend's shoulder. "Come and sit, Turlough. We've slept enough."

He walked over to sit with his back against a moss-covered stone. "When it's light, we'll saddle the horses and ride back to Fanad." The wind has already changed to blow in from *Sruth na Maoile*[1], so it will soon be light. While we wait, let me tell you one of our Irish legends about that sea. It'll take your mind off your dream." MacRory sat in silence trying to control his quivering body, his spirit a wound reopened, while Red Hugh, not waiting for an answer, launched into the story. In that place where some dark entity had invaded his mind, where dark memories were carried on the haunted night wind, the strong, familiar voice reassured.

"It's the story of the Children of Lir, a legend that spans nine hundred years from the time of the Danaan people through pagan Celtic Ireland to the time of Saint Patrick. I'll try not to take so long

---

"The Sea of Moyle," Channel between N. Ireland and Scotland.

in the telling of it and since it's close to dawn I'll give you the shorter version of the legend."

As he recited the story Red Hugh slipped occasionally into the *shanachie's* archaic convention of speech.

"King Lir was King of the Danaan and his wife, Eva, gave birth to four children, Fionnuala, Aodh, Fiachra and Conn. Eva died giving life to Fiachra and Conn who were twins. In time King Lir took Eva's sister, Aoife, as his wife, but the poison of jealousy seeped into Aoife's soul. Like many of the Danaan, Aoife had magical powers and one day as the children swam in Lough Derravaragh she spat on the water casting a spell that turned them into swans. 'By this *geis* (spell) I ordain that you shall spend three hundred years here on lonely Lough Derravaragh, three hundred years on the cold Sea of Moyle, and three hundred years on the wild western ocean. This one thing I will grant. You may retain the power of human speech.' When told their fate by the wicked Aoife the swan-children wept in their hearts for their eyes could not. Fionnuala the eldest child cried out. 'Why, oh mother, do you do this evil thing to us your children?' And Aoife then made this reply. "You are the beloved of Lir and of all the people of the Danaan. That love of Lir for you and for your mother, who was my sister should have been mine. I have not borne you, nor fed you at my breast and in my heart I did never love you.'

"In lonely vigil the years crept on, but the morning came when the swans rose in the air and pointed their long smooth necks to the north to leave Lough Derravaragh and the land of Erin for the Northern Sea.

"Their greatest hardships were out there on the stormy Sea of Moyle. No hardship on Lough Derravaragh compared with the suffering, sorrow, and loneliness that were to be their lot on the wild Sea of Moyle. Far from their own human kind they drifted on the streaming waves that lashed the high dark cliffs of Erin and the bleak, wild shores of Alba. In the darkness of night, mid the roar of the sea, they huddled together on hard grey rocks. Many such nights they endured but in their three hundred years on the Moyle. One night was worse than all others; such was the cold that the very sea itself froze, and as they clung together, Fionnuala sheltered the twins, Fiachra and Conn, one beneath each wing and Aodh in her breast feathers, but they froze to the rock, and when they tried to move, they left their feathers and the skin of their feet on the rock.

And when the ice melted, their fate was to go back on the sea, to return to the biting salt ocean that stung their raw flesh. They suffered, and it took long for their wounds to heal and for new feathers to grow to shield them from the cold. Weary year followed weary year, but this long vigil, too, on the Northern seas ended and they rose in the air and set their ordained course for Erris Head in the Western Ocean.

"And day by day and year by year in slow procession the days passed into years and three hundred years passed behind them. And then, one day, the power of the *geis* was no more and the swans regained their human form. Great was their sadness, for by now no person of their race lived. The people of Danann had been defeated by the people of Mil in a mighty battle and had faded back into the magical kingdom from whence they came. But St Patrick had brought a new faith to the land and as the children of Lir, now incredibly old and feeble; lay dying they were converted to that new faith. As the breath left their bodies they became again the joyous children of their youth and these children of a king, now with angel wings, rose up to heaven."

For the last half hour the stars had been fading in the eastern sky. The Sea of Moyle shimmered silver in the first glimmer of dawn's light and dimly beyond the Foyle the hills of Antrim came up out of the darkness. While MacRory was now more composed, he seemed preoccupied and Red Hugh did not intrude on his thoughts. They rode back to Fanad mostly in silence.

CHAPTER 3

A banquet in Enniskillen castle

Hugh O'Donnell ruled Tir Conaill from his castle at Donegal. Donegal Castle had earlier been a Norse fort, hence the name "Dun na Gall"[1]. Ruling Tir Conaill was not a restful occupation. It required constant vigilance. It also required a good memory to keep track of one's current allegiances and current enemies. His traditional enemy, Hugh O'Neill, was presently engaged in punishing Sorley Boy MacDonnell and the Scots of North Antrim. Years earlier with the help of the English, Hugh had defeated the present O'Neill's rebel uncle, Shane, and caused him to lose his head and rashly flee to the protection of Sorley Boy's MacDonnell relatives in Antrim. The sequence of events, however, was not in the above order, but the outcome was the same, as Shane's severed head had ended up as an English trophy in Dublin. The fact that Hugh O'Donnell's wife, Fionnula MacDonnell, also know as Ineen Duive, was an Antrim MacDonnell may or may not have been of consequence in deciding the fate of Shane O'Neill. Shane himself, had he kept his head, would have been among the first to appreciate the motives of his enemies in removing it. Recently, Shane's nephew, Hugh O'Neill, had been instated as second Earl of Tyrone for exceptional service to the English against rebel Ireland. He was a favourite of Elizabeth. He had made no recent incursions into Donegal, and Hugh O'Donnell did not think any O'Neill mischief was in the offing. With O'Neill engaged elsewhere, he could turn his attention to other matters.

In the late autumn of 1586 Hugh O'Donnell sat his horse on an open, grassy hill above the Glendarragh valley, which separated *Tir Conaill* from the land of the Maguires, a small army of gallowglass and bonnaghts at his back. Beside him on horseback were his son, Red Hugh, his nephew Niall Garve O'Donnell, Don

---

[1] (Irish) "Fort of the foreigner".

Alonzo Cabos, the envoy of Philip II of Spain and Turlough MacRory.

Below and across the Ederney River, Hugh Maguire, son of the Fermanagh Maguire, stood beside his horse, shading his eyes and looking upward at the army arrayed on the border of his father's lands. Behind Maguire was also a small army of gallowglass and bonnaghts. Maguire mounted. He and O'Donnell galloped furiously toward each other. They stopped in the middle of the river, each fighting to control his equally mettlesome horse. After an exchange of words, O'Donnell turned in his saddle and waved to his men. His men turned back into Donegal, except for his mounted entourage who trotted their horses down into the stream.

"Don Alsozo Cabos, my nephew, Hugh Maguire of Fermanagh." O'Donnell made the introductions in English and Hugh Maguire bowed to the Spaniard.

The Spaniard's bow almost brought his head to touch his saddle pommel, and he replied in perfect English looking from Maguire to Red Hugh O'Donnell.

"Certainly a strong family resemblance."

He turned to Hugh O'Donnell.

"Both young men carry your family's traits, red hair, and a noble mien."

While the Spaniard faced Hugh O'Donnell, Maguire adopted what he hoped was a noble mien and winked at his younger cousin. Maguire became aware of the elder O'Donnell's gaze on him.

"If I still have my nephew's attention, may I introduce to him Turlough MacRory, the friend of my son? Even a man as resolute as Eoghan Óg MacSweeney needs the occasional respite, so I have relieved him of his two wilful charges for a few weeks. Niall Garve O'Donnell you already know."

Maguire smiled and extended his hand to MacRory. He acknowledged Niall Garve with a nod.

Niall Garve, also a cousin of Red Hugh, and a proud young man, who was forever conscious that he too could one day be a contender for the O'Donnell chieftaincy, bowed stiffly towards Maguire.

Today, with head inclined attentively to his guests, Maguire was polite and correct as he escorted them with proper decorum to his father's castle at Enniskillen. Their route at times took them close to the north shore of the Erne and here, at the widest part of the lough, five miles separated them from the cliffs of Magho, which rose hazily indistinct over on the farther shore. Occasionally the cavalcade disturbed ducks or other waterfowl that, noisily taking wing, skimmed the surface, their shimmering flight mirrored in the water beneath them. Two fishermen, still as statues, sat in a rough-hewn boat. With that instinctive wariness bred in the humble they had found it was better not to draw attention to themselves in the presence of the proud. Southward toward Enniskillen, the lough narrowed and was dotted with numerous islands, their wooded slopes reaching down to the water's edge where green foliage reflected back from blue water.

As they rode leisurely along a sun-speckled path through tall elms, the path ahead opened up into a meadow of waving grass. Maguire's two large wolfhounds, Bran Mór and Gelert, stalked alongside the horses with all the dignity of their breed.

When the younger Gelert raced off in pursuit of a red fox that had been stealthy stealing along a ditch toward the open meadow, all decorum ceased. Maguire's futile shouts of "to heel" went unheeded. The older Bran Mór looked up at his master, the hound's dark intelligent eyes seeming to deplore Gelert's gaucherie in mistaking a red fox for a red deer. Maguire galloped after Gelert, laughing and weaving through the trees. Soon he too pursued the red blur through the meadow at a full gallop. He leaned forward, arm outstretched with drawn sword as if in pursuit of a fleeing enemy. Some wild indistinguishable war cry floated back. The meadow came to an end at a bank topped by a fringe of *whins*[1]. The fox and the wolfhound disappeared into the whins as Maguire, still yelling, soared over waving his sword above his head.

Fifty yards behind thundered MacRory, Red Hugh abreast to his right, Niall Garve behind to his left. MacRory cleared with room to spare and was aware of Red Hugh on his right also easily clearing the obstacle. Red Hugh's horse, however, was not beneath him. At the same time he became aware of Maguire, sword in hand, sitting his horse saddle-deep in a river and looking back and upward.

---

[1] Gorse

There was not much to be done. He landed with a huge splash almost, but not quite on top of, the heir to the Maguire. Red Hugh, without benefit of his horse, got less distance, landing with outstretched hands, and a lesser splash in shallow water.

A brief pause, an approaching thunder of hoofs which ceased, and Maguire had time to swivel his head the other way as the belly of Niall Garve's horse floated downward toward him. A wave washed over MacRory, as Niall made his splash. Maguire was too close to the horse to be affected by the wave.

They rode on toward Enniskillen only somewhat subdued. Hugh O'Donnell was amused at the behaviour of the spirited youngsters. The austere Spaniard even allowed himself a thin smile.

Maguire apologized for the fracas, and addressed himself to the Spaniard.

"The Irish wolfhound, Don Alonzo, is prized for its faithfulness as well as for its ability in the hunt. They are trained to hunt the red deer, but as you see Gelert is in need of further training. However, he may one day live up to his noble name. I'm sure The O'Donnell knows well the story of another Gelert."

"I seem to have heard of it," Hugh O'Donnell replied, "but I must admit my memory sometimes fails me of late. Perhaps you yourself will recite it to Don Alonzo."

It was rumoured that the once keen intellect of the O'Donnell chieftain was failing and Hugh Maguire inwardly cursed his own clumsiness in having possibly embarrassed his guest.

"Forgive me; it is my memory that is failing. It is, of course, the story of Bran, the famous hound of *Finn*[1] that is so well known in Ireland, but in fact, there is also the lesser-known story of Gelert, which I will recite.

"Llewellyn, a prince of Wales, had an Irish wolfhound called Gelert. The prince one day went hunting, leaving Gelert, his favourite hound, to guard his infant son. On the prince's return Gelert, his jaws covered in blood, leaped up in joy on his master.

"The Prince's son was nowhere to be found, and fearing the worst, the prince in rage thrust his sword through Gelert's body. Later the prince found his son alive among the bodies of five dead

---

[1] Mythical hero, leader of a warrior band called the "Fianna".

wolves. In anguished remorse the prince fell on the same sword that had pierced Gelert."

"It is interesting that in Spain we have a somewhat similar legend", Don Alonzo said. "Our legend relates the story of a Moor, who was captured by pirates and had his tongue cut out. A Spanish ship's captain rescued him and he became the captain's faithful servant. Subsequently he saved the captain's life in a sea battle. The captain became so attached to his trusted servant that he made the Moor the custodian of his household and bequeathed a large part of his wealth to the man. The captain's wife was not happy with this arrangement and sought to poison her husband's mind against his servant. She told her husband the servant was plotting to kill her in order to add her share of the wealth to his own. The servant, who could neither speak nor write, could not refute her lies. Returning from the sea one day, the captain came upon his servant standing with a bloodstained sword over the captain's bleeding wife. Thinking the worst, he slew his servant. Only later did he discover the bodies of several Barbary pirates whom the servant had killed protecting his master's wife."

Two of the horses were lame and being led. Red Hugh rode his horse, which had wisely refused the jump, holding the reins in his left hand. He had a painful swelling of his right wrist. The wrist was deformed and obviously broken. MacRory walked by his side, pathetic in his helplessness to help.

The Castle of Enniskillen was situated on an island in the Erne. Above and below Enniskillen, the river widened into two large loughs. One third of Fermanagh, the land of the Maguires, was water. Here at Enniskillen the approach to the castle was over a wooden bridge across the narrowest part of the river. Another bridge crossed a deep and wide ditch leading to an archway through the eight-foot-thick castle wall. Cuconnaught Maguire, chieftain of Fermanagh, met his visitors in the courtyard of his castle. He greeted his friend, his wife's brother, and his sometime enemy, Hugh O'Donnell, with warmth and affection. The Spaniard he greeted with formal courtesy.

The horses were led away and Maguire ushered his guests through the vaulted castle entrance, along a tunnel-like passageway, and into a large hall. Heavy drapes hanging on the walls and a fire of logs, which burned brightly in a large open grate beside one wall, tempered the austerity of the stone-vaulted chamber. Simple but comfortable-looking, cushioned wooden seats were placed around the fire. Bran Mór and Gelert had already taken their places and lay on the flagstones close by the fire. Servants approached the guests to take their riding cloaks. They were seated and presented with well-filled goblets of an alcoholic brew. Cuconnaught Maguire raised his goblet.

"To our guests, Don Alonzo Cabos of Spain and to my wife's brother, the faithful shield of the Maguires, Hugh O'Donnell, chieftain of *Tir Conaill*. Health to you both and long may you live."

While drinking the toast, Maguire noticed Red Hugh struggling to hold his goblet in his right hand. To use the left hand to drink a toast was unthinkable. Maguire at once called for his physician. Conor O'Cassidy, the physician to the Maguires, arrived presently and unhurriedly, and was introduced to the guests. O'Cassidy's red face and veined nose bespoke a lifelong fondness for *uisce beatha*[1], an indulgence, however, which never seemed to interfere with his duty. He examined the wrist and advised Red Hugh that resetting it would be painful. Next he looked expectantly at a servant, who hastened to provide the physician with a goblet of the potent liquor that had been offered to the guests. The physician took a long and seemingly satisfying draught. Having thus fortified himself against the pain, he suggested to Red Hugh that he do likewise.

Hugh Maguire, standing by the fire, shouted a reassurance across the hall to his younger cousin: "He's a good man, Hugh Roe, and he's sober tonight. I've often heard it said of him that if you were at death's door, you could rely on O'Cassidy, drunk or sober, to pull you through!"

O'Cassidy loudly addressed his patient. "Take a good swig, boy. I don't care much for the stuff myself, but I drink it from time to time to dampen my intellect down to the level of the Maguires."

Aligning the boy's hand palm down, O'Cassidy grasped it in his own right hand and grasped the forearm just above the broken wrist with his left hand. Held thus the deformed wrist exhibited the

---

[1] (Irish) "Water of Life", whiskey

appearance of a dinner fork. Applying traction in this manner, he first bent the wrist slightly upward, then sharply downward while at the same time twisting the boy's hand and wrist toward himself. He then had an assistant continue the traction while he cupped his hands around either side of the wrist, compressing it. He examined the wrist, which, while still swollen, was no longer deformed. The portly physician, red faced from exertion, helped himself to another well-earned draught. Red Hugh, pale and sweating, turned and thanked Cuconnaught Maguire for the ministrations of his physician. A splint was then applied to the wrist.

Servants arrived to show the guests to their rooms where they would rest after their journey. The following night there would be a banquet in their honour.

Oil-burning torches spaced at intervals along its walls lighted the great hall of Enniskillen Castle. Cuconnaught Maguire sat at the top of a huge horseshoe-shaped table. Behind him Bran Mór and Gelert lay on the flagstone floor. Above and behind him in the vaulted apse hung the war banners and crests of his family. O'Donnell and Red Hugh sat on Maguire's right; his wife Nuala, sister of Hugh O'Donnell, the only woman present, and his son sat on his left. Each arm of the horseshoe was sixty feet in length. Silver candelabra were placed at intervals along its length. Servants moved back and forth quietly within the horseshoe, placing food, and drink in front of the guests. Freshly cut green rushes carpeted the flagstones of the dining area. The guests were seated along the outside of the horseshoe so that none would have his back to another. Along the top of the horseshoe to the right and left sat nobles and other Maguires. Beyond them sat the Fermanagh chieftains. Prominent among the latter and in places of honour were the McCaffreys, the MacManuses, the O'Flannagans, and the O'Cassidys. Interspersed among the chieftains were churchmen, bards, poets, Brehons, and shanachies. Some of the men were clean-shaven except for the moustache, reminiscent of the Celts of old. Their hair was worn long at the back with a gleebe[1] in front that

---

[1] (Irish) "Fringe".

fell down over the eyes. The soft flickering light of the torches played on flag-draped walls, on pillars hung with shields, swords, and crests, on green and saffron robes, on silver drinking goblets and silver utensils, on the polished oaken table, and on the large polished flagstones of the floor beyond the dining area.

Across from Maguire, on a pedestal within the horseshoe, sat a large exquisitely worked wood and silver chalice. It stood about ten inches high, supported on four silver legs, a central cylinder of polished yew wood, with an outer intricate latticework of silver. The squared rim, smooth on the inside, was inlaid with Latin inscriptions around the outside. The perfectly proportioned chalice, with its blending of dark wood and silver latticework was beautiful in symmetry and design. This was the "Mighty Cup," a family chalice commissioned by Katherina, wife of the Maguire, in 1493. Wheat-bread cakes soaked in honey were passed among the guests. Wine, mead, and *uisce beatha* were plentiful.

Maguire, on an expedition to Rome, had brought home with him an Italian cook, and this Continental touch was the envy of his neighbours. The cook was of that temperamental disposition common enough in cooks. He resented Nuala Maguire's rare intrusions into "his" kitchen. Despite two years in the Maguire castle, he had never learned to speak Irish but could understand some English. Nuala Maguire herself conveyed instructions to him in English. His responses, in Italian and accompanied by much gesticulation and lively facial contortions, so often ended with the phrase *"tu vacca"*[1] that Nuala Maguire told her chaplain, who had studied in Rome, that the only words of Italian she had learned from her cook were *"tu vacca"* which she took to mean Ma'am, or some such respectful equivalent. When her cook used *"tu vacca"*, for the next and last time, Nuala Maguire happened to be armed with a heavy wooden ladle, whose long handle broke after only two full-blooded clouts to the man's head and well before she had fully expressed her displeasure. When she seized upon another weapon, a yard-long iron poker used for stoking the fire, Italy fled the field uttering a veritable torrent of what might have been Italian invective but which did not however contain the phrase *"tu vacca"*. Among

---

[1] (Italian) "You cow!".

the dishes served were beef, mutton and salmon, and also eel from the Erne. This latter was a delicacy for which a market existed in France.

The Erne's eels had some years earlier been the cause of a bloody little war between Maguire and O'Donnell. O'Donnell had erected a weir at Ballyshannon and had thus captured the largest share of the eels, depriving Maguire farther up the lough of his share. Maguire professed to be particularly upset by the fact that O'Donnell's weir was taking a large quantity of elvers on their way up the river from the ocean and of the mature silver eels on their way back to the Atlantic to spawn, and might thus eventually destroy the lucrative Erne eel fishery. It was possible, however, that Maguire was motivated more by motives of jealousy than concern for the future of the eel. After some months of bloodletting, a compromise was reached whereby O'Donnell did the shipping and Maguire did the fishing. The weir was moved upstream into Maguire territory at Belleek and both chieftains again became amicable neighbours. Maguire captured the small elvers and the larger silver eels while O'Donnell had a two-way trade, shipping Maguire's eels from Ballyshannon to Brest and sometimes further south to Bordeaux and returning with a profitable cargo of wines. O'Donnell leaned over to congratulate his host on the delicious eel and the excellent wines.

The aspirated and sibilant tones of the Irish tongue filled the hall with a loud continuous murmur, periodically punctuated by a louder laugh. Occasionally too, as happens, by some quirk of acoustics, a single word or sentence-fragment floated distinctly out of the background hubbub. No one afterwards would ever say who was responsible but one such sentence fragment that floated out was "That Bollocks McCaffrey". As Hugh Maguire was to comment later, "Like a fart at a wedding, it did not go unheard", but happily it went unheard by old Phelem McCaffrey himself whose hearing was not what it used to be. He would go to his death never knowing that as a result of the acoustics in Maguire's banquet hall he would become widely referred to as "Bollocks" McCaffrey. There was no one brave enough in Ireland to refer to him as such to his face. Knowing that the wild-eyed old brigand would have been enraged had he been aware of his new appellation made it all the more delicious, as well as ensuring that the name stuck like a burr to a blanket. A seated bard played the Uileann pipes. This instrument was similar to, but lacked the volume of, the larger war pipes. The bladder was inflated not by blowing into a chanter as with the war pipes, but by a movement of the elbow. Later all fell silent as the Maguire bard played the large traditional brass-stringed harp.

Toward the end of the feast, the hubbub of voices died away as Nuala Maguire walked to the raised dais off to one side where the harp stood. The Maguire bard vacated his seat. Nuala sat and played the instrument with a confident and sure touch. The strumming music that had stirred generations long dead resonated in each Celtic soul, and was greeted, when she finished, with a thunder of applause. Hugh Maguire then joined his mother on the dais and accompanied the harp with a flute. Its sweet clear tones harmonized wonderfully with the softer muted tones of the harp and once again the performance was greeted with a thunder of applause. Some of the fierce, old faces softened, and the duet continued for some time until Maguire's wife and son rejoined Cuconnaught Maguire at the table. The *file*[1] then rose to recite poetry, which was listened to with attentive and critical appreciation. Cuconnaught rose, and with a scraping of chairs, all the company arose. The distant wail of pipes came steadily closer until the walls and roof of the great hall reverberated with the sound that for four hundred years had led the Maguires into battle. This was not the soft, sad music of the harp or flute, gentle and flowing. This was the loud, wild, thunderous wail of battle, echoing and re-echoing in the vaulted hall. The sweet, gentle music of the harp and the wild, skirling of the war pipes both had a place in the soul of the Gael. The piper stood facing his chieftain and played the proud, martial tunes. Maguire's wife stood with eyes sparkling, a high colour on her cheeks, as stirred by the music as any of the men present.

The piper played the old, well-loved marches and the wailing laments, each following the other without pause. The stirring music echoed in vaulted hall and Celtic soul and evoked memories of battle and glory. Fermanagh's chieftains remembered, their faces fierce and proud, the music of centuries ago, the music of yesterday. At last the music stopped – the sudden abrupt stop, a contrivance to remind those present that the piper, leading his sept into battle,

---

[1] (Irish) "Poet"

was often the first to die. There was a deafening silence during which ears rang. A roar of sound shattered the silence as all assembled cheered with stamping feet, waving tankards in the air. Maguire's wife stamped her small foot and waved with the rest. A servant lifted the Maguire chalice and presented it to Cuconnaught Maguire. He drank from it and passed it to the piper. When the piper had drunk, the chalice made its way down the table, carried across from side to side, and replenished as necessary. At this stage Nuala Maguire retired. The hours passed with music and singing, interspersed with storytelling and poetry recital. Alcohol flowed and the voices grew louder. One guest who was slumped in his chair in near stupor was being assailed by his neighbour with unwonted garrulity. Far down the table a man spoke with vehemence and conviction, until he lost his train of thought! The *file*, having mistaken a polite response to his first offering, for an enthusiastic one, rose to proffer a second. However his eloquence was now blunted by a thickened tongue. His inspiration took a mortal wound when Conor O'Cassidy, seated beside Hugh Maguire, and himself not noted for sobriety, voiced his opinion of the poet's verbal artistry loudly and with some amazement.

"The bastard's drunk, Hugh."

The etiquette of a banquet was exquisite, no part more exquisite than its ending. No chieftain must leave before Maguire, and Maguire must not be seen to leave too soon. Etiquette seemed to have been served as the sun's dawn rays illumined Enniskillen Castle. Even a chieftain as powerful as Maguire went in trepidation of falling short in the matter of correct manners. To be the object of a satirical poem was no small thing. Many an equally powerful chieftain had been satirized by a *file* for a lack of hospitality and manners, and many such chieftains had had their status lowered as much as if their castles had been stormed and taken. The banquet had provided food for body and soul. Each man there was proud of his prince and deemed his chieftain's conduct princely. Niall Garve O'Donnell, however, seethed inwardly. He had been placed below Red Hugh at the table.

Cuconnaught Maguire, with Hugh O'Donnell and Don Alonzo Cabos, rode along the banks of the Erne. It required a robust constitution to be an Irish chieftain. Despite only three hours of sleep, Maguire looked rested, as did the Spaniard. By mutual consent Don Alonzo had absented himself from the banquet of the previous night, and retired early to a room remote from the noise of revelry. He had not wished to advertise his presence in the country. His mission to Ireland was to make known to these Northern chieftains that an armada was being prepared in Spain for the invasion of England.

"We have an especial interest in the intentions of Hugh O'Neill, who I understand is your son-in-law, Lord O'Donnell," Don Alonzo said.

"Ah, yes, that is so, yes" O'Donnell replied somewhat absentmindedly. "He is married to my daughter Nuala ... ah, my daughter Siobhan, of course, I should say."

"And your sister Nuala is married to Lord Maguire. Such alliances between the three most powerful families in the North may not be altogether to England's liking."

"We are becoming increasingly aware that what is to England's liking is seldom to Ireland's benefit", replied O'Donnell. "Our religion comes under a sustained and merciless assault. Patrick O'Healy, the Archbishop of Mayo, was tortured and murdered, and with him, Conn O'Rourke, a Franciscan priest, the son of Brian O'Rourke, Lord of Breffney. Recently Adam Loftus, the Protestant Archbishop of Dublin, had Dermot O'Hurley, the Catholic Archbishop of Cashel, tortured and hanged in Dublin. Loftus sought the advice of an expert in torture, Walsingham, the Queen's secretary in London, who, with the Queen's consent, suggested the 'Iron Boots.' O'Hurley had his feet and lower legs encased in metal boots filled with oil and salt, and then the boots were heated white hot in a fire until the flesh came away from his limbs. His hanging, too, was brutally and deliberately protracted, after which his body was thrown in a ditch.

"Such atrocities are common. Priests and laymen die for their faith on a scale reminiscent of the persecution of Christians in early Rome. And since those in power decree how these things are remembered, if England rules our country one day, the names of those Irish who died for their faith will be forgotten. Queen Mary, who tortured and murdered English Protestants, is known as 'Bloody Mary,' while her sister, Elizabeth, who tortures and murders Irish Catholics, is known as 'Good Queen Bess.' These accursed Tudors, whatever religion they espouse, are an abomination on humanity."

"The ultimate in power is to control the minds of the people. In Spain, too, we have the Inquisition to teach people what they may think and what they may believe. We, too, have buried in our soil the tortured flesh and racked bones of martyrs to their beliefs – many their names unremembered, known but to their God."

"The English attempt to play us off one against the other. Even their favourite, Hugh O'Neill, they hold in check by supporting the claim of his old rival Turlough O'Neill."

"A time-honoured tactic, and one not unique to the English, More than fifteen hundred years ago Caesar employed *Divide et Impera*[1] to conquer your ancestral Celts in Gaul[2]. There's a lesson to be learned there, for Caesar wrote that if the Celts had ever become united, they would have been unconquerable.

I understand also that Sir Henry Sidney took O'Neill, as a young boy, to England where he was educated. He is now a Queen's earl, who sits in the English Parliament in Dublin. He recently helped to suppress a rebellion by another Irish earl in Munster and is presently engaged against England's enemies in Antrim. However, we all know that allegiances can change. I have taken the time to acquaint myself with O'Neill's family and I know that his uncle, Shane O'Neill, led a rebellion that hammered at the gates of the Pale. I also understand that Hugh O'Neill is the able leader of a family that has for centuries manipulated fortune to their advantage. If fortune now favours Spain in her war with England, I'm certain O'Neill would insist on being on the winning side."

Alonzo Cabos came from an ancient Spanish line. Generations of his forebears had been forged in the crucible of perpetual war during Spain's long struggle against the Moors. A soldier of renown in his own country, he was also a shrewd and patient diplomat, a master of the art of intrigue and politics. He had expertly navigated a course through the turbulent and treacherous waters of Spanish politics, avoiding Scylla[3] on the left, Charybdis on

---

[1] (Latin) "Divide and Rule".
[2] Modern-day France.
[3] The trials of Jason in Greek mythology; Scylla ate sailors alive and Charybdis devoured them in whirlpools.

the right. He had advanced ever upward, expediency his guiding light and his only consideration, a sword thrust to the right, a polite word or bow to the left –the velvet glove in the mailed fist.

Late sixteenth-century Ireland was fertile ground for the seeds Alonzo Cabos sowed. It did not require his arrival in Ireland, however, to awaken the Irish to a new danger. They were accustomed for centuries to warfare and accommodation among each other. An Irish chieftain was elected for ability and intelligence. Lacking either, he was soon out-manoeuvred by war or subterfuge. The old Gaelic chieftains were becoming aware of the steady erosion of their power by the English. Each accommodation with England had been to their disadvantage. Instead of the old Gaelic titles, they had accepted English titles. O'Neill became Earl of Tyrone, Maguire, Baron of Enniskillen. They had allowed their traditional lands to be shired[1] according to English custom. *Tir Conaill* became County Donegal; *Tir* Owen became County Tyrone, Breffney of the O'Reillys and the O'Rourkes, Counties Cavan and Leitrim.

More than names, however, had changed. At the same time came a concerted attack against all Irish customs and institutions – the Irish Brehon Laws, which included the laws governing inheritance, the Catholic religion, and the Irish language. Eventually all Celtic customs and manners became distasteful to an increasingly intolerant and arrogant foe. The colour saffron, the traditional colour of the cloaks of the Irish nobility, was banned. The *gleebe* and the moustache, considered "barbarian," were banned. The Irish found that any accommodation was becoming impossible. Increasingly war was the only option, and Spain presented herself as an ally.

Alonzo Cabos hoped to foment a rebellion in Ireland. England would have to divert soldiers there, which would be in Spain's interest. He knew how difficult it would be to get these chieftains, independent and jealous, to act together in any united, concerted action against England. Who, for instance, was powerful enough to lead? O'Neill came to mind.

---

[1] Divided into counties or shires.

It had been five hundred years since Ireland had been united under a single leader when King Brian had rid the country of the Norse. In the intervening centuries the country had again fragmented into petty kingdoms. The Spaniard knew what could be accomplished if the country united under one leader, and O'Neill, if accepted by the chieftains, could be such a leader. Spain, a century earlier, had been what Ireland was today – a nation, if it could be called such, of individual warlords, each jealous of the other. United under the leadership of Ferdinand and Isabella, Spain had driven out the Moors, and now threatened another equally powerful and united nation, England. The Spaniard, with tact, brought these matters to the attention of his two companions and explored the possibilities, as they sat their horses in Fermanagh and looked out across the Erne to Donegal.

CHAPTER 4

The Falls of Assaroe

Red Hugh O'Donnell, with his cousin, Niall Garve O'Donnell, Hugh Maguire, and Turlough MacRory, drifted slowly down Lower Lough Erne. Like its upper counterpart, the lough was a maze of islands; this year the water in the lake was particularly high, partially submerging some of the smaller ones. The islands and the shore were heavily wooded. Oak, beech, larch, elm, and sycamore were the predominant species. The south side of the lower lough, the fiefdom of the O'Flannagans from even before the overlordship of the Maguires, was a remote part of Fermanagh whose wooded hills, and hidden glades, removed from the trodden paths of man, provided shelter, and sustenance for creatures of the wild whose eyes had never gazed on the ultimate predator. The deep blue of the lough reflected the autumn gold, yellow, and brown of shore and islands. Looking down the lough the rounded blue hills of Donegal rose to the right, the wooded slopes of Fermanagh to the left. While still quite wooded, the county had once been heavily so, and Hugh Maguire told his listeners that in the sixth century, in the time of Columcille[1], a squirrel could travel from Derry to Cork without ever touching the ground. Niall Garve O'Donnell who was of the type that would argue with his own shadow, demanded to know what proof Maguire could offer for this exorbitant claim.

Maguire stared for some moments at the young man before turning and addressing Red Hugh and MacRory.

"What is a present day squirrel when compared to those Irish squirrels of bygone days that were capable of such prodigious leaps?"

"You must not leap to conclusions," Red Hugh laughed, slapping his cousin on the back and wincing as he realized he had used his splinted right hand.

---

[1] An Irish monk who founded the monastery of Iona.

"We should none of us leap to conclusions," Niall Garve replied with an oblique, unsmiling glance at Red Hugh.

"Let me acquaint you callow youths with some further facts," Maguire continued. "You will find remnants of many early Christian monastic settlements here on the lower lough. These islands seem to have been favourite sites for monks to pursue their contemplative lives. There's a story of the centuries when the Norse rampaged through Ireland that may stir the blood of brutish young warriors like yourselves. The invaders came in from the Atlantic and sailed up the River Shannon, plundering as they went. Rather than facing an irate and aroused population on their return down the Shannon, they portaged their boats overland to the headwaters of the Erne and continued their depredations on the Erne's island monastic settlements as they sailed down the lough to return to the Atlantic at Ballyshannon."

"You ask us to believe that they moved heavy, seagoing boats twenty miles overland!" Niall Garve demanded.

"You may believe what you wish. These were no puny men. These were men of a formidable race who built boats that could cross oceans to far off lands, men accustomed to overcoming obstacles. Personally, I would like to think they were capable of such a feat."

Niall Garve lapsed into silence and Maguire continued, "The Norse slew all of one settlement with the exception of one monk. Him they took with them in order to ascertain if the falls on the Erne above Ballyshannon were navigable. The monk told them that while an Irishman might negotiate the falls, it was unlikely that they, the Norse, were good enough sailors to do so. So goaded, the Norse attempted the passage and they were all swept to their deaths at the Falls of Assaroe."

About a mile and a half below Enniskillen, Maguire guided them ashore on the southeast side of a large island where stood a round stone tower dating to the twelfth century, and beside the tower, an Augustinian church, and the ruins of an earlier Christian church. Close by the ruins was a scattering of tombstones, some with the traditional Celtic cross design, others of varied shapes and sizes, some bearing Latin inscriptions. These inscriptions blunted with age, bore mute witness to the fact that "written in stone" had, with time, as much permanence as "written in the wind". This island was the site of a monastic settlement founded by Saint

Molaise in the sixth century. As the young men wandered among the quiet ruins, Maguire continued his narration.

"When Saint Patrick tamed the pagan heart of the Celt and destroyed their savage gods, our Celtic ancestors, with unexpected fervour, embraced their new, gentle God. However, Patrick, Ireland's beloved saint was not Irish. In that earlier time, pirates from the West Coast of Britain frequently raided the Irish Coast, raping and plundering. We Irish, too, occasionally crossed over to Britain and to Gaul to make love and to borrow things. One of the things which the Irish King Niall, on one such expedition, borrowed was a young man who was a Romanised citizen living in either Britain or Gaul. He was brought back as a slave to tend sheep for his master on Slemish Mountain in Antrim. In the cold of those mountains, poorly clad and hungry, he became closer to his God, as is said to happen sometimes to those who suffer. He eventually escaped from this rather meagre Irish hospitality and made his way to France. Later, while studying theology on the Continent, he supposedly had a vision in which he saw many hands stretched out towards him and Irish voices pleading 'Come back and walk among us.'

"While this vision may or not have happened we do have authentic details of St. Patrick's life in Ireland from two existing manuscripts written in Latin by St. Patrick himself, the *Confessio* and *Letter to Coroticus*. They reveal a simple man who was looked down on by his fellow bishops in England and on the Continent because of his lack of learning and his clumsy Latin. He had been a late starter in his theological studies due to his earlier years of sheep-herding on the Antrim hills. The names and the deeds of these other learned bishops are now forgotten while the name and the deeds of St. Patrick never will be. Courage, compassion, and a fervent faith in his God seem to have made more of an impression on his Irish converts than the nuances of theology and the nicety of Latin syntax. Both his compassion and his courage, and indeed his less than precise Latin, can be seen in his *Letter to Coroticus*, the latter a raiding prince who had enslaved some of Patrick's converts. He pleads desperately for the return of his newly baptised converts and at the same time minces no words when he calls Coroticus and his men "citizens of the devil" – a brave act by a man armed only with a wooden walking staff to so insult a pirate prince."

Maguire went on to tell them how the centuries intervening between Saint Patrick's conversion of Ireland to Christianity and the Norse invasions were Ireland's golden age. While Europe sank into the Dark Ages and barbarians whose names were to become synonymous with mindless destruction howled around the corpse of Rome's decaying civilization, monks and scholars in remote Ireland kept the light of civilization burning. They preserved and copied priceless manuscripts, and founded monasteries and secular centres of learning at home and abroad. These monasteries became isolated havens of civilization, beacons of hope in Europe's long night of darkness. Saint Columcille, an O'Donnell and, unlike Patrick, an Irish-born saint, founded the famous monastery of Iona and his acolyte, Saint Aidan, the equally famous Lindisfarne. Other Irish monks founded monasteries far from their own land in France, Switzerland, and northern Italy. From Iceland to Italy, and from the Bay of Biscay to the Black Sea, these Irish men nurtured the dying light of a lost civilization until that light could again blaze forth across Europe.

The four young men sat on the island beside the thousand-year-old ruins of a church, eating food, which they had brought ashore with them. Only the smallest breeze rippled the lake and brought its waters whispering gently up the pebbled shore. Here, long before them, others had lived and laboured and died. Here the tolling church bell had regulated the quiet ordered lives of the monks, each mellow, hollow peel fading across the lough as it called them from toil in field or forest; it was a familiar sound also to others laboriously transcribing manuscripts, their sole life's work, in their small, stone-walled cells. The familiar hollow peel that had governed each monk's life would, on his death, punctuate each hollow thud of earth on his coffin. On the island the monks, walking among the graves of their dead brethren, were forever conscious of the transience of the flesh. The tombstones of the dead spoke to the living.

"What you are now we once were. What we are now you will be."

The bell would have peeled also on a fateful day in 836. Responding to the summons of the bell, the monks hurried down to the lakeshore to show the traditional hospitality as a longboat with banks of oars came surging up the lough. The monk in the enclosed bell tower continued to peel the bell as these Norsemen leaped ashore, repaying hospitality with bloody sweeps of sparth[1] axe. Other monks, summoned by the bell from the fields to their duty of hospitality, came hurrying to their sudden frightful deaths. The monk in the cloister wept, before his death, staring with unbelieving eyes to see the loving, irreplaceable work of lifetimes fuelling flames. The terrifying mad marauders rampaged. The monk in the bell tower turned as the light in the dim, stonewalled tower was dimmed further by a huge, uncouth figure with bloodstained battle-axe. The dying echoes of the bell, whispering across the lough, echoed a requiem for Christian Ireland's centuries of peace.

The youths pushed out into the lough, leaving behind the peaceful island and its mute ruins. MacRory had unconsciously elected himself oarsman and seemed most suited to the strenuous task. His large hands skilfully plied the heavy oars, although at fourteen he had that appearance of awkwardness seen when large bones and rapid muscular development have not yet had time to become moulded into the symmetry of a powerful frame.

Maguire was so taken up in explaining the history of the islands of the lough that he would not have had breath for rowing, while the two O'Donnells would not have had much experience in doing so. MacRory's tendency to listen rather than to talk gave Niall Garve the impression that the young man was perhaps shy or somewhat inarticulate – either to Niall Garve, a fault of character. There was nothing shy about Maguire or the two O'Donnells whose voices, raised in argument, discussion, and frequent laughter, floated across the lake. Niall Garve turned to MacRory.

"You don't speak much, do you? You're doing a good job on the oars anyhow. I suppose one doesn't look for conversation to the ox that pulls the plough."

MacRory ceased rowing and the oars trailing in the water made the only small sound in the sickening silence. Red Hugh, appalled, stood in the boat, and moved up to MacRory, putting a hand on his arm to restrain him. Red Hugh stared at Niall Garve as he spoke. "Turlough, I ask you to forgive that comment, and if my cousin is so ill-bred as to fail to apologise for his remark, I apologize for him."

---

[1] Viking battle-axe.

Niall Garve, surprised, looked from Red Hugh to Maguire, whose face was flushed with shame, then to MacRory who sat pale and quiet, holding the oars. Niall's own face reddened in anger. "How dare you offer to apologise for me? You do not apologise for me. Your words are insulting."

"And your words betray your lack of manners. If you take insult – and you should – I offer you any satisfaction that you feel is indicated."

"That I'll have."

"Whenever you wish."

Maguire held up both hands. "Niall Garve, think of who has really offered insult here, and think on the proper course for any honourable person. Your comment to MacRory was a foul thing and dishonors only yourself."

Like ripples disturbing the surface of the lough, changing passions played across the young man's face, then he, too, stood and moved up to stand in front of MacRory.

"Forgive me; the comment was unworthy of me.

There was a long horrible pause, and then MacRory nodded and said "Possibly it was". MacRory's emphasis on the word "possibly" was not lost on Niall Garve, whose face again reddened. MacRory resumed rowing seeming not to see the proffered hand.

The lough now carried them toward Ballyshannon and O'Donnell country. A few miles above the ford of Belleek, the lough narrowed into a fast-flowing river, which below the ford flowed through a deep gorge. Beyond the gorge and close to the Erne's entrance to the Atlantic were the Falls of Assaroe. An O'Donnell castle stood on the north bank of the river guarding another ford above the falls. Their destination, however, was Abbey Assaroe, a Cistercian abbey also on the north side of the river, and a few miles from the castle.

Below Belleek the current was noticeably faster. The vast volume of water of the two loughs, unusually high this year, funnelled into the narrow gorge in its rush to the ocean. They stayed close to the north side of the river as they approached the landing above the Falls of Assaroe, pulling hard to counteract the current and keep the boat on a heading for the landing.

For better control of the boat, Niall Garve now rowed with one large oar, MacRory with the other. Within feet of the landing, Maguire went forward to the bow, rope in hand. Niall Garve first leaned forward for leverage, and then heaved back mightily on his oar to bring the head of the boat alongside the landing. The oarlock lifted out of its socket and Niall Garve fell back, laughing into the well of the boat, losing his grip on the oar, which floated off. The boat drifted past the landing as Maguire leaped for the wooden platform. He gained the platform, rope in hand, only to be pulled back into the water by the heavy, fast-moving boat. He held the rope in one hand, using the other to attempt to swim, pulling the boat to shore.

MacRory threw down his now useless oar and leaped into the water to assist Maguire. As yet there seemed no danger, although the roar of the falls half a mile away could be heard. Red Hugh and Niall Garve, the latter no longer laughing, watched the efforts of the other two. Their efforts succeeded only in keeping the boat from being swept farther away from the bank into the centre of the river. The boat continued to be swept toward the falls. They all now appreciated some danger in their situation, and Maguire shouted to those in the boat that he was losing the battle.

Red Hugh and Niall Garve leaped from the boat and all swam for the shore. Red Hugh, farther downstream, and with a splinted right arm was now in danger. It looked as if the others, swimming and angling toward shore would make the bank, but with little enough to spare. MacRory, seeing O'Donnell's plight, stopped swimming to shore and swam directly downstream to reach O'Donnell. Both were excellent swimmers and used to swimming winter and summer in both Sheephaven and the Swilly.

The roar of the falls was much closer as MacRory, reaching his friend, turned on to his back and grabbed O'Donnell's hair in his teeth. This freed both his hands and allowed both men to swim with powerful backstrokes for shore. MacRory caught a glimpse of the abandoned boat disappearing from sight as it hurtled over the falls. They were now in swiftly moving water immediately above the roaring cataract. The roiling river was master and the efforts of the two to little avail.

Close to shore and a few feet above the falls the current swept them beneath the low overhanging branch of a large yew tree. MacRory threw up both hands, managing to grasp it. He continued to hold on to O'Donnell's long red mane in his teeth, while trying to keep his own head above the water. The falls roared angrily and deafeningly, for the moment cheated. Neither man could do anything to help the other. The swift deadly current pulled on the two bodies.

Maguire, dripping water, came running along the bank, and climbed out along the branch of the yew. The added weight on the branch made it still more difficult for MacRory to keep his head above water, but his teeth held on doggedly to O'Donnell's hair. Straddling the branch, Maguire reached out and was able to grip O'Donnell's left hand. As Maguire pulled O'Donnell towards him MacRory's head disappeared completely beneath the water but his teeth still remained clenched on O'Donnell's hair. Maguire pulled Red Hugh up across the branch which at the same time pulled MacRory's head above water. Even in this moment of extremity Maguire could not resist pretending to believe that MacRory's death grip on Red Hugh's hair was in order to save MacRory's own skin.

"Let go of the man's hair, MacRory, You're safe now. He's kept you afloat. You won't drown."

MacRory opened his aching jaw and let go of Red Hugh. He looked up at Maguire and with difficulty articulated the words:

"Get off the branch, you lard-arsed bastard. You're drowning me!"

Dampened only in body, the group approached the friary to be greeted with alarm by the abbot. They exchanged their wet clothing for warm Cistercian habits. Later in the refectory of the friary, the four new "monks" were the objects of some oblique looks by the bona fide members of the order. Clad in their warm clothes, and cheered by the warmth of the abbot's welcome once he recognized his guests, they were in high spirits. They sat around the abbot at the head of the table, and he offered them food and drink, and inquired further into the manner of their mishap. They regarded the whole episode lightly while he shuddered to think of the consequence had the heirs to Fermanagh and Donegal been swept over the falls.

Maguire took great delight in telling how MacRory had saved himself by hanging on by his teeth to O'Donnell's hair. "And when I finally succeeded in prying him loose from Hugh Roe's hair, he was so rude as to call me a 'lard-arsed bastard'." MacRory humoured him with a twisted smile. "My apologies Maguire if I was inadvertently rude but you misunderstood me. My jaws were aching and I had trouble articulating my words. What I had meant to say was 'you large-arsed bastard'." The gentle, old abbot affected not to have heard the exchange, but some of the younger monks looked with consternation from one to the other, as word of Maguire's celebrated temper had spread to even Assaroe's quiet cloisters. Maguire, who had come to like MacRory, liked him more than ever. The abbot, anxious to change the direction of the conversation, addressed himself to Red Hugh O'Donnell.

"You would not have been the first, Red Hugh, to have been swept over Assaroe. The name of the falls, *Eas Aodh Rua*[1], relates to an earlier Hugh Roe O'Donnell, who lost his life in the falls."

Red Hugh, who knew his family's history at least as well as the abbot, smiled and nodded with polite attention, giving the impression that he was being made aware of this for the first time. He knew that the Red Hugh after whom the falls were named was not a Red Hugh of the O'Donnells, but would never be so impolite as to point out the error to the older man, although he did allow his mind to dwell on how these clergy, accustomed to dealing with people less learned than themselves, could become foolishly pedantic. Having eaten, the abbot ushered them into a separate room that was spartan and spotless with a clean smell, and contained only some leather-bound manuscripts and a large well-oiled pine table and chairs. Here he left them to return with a young brown-robed Franciscan priest. The abbot introduced the newcomer with a certain deference, unusual considering the difference in the ages of the Cistercian Abbot and the younger Franciscan. The eminence of the company did not seem to daunt the Franciscan's assured manner. Educated at Salamanca in Spain, and recently arrived in Ireland, he was the newly appointed Provincial of the Franciscans in Ireland. Lady Nuala O'Donnell, the wife of an earlier O'Donnell chieftain, had brought the Franciscans to Donegal in the 1400s, and in the centuries since, the order had become inextricably associated with the family. Father O'Mulconry's destination was the Franciscan friary beside the O'Donnell castle in Donegal. His intelligent eyes travelled over the black and white Cistercian robes, incongruous on the longhaired group. "The Cistercians' gain is the Franciscans' loss. Certainly we

---

[1] (Irish) "Falls of Hugh Roe".

of the Friars Minor[1] would have been proud had we been able to recruit four such pious-looking noviciates." The young priest's Irish had the soft Galway inflection. Maguire irreverently informed him that they were the vanguard of a new order of untonsured Cistercians, superior in every way to the Friars Minor, and that Maguire himself was the "Monk Major."

The priest had soon engaged them in a conversation that was strangely secular, and for someone who had spent most of his recent life on the Continent, he was very conversant with current Irish affairs. As the Franciscan spoke, Maguire was intrigued to find that this newcomer was already aware of Alonzo Cabos' presence in Ireland.

"The North of Ireland is the only part of the country that is still independent of English rule. The O'Neill's, the O'Donnells, and the Maguires are the most powerful of the northern families. If Don Alonzo Cabos can report back to Philip of Spain that these northern chieftains will unite against England, Spain will support them with arms and fighting men. Hugh O'Neill was groomed in England to be an English earl to rule Tyrone for the English, but it is rumoured that his ambition reaches higher. It is also well known that the O'Donnells and the Maguires are beginning to resent the intrusion of English sheriffs in their lands. The northern chieftains have merely to look south to Connacht[2] to see the result of cooperation with England. An alliance of the northern chieftains under O'Neill would attract others and might unite all Ireland."

"The Irish have not been united under an *Ard Rí*[3] since the time of Malachy[4] and Brian more than five hundred years ago," Maguire mused.

"The country united then to face the Norse, and the country must unite now to face the English. If Ireland does not unite, and unite soon, under its own *Ard Rí*, an English king will rule all of Ireland. Ireland cannot prevail against a powerful country such as England, and England is powerful because England is united. Spain

---

[1] A Franciscan order.
[2] One of Ireland's four provinces, the others being Ulster, Munster and Leinster.
[3] (Irish) "High King".
[4] Malachy and Brian, the last of Ireland's High Kings.

is powerful because Spain is united. Ireland needs a powerful ally, and Spain is willing to be that ally."

The young chieftains listened with interest. Political discussions had been part of their education since childhood.

"Would such an alliance with Spain not be exchanging one master for another?" Red Hugh queried.

The priest nodded and admitted that this was a possibility, but an unlikely one. "Spain's main interest in Ireland is to divert England's attention in the coming Spanish assault on England. In this Ireland's interest could also be served."

This was the first time he had alluded to a Spanish assault and his listeners were doubly interested. The idea of an all-Irish alliance was a novel one, and while they agreed with the merit of such an alliance, they also foresaw the difficulties. A strong leader could oust the English, but at what cost to the others? Which of them would willingly accept an overlord?

The conversation then went on to other matters. It turned out that Maguire had visited the Irish College[1] at Douai in Spain's Flemish territory at a time when Father O'Mulconry had been in residence there as a student. Maguire had also been to Salamanca where the priest had finished his studies, and he and the priest discussed the likelihood that Philip of Spain might establish an Irish College there also.

When mention of the monastic settlements on the Erne came up, the priest commenced a discussion on the early Irish Celtic Church.

"Initially there was little central authority. Each monastic settlement surrounded itself with a religious community. In those early days the system worked well and continued in this fashion into the eleventh century. The Celtic church resembled the Byzantine, and both eventually became at odds with the Roman church. The latter had developed into a hierarchical system of cardinals, bishops, and priests under a central authority in Rome. In 1155 Pope Adrian IV issued a papal bull awarding Ireland to Henry II in order to bring the Irish Church into line with the Roman model."

---

[1] After the Reformation, it became necessary for Irish priests to be educated abroad in Irish Colleges.

"An English Pope awarding Ireland to an English King," Maguire commented. "It's difficult to say whether more harm is done when church and king act in collusion with each other, or when they oppose each other."

"A central authority exerts more power and control," the priest commented, assuming that he was having the last word on the subject.

"The Roman church gave law, the Celtic church gave love," Maguire quoted an Irish saying.

The priest turned and commenced a conversation with Red Hugh, gauging him. He knew this boy was the preferred O'Donnell heir, although under Brehon Law, his brothers, Rory and Donel, and cousin Niall Garve, among others, were also in line. He mentioned how the English were trying to impose the law of primogeniture, whereby the oldest son inherited, and this was often in conflict with the Irish Brehon Law. When Shane had tried to usurp the O'Neill title, it had caused a war among the O'Neills.

Red Hugh, well versed in Brehon Law, eagerly accepted the older man's implied challenge.

"For generations that part of Brehon Law dealing with the election of the chief has served well in Ireland, providing a choice whereby the sept selects the ablest chieftain from among the *Derbfine*[1]. Admittedly this arrangement has sometimes resulted in warfare among the contenders, but the ultimate goal of a strong leader has always been of utmost importance. Indeed, whenever a weak chieftain rules, war is inevitable. While the ancient Celtic custom of killing the chieftain when he became feeble and ineffective is long since only a memory it perhaps had its uses in a warrior society. More recently the election of a *tániste*[2] during the reigning chieftain's lifetime often prevents dissention on his death. What has really caused dissention, however, has been the imposition of late of the English system of primogeniture. How can there be anything but discord, and this is a deliberately fostered discord, when the English support one contender according to the practice of primogeniture and their feudal laws, and the sept

---

[1] (Irish) "Those of the ruling family in direct descent from a common grandfather".
[2] (Irish) "Heir apparent".

supports another according to the usage of our Brehon Law? The automatic succession of the eldest son makes no sense. By what reasoning is the eldest son necessarily the ablest to rule?"

Maguire interrupted.

"Speaking of chieftains in times past, what has become of the custom whereby the chieftain had to be "without blemish"? Apparently it no longer applies, as witnessed by the election of the lame Con Bacach to the leadership of the O'Neill. It certainly was no hindrance to his being awarded the English title of First Earl of Tyrone, nor to his present grandson's acceptance of the title of Second Earl!"

"Interesting point, Maguire. I suppose some things have changed a bit since ancient times, but let me continue about the Brehon Law.

"Under Brehon Law, the sept owns the land and every member of the sept has as much right to the land as has the chief, but under English feudal law, the chief owns the land and on his death, his eldest son inherits the title to the land. Such a system must eventually lead to discontent among the people, who living and working on the land, are merely slaves without any share in the land. When the Earl of Kildare, and more recently the Earl of Desmond, were declared traitors, their lands reverted to the English monarch under England's feudal laws. Their people were dispossessed and the land parcelled out among English settlers. Such injustice to our people would never have been countenanced under Brehon Law."

The priest decided to play the devil's advocate.

"The English have never held Irish Brehon Law in any high regard. In the Statutes of Kilkenny they outlawed the Irish system of justice, stating that Brehon Law 'reasonably ought not to be called law, being a bad custom'."

"Brehon Law was outlawed because it stood in the way of English conquest. The Statutes of Kilkenny were formulated in 1366; two hundred years after Strongbow and his Normans invaded Ireland. The Norman-English invaders of 1169 had, by 1366, become Norman Irish. They spoke Irish, adopted Irish customs, and abandoned the English law for the Irish Brehon code. The Statutes of Kilkenny were an attempt by England to re-impose English law. Is it not of significance in itself, Father O'Mulconry, that the English King Edward felt it necessary to proscribe our

Brehon Law? Why was this archaic law, this mere 'bad custom' so dangerous and so seductive? Why, in our own times, have hundreds of families left the Pale to live under the Brehon code?

"These laws were evolved by our people, for our people, and have stood the test of generations. They have become suited to and interwoven in our culture. Our people obey these laws because they are our laws. Our pagan ancestors obeyed our Brehon Laws, our Christian ancestors modified those laws, and we still live by them today. In the more than three centuries from Ireland's conversion to Christianity until the Norse invasions in the late 8th century, our people lived by these laws and lived in peace both at home and with our neighbours beyond our shores. The only conquering armies we sent abroad were monks to conquer paganism and scholars to conquer ignorance."

Maguire, ever in favour of an argument and fearful that O'Donnell's persuasiveness might silence the opposition, leaped in on the side of the priest and the devil.

"All very well, O'Donnell, but in addition to being just, the law should be easily understood by all. Of what use is a law that has become so complex that only a special elite can comprehend and interpret it? Under our law the Brehons levy one *eric*[1] for a blow to the cheek, another for a blow to the chin, one penalty for a blow that breaks the skin, another for a blow that does not. Different levels of compensation if a man bitten while separating a dogfight is the owner, with a bias toward his own dog, or an unbiased spectator, or some meddlesome passing idiot."

"I admit the Brehon Law has its faults, and complexity is one of them, but can you devise a better code? In seeking justice, all aspects of a problem have to be explored. Justice is difficult to achieve and rarely attained, but should we not strive for it? Few people, even the Brehons, are capable of knowing all of the law. In many walks of life we need the help of people with special knowledge. Your own family, Maguire, and mine need the services of physicians, shanachies, and teachers."

---

[1] "Penalty" or "Fine"

"Don't forget the priests whose function it is to remind us that everything we enjoy is sinful, immoral and illegal, Is it true, Father, that sex is only a sin if you enjoy it?"

"As a priest I am supposed to be somewhat of an authority on sin, but as a celibate not much of an authority on the enjoyment of sex. We Franciscans are taught to curb our appetites." The priest smiled at Maguire, feeling that with this veiled chastisement he'd had the last word on the subject.

Maguire smiled back and quoted an Irish proverb: "*Is maith an t-anlann an t-ocras.*"[1]

Neill Garve now also joined the argument, predictably opposing his cousin.

"Once the Brehon gives his decision, who will enforce that judgement if the miscreant chooses to ignore the decision of the Brehon? The sheriff and the constable enforce English law, but we have no such means of enforcing Irish law."

"The people themselves enforce the judgements, and anyone ignoring a judgement is branded an outlaw, an outcast, destined to live and die without the protection of his sept. Who better to enforce a judgement than the people themselves? You know how much the people value justice and love to see justice done. You know how much they respect the Brehons. How often is the Brehon's decision ignored? Who has the courage to ignore it? Not even a chief dare ignore the judgement of a Brehon."

"They are a respected and respectable group, and their judgements are usually just," Maguire admitted. "There's a story of a Brehon in olden times who wore a solid gold torque[2] around his neck. If he gave a false judgement, the torque tightened, choking him until he revised his decision. Sad how mundane our world has become! One so seldom nowadays sees a choking Brehon! Perhaps they're getting the hang of getting it right. Interesting to be present when that Brehon gave a judgement unfavourable to his chieftain! Surely a tricky decision – whether to be choked by your own collar now, or by the chieftain's noose later!"

---

[1] "Hunger is the best sauce".
[2] Collar

It had previously been arranged that Red Hugh and Niall Garve were to accompany the Franciscan to Donegal while Maguire and MacRory returned to Fermanagh, MacRory to meet his uncle, Donagh, who was a captain of the Maguire gallowglass.

Again dressed in their own clothes and supplied with horses at O'Donnell's castle above Assaroe, the two groups parted at the ford below Belleek. Red Hugh called back to MacRory that they would again meet at Sheephaven in four weeks. Much would occur in each man's life before they again met in four years.

CHAPTER 5

Brookeborough Raid

The town of Brookeborough in Fermanagh was small and dreary, consisting of one main street and no others. Close to one end of the street stood the police barracks of the Royal Ulster Constabulary. Police elsewhere in the United Kingdom operated out of police stations, but in Northern Ireland they sallied forth from "barracks." The R.U.C., all tall men, in accordance with the forces' minimum height requirement, went about law enforcement armed with a heavy Webley revolver strapped at the waist and an arsenal of rifles and sten guns stored in the barracks. Another armed force called the "B Specials," who trained weekly and were available for emergencies, backed up the R.U.C. The R.U.C. and the "B Specials" functioned to enforce the laws and the policies of the Unionist government at Stormont in Belfast, and to act as an armed deterrent to any I.R.A. militant nationalist aspirations for a united Ireland.

Close to the village was Colebrooke, the residence of the Brooke family after whom the village was named, and the current Brooke, Sir Basil, was Prime Minister of Northern Ireland. Sir Basil was the nephew of Alan Brooke, or to give him his full, and fully merited, title: Field Marshall the Rt. Hon. Alan Francis Brooke, 1st. Viscount Alanbrooke, KG, GCB, OM, GCBO, and DSO & Bar.

Alan Brooke had chosen to be born in Southern France where the climate was better. In the recent war Alanbrooke had been Chief of the Imperial General Staff and a respected confidante of Churchill, with whom he did not always see eye to eye, and by whom he was not overawed. The Brookes were not accustomed to being overawed by anyone. Churchill said of him that when he, Churchill, wishing to dominate in an argument, pounded the table and thrust his face forward "that stubborn Ulsterman pounded the table twice as hard in response". In his memoirs Alanbrooke had no hesitation in criticising many of Churchill's wartime decisions. Montgomery called Alanbrooke England's finest soldier, a somewhat surprising accolade as one would have imagined Montgomery would have reserved that pedestal for himself. Perhaps the fact that they were both Ulstermen swayed his judgement. As Churchill's military advisor and England's foremost soldier Alanbrooke worked closely with and was widely respected also by the American allies. Perhaps after the passage of more than a century Eisenhower could jokingly remind Alanbrooke of how a Brooke relative, Colonel Arthur Brooke, had helped burn down the White House in the war of 1812. What was now Colebrooke had once been *Aghalun*[1], a Maguire residence.

The Brookes came to Ireland in Elizabethan times. An earlier Sir Basil had taken over the O'Donnell castle in Donegal after the defeat of the Irish chieftains in that time in Irish History known as the "Plantation of Ulster." A son of this earlier Sir Basil was granted 30,000 acres of land in Fermanagh when the previous owner the "Traitor" Lord Maguire had been hanged at Tyburn for attempting to regain his ancestral lands in the rebellion of 1641. The Tyburn hangman was kept busy plying his craft on Irish traitors. In the intervening centuries the Brookes had fought in all of England's wars. Some rested in far off battlefields, including two of the Prime Minister's sons who had been killed in action in WW 11. The Prime Minister himself had fought with distinction in the First World War, winning the Military Cross and the Croix de Guerre. One of his sons had also won the Military Cross. Of the 23 Brookes who had marched to war in two world wars, eighteen had died. For three and a half centuries this distinguished Northern Ireland family had valiantly fought for England.

Would that this had been for Ireland[2].

Traffic from Enniskillen to Belfast passed through Brookeborough, but usually found little reason to stop. On New Year's Eve in 1957, a gravel lorry, carrying a group of men and a Bren gun stopped close to a pub near the barracks. Some of the men got out, passed by the pub, and continued down the street. One of the men carried a mine intended to blast down the door of the police barracks. The others were armed with Thompson submachine guns. Sean South, one of the five men who remained in the back of the lorry, opened fire on the barracks with a Bren gun mounted on a tripod; the others opened fire with submachine guns. There were three constables and a sergeant in the barracks. From an upstairs window of the barracks Sergeant Cordner pushed a sten gun over the window sill and poured the contents of a magazine down onto the lorry below. The sten gun was a fairly inaccurate weapon that merely threw out a fan of bullets, but its deterrent effect was considerable. The metal sides of the lorry gave no protection from the fire from the upstairs windows, and now also a Bren

---

[1] (Irish) "Field of the Blackbirds".
[2] The exiled Patrick Sarsfield, Earl of Lucan, dying on a battlefield in Flanders in 1693, was reputed to have said. "Would that this had been for Ireland". Sarsfield had led the Irish forces at the Boyne, Aughrim and the Siege of Limerick. His ancestors were "Old English Catholic" who had come to Ireland five centuries earlier with the Normans.

gun returned fire from the barracks. Sean South, groaned as a bullet struck him, and three more raiders were also wounded. One raider threw a grenade at the barracks, which bounced back from a windowsill and exploded beneath the lorry, hurtling one of the wounded men from the lorry to the pavement. The mine placed at the door of the barracks failed to go off and one man made a suicidal dash back to get another mine from the truck. This one also failed to explode, even when urged to do so by having submachine gun bullets pumped into it.

The men, having failed to gain entrance to the barracks, raced back and scrambled into the back of the lorry amidst what was now a leaden hail from the upstairs windows. The late-evening peace of the sleepy little town was shattered with the rattle of gunfire.

The shattered safety glass of the windshield made it impossible for the driver to see out and he hammered a hole in the glass with a rifle butt. Gunfire had damaged the tipping mechanism of the lorry, further exposing the men in the lorry to the fire from the police. The lorry, with two flat tires, raced along a narrow by-road up a mountain heading for the border with the Irish Republic seven miles away. The R.U.C. and a force of B Specials pursued in jeeps.

In the back of the truck, Sean South was dying and Fergal O'Hanlon would require early medical treatment if he were to survive. Four others were also wounded. It was almost certain that the police at the town of Rosslea on the road ahead between them and the Monaghan border would have already been alerted. The only safety lay in abandoning the lorry and heading across the fields to the nearby border. Vincent Conlon, the driver, stopped at a crossroads, known locally as Moane's Cross, for a quick conference with the men in the back. Sean South and Fergal O'Hanlon were now both unconscious. The others carried the two dying men into a disused, stonewalled cow byre close to the crossroads. Sean Garland, himself wounded, asked to be left with his two unconscious comrades, but the others would not allow it. The distant sound of the pursuing jeeps came faintly from the road below.

Having said a last farewell to the two dying men and supporting their wounded comrades, the remainder set out across the moor for the County Monaghan border. Ten minutes later they stopped and looked back as they heard several minutes of sustained sten gun fire, then after a pause one further long burst. Later the body of Sean South was sent back to his home beside the Shannon. He and Fergal O'Hanlon had joined the long list of martyrs, and in the Irish tradition were soon immortalized in the song, "Sean South of Garryowen."

For years afterwards the story circulated that the R.U.C. and B Specials had so riddled the bodies of the two dying men, or possibly their already dead bodies, that the bodies were unrecognizable. This was later found to be incorrect, but only after it caused years of resentment in the nationalist community.

The Brookeborough raid in 1957 typified the blood sacrifice ideal of a prior generation, the ideal engendered by the men of Easter Week of 1916, whose fatalistic but gallant efforts had aroused the conscience of the country. The Brookeborough raid also typified everything that was lacking in the training and organization of the I.R.A. of the fifties.

The I.R.A. men of the fifties – poorly armed and knowing only the end they wished to achieve, but with no clear perception of how to achieve it – were one generation removed from the struggle of their fathers who had secured a republic for the south of Ireland. They regarded the situation in Northern Ireland as unfinished business, and were quite willing to die for the cause of a united Ireland. The authorities in Northern Ireland showed willingness, and indeed an eagerness, to help them die for that cause. The lack of organization, training, and equipment of the I.R.A. of those days made this work of the authorities easier.

During the Second World War, members of the I.R.A., on the premise that England's enemy was Ireland's friend, sought help from Nazi Germany. This did not endear the I.R.A to Irishmen north and south fighting in the British Army or to Americans, Australians, and Canadians of Irish descent fighting Hitler's obscene regime.

The Northern Ireland government in Stormont, overwhelmingly Unionist and Loyalist, English in sentiment and by long tradition, looked to London and wished to have nothing to do with the Dublin government south of the border. The thought of breaking ties with England and joining in a United Ireland was enough to send any staunch Scotch-Irish Presbyterian into laager mode. Yet Unionists and Nationalists seemed to have forgotten that Wolfe Tone, a Belfast Protestant who had led the United Irishmen Rebellion of 1798, had planted the first seeds of a United Ireland and that the two creeds had at that time fought together for the common goals. Ever since, however, for close to two centuries, the Ulster Loyalists had entrenched themselves as an English enclave in the northern part of the island. These Ulstermen were Irish only to the extent of being strongly influenced in the present by events of the distant past. They were not Irish, nor did they wish to be, in any other respect. They were hyphenated Irish preferring to be known as Scotch-Irish or Anglo-Irish in order to distance themselves from the unhyphenated mere Irish. Despite the fact that three hundred and fifty years separated them from their Scottish and English forebears, they were prouder of their ties to Scotland and England than of any ties to the rest of Ireland.

In Northern Ireland 12 July until 12 August was known as the "marching season." William III had defeated James II, the Catholic King of England, at the Battle of the Boyne in 1690 in Ireland. The Irish were on the wrong side of the Boyne and some said on the side of the wrong English king. William led from the front, while in the words of one Irish historian, "James did all that was possible to secure a defeat. He contrived to be first in the retreat which he had anticipated, and for which he had so carefully prepared."

Each year on the "Glorious Twelfth" the Unionists, whose ancestors had fought alongside William of Orange, marched with banners flying and drums beating, remembering the Boyne. The air in many a town throughout Northern Ireland reverberated to the thunderous beat of the large Lambeg drum and to the tread of marching Protestant feet as the flute and pipes played "The Protestant Boys", "The Sash", and "The Green Grassy Slopes of the Boyne."

Would the marching feet have faltered, and would the flutes have hit a sour note if those sash-bedecked marchers had chosen to remember the events of 1690 more accurately? Due to the vagaries of European politics, Pope Alexander V111 and William of Orange were allies against the French King Louis X1V and his protégée, the deposed King James 11. In honor of William's victory at the Boyne, the Pope celebrated a pontifical high mass and ordered the singing of a Te Deum?

The Nationalists saw this celebration as an annual rubbing of the Nationalist nose in it, or to use a word frequently heard in Ulster, "Triumphalism."

The Unionists regarded it as their right to annually celebrate the events of the "Glorious Twelfth". If Nationalists were thin-skinned enough to be upset by some of the lyrics of "The Protestant Boys", then that was their problem – the problem of the present generation and the fault of past generations.

> "When treason was rampant and traitors were strong,
> And law was defiled by a vile rebel throng,
> When thousands were banded the throne to cast down,
> The Protestants rallied and stood by the Crown."

A man had to be exceedingly brave or exceedingly foolish, or possibly both, to go up to one of those proud descendants of the victors of the Boyne, who wore the traditional blue-and-orange sash, together with that other relic of a bygone era, the bowler hat, and ask: "Would you give us 'Sean South of Garryowen' next? It's the same air as 'Roddy McCorley'".

CHAPTER 6

A Gallowglass captain

The illness, which prevented MacRory from returning to Sheephaven, commenced soon after he returned to Maguire's castle. Looking back, however, he was aware of having felt unwell for some time. He had suffered from occasional abdominal pains, nausea, and the flux, and these symptoms now progressed to a disinterest in eating and weight loss.

O'Cassidy's services were enlisted and the old man questioned him in detail, wanting to know when his sickness had started, what were his bowel habits, and what had he eaten recently and what was he in the habit of eating. O'Cassidy had even been interested in what his diet had been at MacSweeney's household. Were the beef and pork and fish well cooked?

MacRory, already ill, had difficulty in replying with the requisite politeness to some of these irrelevant questions, and for someone who was somewhat fastidious, he found his patience and sense of propriety further assailed when the old man insisted on examining daily samples of stool and urine. If MacRory happened to vomit, he had to save some for O'Cassidy's perusal.

The physician finally seemed to have come to a conclusion. MacRory was not allowed anything to eat for two days, after which the doctor increased his patient's discomfort by giving him a salt purge. The following day he was given two tablespoonfuls of a bitter and foul tasting liquid, which the physician referred to as "extract of male fern," and which was used for tapeworm infestation. It may as well have been a poison, for the pain only worsened overnight and settled in the right lower abdomen. When MacRory commenced vomiting and developed a distended abdomen, O'Cassidy felt his forehead with the back of the hand, checked the pulse, looked at the tongue, looked at the abdomen, felt the abdomen, percussed the abdomen, and even laid his ear to the abdomen. He then stood and looked at his patient with a grave face.

MacRory had little remembrance of events after this until some weeks later, and had only learned of them subsequently from Hugh Maguire. Apparently MacRory had been near death with a high fever and delirium. He had a memory of some events, but in a disjointed fashion. He seemed to remember Maguire and O'Cassidy sitting beside him. O'Cassidy's red face swam often into his consciousness. In a delirium he relived his nightmare in the Hebrides. He floated in and out of consciousness, but over weeks between life and death, the balance slowly tipped in his favour and he had lived. His bloated abdomen subsided and O'Cassidy gave him sips of warm water with dissolved honey and salt to drink. Initially his urine was scant and dark amber in colour, but as it increased in quantity, O'Cassidy seemed pleased. MacRory gradually regained his strength.

"You've milked your illness for all the sympathy you'll get. You can't lay there like some, some ... some lard arsed sloth forever." Hugh Maguire stood over him, a mock scowl on his face.

Several days earlier O'Cassidy had pronounced the patient would live, but the patient himself was of the opinion that the doctor's prognosis was rash and uninformed. When MacRory stood, his legs would not support him and he felt light-headed and weak. He sat on the side of the bed and drank a salty broth O'Cassidy held out to him. When he finished, Maguire helped he patient to his feet, and addressed the doctor.

"Did you know, O'Cassidy that in China the physician is only paid a fee if his patient recovers?"

O'Cassidy, supporting his patient, had is back to Maguire, but if such a thing as an audible smirk were possible O'Cassidy's response came close to achieving it.

"I suppose it would be a bit more difficult to collect one's fee from a dead patient," was O'Cassidy's smug response.

"Did you also know, O'Cassidy, that when Hephaestion, the friend of Alexander the Great, died of an illness, Alexander had the physician castrated and then crucified?" Maguire smiled at the older man.

"That seems a mite testy to me. I hope he didn't also withhold the man's fee."

O'Cassidy pretended to be preoccupied in examining his patient, lest it appear that he paid much attention to his tormentor, or that his replies required much in the way of mental effort.

"I have often thought that the threat of castration would keep a physician on his toes – a sobering thought, O'Cassidy."

O'Cassidy straightened and turned to look directly at Maguire.

"Certainly food for thought, Hugh, but don't you think that such a threat might poison the doctor-patient relationship? And speaking of food for thought, have you yourself ever considered employing a food taster? You've heard how the English attempted to have Shane O'Neill poisoned by his own physician."

Feeling he had won the battle, if not the war, he turned and beamed on his patient. "Walk a little more each day. You'll feel weak for a while, but soon you'll be as strong as ever."

But Hugh Maguire rarely conceded any battle. "They're a sinister race, these English, and no doubt about that. Imagine having a physician poison a man – and poison him on purpose! Of course, not a difficult task for any physician, since they regularly poison us by accident."

MacRory's strength did return as predicted, and in a few weeks he was able to sit a horse and joined Maguire on a trip to the Maguire castle of Lisnaskea. The castle was ten miles from Enniskillen and set back about two miles from the shore of the Upper Lough. Lisnaskea, not Enniskillen, was the ancient seat of the Maguires, and it was here also that past generations were buried close by at the Maguire graveyard of Aghalurcher. In 1430 the Maguires split into a senior branch in Lisnaskea and a junior branch in Enniskillen. From that time the chief of the sept had been elected from one or the other branch, but since 1540 all the sept chieftains of the Maguires, with the assistance of the powerful O'Donnells, had come from the junior branch of the family in Enniskillen.

"In Lisnaskea you'll meet some of your MacRory kinsmen from the Isles," Maguire told him. "Donagh MacRory, your uncle, is a Consupal[1] of the MacRory gallowglass there, as was his father. His father, your grandfather, was killed in a skirmish with the O'Reillys. Your uncle has earned a reputation in this part of the world. He demands much of his men, including implicit obedience. He forbids them to loot, and once, after a battle, he took the dangerous course of interposing his gallowglass between the Irish, eager for revenge, and the enemy he had helped defeat. When one of his men defied his orders and raped a woman, he invited the man

---

[1] Captain

to a sword fight, and of course such an invitation from any captain of gallowglass was an invitation to death."

"While at Fanad I heard a rumour that my uncle Donagh had gone to the Isles to seek Alistair MacDonald."

"He did, and he found him. I'll tell you the story as I myself heard it from a soldier in the employ of the Duke of Argyle. Donagh has never spoken of it.

"Your uncle informed my father that he was returning to the Isles where he had some business to attend to. There he sought out Alistair MacDonald on Uist, but MacDonald, knowing Donagh's reputation, had fled to Argyle on the Scottish Mainland where he enlisted in the army of Archibald Campbell, the Duke of Argyle. Donagh crossed over to Argyle and also enlisted as a soldier in the Duke's army." Maguire smiled at his companion. "I imagine, though, that Donagh was not contemplating any long term commitment to the Duke.

"Some say that when they met, your uncle killed Alistair MacDonald, but I have also heard that MacDonald died later from his wounds. Argyle, who at that time commanded an army larger than any other in either England or Scotland, was displeased at this unauthorized loss of even one man, and decided he would accept the loss of two. Your uncle was imprisoned in Inveraray Castle awaiting hanging.

"When Donagh escaped, killing his jailer who was a MacDonald, the Duke lost another man. Now armed, Donagh fled westward. Archibald Campbell, more than ever determined to hang the fugitive, sent twenty men in pursuit. Of these twenty, seventeen were MacDonalds who had volunteered in order to avenge their kinsmen. His pursuers caught up with Donagh as he was crossing from the mainland to the island of Jura in a coracle which he had commandeered. They were closing on him in a larger boat and rashly followed him into the Corryvreckan maelstrom between Jura and Scarba. The smaller coracle survived the maelstrom. The larger boat did not. Three days later two more of Campbell's soldiers, one of them a MacDonald lost their lives. These two were unfortunate enough to come on Donagh as he was getting into a small boat at the tip of the Isle of Isla within sight of the Irish coast twenty-three miles away. The muster of the Duke's army was now short twenty-three men, indeed twenty-four if the reluctant recruit sailing for the

Irish coast be counted! The MacDonald clan muster was short by twenty men."

In the courtyard of Lisnaskea castle a tall man of about thirty-five walked toward Turlough MacRory with outstretched hand. Turlough had a moment of shocked disbelief. It was his father! The lean body and the loose-limbed walk. The blue eyes in the lean angular face. But apart from the startling resemblance to his father, Turlough had seen this man before. The Hill of Aileach! How could this be! Why this torment? He shuddered as he saw again in his dream the man who, with his sword, had released him from Alistair MacDonald's grip.

But the strong hand that gripped Turlough's was of flesh and blood. Everything about his uncle, from the slow smile to the mannerism of tilting his head as he talked, brought to the younger MacRory an aching recollection of his dead father. Turlough had never before met his uncle, who had been for many years in Ireland, but the man's resemblance to his father awakened in him a yearning remembrance of the life and the people he had deliberately exiled from his thoughts. In the man's presence the younger MacRory again experienced the same sense of security and safety that he had in his own father's company.

In the months that followed, Turlough MacRory frequently spent time with his uncle at Lisnaskea. When the exiles spoke of their home in the Isles, Turlough learned much from his uncle that he had never known of his own father's life before he himself was born. Amazingly he had never before been told that his father and Donagh were twins.

Turlough and his uncle stood on a hilltop called the Moate, one of the inaugural sites of the Maguire chieftains, and looked across at the castle of Lisnaskea half a mile away.

"Did you think your parents had no life prior to your arrival? Three quarters of their lives had passed behind them before you were born. When your mother, Oona MacDonald, eloped with your father, it caused a clan war that left few MacRorys alive on Uist. She was betrothed to another of the MacDonald clan. After the elopement she and Rory fled to Argyle where your oldest brother, Ian, was born.

"But your father was stubborn and he insisted on returning to the Isles where he lived a dangerous life surrounded by MacDonald enemies. After he killed Randal MacDonald in a sword fight, it was only a matter of time before the MacDonalds exacted their cowardly revenge. Rory was always headstrong and our father could not prevail on him to come with us to Ireland as a gallowglass. Your mother, God have mercy on her soul, was a gentle woman, and the constant conflict put her in her grave before her time. You and I are now all that are left of our immediate family. Even though the MacDonalds trace their blood back to ours, they have shed the blood of many of our sept and put many a MacRory in his grave."

When his uncle went on to speak of the bad blood between the MacDonalds and what was left of the MacRorys, Turlough noticed there was an element of fatalism in the older man's attitude. It was as if no compromise or accommodation could ever be possible, and the dictates of blood feud had a life and inevitability of their own. Turlough wondered how this attitude could have been bred into an otherwise humane and intelligent man. He noted, though, that Donagh MacRory sought no revenge for his own father's death at the hands of the O'Reillys. Such a death in battle was accepted as the inherent fate of any gallowglass.

Donagh MacRory had once married, but his wife died in childbirth. The baby had been too large, and Donagh watched helplessly as his wife suffered the slow death of an obstructed birth. The obscene agony ended when Donagh ordered the midwife to leave the bedside and instructed her to leave behind the bottle of laudanum[1].

His gallowglass were now his life. He shared the same spartan barracks, cared dearly for the welfare of each of his rough charges, and after a battle, he mourned the losses as if they were his own children. He sought to minimise those losses by ensuring that no lack of skill in their profession contributed to their death, but often skill alone was not sufficient. Their lives were often squandered by the rashness of a chieftain and their deaths accepted with a strange professional fatalism by both the captain and the men.

On occasion, at the end of the day, he joined with his gallowglass in the songs of the Hebrides; the lilting plaintive tunes, sad and soothing, and the clear strong voice that rallied his men in battle could be heard above the others drifting out from the

---

[1] A morphine-derived analgesic.

quarters of these mercenary exiles. His profession had not brutalized the tough and capable mercenary, a soldier since early adulthood and a captain of soldiers, nor did any soldier under his command ever engage in the senseless, brutal slaughter so often the aftermath of a battle. There was something incongruous in the sight of this hardened soldier kneeling with child-like simplicity beside his bed in the barracks each night to pray. He prayed the prayers he had been taught in childhood. He prayed also for forgiveness for ending his wife's life, although his own conscience forgave him for ending her suffering.

As his strength returned, Turlough engaged in daily sword and pike practice with his uncle's gallowglass. His uncle, in his capacity of Captain of gallowglass, was a ruthless professional whose dictates were never questioned. Likewise he was painfully merciless in exposing any weakness in his men's technique with sword or halberd. There was much realism to these practice sessions and any man whose guard was faulty was made to feel something of what he might experience should a similar lapse occur in battle.

"If you mean to be a gallowglass, sword play will be your life, learn it well for your life will depend on it. Admittedly, though, you could nowadays as likely die by a musket ball sent your way by someone whose only skill is the ability to squeeze a trigger. If you lose your concentration and do not apply yourself in sword practice, you may get injured," Turlough told his men. "If you lose your concentration in battle, there is the absolute assurance of injury, and usually of mortal injury."

Donagh made no exception for his nephew, who, often bleeding from several non-lethal wounds, defended himself with desperation born of that hint of uncertainty as to whether his opponent's next slash or thrust might be lethal. However, it was exactly this uncompromising element of danger that Turlough MacRory found challenging and exciting. He also found as time went on that he was better than most with sword and halberd. With practice his defence became less frantic and he seemed to fall naturally into an almost relaxed state, which was also, however, at some instinctive or involuntary level a state of focused deliberation.

The older MacRory was a patient but unrelenting coach. "Relax your shoulders; relax your arm, your wrist, your hand. Relax your body. The mind, not the hand, guides the sword. You don't believe me! You refuse to learn! Then pay the cost."

The cost was usually a painful one.

Initially, the younger MacRory found it difficult to relax while defending against a slashing sword edge ready to deal pain or death. With practice, however, he did find that as he relaxed, his movements became faster, more fluid, and more precise. His sword became an extension of his arm and ultimately of his mind.

From childhood MacRory had felt awkward interacting with others. Such things as figures of speech and humour, that were easily understandable to others, were complexities to him. He himself could not easily dissemble or tell a lie and he could not detect a lie in others. Consequently to make sense of his world he unconsciously absorbed the body language that accompanied speech. Now in practicing swordmanship he found that he could instinctively read body language. He could predict his opponents actions, and felt as if, on occasion, he was reading the very thought that heralded the action. The day came when; with surprised satisfaction, his uncle realized that his pupil's expertise matched that of his teacher. His uncle's only edge was experience.

Hugh Maguire was born to a life of privilege, and until his father's death, a life of leisure. While his father ruled Fermanagh, the young Maguire's life was untrammelled with any great responsibility and he had ample time for leisure. He was an accomplished swordsman and horseman, as were all members of the chieftains' households. From early days, they were taught martial skills. Maguire practiced with all weapons, spear, crossbow, longbow, musket, and the heavy, two-handed broadsword, but the weapon of choice for the nobles was the rapier type of sword, sometimes referred to in Ireland as a 'claybeg', popular as a dress sword because of its light weight and shorter length. The sports and leisure pursuits most enjoyed were those with an element of danger, and when the ultimate sport of war was not available, duelling, sword practice, and hunting from horseback were favoured.

Hugh Maguire, Turlough MacRory, and Conn O'Neill sat their horses and listened to the shouts and cries drifting down wind toward them from the beaters in the woods, who were still a mile away. Each man had a long spear couched under his arm, but as yet they sat relaxed without any anticipation of any immediate action.

"I don't think we give the boar much of a chance, three men on horseback against one small pig on foot," Maguire mused.

"One large, fast pig, nimble and well-balanced on four feet, with tusks that can slice as cleanly as this sword," Conn O'Neill replied.

"What's your opinion Turlough?" Maguire turned to MacRory. "Myself, I think O'Neill lacks a sense of fairness. It would be fairer if we dismount, get down on all fours, and bite the pig, but only fairer if we do so one at a time"

"If you carried justice and fairness to that extreme, the pig would win," O'Neill replied, and then murmured: "*Justitia et porci invincibilii sunt.*"

Maguire stared at him in disbelief. The Maguire family motto, *Justitia et Fortitudo Invincibilia Sunt*[1] had just been rendered into "Justice, and the pigs are invincible."

A crash in the underbrush and a large tusker burst into the clearing below. It stood, head moving from side to side, shaking a yellow froth from his mouth, and then a pair of small eyes focused on the horsemen above. For a moment the pig glared malevolently at its foes, and then darted into a thicket to one side.

Maguire dismounted, handed his reins up to MacRory, and walked to the thicket with spear in hand. The boar's small eyes watched his approach, then, head down, slavering and grunting with rage, it charged the man on foot. Maguire, although somewhat taken by surprise at the speed of the animal, still had time to leap aside to avoid the venomous snorting rush, and as he did so, he stabbed with his spear. The animal squealed as blood sprayed from its flank and wheeled around in a short semicircle, short stout legs churning madly. Maguire discarded the spear and waited with drawn sword.

A thunder of hooves and O'Neill on horseback cleanly speared the boar, which lay kicking and squealing. O'Neill dismounted and, holding on to the reins of his rearing, shying horse, drew his sword and finished the work of the spear.

---

[1] "Justice and Fortitude are invincible."

Wordlessly, Maguire sheathed his sword, walked over and took the reins from MacRory, and mounted.

Conn O'Neill, excited and flushed with exertion, called over to him. "Had I not intervened, your pig would have rewarded your fairness and your foolishness by ripping your belly open. Only a fool fails to distinguish between bravery and folly, and only a fool would face a pig with a sword. Good manners might warrant a word of thanks."

O'Neill remounted and Maguire turned on him a face pale with anger.

"You're an ill-bred cur."

The colour drained slowly from O'Neill's flushed face.

"You call me ill-bred?"

"I called you an ill-bred cur. I did not need the help of one pig in dealing with another."

O'Neill drew his sword and Maguire pulled his horse around and turned his back on him, saying over his shoulder:

"Later, at Dungannon[1]."

All three rode back to Dungannon in silence. MacRory was accustomed to these often lethal confrontations and always found them disturbing. Some trivial matter became a point of honour, ending in some young man's death and his burial in the family vault.

As they dismounted at Dungannon, O'Neill said curtly to Maguire, "Whenever you feel your courage is up to it."

Maguire drew his sword, and MacRory moved over to him. "It was a hasty word, Maguire, and a rash deed. There's no need…"

A different Hugh Maguire stared back at him. "No need? Do not presume to tell me how I should behave. This matter is no concern of yours." He turned to O'Neill. "For the second time today, I face a pig with my sword."

Others, seeing the confrontation, gathered in the courtyard, but no one made any attempt to intervene. Conn O'Neill was older than Maguire, a veteran of many battles who had killed two men in duels. He was now intent on killing another and was confident in his ability to do so. No man called an O'Neill an ill-bred cur and lived.

---

[1] The stronghold of the O'Neills.

As they fought, however, his confidence faded to be gradually replaced with the shocking realization that the younger Maguire was the better swordsman and it was he himself who might die. Maguire deliberately fought with an insulting negligence. Conn O'Neill fought with increasing hopelessness, and eventually with the desperation of a man looking for some lucky chance that might redeem where skill had failed.

No such chance was afforded him, nor would be. Maguire, as well known for his generous nature as for his quick temper, and realizing the other was at his mercy, might, in other circumstances, have shown mercy and allowed his opponent to withdraw with an honourable wound. However the words, "Whenever you feel your courage is up to it," had implied a possible lack of courage that Maguire would never forgive and he was determined to kill O'Neill. The opportunity came and Maguire lunged. His sword passed through O'Neill's chest.

O'Neill stood for some moments while his hand, still clutching his sword, fell limp by his side. Then his knees buckled and he sank to a kneeling position, blood trickling from the corner of his mouth. He tried to look up, but his strength failed him and his head fell forward on his chest. Air rattled in his throat.

Maguire knelt on one knee beside the dying man, and turned to the spectators in the courtyard.

"Find the priest and have him attend here."

O'Neill's head came up part way and his eyes looked up at Maguire. "Damn you, Maguire. Damn … you …"

The dying man's body toppled backward and a convulsive heave filled his lungs with their last breath. The eyes remained looking up at Maguire as that last breath sighed out from the body and the light of life faded from the eyes. Hugh Maguire remained kneeling by the body, then placed his sword on the ground before reaching down to close the dead man's eyes.

Maguire and MacRory were guests at Dungannon, and Maguire had killed a kinsman of his host, Hugh O'Neill. Indeed the man he had killed was the cousin of his own wife. The duel had been a fair fight, fought on a point of honour, and no one in O'Neill's household displayed any great animosity toward Maguire for the death. Most thinking of the death of Conn O'Neill would have regarded it as an honourable departure and preferable to death by some of the other eventualities available, such as death by accident or disease.

It was shortly after the death of Conn O'Neill, and while Turlough MacRory and Maguire were still guests of O'Neill's, that a horseman pulled a lathered horse up on its haunches and shouted the fateful news to a sentry on the wall of Dungannon Castle.

"Red Hugh has been captured. Imprisoned in Dublin! A ship anchored in the Swilly off Fanad. MacSweeney of Fanad and Red Hugh were lured aboard. On the ship armed men surrounded them. Red Hugh is now a hostage in Dublin Castle."

While there were others in contention for the chieftaincy, young Red Hugh had always been the most widely accepted choice for O'Donnell chieftain. From an early age he had displayed an easy grace and intelligence that had placed him well ahead of any other contender. The time-honoured prerequisite of the Celtic chieftain, "without blemish," seemed exemplified in both body and mind in the young Red Hugh.

The capture of the O'Donnell heir put the north in turmoil. Next to the O'Neills, the O'Donnells were the most powerful sept in Ulster. Now the uncertainty engendered by the capture of Red Hugh had a destabilizing effect on all the northern septs, not only the O'Donnells, but also neighbouring septs. If he were ever allowed to return to Donegal, it would only be as a puppet ruling for his English masters, and if, as was certain, Red Hugh would never suffer himself to be moulded into such, he would never again see the dark old hills of his native Donegal.

The voluntary giving of hostages or pledges to insure good faith was a custom frequently employed, but in this instance the hostage had been seized involuntarily and there were no guarantees for either his life or safety. Despite the fact that Brehon Law clearly delineated the proper treatment of pledges, these pledges lived a dangerous existence in captivity. They could be hanged by their "host", whose only regret might be that he had lost his pledges as a bargaining tool, and would possibly have to seek new ones. This could happen if there was any perception that the good faith they were held captive to ensure had been broken. When Sorley Boy displeased the Lord Lieutenant by his conduct in Antrim his son Alistair, a hostage in Dublin, was executed by Perrot. When Sorely Boy was later brought temporarily to heel and on a visit to Dublin was brutally shown his son's head he is reputed to have said. "My son hath many heads" On hearing the news of his friend's capture, Turlough MacRory sank into a despair he had not known since the death of his family. He turned instinctively to his uncle for solace in this new grief. He grieved, too, for MacSweeney, knowing how he must feel, and how he would blame himself for the capture of his foster-son. MacSweeney was the bravest of men, but how would he face Ineen Duive?

Maguire decided Turlough MacRory would stay in Fermanagh and that he would be inducted into Donagh MacRory's gallowglass. MacRory found himself in the strange position of being both a mercenary soldier in the employ of Maguire and also the personal friend of Maguire. When he was in the gallowglass barracks, he was merely another soldier and treated as such. When he was with Maguire, he was as much a Maguire family member as any other in the family.

Cuconnaught Maguire died peacefully in his bed in 1589, this mode of death not altogether to his own liking. Conor Roe Maguire of the senior branch in Lisnaskea, contested the election of Hugh to the chieftainship, but Hugh, with the assistance of the O'Donnells, was elected chief. One of his first acts was to expel the English sheriff, Willis, from Fermanagh.

When the Lord Lieutenant in Dublin had informed Maguire that an English Sheriff was to be installed in Fermanagh Maguire's response had been. "Then tell me the price of his *eric* [in Brehon Law, blood money atonement] so that I may levy it on my people when they remove his head."

Twenty years earlier his father had accepted an English title and allowed the territory of the Maguires to be shired by the English Lord Deputy, Sir Henry Sidney. The Irish chieftains over the centuries had donated extensive lands to the old church and the monasteries, and the abbeys on these lands scattered throughout Ireland had amassed a good deal of wealth. Often too, the well-constructed, stone buildings of the abbeys and monasteries provided easily fortified bases from which the English could conduct military operations against the very chieftains whose generosity to the church had been responsible for their construction. These abbeys and lands with their wealth were an inviting target for the more rapacious of the English, who in any event had little time for the old religion of Ireland. The Tudor English in Ireland loyal to Henry VIII, and later to his daughter, Elizabeth, were upholders of the Reformation, and the ugly scars and divisions engendered by that religious upheaval were still fresh.

Willis, the English sheriff in Fermanagh, was of the more rapacious breed of Englishman. The new Maguire chieftain was not willing to tolerate further English depredations against the monasteries and church properties in Fermanagh, bequeathed to that church by the piety of generations of Maguire ancestors.

CHAPTER 7

Maguire expels England's Sheriff

Across the river from Enniskillen Castle, one hundred gallowglass in battle armour had formed up under the critical eye of their captain, Donagh MacRory. Hugh Maguire on horseback, attended by some of his Fermanagh chieftains, rode ahead as the armed convoy set out heading westward from Enniskillen. Turlough MacRory rode with them, while his uncle marched at the head of his *corrughadh*[1] of gallowglass.

Proceeding slightly to the north of west they traversed an elevated moorland that paralleled the lower Lough Erne and a few miles to the south of it. They crossed and re-crossed the meandering Sillees as it wound down from its source in the pine-clad hills above Glen na Sheevaar.

They passed south of the stronghold of the O'Flannagans at Aghamore and toward evening descended into the Correl Glen. Here they were joined by fifty of O'Flannagan's men from the nearby fortress of Aghamore. They bivouacked by the banks of the Sillees, sheltered in the narrow glen from the winds that, blowing in from a storm in the Atlantic, moaned among the swaying tree tops in the slopes above.

Next morning they climbed along the mountain pass of Glen na Sheevaar, (the Sorcerer's glen) traversing a windswept moorland of waving heather, interspersed with white tufted bog cotton that bobbed and weaved in the stiff upland breeze. Scattered groves of mountain ash and willow grew by the banks of the Sillees, and among the heather were small dark ponds, some patched with white water lilies.

The bunched, blood-red berries of the mountain ash contrasted vividly with the muted shades of brown and purple heather. A MacManus chieftain reined in his horse, reached out to

---

[1] (Irish) "Military formation of one hundred"

pick a berry from the mountain ash, or rowan tree, and commented that the tree had been sacred to the Druids.

"So it was, Manus," Maguire agreed. "All trees were sacred to them, especially the oak. They saw all living things, plant and animal, as a manifestation of some all-powerful, life-giving force. The Druids were healers and philosophers, as well as priests. They had knowledge of the medicinal value of herbs and used mistletoe for healing and in their sacred rituals. I'm sure they'd have found some medicinal ingredient, too, in the berries of the rowan."

"Certainly something that tastes this bitter must have great medicinal value." MacManus grimaced, spitting out the pungent-tasting red berry, which he had gingerly crushed between his front teeth.

"I wouldn't make a feast of them." Maguire laughed. "What's medicinal in small quantities can be poisonous in larger amounts.

"It's said that it took twenty years of study to become a Druid, and only a select elite were initiated into their ranks. Because they guarded their secrets closely, they were believed to have magical powers and were regarded with reverence and awe."

There was nowhere any sign of human habitation, but bird and animal wildlife were plentiful. The flute-like call of the great northern loon floated out from some hidden pond quite close by in the heather, and was answered by a series of musical lonesome wails. Two deer stood beside a copse of pine trees, heads high and alert with ears twitching. Their large, gentle eyes watched curiously as the column of men passed. A hare bolted from cover, its powerful, rear legs propelling it in a series of erratic leaps, until it disappeared over a hillock. MacRory, watching the flight of the hare nearly became unseated when his horse reared and shied violently to the side as a grouse, in a blur of brown and yellow plumage, exploded from the earth almost beneath his horse's hooves. After a short burst of flight, the bird landed again and darted with outstretched neck for a new hiding place. A red fox, black snout smeared with red blood and white feathers, loped off through the heather, looking back over its shoulder at the passing intruders.

After some hours of uphill progress, and having crossed the Sillees one last time, close to its source in Lough Achork and now no more than an eager streamlet, they crested the west rim of Glen na Sheevar and looked across the lowland to the distant, thin, white lines of Atlantic breakers beyond Ballyshannon. To the west a low mountain range marked the boundary between Connacht and Ulster. The ridge of the dark blue mountains stretched into a haze to the left and to the right sloped gently down to the Atlantic. The concave slope of the mountains, sweeping down to meet the ocean, was broken by two up thrusts of rock, "McGlanagh's Bubs," which jutting up in profile interrupted the smooth flow of land to sea. A few miles inland from the ocean, the blue waters of Lough Melge[1] lay placid beneath the slope of the Leitrim Mountains.

Leaving the upland they descended, following the course of a small river, which emptied into the lough. In the lower elevations the land was more heavily wooded, and closer to the lough they rode through a grove of venerable oaks that dwarfed the lesser giants of the forest. Massive trunks sprouted massive convoluted limbs, which branched outwards and upwards to spread a canopy high above. The majestic oaks tolerated no growth of any lesser species beneath the shade of their leafy domain.

Some of these trees could have begun their lives when St. Patrick walked among us, thought Maguire as they passed silently over the mossy ground through the gloom of the vaulted caverns of the forest.

The monastery of Cill Cou stood on a hillside overlooking Lough Melge, and peeping through the trees of a wooded island in the lough below was the small church of Inish Temple. The English sheriff, Willis, and his men, having expelled the monks, now occupied the monastery. Willis' men had used a small, walled-off graveyard nearby as a horse enclosure, and straw mixed with manure was scattered among the gravestones Maguire and Willis faced each other, and Maguire spoke with a deceptive gentleness.

"I will have to ask you to leave the land of the Maguires. You are no longer welcome here."

"No longer welcome! I need neither your welcome nor your sufferance. I will remind you that I am in Fermanagh as the representative of the Lord Deputy, who in turn is the representative of the Queen of this country."

---

[1] (Irish) Lough Melvin.

Maguire turned to look off beyond the hill of Dartry. "Surely you are mistaken. The last Queen of Ireland sleeps under a very ancient cairn, on a mountain top some thirty miles south of here."

"What do I care for your Irish Queen? I serve the Queen of England and I stand protected by her soldiers, the best in the world"

Maguire smiled. "An empty boast when you stand facing my gallowglass."

"No empty boast. These men of mine have taught lessons to your Irish rebels in Desmond that they won't soon forget."

"Perhaps, but now they face soldiers. Would you care to pit one of your heroes who fought so bravely against women and children in Munster against one of my men, ... or perhaps you and I?"

Willis looked startled but conferred with a lieutenant before selecting one of his men. The man donned a cuirass and then stepped forward.

Maguire turned towards Donagh MacRory who unsheathed his claymore, but instead of offering himself as the champion walked over to his nephew and handed him the sword. Disbelief, pride, and consternation warred with each other in Turlough's racing heart as he accepted the sword from his uncle. To be selected in front of all of Maguire's gallowglass! But to fail! But he knew that Donagh would not have chosen him if he had any doubts about his ability. His uncle's confidence in him buoyed his own and any apprehension ebbed away. Turlough spoke quietly to his nephew.

"You have never killed a man. The man you face I know. He deserves killing. He butchered innocents in Munster. However if you cannot bring yourself to kill, disable him quickly for he means to kill you".

As he walked forward relaxed and focused, he remembered his uncle's often repeated advice. "The mind, not the hand ..."

His huge adversary, seeing this youth who wore no protective armour, advanced sneering and twirling his sword in a gesture of bravado. He stretched out his left hand, palm upwards, and moved the cupped fingers in a "come hither" gesture.

"Come on lad, come to your death. This blade is no stranger to Irish blood".

Mac Rory was already enough of a professional to know that the man's bravado could be a fatal error. Proud to have been chosen as the champion, he was heedful of his uncle's advice and determined to bring the contest to a quick end.

Contemptuously, Willis' champion half turned away only to pivot suddenly, his sword scything a vicious arc aimed to decapitate. MacRory, knowing what was in his opponent's mind, at about the same time that the man himself did, also pivoted, and dropped to his heels. His opponent's sword passed feet above his head. MacRory's body uncoiled, and trunk, arms, and wrists co-coordinated in a fearsome two-handed slash. The heavy claymore sliced through flesh and bone, to completely sever the other's leg below the knee. A cheer arose from the assembled gallowglass and a murmur from Willis's men some of whom placed their hands on their swords. The corrughadh of gallowglass had been standing at ease, feet apart, one hand on sword hilt, with the long blade resting on the shoulder. Donagh MacRory, uttered a sharp "Aire," ("Ready") and punched his fist in the air. In unison each gallowglass slapped his other hand to his sword hilt. At the same time, with a sound like a single muffled drum beat, each man stomped his left foot forward.

Maguire drew his light sword and rested the point on the notch where Willis's neck joined his torso.

"I now demand that you leave the land of the Maguires. You may make whatever explanations you see fit to your Lord Deputy and your Queen."

Willis stared along the length of the shining blade to Maguire's resolute face, and realized that here on the shores of Lough Melge, with a sword at his throat he was far from the protection of Lord Deputy and Queen.

"We'll leave Fermanagh as soon as my men and I can make preparations, but I must warn you that your act will be construed as treason."

Willis barely managed to choke out the words. An unsteadiness in his voice betrayed his bluster and an increased pressure of the sword on his windpipe caused the word "treason" to be uttered in an unfortunate high-pitched squeak. Maguire still stood relaxed.

"You'll leave now, and you'll leave without horses or arms." Maguire returned his sword to its sheath and, turning his back on Willis, said to Donagh MacRory. "Remove their arms."

When the arms were stacked, Maguire pointed to the Southeast.

"The Pale is in that direction sir, but I must warn you that in that direction also are some Irish septs capable of further foul treason against an English sheriff. If you do reach the Lord Deputy in Dublin, you may have much treasonable activity to report. You may be shy about entering the territory of these chieftains uninvited, so I'll provide you an escort to the borders of Maguire lands.

"Take twenty men, Donagh, Turlough go with him. See England's sheriff to the far side of the lough. Meet me later at O'Donnell's castle of Ballyshannon." He turned to the McManus chieftain. "Ride ahead, Manus, and inform the warden that I'll be there before nightfall."

The two MacRorys, Donagh now also mounted and at the head of twenty of his gallowglass, escorted Willis and his men to the south side of Lough Melge and saw them into the territory of Breffney-O'Rourke.

Night was falling, and although they were only a few miles South of Ballyshannon, Donagh MacRory decided to camp on the shores of Lough Melge and make the short journey to O'Donnell's castle in the morning. He felt that long marches and a bed beneath the stars toughened the men and thus increased their chances of survival in battle.

Donagh MacRory awoke, and lying perfectly still, moved only his eyes. The slowly drifting clouds overhead partially obscured the dim light of a crescent shard of moon. It was close to dawn, but the only light yet cast was the wan light of the moon, reflecting a muted sheen across the still waters of the lough. The Drowes, flowing out from the head of the lough, murmured peacefully as it coursed its eternal way to the sea. Around him on the ground in the small clearing among the trees lay the vague shapes of his men as they slept covered by their cloaks, swords by their sides. Their sparth axes were piled in the centre of the glade. The two horses, large, blurred shapes, stood tethered to one side. They moved fretfully. MacRory moved only his eyes to take in the shape of the sentry hunkered down with his back to a tree at the camp's periphery.

Some of the men snored softly, others turned restlessly on the hard ground. Was it this sound or this movement that had awakened him? Perhaps, but he did not think so. Over the years he had developed a sense of the presence of danger, and knew that it was this sense that had awakened him. His eyes again looked toward the sentry. Was the man asleep? The sentry's head was flexed forward on his chest, and he had not moved since MacRory had first looked in his direction. Where was the sentry's sparth axe? The captain's hand, beneath his cloak, closed around the hilt of his sword. The clouds parted slightly and the moon's pale light illuminated the just discernable shapes of many men silently standing among the trees.

"Arms!" Donagh MacRory's hoarse, drawn-out howl disrupted the quiet night. One of the horses startled by the sudden bellow, reared, and neighed. Donagh MacRory himself had thrown aside his night cover and was on his feet sword in hand. His men were well trained. Some were already on their feet to meet the enemy rush, and others knelt on the ground, but all with swords in hands.

The sentry alone did not rise, having already paid with his life for his lack of vigilance. His comrades, fighting for their lives, seemed about to pay the same price. Despite the instinctive, disciplined response of MacRory's gallowglass, the enemy's advantage of surprise was devastating. In the first few moments the rush of pike men killed many gallowglass before they gained their feet. Two of the enemy were mounted, and MacRory recognized one of them as Willis. The enemy strength seemed to be somewhere around forty.

Donagh MacRory and Turlough MacRory fought with their backs protected by the trunk of a large beech tree. They fought side by side and soon each new assailant to engage them had to step over the bodies of several dead comrades, but eight of the twenty gallowglass were already dead and others wounded. The two men on horseback made a concerted effort to take the two MacRorys out of the fight.

"We cannot hold out here. I'll attempt to hold them, while you to try to get to Ballyshannon and Maguire," Donagh yelled over the din of the battle. "If I can unseat one of these horsemen, you can use his horse, or perhaps you can reach one of our own."

Turlough MacRory knew that long before he could return with help, this superior force would overwhelm his uncle and his gallowglass. He also knew his uncle was aware of this, and offered him the only slim chance to save his life.

"That will not happen, Donagh. We remain together."

Both Donagh MacRory and his nephew knew that they could not win this fight. Turlough, fighting for his life, was aware of a sudden change in his uncle. They had both fought side by side, and even in this moment of extremity, Turlough found time to marvel at his uncle's ability with the large two-handed sword. Donagh, now uttering an animal-like guttural roar, threw his sword at Willis, and picking up a sparth axe, advanced whirling the fearsome weapon in an arc around his head, killing anyone who came within its deadly radius. Men fell back before the wild fury of this deadly assault. He seemed larger and more than human as he rampaged among the enemy, a primeval force, awesome and invincible. He had the appearance of one possessed, eyes wild and staring with flecks of foam falling from his lips – a Cuchulainn[1] in a battle rage, a Norse berserker of old. Willis reined his horse to the side and out of range, and called to his men to fall back. He signalled to two men with muskets, who ran forward and fired hastily at the raging gallowglass. Both musket balls found a target. A ball struck one of Willis's men, who was slow in getting out of the line of fire. The man fell dead. The other thudded into Donagh MacRory's side.

Donagh seemed unaware of having been hit. He continued his frightful advance toward Willis, who pulled his horse back on its haunches, and only saved himself from the whirling sparth axe by falling off his rearing horse. Turlough MacRory shouted a warning as the second horseman galloped from the rear and raised his sword for a blow that would have ended his uncle's life. Donagh, however, seemed already aware of the danger and swung his sparth axe with such force that the other man's sword broke at the hilt. The berserk gallowglass again turned his attention to Willis.

At a shouted command from the man on horseback, the enemy soldiers fell back on all sides. The sudden change in tactics surprised Turlough. However, the reason for this sudden, apparent capitulation soon became evident as a group of men knelt in a semicircle with muskets aimed at the gallowglass within the clearing. A second group of musket men ran up, and formed up, standing behind the first.

---

[1] Mythical Celtic warrior

"Surrender at once," the man on horseback shouted to Donagh MacRory.

Donagh turned his head; his chin flecked with foam, eyes wild and uncomprehending, a fearsome figure, and stared at the horseman. He seemed not to hear the command. His sparth axe was raised to strike. His lips were drawn back from his teeth, and he uttered an inhuman howl as he turned back to Willis, who lay on the ground at his mercy.

"Fire!"

The roar of the muskets was almost simultaneous as the kneeling men in the front rank fired. Donagh MacRory, struck by many musket balls, seemed first to jerk up to his full height then fall forward. Willis just managed to roll aside from the blade of the sparth axe, which buried itself in the ground beside his neck. Most of the musket fire had been directed at Donagh MacRory, but two more gallowglass also fell under the close range fuselage. The kneeling men commenced reloading their muskets, while the second rank aimed.

"Surrender!" The horseman directed the command to Turlough MacRory.

MacRory stood with bloodstained sword amid the handful of remaining gallowglass. He stared at the horseman waiting to hear the command "Fire" repeated. Seeing his uncle die had reopened the wound of his father's death and a musket ball would not have been unwelcome. For himself he cared little, but with the instinctive reaction of a leader, he thought of the others.

The man on horseback seemed to read his thoughts.

"Most of your father's gallowglass are dead. I would prefer to spare those left and do not wish to kill them from a distance with muskets."

Turlough MacRory let his sword fall to his side.

"He was my uncle, not my father."

"I have seen men fight like that before," the horseman replied. "They are difficult to kill."

As Willis walked over, leading his horse, the man on horseback said,

"I am St. Leger, and I believe you already know Captain Willis. We are not normally in each other's company but by fortuitous chance my men and I came on him as he furtively tiptoed around Leitrim. He was lucky he did not blunder into Brian

O'Rourke. O'Rourke and Maguire show more hospitality to shipwrecked Spanish sailors, who are England's enemies, than they do to England's sheriffs. Your mercenary gallowglass fight well. Would you perhaps consider payment for your services in English gold?"

Warham St. Léger! The English Hugh Maguire! The gallowglass knew him by reputation.

"My men are mercenary soldiers as you say. They are Maguire gallowglass, and will fight and, if necessary die, as such, as did their comrades." MacRory unconsciously accepted the role of leader of his uncle's men.

"If you will not fight for us, then die you certainly will." The words were not St.Leger's, but Willis's. Willis turned to the musket men and shouted, "Aim."

St. Leger placed his horse between the musket men and the remaining gallowglass and said quietly,

"Belay that. As you were." Then he smiled at Willis. "You are, no doubt, eager for revenge, but any orders to my men will come from me."

MacRory wondered if, once this matter of protocol had been settled, the order would still be the same. However, after a moment's pause St. Leger turned to him.

"Normally we have no use for captives, however, you and your men fought well, and I will not allow what's left of you to be massacred. In any event you may be useful as an exchange. This is an unruly part of Connacht, which we have not yet pacified. Pass me your sword and have your men put down their weapons at once. My comrade here would be glad to shoot you all, and I myself will not stand in his way if I do not have your immediate compliance."

MacRory handed his sword to the man on horseback and nodded to the gallowglass, who laid down their weapons. Their captors escorted MacRory and the remnants of the gallowglass toward Sligo Castle, which was held by the English.

Earlier in the year, the Governor of Connacht, Sir Richard Bingham, a man whom the Irish hated and feared, had sent a punitive expedition into the territory of Brian O'Rourke in Northern Connacht. O'Rourke was accused of harbouring shipwrecked Spaniards after a storm had driven ashore ships of the Spanish Armada off the Irish coast. Bingham had rampaged through Breffney/O'Rourke, destroying homes and hanging men, and O'Rourke himself was forced to flee to the refuge of the MacSweeneys in Donegal.

His son, Brian Óg, despite the fact that he had been educated at the newly formed University of Oxford in England, had no reason to love the English. They had executed his brother, Conn, for the crime of being a Franciscan priest, and now his father, Lord of Breffney, had been driven like a common outlaw from the land of the O'Rourkes. It was this young man, who making no attempt at concealment, sat his horse on a hilltop, surrounded by his sub chieftains, and watched the procession below him progressing towards Sligo.

Willis and St. Leger stopped and spent some time in discussion with frequent glances at the men on the hilltop above them. St. Leger ordered his captives off to one side and again had his men train their muskets on the gallowglass. He then wheeled his horse and rode up the hillside. While he was still half way up the hillside, O'Rourke and about fifteen horsemen galloped down to meet him. The future began to look increasingly grim for Willis and St. Leger, and indeed for their captives, as with a wave of his arm O'Rourke caused some twenty gallowglass to materialize on the hilltop. These started down the hillside in a loping run. O'Rourke and his horsemen escorted St. Leger back down the hill.

With respect to numbers Willis and St. Leger had a slight advantage, but this was greatly outweighed by the presence of O'Rourke's fifteen armoured horsemen. Willis and St. Leger knew they did not stand much chance of reaching Sligo alive.

"Let me understand. You offer us the lives of a handful of captured gallowglass. You will lose your captives shortly when you lose your own lives. Why should we bargain?" O'Rourke's question was not rhetorical, but asked as if he were genuinely puzzled.

"As you can see the captives will be the first to die, and we ourselves, if we are to die, will sell our lives dearly,"

"We expect you'll do your best."

By now his gallowglass were formed up behind him. MacRory, watching the exchange, knew that he and the captive gallowglass would be first to die if O'Rourke attacked. He also knew this consideration was unlikely to prevent O'Rourke from attacking.

"Bingham will hang your pledges." St. Leger played his last card and hoped that Brian O'Rourke did not know that the Governor of Connacht had already hanged them.

O'Rourke stared thoughtfully at St. Leger. The young chieftain had assumed Bingham had long since hanged his O'Rourke pledges, but now St. Leger's words introduced some uncertainty. Perhaps his father's pledges were still alive. If they were, they would not be for long if he killed these Englishmen. Abruptly he made up his mind. "Hand over your captives and your weapons to me, and you may proceed to Sligo. You have my word on it."

"I accept your word and your offer," St. Leger replied at once.

"Never," Willis shouted, turning to St. Leger. "Once we are disarmed, what guarantee do we have that this Irish savage, who knows nothing of honour, will keep his word? We'll shoot the captives one at a time and see if that does not change his mind." O'Rourke turned his attention to Willis.

"The first captive to die will be followed by your own death. The choice is yours, and if you choose to resist, it's the choice most to my liking. I'll ensure that one or two of you are left alive to carry the news to Sligo that I offered the option." O'Rourke, with his hand on his sword, advanced on Willis. "You, sir, will not be one of those left alive. You have my word on that."

"Wait!" St. Leger shouted, and then turned to Willis.

"I'll remind you again that I command my own men here and will make any decisions regarding their welfare. I can understand your reluctance to part with your arms twice in as many days, but you will not endanger my men with your rashness."

St. Leger started to unbuckle his sword hanger explaining to O'Rourke that he had lost his sword recently. At the same time he ordered his men to lay down their weapons.

O'Rourke turned to St. Leger telling him to retain his sword hanger.

"Your word alone, sir, is of course acceptable."

O'Rourke then drew his own sword and reined his horse around to face Willis "You need not let your friend's decision affect yours, nor need our men now become involved. This is a matter between you and me."

Willis stared for some moments at the other before reaching for his sword. He held the weapon out to O'Rourke, who looked in amazement at the proffered sword, then turned away in disgust.

He spoke over his back to Willis. "Your courage, sir, seems on a par with your manners. Your sword you can throw on the ground."

Before meeting Maguire at Ballyshannon, Turlough MacRory returned to bury the body of his uncle and his comrades in the beech wood clearing by the shores of Lough Melge.

CHAPTER 8

Maeve O'Rourke

"Maeve O'Rourke, the gallowglass Turlough MacRory." Hugh Maguire made the introductions with an exaggerated bow. "Oh! A Scottish warrior come here to Fermanagh to protect us all?"

The brown eyes across the table mocked Turlough. He felt his face flush, looked away – no that was rude – looked back again into the brown eyes still mocking him, looked at the smiling mouth and white teeth, looked at the table and swallowed with an audible gulp. The sound must have been heard by all. In order to do something, he picked up his pewter and drank some water. He held the water in his mouth, now afraid to swallow. The brown eyes continued to look at him with steady amused interest. Was he going to reply? His discomfort was acute. He felt oafish, uncouth, ill-mannered. He had to make some sort of reply, but first he had to get rid of the water in his mouth. Another disastrous and audible gulp. He opened his mouth and his voice failed him.

Seeing his discomfort, Hugh Maguire rushed to his aid. "I think Turlough has just choked on something."

Not only the lovely brown eyes, but now also all other eyes at the table, turned on him. Finally he croaked out the strangled reply, "Aye, ma'am."

Dear God, what had he said! Had he confirmed that he, nineteen years of age, did indeed consider himself the saviour of Fermanagh, or worse still, would she consider his reply curt and rude.

Her mouth widened in a gurgle of laughter. "Ma'am, indeed! Chivalrous – and modest."

Maguire murmured sententiously, "In MacRory you will find the personification of selfless chivalry and taciturn modesty."

MacRory, feeling that he could only hurt himself by further speech, and too dry-mouthed to attempt any, lapsed into a miserable silence.

When Brian O'Rourke, chieftain of Breffney-O'Rourke, had fled to the MacSweeneys of Doe in Donegal for sanctuary after he was found guilty of harbouring shipwrecked Spaniards of the Armada, he had taken his daughter, Maeve, with him. She now visited the Maguires in Enniskillen, and it was she, who was the source of MacRory's present embarrassment. MacRory, silent throughout the meal, was aware of the brown eyes turned in his direction from time to time while she discussed with Maguire the events that had led to her father's flight.

"Three of their ships were driven ashore on Streedagh Strand. A Captain de Cuellar and eight Spaniards reached Tadhg McGlanagh's castle at Rossclougher in my father's land."

"I know the McGlanagh castle at Rossclougher, for in the past Maguires have not always been friendly with the McGlanaghs. It's a crannog[1] fortress in Lough Melge and virtually impregnable if held by a resolute foe. De Cuellar's defence of Rossclougher, where with eight men he held out against Fitzwilliam, is already a legend. It's well known the Spaniards are formidable soldiers. In the New World, Cortez and Pizarro, with a few hundred men, are said to have conquered an area larger than Europe. But, eight to hold off seventeen hundred!"

"My brother, Brian, said the English tortured and hanged two other Spanish prisoners in front of their comrades in the fortress, but finally gave up the siege. Before reaching McGlanagh's castle, de Cuellar had sought refuge at Staad Monastery, but when he got there, he found Bingham's soldiers had arrived first, and twelve of his comrades together with the abbot were hanging from the window gratings. How could men be so cruel?"

"Both Fitzwilliam and Bingham seem to have an appetite for cruelty that needs to be sated daily. The Lord Lieutenant has circulated a copy of his orders. He has ordered the execution of all Spaniards, and suggested the use of torture in obtaining information as to their whereabouts.

"As many as twelve ships of the Armada were wrecked on the Irish coast. He sent armed men to the west with orders to help Bingham hunt down and hang all survivors and any Irish who harbour them. Fitzwilliam is one of the more avaricious Lord

---

[1] (Irish) A fortified dwelling on an island, sometimes man made, and often approached by a submerged, winding causeway.

Lieutenants that England has, to date, bestowed on us, and I suspect greed also motivates his zeal on his queen's behalf. It's rumoured that some of the Spanish ships held quantities of gold.

"Three hundred Spaniards who were shipwrecked in the north were put to death after being offered honourable terms of surrender, but Fitzwilliam had some noblemen among them taken to Dublin to be held for ransom. Word of de Cuellar's brave defence of McGlanagh's castle is told around firesides all over the west. It's rumoured he eventually succeeded in reaching Scotland, but sadly I have also heard that Bingham recently captured Tadhg McGlanagh, and had his head sent to Dublin. "

"Oh no! Poor Tadhg!" One small hand went up to her mouth. "How sad to hear he has paid such a price. The McGlanaghs of Dartry have always been loyal to my father. Is it true, Hugh, what's being said that the Irish, too, looted and robbed the shipwrecked Spaniards?"

"I'm ashamed to say it, but in some instances our own people aided Bingham and his English settlers. Many Irish, however, sheltered the Spaniards, and, like Tadhg McGlanagh and your father, risked their own lives in doing so. As you know, many of our chieftains are allied with the English, but had they been as opposed to the English as was your father and had they united with the Spaniards, who came ashore, we could have driven Bingham from Connacht, and perhaps the English from Ireland."

Bran Mór and Gelert sat and watched as their master sweated with concentrated effort as he parried and slashed with the large, two-handed sword. It was not his favourite weapon, but he manfully strove to master it. Facing him, the gallowglass fought with a relaxed, easy style, parrying each stroke away from his body with a minimum of excess movement. His uncle had taught him it was only necessary to deflect the blade inches from the body, and excess movement was not only unnecessary, but also wasted strength and compromised balance.

They had risen early and proceeded to a broad meadow on the south side of the castle used for practicing horsemanship, and used by the gallowglass for practicing their war skills. Two groups of gallowglass were engaged in the same sword practice as Maguire and MacRory.

Despite the strenuous exertion, Maguire was still able to gasp: "Your skill with the sword is only equalled by your skill with the ladies, Turlough. What a silver-tongued devil you are. 'Aye, ma'am.' I wish I had thought of that, terse, concise. It certainly says it all. Establishes you right from the start as a man of few words. I waited in hope throughout the evening for any further lyrical utterances, but alas in vain."

The gallowglass remained silent, which long ago he had learned was the best defence against Maguire. He had also learned the best defence was a good offence, and with a sudden flurry of movement, he ensured that Maguire, busy defending himself, had no energy for speech.

"Enough," Maguire gasped. "I think you mean to kill me."

"If that's what it takes to silence you, but then, what guarantee do we have that even death would silence you?"

"Talk of the lady seems to have energized you, and speaking of the lady", Maguire nodded his head toward where Maeve O'Rourke came galloping across the meadow toward them, long, brown hair flying out behind her. She pulled her horse up, and Maguire held the bridle.

"Good morning to you, Hugh Maguire. Are you practicing with that great sword to smite Bingham?" She smiled at him, and MacRory envied Maguire.

"Aye, Ma'am." Maguire smiled, looking at MacRory, and MacRory hated Maguire.

This was too much and he hoped never to hear the two words again, but it was not to be.

She now smiled at MacRory. "Ho! Sir Scottish Knight, wouldst help an old ma'am from her horse?"

"'Aye, ma'am' is the response of the knight," Maguire whispered in his ear as MacRory dismounted and held up his hand to her.

For someone who rode so confidently, she dismounted clumsily, falling forward and ending up in the arms of the gallowglass. Red-faced, he placed her gently on her feet, embarrassed and sure the clumsiness was his. She seemed not too upset and with a small "Oh my!" rearranged herself.

Later, they walked back to the castle, Maguire leading the horse. Maeve O'Rourke walked beside the gallowglass. She seemed unable to resist an urge to tease him.

"My brother, Brian, has many MacRory gallowglass. They are mostly from the Isle of Uist."

"Most of the MacRorys are from that island, although others are from Barra and Skye,"

"Why do the English call you Scots 'Red Shanks'? Is it because you keep falling off your horses and scraping your shins?"

The laughing eyes again mocked him, but it was a gentle mockery. He smiled politely, knowing it was unlikely the sister of O'Rourke was so ill-informed about her brother's mercenaries.

"It's because some of them fight barelegged below the knees,"

"And do you, too, fight barelegged below the knees?"

"Those of us who fight on horseback wear protective armour, which also covers our legs. On horseback a rider's legs are vulnerable, so it's for that reason"

He felt he was babbling and should be succinct. To his horror, he heard himself say:

"On horseback, bearing arms, we do not bare our legs."

Maguire raised his eyebrows and looked across at him with a smile that managed to convey some pity and much delight.

The small, gloved hand went to her mouth, which gurgled with laughter, and she laid the other hand on his arm in an unconscious gesture. She ceased laughing, catching her breath with another 'Oh, my,' only to again burst forth in convulsive, bubbling laughter.

Each morning Maguire and MacRory practiced swordsmanship in the broad meadow. They practiced the tactics of war on foot and on horseback. On horseback, they practiced the manoeuvre of guiding the horse by pressure from the knees alone, using sword in right hand and shield in left. They spent many patient hours training the large horses to rear and turn to right or left.

It had become a routine for Maeve O'Rourke to ride out each morning to watch. On one such occasion, watching as the gallowglass reared his horse around and gained the advantage on Maguire, she clapped her hands and shouted, "Bravo, Sir Gallowhad."

After a time, the gallowglass's formal "Ma'am" became "Maeve, ma'am" and eventually "Maeve." To her, depending on her mood, he became "Turlough" or "Sir Gallowhad."

Apart from her morning visits to the meadow, he saw her often around the castle, and when she was not in his sight, she was seldom far from his mind. Indeed, she was nearly always in his mind. She cut a large swathe though his mind. She was the most unique person he had ever come in contact with, and he found it difficult to understand how others could speak of her as if she were just another mortal. Maguire spoke and laughed with her, then went about his business as if he had forgotten her. To the gallowglass the name of, the appearance of, the thought of Maeve O'Rourke, brought with it a surge of happiness. He was amazed and delighted with the series of coincidences that gave him the opportunity to be in her company. With amazing frequency, in the castle or by the river, he came across her.

There, suddenly, was the very object of his thoughts, the smiling face, and the now welcoming brown eyes. On one occasion, he was riding well west of the castle at a place where the river widened to form the lower lough below Port Toura, when his horse pricked up his ears and turned his head to the side.

"Sir Gallowhad." She waved and galloped up. She seldom walked or trotted her horse, usually proceeding at a full gallop. Life for Maeve O'Rourke was a full, joyous gallop. She now reined in beside him. While she did not say so, he got the impression that she had become lost, although it soon became apparent she'd had the foresight when setting forth to supply herself with food and even with some wine. She dismounted and produced from her saddlebags a linen sheet, which she spread on the ground. Next came wheaten cakes baked in honey and an earthenware jug of wine. She sat with her legs tucked up beneath her and smiled at MacRory. They sat by the lough in the long twilight.

"We must come to this place again, Turlough, for the lough here reminds me of Lough Gill near Dromahaire.[1] That little island out there could be Innisfree, and the swans by that headland could be the swans of Slish wood. I don't know if I'll ever return to the

---

[1] The O'Rourke Breffney castle.

life I knew in Breffney. It seems so long ago, away in another life, when Conn took me to see Lough Gill for the first time."

A wave of jealousy swamped MacRory's happiness.

"I must have been around four. It's one of my earliest memories."

"Who is Conn?" Jealousy seeped away like an ebbing tide.

"Conn ", her voice was strange and unsteady, and she stared at her hands, and swallowed. She tried again. "Conn, Conn ... he was my brother. I thought you knew. He died six years ago. I was eleven at the time."

She looked up and defiance steadied her voice. "Bingham's men hanged him."

"Bingham hanged the son of the chieftain of Breffney!"

"For being a Franciscan priest."

MacRory reached for her hands, and she placed them in his. "But that was insensitive of me to mention this. I know about your other brothers and your father. Nuala Maguire told me."

They sat in silence, each anguished by the other's sorrow, until Maeve shook her head as if to rid it from her thoughts." Now we'll talk of other things. We'll talk about you. Tell me about yourself, Turlough."

"What can I tell you? What, what do you want to hear?"

"Everything, Turlough, anything. Tell me of the girls you have loved. No, don't tell me of that." She took one of her hands from his and placed her fingers on his lips.

He held the hand to his lips, reluctant to let it go, reluctant to make any reply that would dispel the moment.

She allowed him to hold her hand for some seconds before removing it to pour wine for them both. She handed the wine to MacRory and remained leaning forward looking up at him.

"Then I'll tell you of the man I could love." She again placed her hand on his lips, tracing their outline with her fingers.

"If he were gentle, I would see it in his eyes. If he were kind, I would hear it in his voice. If he were brave as a gallowglass, he need not be eloquent, and if he loved me, my heart would tell me, without his speaking it."

She reached up and kissed him. "And if I loved him that first moment that I saw him, I'd love him till I die."

The sun cast long shadows across the lough before they arose to return to Enniskillen.

MacRory lived in a bright new world of almost tangible joy, and Maeve O'Rourke was the sun and heart of that world. His natural taciturnity deserted him. Maeve listened with interest to all details of his short life, and gurgled her laughter at his feeblest jokes. In her presence he felt gallant and witty. She already seemed to know quite a lot about him. She knew in surprising detail about his early life in the Hebrides, and subsequent years in Ireland, and even knew his age. He listened with rapt attention to all details of her life, delighted in her presence, and loved each and every thing about her.

Initially, the interaction between the two was a source of amused interest to Maguire, and MacRory stoically endured his witticisms. Indeed he was so preoccupied with his new and wonderful life that he was scarcely aware of them.

Maguire's amusement and witticisms ceased in time, and as he and MacRory rode across to the broad meadow one morning, Maguire casually brought up the subject of the O'Rourkes. "The O'Rourkes have always sought alliances with the O'Connors and O'Reillys through marriage. It's true that at present the O'Connors and O'Reillys are on the side of the English against O'Rourke, but these things change. Before Bingham commenced devastating Breffney, Brian O'Rourke was arranging a marriage between his daughter and Miles O'Reilly."

Two simultaneous thoughts entered MacRory's mind. An arranged marriage for Maeve! Long live Sir Richard Bingham! His happiness vanished like a light extinguished. He had given little thought to anything of late other than when they might again be together, but Maguire's words brought with them a chilling reality.

In one world both Maguire and O'Donnell treated him as a friend and in every way as an equal, but another world separated him from them. They were chieftains of their people, as was O'Rourke. He was a mercenary soldier serving them. Some mercenaries, by merit and prowess in battle, had risen to be sub-chieftains, but there was the saying "A chieftain, whose father was not a chieftain, is a lesser chieftain." The best he could ever offer her was "a lesser chieftain," and Maeve was to be betrothed to an O'Reilly chieftain, to a member of a family that had ruled Breffney for centuries.

An arranged marriage, betrothed to someone she might not even like! He would elope with her, as his father had done with his mother, but where in Ireland could they go?

Hugh O'Neill had eloped with the daughter of Sir Richard Bagenal. But Hugh O'Neill was Earl of Tyrone and chieftain of the O'Neills, and had taken his wife back to his Dungannon stronghold.

What was he thinking? Elopement and marriage! He was Turlough MacRory, a gallowglass, and she was the daughter of a chieftain of Breffney. There would be no place in Ireland that he could take her. Back to the Western Isles? Maeve would be a widowed bride, for these powerful and ruthless men would pursue them to the ends of the earth. Not love, but the madness of love, would allow such a thought, would inflict such jeopardy on the one he loved. Maeve loved him, she had told him so in a thousand ways, and he loved her, but marriage? Another rush of chilly reality overtook him. He knew Maguire's reason for bringing up the subject and knew Maguire had his interest in mind, but he nevertheless wished that Maguire had never spoken of it.

Maguire on his part rode along also in silence. He had hated to dampen his friend's spirits. He had a genuine liking and respect, as well as a good deal of admiration, for the quiet young gallowglass who was his frequent companion, his preferred protagonist in sword practice and the patient foil for his wit.

"It's necessary, Turlough, these alliances, cemented by marriage or by fosterage. It's been so between the septs for many centuries throughout Ireland and Scotland. There are frequently such alliances by marriage between your own Western Isles and the northern part of Ireland. The O'Donnells have ties of marriage to both the O'Neills and the Maguires, although it has not always kept us from each other's throats."

When they reached the broad meadow, the gallowglass's sword practice was as efficient as ever, but mechanical. No matter how preoccupied, he always fought with a focussed intensity. By both training and instinct he could never allow himself to be distracted.

Some days later the gallowglass came into the courtyard to find Maguire in conversation with a young man. A grim-looking Maguire beckoned the gallowglass to join them. MacRory noticed that the man speaking to Maguire was stamped with the same air of easy authority as the gallowglass had observed in Maguire and

O'Donnell. What indefinable quality, he thought, can thus give a man such an intangible aura?

As Hugh introduced them, MacRory recognized the man, who had intercepted Willis and St. Leger outside Sligo.

"This man is Brian Óg O'Rourke, Maeve's brother. He brings news no man wants to hear. As you know Bingham drove Maeve's father from Breffney for harbouring shipwrecked Spaniards of the Armada, and he sought refuge with MacSweeney of Doah. A few weeks ago O'Rourke crossed to Scotland, but King James, no more than a lackey of Elizabeth, handed him over to the Queen's soldiers. He was brought to Tyburn where he was hanged, drawn, and quartered. My mother is with Maeve now."

The words, spoken with brutal brevity, made the gallowglass reel. The terrible death! Hanged, drawn, and quartered. Not hanged, but vengefully and brutally tortured in death. Choked by the hangman's noose until nearly dead, taken down from the gibbet while still alive, and the belly opened and the entrails drawn forth. The carcass quartered and a quarter of the dead body staked at each of the four gates to the city. The Queen's men dealt sternly with the Queen's rebellious subjects.

"Where are they?" MacRory was rude in his abruptness.

"They are in the river garden. Turlough–"

But the gallowglass had turned and was striding away. As he opened the gate and entered the garden, Maeve arose from the bench where she sat with Nuala Maguire and ran toward him.

"My father! Oh, Turlough, my father!"

He held her, and hoped she did not know the manner of her father's death.

"And such a death," she sobbed. "I know the fate of all of us is in God's hands, but what could God have been thinking of to allow such a thing? First Conor, and now my father."

The helpless face of a hurt child looked up into his, tear-filled eyes pleading for consolation; empathy for her sorrow welled up from the depths of his own long-submerged hurt. He held her closer as rivulets of tears ran down her face, and his own tears fell on her brown hair.

After an hour or so, Maguire and Brian Óg entered the garden. Maguire came and sat by Maeve O'Rourke and took her hand, but for once could find no words to say. After some time he arose, placing a hand on the gallowglass's shoulder.

"Come with me a moment, Turlough." The three men walked to the gate, and Maguire spoke quietly. "Brian Óg will avenge his father's death by laying waste the lands of Bingham's English settlers in Connacht, and I'll assist him. Bingham, in retaliation, could well enter Fermanagh and may even lay siege to this castle. The O'Donnells no longer control Donegal. Brian Óg feels, and I agree, that Maeve would be safer with the MacLeods in the Isles, and while there is no immediate danger, she should leave as soon as preparations can be made. She will sail from Sligo, and my mother insists on going with her that far. I think Maeve would wish you also to accompany her."

The gallowglass nodded. Nothing could prevent it.

CHAPTER 9

Ambush at the Ford of Belleek

A week later Brian Óg and a contingent of O'Rourke gallowglass rode at the head of an escort of fifty men as the two women set out for Sligo. The escort consisted of O'Rourke's own men, twenty mounted gallowglass, and the rest unmounted gallowglass and kerns. Four hobilars[1] went with the party. They set out early in the morning, as the journey to Ballyshannon would take two days, with Sligo a further day's journey beyond. The unsettled state of Fermanagh dictated the size of the escort. Both MacRory and Brian Óg were armed with the lighter basket-hilted swords. As the day promised to be warm, both had their battle helmets slung from the saddle and MacRory also had a light-weight targe, or shield, slung from his.

It was deemed safer to travel the longer route along the south shore of the Erne by way of Ballyshannon rather than the more direct route through Breffney O'Rourke. Conor Roe Maguire had allied himself with the English, who were known to raid in south Fermanagh.

The gallowglass rode weighted with sorrow. Beside him, Maeve O'Rourke and her brother rode silently. In his concern for Maeve, MacRory had tended to forget that Brian Óg also grieved the death of his father. Neither MacRory nor Nuala Maguire attempted to intrude on Maeve's thoughts. They had already said all that could be said. It was piteous to the gallowglass to see her attempted smile as he had helped her back on her horse after one of their brief rests. It was not the smile he had known.

They moved steadily throughout the day along the southern shore of the Erne, sombre and silent except for the creaking of saddle leather, the soft clump of the horses' hooves, and the rhythmic tramp of the soldiers.

Around them on every side, all nature seemed alive on the late spring day. The air was warm. Bright sunlight glistened and

---

[1] Mounted scouts.

shivered on the waters of the island-studded lough. The breeze that rippled the lough whispered through the forest and stirred branches clothed in a full green splendour of foliage. Lavish nature had scattered on the earth its glorious profusion of spring flowers; yellow buttercups and cowslips reached up through the new green grass to smile back to the warmth of the sun. Everywhere there winked gems of small white daisies. Delicate bluebells peeped shyly from their hidden nooks. Clumps of yellow primroses, scattered generously on the earth like handfuls of gold, perfumed the air. Butterflies floated like wisps of gossamer on the scented air.

As they rode through the long grass of a meadow, still damp with remnants of morning dew, a lark leaped into the air, trilling and soaring straight into the blue sky. A corncrake, the skilful ventriloquist of the meadow, croaked its hoarse cry, now here, now there, slyly concealing its meadow nest. Ahead and to either side, finches, swallows, thrushes, and robins sang their mating calls, some unseen in shrubs and trees, others gliding and banking around the meadows and woodland. Only the distant, sad, plaintive call of a curlew seemed in tune with the mood of the riders.

Brian O'Rourke reined in his horse and pointed ahead to where a silent, deadly pantomime was being enacted. A peregrine falcon floated in the azure sky, and beneath, a dove, with frantic wing beats, fled for the safety of a copse of trees. The predator stooped with folded wings. The two birds merged and feathers floated down into the grass behind the doomed prey. The falcon glided down to earth behind the stricken dove, and cruel talons casually controlled its quivering prey while its razor-sharp beak shredded still live flesh. The young of the predator would gorge. The young of the dove would not survive without a mother. Indifferent nature – exquisite in its beauty, revolting in its cruelty. The raw savagery of the scene another hammer blow to Maeve O' Rourke's already wounded spirit.

In the late afternoon, they came upon Bartholomew O'Flannagan and some of his men, waiting for them by the shore of the Erne. The gallowglass, a stranger to O'Flannagan, was surprised by the sensitivity with which the gaunt, uncouth-looking man expressed himself as he took Brian O'Rourke's hand in one of his, Maeve's in the other.

"O'Rourke, Maeve ma'am. The condolence in my heart needs no utterance. No indignity done to your father can diminish the honour of his life. He died alone among enemies, but he lives on with love in the memory of his friends."

O'Rourke nodded his thanks, but it was Nuala Maguire who replied.

"A brave and Christian man. I'm told that at his death, his courage shamed his executioners. That courage lives on in his family. He'll not be forgotten. Our condolences to you, too, O'Flannagan. You have your own sorrow."

"We have. The presence of your son honoured our family at her graveside on Devenish. She now rests beside little Eileen. It was the consumption that took them both, God rest them. It's a hard thing to see the ones you love waste away before your eyes. God asks us to endure a lot, but without our faith in God, where would we be?" He passed a gnarled hand through his hair and looked up the lough in the direction of Devenish Island. "Mother and child are together again out there. Carmel never got over" – a bout of coughing racked his emaciated frame, and the gallowglass had the uncomfortable thought that it might not be long before this man, too, would join his wife and daughter on Devenish Island – "the loss of Eileen, but now they rest together."

The O'Flannagan chieftain escorted them inland into the hills. The sun cast long shadows by the time they crested a ridge and descended into a valley toward the O'Flannagan stronghold by little Carrick Lough. As they descended the south slope of the ridge, the gallowglass looked over to where a lone horseman, one of O'Flannagan's men guarding this northern route into the valley, sat silhouetted on the hill of Minran off to their left.

On arrival at Aghamore Castle, Nuala Maguire insisted that Maeve O'Rourke retire early and O'Flannagan's sister showed them to their sleeping quarters.

Bartholomew O'Flannagan, smoking a clay pipe, sat outdoors in the waning light of the warm spring evening together with Brian Óg and the gallowglass. O'Flannagan explained that both the pipe and tobacco were a gift from Hugh O'Donnell.

"A Spaniard introduced O'Donnell to the custom, but he couldn't seem to master the knack of it and gave it to me. It's something the Spaniards brought back from the New World. The natives there inhale it. It's called tobacco. I myself find it relaxing." Between sentences, he puffed on the pipe to demonstrate his mastery of the art and with each inhalation of smoke, the embers in the bowl momentarily glowed red.

MacRory, watching his host constantly tamping the contents of the bowl with a callused thumb and periodically removing the pipe from his mouth to spit, wondered what could be so relaxing about this gift from across the ocean.

"Here, have a try." O'Flannagan graciously passed the pipe to his guests.

"S-somehow, O'Flannagan, I have a feeling this tobacco smoking w-won't catch on in Ireland," O'Rourke gasped after a few puffs.

"You try it." He hastily passed the pipe to MacRory

"I'd have to agree with O'Rourke." MacRory, coughing, apologetically passed the pipe back to its owner, and all three reverted to a peaceful silence.

Shadow crept down the valley as the sun sank below the rim of Glen na Sheevaar to the west, and gradually the lough changed from silver to black. The silent shadow marched up the eastern slope of the valley, and as it reached the uppermost ridge, an owl hooted in the trees by the lough, as if to punctuate the final curtain of darkness. A servant came with a rush torch soaked in pitch and set it in a wall bracket, and the three men sat in their contracted world of flickering torchlight.

The gallowglass, remembering his journey of two years ago with Maguire, broke the silence.

"Now that we have come this far inland, maybe we should continue on by the mountain route through Glen na sheevaar. Wouldn't it be quicker than returning to the Erne?"

O'Flannagan, his face etched in the yellow torchlight, inclined his head to MacRory.

"It would be the shorter way, but I would not advise it. A few days ago a herdsman up on the bar of Wheaut reported seeing Conor Roe's son, Conor Óg, and a party of Queen's O'Connors from Connacht camped in Glen na Sheevaar."

"O'Connors", Brian Óg spat the word, "and this far north! Do they mean to attack Aghamore?"

"No, I wouldn't suspect it. They did not have the numbers, and I don't think they'd be foolish enough to attempt it. But with Conor Óg Maguire as their guide, they could be scouting out the land." He smiled. "Certainly they'd be foolish to attempt it tonight.

Were they to disturb Nuala Maguire's sleep, she'd hound them back to Connacht like a wolf chasing sheep. There's brave men in Connacht right enough, but none that brave!"

His gleebe bobbed in front of his eyes as his large head nodded, affirming to himself the truth of his remarks. "But you can all sleep soundly tonight. My men guard every pass into this valley. My family has held this stronghold for five hundred years, even back before the days of the Maguires. From here to Belleek and from Lough Erne to Lough Melge is our little kingdom of Toura, which we hold for Maguire. I do not contemplate yielding it up to any of Bingham's bastards from Connacht."

He paused to puff on his pipe.

"But our world is changing, O'Rourke. MacMahon is dead, hanged in front of his own castle walls because he defied an English sheriff, who wanted his lands. Red Hugh, *Tir Conaill's* hope, rots away his young life, a hostage in Dublin. If our chieftains do not meekly yield up their people's heritage to these strangers they will ravage the land and its people as they have done in Desmond. Only O'Byrne in the south and you and Maguire and the Scottish woman here in the north continue to hurl back our defiance. What has become of our warrior race when a woman stands in the *bearna baoil* while our chieftains rush around her to bend the knee and yield up their heritage to the invader?

"Aghamore has stood for five hundred years, but for how much longer? When the storms brew out there over the Atlantic, here in this sheltered valley we hear only the whisper of the wind. But I tell you, it is more than a whisper the storm that is brewing for our people and in the shriek of that storm, I hear the Banshee's wail for our race. Like the shadow of night, these English close in around us, and we do not see the danger. But the danger is not only out there in the darkness. The danger is within ourselves. I know you have no love for the O'Connors, who follow Bingham, but sad the day when a name such as O'Connor, a name borne by kings of Ireland, is spoken in the same breath as that of Bingham. The names of kings of Ireland are now the names of English earls, holding Ireland for England's queen – O'Briens, Earls of Thomond; O'Neills, Earls of Tyrone.

"Is it an evil omen to find an O'Connor and a Maguire allied with the Sassenach up there in the sorcerer's glen?[1] Will it be our own people leading a Sassenach army down that glen that takes Aghamore?" O'Flannagan tapped out the cold ashes from his pipe on a flagstone by his feet.

The next day he accompanied the party for some way along the shore of the Erne before wheeling his horse and waving farewell beneath the Bar of Whealt. The Bar, paralleling the lower lough, rose up some four hundred feet as a sheer cliff face. Inland beyond the bar was the mountain pass of Glen na Sheevar, and beyond that, a desolate, unpeopled moorland stretching off into Breffney-O'Rourke.

The gallowglass, glancing up from time to time at the impressive rock formation to his left, became aware of a flash, as if the sunlight reflected off some mirrored object up on the bar. Then he thought he caught a glimpse of another flash far down the lough on its opposite shore. Perhaps the sun's reflection off some metal object, but what metal object up in that remote place, and had there been a second flash further down the lough? He stopped and he and O'Rourke scanned the cliff top for some time, but saw nothing further. He felt a vague unease as his eyes strayed toward the woman and the girl.

The route by Ballyshannon, although safer, was not devoid of danger. Parties of English raiders moved freely in O'Rourke's Breffney close by, and some had raided into Fermanagh and Donegal. For that reason he had a substantial and well-armed force. He was now only about twelve miles from O'Donnell's Ballyshannon castle. hobilars had been scouting ahead and reporting back from time to time and had not reported any sightings of horsemen on this side of the lough. In order to reach the castle, they would ford the Erne at Belleek as the castle was on the north side of the river three miles below the ford. There was another ford farther downstream from Belleek at Assaroe, which was closer to the castle, but that ford was a more difficult crossing.

They reached the Ford of Belleek with several hours to spare before darkness. The water here was fast flowing and stirrup high,

---

[1] Glen na Sheevar.

but with MacRory holding the bridle of Maeve O'Rourke's horse and O'Rourke doing the same for Nuala Maguire's, they reached the north shore and waited with their horses dripping water while the mounted gallowglass entered the ford.

MacRory was looking back across the ford when he heard a warning cry from O'Rourke and at the same time became aware of a commotion to his rear. Horsemen with drawn swords poured from the concealment of the woods and surrounded the small group on the bank, while a larger force galloped past them into the ford and engaged the gallowglass there. O'Rourke had his sword out and lunged at a man whom he recognized as Conor Óg Maguire. The gallowglass, fending off the determined attack of an Englishman, shouted to a hobilar across the ford: "Get to the castle. Cross at the Assaroe ford."

The man wheeled and galloped along the south side of the river. MacRory had time to see Nuala Maguire strike a man heavily across the face with her riding crop, giving added weight to the blow with a most surprising and unlady-like expletive. The man, who had been reaching for the bridle of Maeve O'Rourke's rearing horse, cursed and raised his arm to protect his face from a second lash.

The ambush was well planned. No one had anticipated an ambush almost within sight of the castle. The two men, fighting desperately for their lives, were isolated on the north side of the ford, while the remaining mounted gallowglass and foot soldiers were prevented from helping them as they themselves fought with equal desperation in the ford. Armed horsemen surrounded both men on the bank, but the ambushers had already learned respect for their adversaries and now manoeuvred more carefully. MacRory's opponent called to the man who had attempted to grasp the bridle of Maeve O'Rourke's horse.

"Here, lend a hand and help me. I'm having trouble skewering this one."

Nuala Maguire was still belabouring the man, and had her riding crop been a sword, his wounds would have been many and grievous. MacRory tried to prevent this new antagonist from manoeuvring behind him, noting with grim satisfaction that the man's left eye was swollen shut and that a red weal crossed his face from Nuala Maguire's ministrations. O'Rourke, himself wounded, had wounded Conor Óg. O'Rourke now faced several attackers, as did the gallowglass, and they now fought back-to-back, attempting to deny the enemy the advantage of any approach from the rear.

The fight raged on and both men inevitably, against such odds, sustained wounds. The result of the uneven battle seemed in little doubt. Help from the castle could not arrive in time to alter the inevitable outcome.

However, O'Rourke's mounted men, fighting with the disciplined expertise of the gallowglass, steadily advanced across the ford. The enemy outnumbered them, but some factor of either training or motivation tipped the balance in the gallowglass's favour. They pushed the enemy up the north bank of the ford, and the foot soldiers, following, advanced across the river. The momentum carried the fight onto the bank around O'Rourke and the gallowglass.

In the furious melee of rearing horses and slashing, stabbing swords, one of MacRory's antagonists disengaged and wheeled suddenly. This time he succeeded in grasping the reins of Maeve O'Rourke's horse. Leaning low in his saddle, he galloped off in the direction of Ballyshannon. Another horseman disengaged and galloped off with him. Two swordsmen were between MacRory and the retreating horses. He parried a blow from one and spurred his horse straight at the other man, who surprised at the sudden, unexpected tactic, was late warding off the sword thrust. The man gasped as MacRory's sword passed through him. The momentum of the charging horse lifted the man backward out of his saddle. The huge sword had penetrated almost to the hilt through the man's body. MacRory's arm was pulled back behind him and the sword, impaled in his adversary, was torn from his hand.

The gallowglass gained slowly on the retreating riders. Sods of earth flew up around him from their horses flying hooves. Maeve looked back as did the rider behind her. This man now pulled on his reins and, dropping back, turned his horse to face the gallowglass. MacRory, at full gallop, swerved around the other, fending off a slashing blow with his shield as he continued to close on the horseman ahead. He closed in on the man's left side and leaned down in his saddle, attempting to wrest the reins of Maeve's horse from his grasp. The man struck across at him. The gallowglass brought his targe[1] up with his left hand to fend off the blow, but the sword blade glanced off the targe and bit through his helmet into the bone beneath. He fell beneath Maeve O'Rourke's horse.

The gallowglass had a vague memory of horsemen galloping past and he next became aware of someone speaking close by.

"… As possible in the morning and get word to Hugh. If my son doesn't hang Conor Óg, I'll hang the cur myself." The voice was Nuala Maguire's.

He lay on a mattress of some sort, in a torch-lit vaulted room. Another voice he recognized was O'Rourke's.

"Some of O'Donnell's men will ride to Enniskillen and let Maguire know. We'll follow the coast to Sligo at first light."

MacRory sat up and groaned. The lighted room dimmed around him, and someone laid him back on the mattress. His head throbbed, and he felt that his lungs could not supply him with air. Brian Óg's face loomed over him.

"You're a brave man gallowglass, but if you're a vain man that wound could be your undoing."

As MacRory lay there, he gradually became more orientated. Flickering torchlight illuminated wooden beams spanning a stone-vaulted hall. He lay on a straw mattress on a wooden cot, elevated about six inches off the stone floor. He heard the roar of a nearby waterfall. A memory came to him of having crossed the ford and being surrounded by armed horsemen, but he had no clear memory of any subsequent events. He heard Nuala Maguire's voice and sat up to look for Maeve. Again, his surroundings went out of focus and he sat on the edge of the bed, supporting his bandaged head in his hands. The movement brought a groan as a pain stabbed in his left chest. He looked up and around. "Is Maeve here?"

Nuala Maguire came over and knelt on one knee beside him, putting a hand to his shoulder. He turned toward her, and the pounding in his head increased.

"Maeve was captured at the ford, Turlough. You sustained a bad wound to your head pursuing her captor. We found you on the road and brought you here to the castle."

---

[1] Shield.

As he became vaguely aware of what she had said he groaned again, and not realizing that he made little sense asked. "Where is she now?"

Briefly, Brian Óg told him of the fight at Belleek Ford and of his pursuit of Maeve's captor. "A hobilar forded the river downstream here at Assaroe and alerted the castle of the ambush. Our men held on, but scarcely, until O'Donnell's men came from Ballyshannon. These men saw you lying on the path, but thought you dead on their way to Belleek. In any event they were in too much of a hurry to check. We can do nothing for Maeve until the morning. I expect they crossed to the south side of the Erne at one of the fords below Belleek, all of them dangerous crossings except for here at Assaroe, and are headed for Connacht by way of Sligo. Her captors mean to deliver her to Bingham. With my sister in Bingham's hands, my own hands would be tied."

Seeing the look on the gallowglass's face he continued. "I know. Indeed no one knows better than I that Bingham has no respect for any Irish woman, man, or child. I will be dead, as will every O'Rourke in Breffney, before my sister is allowed to fall into his hands. We'll follow at first light, and Hugh Maguire will send his men, too. We'll follow to the walls of Ballymore if necessary."

Before dawn the horsemen assembled in the courtyard. MacRory sat his horse with pounding head and aching ribs. His vision blurred intermittently. O'Rourke had lost six of his mounted gallowglass at Belleek, but another thirty mounted O'Donnell men now augmented his force. A party of five hobilars galloped out the entrance and rode off into the dim light of the dawn.

They already had their instructions from O'Rourke. Three were to ride as fast as their horses could carry them toward Sligo. If any of them saw O'Rourke's sister and her captors, they were merely to keep them in sight and to send one of their number back with all speed to inform the main force. Two hobilars were to scout inland toward Dartry Mountain in the unlikely event that Maeve's captors had taken that route.

O'Rourke and his horsemen rode south from Ballyshannon, the chill dawn wind, ripe with the sharp tang of the salt ocean, awakening their sleep-drugged senses. On their right, the rhythmic, surging roar of the Atlantic, on their left, the silent, brooding, mountainous land of Breffney/O'Rourke. As the sun came up, Ben Bulben ahead cast its long shadow toward the ocean.

By noon the day was warm. The moisture-laden winds, blowing in from the Atlantic, formed fleecy little grey clouds above Ben Bulben, each cloud forming, enlarging, and trailing off inland. Briefly the sun was blotted out and a warm rain shower drenched the riders. MacRory rode, aching in body and spirit. His head pounded and rivulets of rain ran down his face. He wiped the red rain off his face with the back of his hand and rivulets of blood ran down his face. He glanced at Ben Bulben and the whole mountain turned on its side as he fell from his horse.

O'Rourke reined in his horse above him and dismounted. The blood-soaked bandage had loosened, and the wound, reopened, steadily poured blood down his face as he sat on the ground in the rain. O'Rourke, his own arm bound with a bloody bandage from the fight the previous day, reached up to one of his saddlebags, took out a shirt, and instructed one of his men to rip it into several pieces. This man brought the edges of the wound together as much as possible, then rolled one of the lengths of shirt into a soft bandage and placed it over the wound. He tied another length of the shirt tightly around MacRory's head, compressing the bandage. O'Rourke then removed his own helmet and placed it on MacRory's head, which further helped to hold the bandage in place.

As he did this, a hobilar rode up and shouted to O'Rourke that they had ridden to "within sight of Maeve's grave," but had seen nothing of his sister's captors. The gallowglass groaned in anguish at the news and O'Rourke reached a hand down to his shoulder.

"A different Maeve, gallowglass, Maeve, the legendary Queen of Connacht. The large cairn on Knocknarea[1], which can be seen for miles around, is supposed to be her burial place. It's not good news, though, for they must still be far ahead of us. We must go on, but you rest here, and if you feel better, follow us. If not, return to Ballyshannon."

O'Rourke did not wait for any answer or remonstrance, but mounted and galloped off, signalling the others to follow.

The gallowglass sat dejectedly on a wet mossy bank. His head still pounded, but there seemed to be no further bleeding. His

---

[1] (Irish) "Hill of the King".

thoughts tormented him and caused him more pain than his head wound. He should have foreseen the possibility of an ambush at the ford, which was the ideal site for such. He should have sent a contingent of mounted gallowglass across the ford, ahead of the main force, to secure the north bank. He should have taken more heed of the ominous signals from the Bar of Whealt. He had delivered the life he loved more than his own into an ambush and the hands of a ruthless enemy.

The shower stopped as quickly as it had started, and the sun warmed him and brought steam rising from his horse, which stood by nuzzling his hand. The horse lifted its head and, with ears pricked, looked up the valley that ran up the side of Ben Bulben. It neighed softly, and the gallowglass, immediately alert, placed his hand over his horse's muzzle.

The sudden tension caused his head to throb even more. He was well familiar with this reaction from his horse, when other horses were nearby. He led the horse, still holding his hand over its muzzle, up the timbered slope of Ben Bulben to his left, careful to stay well hidden among the trees. It took him fifteen minutes of careful upward advance to reach an eminence with a view of the valley below. There, he tethered his horse back in the trees and crawled along the slope to the edge of the wood.

A small stream twinkled down the valley, and three riders made their way up the stream. His heart gladdened and his head pounded as he recognized one of the three as Maeve O'Rourke. The stream bed, which they followed, curved around beneath Ben Bulben on the slope on which he lay. His gaze followed its course around to his left.

Maeve O'Rourke rode with both hands tied in front. Her two captors rode ahead, a rope linking her horse to one of theirs. They had ridden all night, stopping only briefly for an hour's rest when they had ridden into a wood. Here they had untied her hands and shared with her what food they had in their saddlebags. Leading their captive's horse had slowed their progress and earlier, when they had heard galloping horses behind, they had quickly turned inland up the valley of Glencar.

One of the men spoke in English, but with an Irish accent. "It may have been O'Rourke's men, but they did not sound like heavy horses."

His companion, an Englishman who had one eye swollen shut and a red wheal across his face, replied, "I doubt O'Rourke survived, although he and that gallowglass fought like devils. I'll expect to become a famous and well rewarded man for this day's work; killing O'Rourke and delivering his daughter to the Governor of Connacht."

"Do you know who that gallowglass was? He was the captain of Maguire's gallowglass although he's known as O'Donnell's gallowglass. He and Red Hugh O'Donnell were childhood friends. You are lucky to be alive. The woman with the eloquent tongue and the sharp whip was Nuala Maguire, mother of Hugh Maguire."

"The Englishman reached up and gingerly felt the side of his face." I'll tell you this, I'd have no wish ever to meet him, or that bitch of a wildcat again. All the same, it's better to be careful. No O'Rourke would treat us kindly if we were overtaken while delivering their chieftain's sister to Bingham. It's too fine a day to hang. We'll make our way further to the east, but this is his country and we'll have to travel with care."

"I don't know whether it's his country or Bingham's nowadays. We're as likely to run into Bingham's men as O'Rourke's," the one with the Irish accent replied.

"Pray that it's Bingham's. The O'Rourkes I hear are an unkind lot," the Englishman said.

"Not at all like us civilised and hospitable O'Connors," the other laughed.

"I hear much about your Irish hospitality, but have seen little of it, and precious little civility either since coming to this cursed land. These O'Rourkes and Maguires are as hostile as hornets. Mind you, Sir Richard has done his part in stirring up the hornet's nest."

They both turned as Maeve O'Rourke, sagging wearily in her saddle, said quietly, "You speak of hospitality. My father took poor, shipwrecked Spanish sailors into his own home in his own land. For this, which would be an act of mercy in any civilised land, he was hanged and mutilated. My brother, Conor, an innocent priest, you murdered for the crime of professing a faith that you English tell us we must abandon – that same faith that you yourselves, like slaves, rush to abandon at the whim of your queen. Your noble knight, Bingham, spreads famine throughout our lands, and daily demonstrates England's honour by hanging and terrorizing men whose only ambition is to prevent their children from starving."

"The Spaniards, ma'am, are our enemies, and had their Armada been successful, would have imposed on us a foreign monarch, as well as a foreign religion and foreign laws. From what I hear, Spain is not Ireland's enemy, yet when others of their ships foundered off Galway and Mayo, their sailors were met by O'Malleys and O'Flahertys, who hacked them to death in the waves before they could even stagger ashore. As for your priests, they might live longer were they to refrain from preaching treason."

"If what you say is true, then those Irish who treated shipwrecked Spaniards with such brutality are no better than you English, but quite likely, you are merely repeating a rumour your masters spread deliberately to discredit us with the Spanish.

"Is it now treason to live as we have always lived in our own land according to our own laws and to worship our own God as we have done since St. Patrick made Him known to us? You mention a foreign monarch, a foreign religion, and foreign —"

The gallowglass burst from the trees twenty feet ahead, while the two men were turned back looking at her. O'Connor's sword never cleared its sheath and his arm was nearly severed at the shoulder. The Englishman, managing to rein his rearing horse to one side, pulled his sword in time to deflect the backward blow from the gallowglass, but such was its force that his sword went flying from his hand. He leaned low over his horse's neck and spurred desperately. His horse leaped out of the stream, and Maeve O'Rourke's horse lurched as the rope from its bit to the other's saddle broke. She fell from the horse into the stream, hands bound, unable to help herself.

The gallowglass leaped from his horse and knelt beside her. He was only vaguely aware of the sound of rapidly receding hooves as Maeve's captors galloped for safety. She lay still in the rocky streambed, a small hapless bundle with bound hands, and his heart sank, seeing the red blood that stained her brown hair. Was he destined to have caused the death of the one he loved? He threw his sword aside and cupped her head in his hands.

She opened her eyes and looped her bound hands behind his neck and, with something of her old spirit, whispered, "Sir Gallowhad!"

The *Inish Saimer* sailed from Sligo Bay on a full tide. Maeve O'Rourke attempted to control her windblown hair with one hand, as she waved from the bow with the other. The gallowglass on the pier waved back, and stood watching for more than an hour until the ship became an indistinct dot on the white-capped ocean. His vision blurred and he turned away. When he looked again, the ship that carried Maeve O'Rourke away from him and from Ireland could no longer be seen.

    The ship ploughed into heavy seas as she beat steadily up the coast of Donegal. Past Tullan's curving yellow strand where endless serried ranks of ocean waves rolled ashore to collapse in foaming futility, mighty waves of the Atlantic tamed and exhausted after an unbridled rampage across thousands of miles of wild ocean. The *Inish Saimer* sailed on past the island of Inis Saimer at the mouth of the Erne – the fabled island purported to be the landing place of Partholan[1] and his men, on past the wave-lashed sea cliffs of Slieve League, rising up from unknown ocean depths toward a slate-grey sky above, on past Mount Errigal rearing aloft inland into a lowering sky, on past Tory Island grey-veiled to starboard in wind-whipped sea-mist, on into a freshening northwest wind, and a gathering Atlantic storm

---

[1] Ireland's earliest invaders, reputed to be Scythians.

CHAPTER 10

Red Hugh returns to Donegal

In the year 1592, Hugh Maguire, Eamonn MacCaffrey, and the gallowglass – all in armour – rode at the head of a troop of fifty armed cavalry. They rode fast and with purpose along the north side of Upper Lough Erne, in response to an enigmatic message from Hugh O'Neill: "The wolf cub is uncaged."

Close to the head of the lough about ten miles from Lisnaskea, they reached their destination and found a group of O'Neill's men waiting by the shore. Maguire leaped from his horse and strode towards them. From amongst the men, Red Hugh O'Donnell limped forward and the two men embraced.

"Welcome home, cousin. Many a heart in Donegal will rejoice to hear that you are back among us, and may many a Sassenach heart rue the day."

"I was on my way to Donegal a year ago, but the Lord Deputy insisted on my staying and enjoying his hospitality at Dublin Castle. I had trouble dragging myself away on this occasion." O'Donnell smiled. "I owe my English hosts a debt of hospitality, which I intend to repay."

Four years of captivity in Dublin Castle, the last year in manacles following an earlier abortive escape attempt, had left the young chieftain's body gaunt and his face pale – a paleness exaggerated by the mane of his red hair. No trace of boyhood remained on the pale strong face. The promise of the boy had come to fruition during his years of captivity, and the experience of his captivity had in no way diminished that promise. In any company, eyes would have been drawn to him as someone exceptional.

Looking beyond Maguire, he saw the gallowglass standing by his horse and with a cry of gladness hobbled toward him. MacRory's natural reticence and a sense of propriety had prevented him from giving in to his first instinct and rushing forward to greet his friend. But also he hesitated, seeing a different Red Hugh from the one who had parted from him four years ago at the ford of Belleek. O'Donnell was no longer a boy, Wide-set eyes looked out of a large bearded face and that face had an air of purpose and almost of asceticism.

There was only joy, however, on O'Donnell's face as he embraced his friend. O'Donnell, too, saw no longer the boyhood friend he remembered. He saw a soldier, armed and formidable-looking, a gallowglass, six feet tall, wide-shouldered, and muscular. The hand that held his firmly, without wanting to let go, was large, hard, and callused. A scar obliquely traversed his forehead to disappear in the black hair beneath his helmet. They stood for some moments, boyhood friends, each trying to reconcile with his boyhood memory this man now standing before him.

O'Donnell finally broke the silence. "Ah Turlough, How good to be together once again. In chains in Dublin, I often thought of our days at Sheephaven. Stay away from prisons, Turlough. They poison the soul. As boys, when we roamed in the mountains free as God meant man to be, we had no regard for that freedom because we had never experienced the lack of it. Only a prisoner can truly appreciate freedom. Four years of life wasted! Yet I do not blame Perrot. He did what was in his interest and that of England. And now I will do what is in mine and that of my people."

MacRory noted that Red Hugh spoke as if he were already the O'Donnell chieftain.

The sombre shadow passed from Red Hugh's face, and he smiled at his friend. "Eoghan MacSweeney would be proud of you – a gallowglass in his own image."

They stood looking at each other, the moment both thrilling and awkward. MacRory merely said, "God be thanked for your escape, Hugh."

O'Donnell laughed, "God, my mother, and the Earl O'Neill." He was walking back to Maguire when he turned to say, "I have work for a gallowglass. I have work for both you and MacSweeney."

Something, an unspoken change in relationship between them, made the gallowglass draw his sword in reply and salute O'Donnell by pressing its hilt to his forehead, with the words, "Aye, O'Donnell." He would not again, as in their boyhood, address O'Donnell as "Hugh." It would always be the more honorific "O'Donnell."

Red Hugh agreed to go by boat down the Erne to Maguire's Enniskillen Castle, as his feet made it difficult for him to ride.

"Come with me, Turlough. We have much to tell each other." O'Donnell gestured toward the boat, where a MacManus chieftain waited to ferry his guest to Enniskillen Castle.

O'Neill's men galloped back toward Tyrone. McCaffrey took one half of the armed escort and rode off to cross the Erne higher up at the mouth of the Turbet River, and return patrolling down the East shore. The other half under Maguire followed the nearer shoreline, as closely as possible, paralleling the boat's passage. There was need for these precautions. Red Hugh O'Donnell, England's prized hostage, had escaped his English captors.

Initial skirmishing had now broken out into open warfare between Maguire and the English. In the ensuing fighting, the easy-going, erudite Hugh Maguire had proven himself an able leader. He was becoming more and more an inveterate enemy of the English, who were attempting to colonize the ancestral land of the Maguires with English settlers.

"Well, Turlough, much has changed and not just you and I. Some news of Donegal filtered through to me in Dublin, but only scraps. My mother was able to have an agent reach me from time to time with information."

Red Hugh lapsed into silence, and they both remained quiet as they were rowed down the Upper Lough toward Enniskillen. O'Donnell seemed preoccupied and MacRory was loath to disturb him. The easy familiarity of earlier years had gone, although an unbroken and unspoken bond remained, and always would.

The gallowglass knew, as did all Ulster, of the circumstances of O'Donnell's capture and imprisonment in Dublin. Six months after he and Red Hugh parted at Belleek, a ship had sailed up the Swilly, anchoring beneath MacSweeney's castle. The captain had invited MacSweeney and his family aboard to sample some Spanish wines, Red Hugh with them. MacSweeney's group was overpowered in the captain's cabin. The ship put out to sea. When well offshore, MacSweeney and his family had been released and put in a boat. Red Hugh had been brought to imprisonment in Dublin; The English Lord Lieutenant there had sent an exultant message to London. "We have caged the wolf cub."

The young Red Hugh was held hostage against his father's co-operation. Two others, Henry and Art, the sons of Shane O'Neill, were held with him. The gallowglass knew also, as did all Ulster, of Red Hugh's escape after three years of imprisonment, of how he had made his way to the Wicklow Mountains south of the city. There, Phelim O'Toole betrayed him. It was suspected, though, that O'Toole, outnumbered by a superior English force and seeing no alternative, had surrendered Red Hugh. The captive was returned to Dublin Castle, where he was then held in manacles to prevent any further escape attempt.

Now all Ireland would know that Red Hugh O'Donnell had escaped, and the English in Ireland would soon know that they had gained for themselves an implacable enemy in the north.

They passed along the island-dotted Upper Lough within sight of stark Cuilcagh Mountain, one of the traditional inauguration sites of the Maguire chieftains. From the top of Cuilcagh could be seen all of Fermanagh; not only Fermanagh but also, gazing across the lough to the north, could be seen the distant blue hills of Donegal. To the north and east could be seen Tyrone of the O'Neills, to the east the territory of the MacMahons, and to the south lay Breffney-O'Reilly and Breffney-O'Rourke. Some of these often-troublesome neighbours were now becoming united and following Hugh Maguire in his war with the English.

O'Donnell awoke from his reverie. "Forgive me Turlough, I have been thinking of my time in Dungannon with O'Neill, and of what lies ahead of me in Donegal. Tell me of your years with Maguire. We heard at Fanad of your sickness, but of your life afterward not much reached me in Dublin. Tell me all of it, Turlough, everything."

MacRory described the illness that had nearly claimed his life.

When he had finished his narrative, O'Donnell nodded. "I, too, have had somewhat similar symptoms, but nothing that gave me such a close brush with death as that."

He pointed to the gallowglass's scar. "It was not your only brush with death?"

MacRory went on to describe his subsequent training as a gallowglass with the MacRorys in Fermanagh, eventually becoming a captain of gallowglass. He spoke unassumingly, but O'Donnell knew well that their captain was elected by the gallowglass themselves on merit and merit alone. A captain of gallowglass at the age of nineteen! No friendship with either an O'Donnell or a Maguire chieftain would have been allowed to influence that choice. A captain had not only to be the most capable soldier, but also to have had considerable experience in battle. He knew that his friend had lived a busy and dangerous life during his own years of captivity.

"Many things have changed since we parted at Belleek, but those bonds of our early years will never be broken. In the coming years, I will need you as a captain of my gallowglass, but above all I will need you as a friend. In captivity, surrounded by enemies, it was the memories of friends that sustained me, and yours was the memory that burned brightest in my mind – memories of those early days in Sheephaven, of galloping neck and neck on the strand in the bay, of racing each other barefooted in the hills, free as young hares in the heather. Alone, we enter this world, Turlough, and alone we depart it but the true friends God sends us on our journey are gifts beyond price. It's only the things of the spirit that have true value, things that have no material substance, things like, honour, courage, justice, love. Unlike gold, their value is inherent and not depleted by a surfeit. What is the value of gold? In itself it is worthless. Its value is whatever value we place on it. The more abundant it is the less its value.

"In prison, too, I had ample time to observe our English enemies. They are a worthy and dangerous foe. Our countries are close; our cultures are not. They are willing to accept some loss of personal freedom in their loyalty to further the ambitions of their queen. This is their strength, not their weakness. Their queen's ambitions, though, will result in the loss of that personal freedom we so value. Our proud Irish chieftains, chieftains whose ancestors were princes when theirs were swineherds, accept bauble English titles in exchange for their freedom. They manipulate us with contempt, and we follow with the dumb ignorance of cattle. If our chieftains must be led, it will not be by the English."

O'Donnell again lapsed into silence, and MacRory had no doubt as to whom Red Hugh felt should lead. MacRory marvelled at the confidence and assurance of his nineteen-year-old companion, who had spent the last four years of his life in degrading captivity. His body may have been held in chains, but the mind and the spirit that shone out from the compelling eyes had not.

They rowed within sight of the east shore of the Upper Lough, occasionally catching glimpses of Maguire and his men following along the shore. Four hours after leaving O'Neill's men, they came ashore at Enniskillen.

CHAPTER 11

Story of a Daring escape

"Now, Hugh, we want to hear of your escape, and leave out no detail."

Each holding a goblet of wine, they sat by the leaping flames of a fireplace in Maguire's castle. From fragments of the story that had already reached the north, the men sensed a legend in the making. Red Hugh sat with both feet elevated on a cushion while Maguire, Eamonn McCaffrey, and the gallowglass sat inclined forward in anticipation, awaiting the story of his escape from Dublin Castle.

"I'll get to my story, but first I must know how things stand in Donegal. I have heard that Donel divided the O'Donnells and took the chieftainship from my father."

"Donel is dead," Maguire said quietly, unsure if Red Hugh had as yet been told of his half-brother's death. "Your father had become weak. Donel deposed him and tried to have himself accepted as The O'Donnell. Hoping to hold the chieftainship for you, your mother opposed Donel. The MacSweeneys of Fanad, the MacSweeneys of Doe, and the O'Dohertys stayed loyal to her and to the old chieftain. The MacSweeneys of Banagh, the O'Boyles, and the O'Gallaghers supported Donel.

. Your mother went to Scotland and recruited a force of gallowglass, and a battle was fought at Derryleathan. Donel was killed along with three hundred on both sides.

"I know, Hugh, of Donel's death and I know that you favoured his chieftainship. In your place it's what I myself would have done. Our people needed a chieftain and I was a prisoner in Dublin castle from which no prisoner had ever escaped, Donel was the right choice."

Maguire himself had indeed mourned Donel's death. Donel was a capable leader, and what had now befallen Donegal would never have occurred had he lived. Maguire had agreed with Donel's attempted usurpation. They had been friends and allies. When Cuchonnacht, Hugh's father, had died three years ago, Conor Roe Maguire had sought the chieftainship of the Maguires, but it was

Hugh Maguire, with the assistance of his cousin Donel O'Donnell, who had been installed as the Maguire.

"I'm afraid, Hugh, I have further news of Donegal. Your father is barricaded in his castle at Donegal with a few men, while two English captains are raiding freely throughout *Tir Conaill*. They have driven out the friars and have taken over the friary within sight of your father's castle. Your castle at Ballyshannon is still in O'Donnell hands, but no O'Donnell rules in *Tir Conaill*."

Red Hugh was lost in thought for some time. Coming out of his reverie, he made no comment about his brother, but merely said,

"If the people do not know their chieftain, the fault is not the people's'. I'll return to *Tir Conaill* tomorrow."

He then started on the story of his recent escape, although not in the type of detail that would have satisfied his audience.

"You know the story of my capture at Fanad by Perrot."

"I have heard that Perrot was the bastard son of Henry the Eight, but I understand that he was also a bastard in his own right," McCaffrey interrupted before Red Hugh had gotten very far in his story.

Maguire raised his eyebrows. "A legitimate bastard! A self-made man! We Irish have some of those. There are many such among the O'Neills. Hugh O'Neill, my father-in-law comes to mind. Yet Perrot was not the worst of England's Lord Deputies. He was certainly more honourable than his successor Fitzwilliam.

"Perrot died in the Tower, awaiting execution on some charge or other. If he were indeed the bastard son of Henry the Eighth, then he would have been the half-brother of Elizabeth, yet he died in his sister's prison. Henry, her own father, the same father who murdered her mother, declared Elizabeth illegitimate. When Elizabeth became queen, she had her rival, Mary Queen of the Scots, beheaded.

"Henry's new wife, Anne Boleyn, came close to persuading Henry to have his first daughter, Mary, beheaded, but as it transpired, it was Anne herself who lost her head, the first of Henry's wives to do so. Henry finally had a son by his third wife, Jane Seymour, and to this son he bequeathed the crown of England, but some say he bequeathed more than that to his unfortunate son, for Edward died at the age of sixteen covered with sores. Henry may have acquired syphilis, which had just become available in

Europe, and passed it on to his son, although some say the disease was consumption[1]. Elizabeth's half-sister, Mary, Henry's daughter by his first marriage, who was known as 'Bloody Mary' for her persecution of Protestants, had her predecessor, Lady Jane Grey, beheaded. An exemplary family, the Tudors!"

"One can understand, indeed, why the behaviour of the offspring, legitimate or otherwise, might be erratic, since their father Henry was somewhat of a reprobate," Eamonn McCaffrey agreed.

"Erratic! Somewhat of a reprobate! What a way you have with word, Eamonn." Maguire exploded in laughter. "Describing the offspring of Henry the Eighth as 'erratic' and the father as 'somewhat of a reprobate' is akin to describing the horsemen of the Apocalypse as 'scallywags,' and Satan himself as 'a bit of a rogue.'

"These Englishmen serving their queen in Ireland must know that serving such a fickle monarch can be dangerous to their health. Walter Devereux, the First Earl of Essex, that nobleman who so pleased his queen by his vigour on Rathlin, died in Dublin in disgrace and out of favour, but I hear his son is the current favourite of Elizabeth."

"He will remain Elizabeth's favourite for as long as he furthers Elizabeth's ambitions," O'Donnell commented. "Being the favourite of a capricious monarch can be a two-edged sword. If he displeases Elizabeth or if she were ever to see him as a threat, that sword could remove his head, as it did the head of Mary of Scotland. I wish the younger Essex no harm, for I do not blame the deeds of the father on the son, but what his father did to my mother's people on Rathlin was an act beyond the pale of humanity. But let me continue my story.

"Following my first escape attempt a year earlier, the two O'Neills, Henry and Art, and I were kept in chains. On this occasion, on Christmas Eve, we managed to overpower a guard when he removed our manacles to eat. We then lowered ourselves down the castle walls by a rope that an accomplice had earlier managed to get to us. This accomplice was to meet us outside the walls with horses, but he was unable to procure them, so the four of

---

[1] Tuberculosis.

us set out on foot and following the route of my earlier escape, we headed south toward Wicklow and the mountains.

"Fiach MacHugh O'Byrne, we knew, would shelter us if we could reach Glenmalure. When we reached the mountains south of the city, it began to snow. We were lightly clothed and wearing only indoor footwear. We stayed well away from the main road south. The night became black as pitch and Henry O'Neill wandered off in the snowstorm and the darkness and we were never to see him again."

O'Donnell warmed his hands by the fire and seemed to relive again the chilling cold of that night. He then told them of how Art O'Neill, given little opportunity for exercise during his long captivity, began succumbing to cold and exhaustion.

"I tried as best I could to sustain him and help him along. My own feet I could no longer feel, but we struggled on. Neither of us could bear the thought of returning to captivity. Neither of us would again accept it. We felt it better to die in the cold of the mountains of our own land than to live in shackles in an English prison. No man should live in captivity, and any man who has, does not easily forget it."

O'Donnell paused, staring into the fire, and Maguire was reminded of a story that had made its way back to the north regarding Red Hugh's captivity in Dublin.

Following his first escape, the Lord Deputy Fitzwilliam had had the eighteen-year-old Red Hugh tortured in the hope that he would implicate Hugh O'Neill in the escape. Weakened by torture and by an illness similar to that which had nearly claimed MacRory's life, Red Hugh had continued to resist his captors. When they had offered, in exchange for the information they wanted, to remove his shackles and have him treated by a physician, he had replied, "If death is the only door to freedom, then I'll pass through that door." He survived the torture, and the illness, and a year later found another door to freedom.

"We staggered on through the snow all that night and the next day, and on into another night. When Art could no longer go on, we lay down in the shelter of a rocky ledge in the mountains above Glenmalure. I'm told we travelled a distance of forty miles. Our accomplice, better clothed for that winter night, continued on to try to reach O'Byrne."

Maguire interrupted to ask who it was that had helped them.

"I do not know his name," O'Donnell replied: "Some kern my mother had engaged. Fiach MacHugh told me later that when our messenger arrived, he at once sent some men back with him to find us. When they found us, they thought they had come too late, for we appeared to be dead. We had huddled together with our arms around each other for warmth. We lay thus, our thin clothing iced over and our bodies frozen together.

"Art O'Neill was indeed dead and I myself close to death. They buried Art in that place. I could not walk as my feet were frozen, and they carried me down off the mountain to MacHugh's stronghold in Glenmalure. O'Byrne restored me to health, except for my feet.

"The English knew I had reached O'Byrne. Glenmalure is a remote and secure fastness, and the English seldom venture there, but for extra safety, he hid me in a secret place in the woods. Later, O'Neill sent his brother, Turlough O'Hagan, to assist me back to the North. O'Neill, as you know, was fostered by the O'Hagans.

"The fords across the Liffey were now guarded to prevent my return and in any event, I was not sure I could ride a horse, but as you see I made it back." O'Donnell then concluded the narrative with brevity that was not at all to his listeners' liking. He told them how O'Byrne had sent a troop of horsemen with him as far as the Liffey. Among these horsemen were Phelim O'Toole and his brother.

"Not Phelim O'Toole, the traitor who betrayed your first escape attempt!" McCaffrey interrupted.

"O'Toole was no traitor. Do you think Fiach MacHugh O'Byrne would have let him live to betray me a second time? I want to put to rest the rumour that he handed me over to the English when I was recaptured after my first escape. On that occasion, Phelim was escorting me to O'Byrne's castle, when we were surrounded by a superior force of English. Seeing that the situation was hopeless, he acted with an intelligence that I could only admire. He made the pretence that I was his captive and that he was returning me to Dublin Castle, a story the English captain found a bit difficult to swallow, as we had been heading into the Wicklow hills and away from Dublin, but Phelim O'Toole is a persuasive man, a brave man also; so is his brother, as they proved at the Liffey's ford.

"To my shame, though, I did have a moment of doubt as we approached the Liffey two weeks ago, and O'Toole and his brother galloped ahead across the ford, shouting to the English guards. But then I heard what they were shouting. 'O'Byrne's men and O'Donnell are attempting to force their way across the river downstream.' They had not informed me of their plan, knowing I would not have allowed them to take such a risk. I last saw these two brave men as they, and the English guarding the ford, galloped off downstream, while we crossed the now unguarded ford. They're brave and resourceful men, and I only hope that somehow they were able to escape back to the Wicklow side of the river, for if they did not, their deaths will be slow and painful."

Red Hugh's sole companion, once across the Liffey, had been O'Neill's agent, who had guided him north to the safety of Red Hugh's father-in-law, the Earl of Tyrone, and the stronghold of Dungannon.

When O'Donnell concluded his narrative, no one spoke for some time. Each was aware of the hazards of the journey described so matter-of-factly. O'Donnell, barely able to sit a horse, had travelled some one hundred miles through enemy-held territory. He had crossed several well-guarded fords and evaded an enemy determined to thwart his escape back to the North.

CHAPTER 12

Red Hugh is elected the O'Donnell Chieftain

ed Hugh sat his horse in the courtyard of Maguire's castle. A mounted guard of his own men, led by his younger brother, Rory, had come to escort their future chieftain back to Ballyshannon. Red Hugh had refused to continue his journey to Ballyshannon by boat and insisted on riding at the head of his men. He already acted as if he were the O'Donnell chieftain, and already he seemed to be accepted as such. He turned and spoke to MacRory beside him.

"Good luck, Turlough. If you get through to Donegal Castle, tell my mother that as soon as I collect sufficient forces at Ballyshannon, I'll rid Donegal of those two Sassenach swineherds, and no O'Donnell will again have to cower behind his own castle walls."

He waved to Maguire and, taking his place at the head of his armed men, trotted out of the courtyard.

The gallowglass followed across the bridge before turning and galloping off to the right. MacRory followed the route, in reverse, that he had taken four years earlier with Red Hugh's father. He urged his horse briskly along in the cold early morning. His horse was the large war horse that could carry a man, armed with hauberk[1], helmet, and heavy sword. The gallowglass, on occasion, rode the heavy war horse, or destrier, with saddle, according to the English mode, rather than the lighter saddle-less Irish cavalry horse.

Few went these days unarmed in this part of Ireland. Maguire controlled Fermanagh, but was at war with the English. Donegal was controlled by whatever force – Irish or English – that prevailed from day to day.

MacRory rode steadily throughout the morning without encountering another person. His path wound through the small rounded hills, a geological formation called drumlins, the leafless branches on their wooded slopes still shiny with frost even at noon.

---

[1] Mail armour.

By late afternoon he was close to O'Donnell lands and stopped by a small stream. The gallowglass dismounted and, taking some food from his saddlebag, sat on a rock by the stream bed. He was temperate and disciplined by nature and seldom ate more than twice a day, one small meal in the morning and a larger meal toward evening. On occasion he drank wine or mead, but always in moderation. *Uisce beatha*, popular with so many soldiers, he avoided. He had been induced to drink it once, and his abstemious nature abhorred the sense of loss of control the potent liquor induced.

His horse lowered its velvet muzzle and drank daintily from the cold stream. The gallowglass gazed into the slowly moving water. Exquisitely delicate slivers of silvery ice had formed jagged halos around the stones protruding from the stream. As he ate, he watched idly as little bubbles of white froth escaped the current to dally and circle in the eddies before being again caught up in the stream and swept away beneath the trailing branches of an overhanging willow.

With a flurry of drumming hooves, six horsemen swarmed down on him from the hillside above. They galloped into the stream, surrounding him, on their small shaggy-looking mounts. They were hobilars, lightly armed scouts, mounted without saddle on the agile little horses called "garrons."

The gallowglass looked up, but remained seated on the rock and continued eating. "Heavens above! If it isn't a squadron of MacCaffreys mounted on sheep! You're a shrewd and resourceful man, Phelim, using a beast that provides both transportation and wool. Judging by the luxurance of the fleece, you'll be a rich man, too, come the spring shearing."

Their bald-headed leader, "Bollocks" MacCaffrey, had a scar along the left side of his face reaching down to his mouth and his wry attempt at a twisted smile merely made the villainous old chieftain look almost comically piratical. He seemed disappointed to have come upon a friend rather than an enemy.

"Oh, it's you, captain. Sorry," was his less than warm greeting. "From the hill yonder we thought that perhaps you were one of Willis' or Conwell's men, or perhaps one of the brave captains themselves, come across from Donegal to test the waters in Fermanagh."

"I suppose it could have been one of the brave captains, Phelim, luring you and your shaggy group of overeager bandits into an ambush. I've appreciated your sly escort for the past half-hour or so. You'll never be a success at ambush, Phelim, unless you take to wearing a helmet to cover that shining pate. The English gentlemen's romp through Donegal is about over, though. Red Hugh is gathering an army at Ballyshannon."

"Red Hugh? Red Hugh is back in Donegal! He has escaped again!"

"This time he reached O'Byrne in Glenmalure. The sons of Shane O'Neill escaped with him. Art died in the cold and Henry did not make it back. O'Neill sent O'Hagan to help Red Hugh back to Dungannon and sheltered him there"

"Man, that is news to warm the heart. The MacDonnell woman will have him elected chieftain within the week, and then any of the Sassenach left in Donegal had better learn to speak Irish. Ineen Duive, of course is close kin to Sorley Boy, and will never forgive what Essex and Drake did to her family on Rathlin. She stands by Old Hugh, despite his earlier alliance with the English, but The O'Donnell is not the man he was. The man sheltering in Dun na gall Castle is not the man who drove Shane O'Neill to seek sanctuary in the arms of his enemies. Donel, had he lived, was a chieftain. Niall Garve lusts to be chieftain, but he has too much ambition in him. He's all ambition, but has no vision. He'd deliver Donegal to the Sassenach if they promised him the chieftainship and Ireland to the devil if that gentleman promised to make him *Ard Rí*. Donegal needs a chieftain, and from all I have heard of Red Hugh, he was born to be that man. The legend speaks of the English being driven out of Ireland when one Hugh of the O'Donnells succeeds another in lawful succession. But has he the support, do you think?"

The gallowglass mounted and turned in his saddle before urging his horse up the bank of the stream. "He's always had the support, even as a captive in Dublin and Donegal will have a chieftain that Donegal will remember."

The sun was low in the sky by the time he sighted Donegal Castle. The castle, built on a rocky outcrop overlooking the Eske River, commanded a view of Donegal Bay. The square, four-storied fortress, stronghold of the O'Donnells for the last two centuries, stood silent and sombre in the fading light. It was surrounded by a bawn, an outer protective rampart of stone that was ten feet high and three feet thick, and in places the slanted roofs of thatched dwellings abutted the inner aspects of the wall. The cold winter sun, setting out in the bay, cast its flat rays on the grey battlements.

The gallowglass reconnoitred for a half-hour. He sat his horse on a small wooded hill three hundred yards from the castle. He saw two sentries posted on the walls. Beyond the castle, where the Eske flowed into the bay, was the Franciscan abbey, now occupied by the two English adventurers, Willis and Conwell, and their men. MacRory's gaze, however, was fixed on two English soldiers positioned behind a breastwork a few hundred yards from the castle gate. He knew they were positioned there, protected by the breastwork from arrows, to monitor the castle and activities within.

He took a mirror from his saddlebag and angled it to deflect the sun's rays toward the sentry on the castle wall. After some time he was successful in gaining the sentry's attention. MacRory continued to flash the mirror on the sentry for some minutes more. He then replaced the mirror and rode out of the copse, walking his horse toward the breastwork.

The soldiers there saw him almost immediately. The gallowglass waved and continued to walk his horse toward them. The soldiers stared at him uncertainly. He was now about two hundred yards from them. He walked his horse toward the breastwork, looking around, and even stopped to reach down to adjust a stirrup. The two soldiers stared in his direction, still uncertain of the approaching horseman.

He continued his casual approach. He was fifty yards from them when he heard their shouts of alarm. They had recognized him as a gallowglass. The war horse thundered into them. One soldier managed to raise his halberd, but the gallowglass severed its wooden staff with his sword before slashing the sword down on the man's shoulder. Normally, a horse will try to avoid trampling on a fallen man. The war horse, however, rearing, stamping, and biting, was often as fearsome to a man on foot as was its rider. The one remaining man, who had stumbled and fallen in the melee, kneeling, looked up in mute despair before he died beneath the iron-shod hooves of the heavy war horse.

An entrance gateway in the bawn swung open and MacRory called, "I'm Turlough MacRory, O'Donnell's gallowglass." Or perhaps Maguire's, he thought.

Ten or fifteen gallowglass were visible within the bawn, each armed with a halberd.

A group of mounted men wheeled from the friary and galloped toward the castle, but MacRory, saddened to see the O'Donnell castle impotent before this band of marauding English, did not feel like running for the shelter of the castle. He shouted to the gallowglass in the courtyard to form around him in the castle entrance. The words "O'Donnell's gallowglass" had their effect, for the disciplined men formed up on either side of the captain, each kneeling on one knee and holding his halberd, butt on the ground, shaft angled upwards.

The halberd, with its long curved blade attached to a long staff, was an effective weapon against cavalry, and the setting sun glinting on the shining blades presented a chastening sight to the charging horsemen. The small group stood quietly just outside the castle entrance as the horsemen thundered down on them. A premature hail of arrows from the castle walls whooshed overhead, most of them landing short of the charging horsemen, but one did find its mark and a horseman, who had been well out in front, reared back in his saddle, an arrow piercing his right eye. His rider less horse galloped, angling to the left across the line of charging riders.

A woman's voice shrilled from the courtyard within, berating the captain of the archers on the battlements above.

"O'Daley, you dung-brained imbecile, and them not wearing armour! Couldn't you have waited – Oh, you witless *amadhaun*[1]! If they ever let you breed, Donegal is done for."

The woman's voice was heard giving orders within the bawn, and soon a second group of men armed with halberds arrived from within the castle, and formed a second line of steel behind their comrades. The charging line of horsemen wavered, and then broke into a disorganized melee of rearing, whinnying horses. Quickly, the horsemen withdrew beyond the range of the arrows. The situation was a stalemate. The mounted men could not effectively charge, nor could they outflank the gallowglass, who knelt with the castle entrance at their backs. The gallowglass were too experienced to be drawn out. On foot, away from the castle, they could be surrounded and be easier prey for the men on horseback. The English

---

[1] (Irish) "Idiot".

horsemen, drawn up out of range of the arrows, commenced taunting the gallowglass in an attempt to lure them out.

"Tell the MacDonnell woman to feed you some *uisce beatha* to stiffen your courage!"

"Come feel the English steel we fed to your papist monks."

"A new breed of bird comes to Ireland? The yellow-livered red-shank!"

With a quiet "stand fast" to the men behind him, MacRory walked his horse forward some twenty paces and sat facing the horsemen from the friary.

"Is the coward, Willis, among you, and will he choose to decline my invitation as he did that of Brian O'Rourke?"

It would seem that Willis had little choice. In front of his men he could not ignore the challenge or the insult. After an interval a horseman charged out screaming from among his comrades. MacRory sat immobile on his horse, his two-handed sword in his right hand by his side. The horseman bore down, sword arm outstretched, leaning low on his horse's neck. He passed, cursing, on the gallowglass's right, pulling his horse up on its haunches, and slashed backward with his sword. The gallowglass leaned sideways, sword still by his side, as his horse with a slight pressure from his rider's knee also moved to the side. The man's slashing sword missed, not by much.

The gallowglass manoeuvred his horse with his knees only, the tactic the result of months of patient training. The horse made a rearing turn to the right that brought MacRory around behind and to the left of the other man, both men facing the castle. Willis turned desperately around in his saddle, and awkwardly raised his shield for protection, the sword in his right hand now useless. The eyes of the two men met, but the words "For Donagh" may never have reached the dying man's consciousness. If they did, they were the last that would ever do so.

A scything two-handed slash removed the man's head from his body. The truncated body fell forward on his horse's neck, severed arteries pumping two small fountains of blood. The body remained in the saddle as his horse and its bloody burden galloped back toward the friary. Finally, the body toppled from the saddle in front of his comrades.

The gallowglass dismounted and picked up the head. The head however was not that of Willis. Remounting he galloped toward the horsemen, as if he meant to charge them, but wheeled his horse in a wide circle within the protection of the archers on the battlements and, throwing the head of their comrade toward them, shouted, "A gift from Red Hugh O'Donnell."

He rode back through the line of gallowglass, gesturing at them to follow as he entered the castle. He dismounted in the courtyard, and bowed as a lady approached him.

"A gift from Hugh Roe!" She held both his arms and looked at him with glittering blue eyes. "Is Red Hugh safe, Turlough?"

"He's safe, ma'am, and collecting an army at Ballyshannon."

She gasped, and the grip on his arms tightened as she continued to stare at him. The blue eyes glittered with tears. "He's back in Donegal! We've been shut up in the castle with no news from outside" Quickly she composed herself. "We must get word to the MacSweeneys, the MacSweeneys of Fanad and Doe, and the O'Dohertys."

"O'Neill will have already done so," the gallowglass replied.

"O'Neill knows of his escape?"

"He assisted in it, ma'am. Turlough O'Hagan brought Red Hugh through the Pale and safely to O'Neill's castle at Dungannon."

The old lady smiled. "O'Neill plays a dangerous game. The Earl O'Neill rescues his O'Donnell kinsman from the Lord Deputy, who is the Earl O'Neill's English friend."

"Red Hugh instructed me to say that he intends to rid you of your English guests in Donegal, ma'am, as soon as he can collect sufficient forces at Ballyshannon."

"God hasten that day! I was visiting here from Mongavlin when those two pieces of English offal arrived to desecrate the friary and butcher the monks. Some managed to reach shelter here in the castle. Others fled inland to hide in the woods around Lough Eske. Willis and Conwell have also taken the O'Boyle castle on the harbour. They kill and plunder our people. They take what they wish and ride where they will throughout Donegal. Like vultures these Sassenach scavengers and their friends share in the spoils."

"And The O'Donnell?" MacRory murmured.

She turned away abruptly, only to turn back smiling and holding out both hands. "Forgive me, Turlough, I forget my manners. The Sassenach are eroding our manners as well as our customs."

MacRory felt vaguely uncomfortable. Had his question about the old chieftain been inappropriate? Had Ineen Duive just reminded him that he, too, had forgotten his manners?

"My husband has become frail. He can no longer protect Donegal, but his son, -and mine, was born to rule *Tir Conaill*, and perhaps all Ireland." She reached up, placing both her hands on his shoulders. "Turlough, it's many a year since I've seen you, and in those years you've become a man, a man who brings me good news. My son's dearest friend is dear to my own heart. Out there it gladdened that heart to see you send that mongrel son of a mongrel mother to hell in two pieces. May he suffer twice the torment there. My only regret would be that you didn't leave his head on his shoulders for my son to remove."

"He may yet get the chance, ma'am; Willis still lives and is still a coward. He sent a henchman"

"Perhaps then my son may not wish to taint his sword."

She turned and shouted up to the battlements. "O'Daley there, keep your eyes open for any more activity from the friary."

"That I will, ma'am. If they come at us again, we won't make the same mistake. We'll be grappling hand-to-hand before the archers let them have it next time."

"WHAT! Oh Christ Almighty! Where does the likes of him come from? Why his mother didn't drown him at birth!"

She took the gallowglass by the arm and led him towards a stone stairway which led to the second-story living quarters. "Come and tell me about my son's escape, and of your life among the Maguires. I'll have the servants bring us food and wine."

On May 3, 1592, Tir Conaill's chieftains gathered at Carraig an Dun to elect Red Hugh O'Donnell, chieftain of the O'Donnells. Many of the chieftains attended; some, including Niall Garve O'Donnell, did not. Eoghan MacSweeney, Red Hugh's father by fosterage, was present, as was Donal MacSweeny of Fanad. Old Hugh O'Donnell, in the presence of his wife, Ineen Duive, and the assembled chieftains, ceded the chieftainship to his son.

Within days of Red Hugh's arrival at Ballyshannon enough forces had rallied to him that he was able to drive the English raiders out of his father's territory. Most of Donegal had rallied with joy to one who promised again a strong leadership.

On the day of the ceremony, Red Hugh, standing on the Rock of Doon and holding the white wand of chieftainship in his right hand, took advantage of the assembly of chieftains to call a council of war. "A quarter of a century ago, my father, Hugh O'Donnell, was known as a 'Queen's O'Donnell' when he enlisted English help to defeat Shane O'Neill. A leader does what he must. The past is the past. Shane O'Neill was an unpleasant and quarrelsome neighbour, but Shane O'Neill never bowed to England. The English assist us in destroying ourselves. Never again will there be a 'Queen's O'Donnell' in *Tir Conaill*.

"You have elected me to rule *Tir Conaill*. I am your lawful chieftain. In three days, when we reassemble here at Carraig an Dun, I will expect each of you sub-chieftains to stand at the head of three hundred of his men. We will first march against Turlough O'Neill, who with the help of the English raids on our eastern border. Donal MacSweeney will marshal the MacSweeneys of Fanad and the O'Dohertys of Inishowen and meet us at my Lifford castle.

"No longer will our people, in their own hallowed homeland, bow to some petty English tyrant. No longer will the Saxon swine defile this holy land of our fathers. Whose sword will avenge our broken altars and our slain priests? Whose sword is unsheathed for *Tir Conaill*? Who remembers Clan Conaill's ancient glory? Who stands with his chieftain?"

A roar of acclaim greeted his words as each chieftain drew his sword. The O'Donnell war cry "*O'Donnell Abú*" echoed and re-echoed from the hills around Carrick an Dun.

Ineen Duive rose, her blue eyes gazing steadily at her son, her head nodding almost imperceptibly in approval.

His words at Carraig an Dun effectively portrayed Red Hugh's attitude toward the English and anyone, English or Irish, who stood against him. Within a week, he led his men against Turlough O'Neill.

Energetic and single-minded, he pursued his purpose. Within months no enemy threatened his frontiers. O'Gallaghers and O'Boyles were made to know who their lawful overlord was. By whatever means necessary, subtlety or the sword, generosity and gracious forgiveness or unrelenting war, by the force of his will, the nineteen-year-old chieftain united Donegal.

Men were drawn to him as steel to a magnet. He engaged Hugh O'Neill's assistance in arranging a meeting with his recent captor, the Lord Lieutenant. Red Hugh, surrounded by his sub-chieftains, apprised the English Lord Lieutenant that an O'Donnell again ruled in *Tir Conaill*.

Again, as in the past, from Inishowen to Inish Saimer, from Tory to the Foyle, the war cry of the O'Donnells brought fear and swift vengeance to the enemies of *Tir Conaill*. Secure in his fastness in Donegal, he looked southward to Connacht, and Sir Richard Bingham's English colonists.

CHAPTER 13

Battle of Atha Culainn

acRory had again reason to question his status as an O'Donnell or a Maguire gallowglass. He was in Connacht, the territory of neither, as he rode in a flat gallop in pursuit of Richard Bingham's cavalry. A horse-length ahead rode Hugh Maguire, screaming his war cry as his faster horse closed on an unfortunate soldier. The soldier would have been unfortunate "unto death" had not the pursued and the pursuers galloped into Sir Richard Bingham's fortified camp.

Horses were pulled up rearing and plunging. In a fast reassessment on both sides, Maguire considered himself well outnumbered, and Bingham, by his action, seemed to concur. Maguire now had to rein in his excellent horse to hold his position, protecting the rear of his fleeing cavalry. Some of Bingham's pursuing horsemen wore mail hauberk and were mounted on fresh horses. These now came in contact with Maguire's rearguard, and indeed there was no clear line of demarcation between the two groups of galloping horsemen.

There was seldom a Maguire battle in which a McCaffrey was not present. Phelim McCaffrey and Maguire fought, screaming and yelling their war cries; the gallowglass fought with silent expertise. The battle was waged at a full gallop with horsemanship as important to life as swordsmanship. The peaceful plains of Connacht reverberated with the thunder of hooves, the ringing clash of swords, and the wild and screaming yells of the protagonists. Occasionally a gurgling groan and a heavy thud cut off the yells as a man fell from his horse.

As they came within sight of Maguire's camp and of his main force, the pursuers fell back, except for a small group, which had surrounded McCaffrey. McCaffrey, engaged with one of Bingham's men, had fallen well behind the fleeing horsemen and was now fighting, surrounded by half a dozen of the enemy. Maguire raced back toward him, shouting over his shoulder, "Back with me, MacRory."

As he did so, Bingham's men disengaged, and MacCaffrey sat his horse to look after them. As Maguire reached him, McCaffrey fell from the saddle, bleeding from his many wounds and dead.

Maguire's men returned from their raid into Connacht, exulting at how their success must enrage Bingham. They brought with them the spoils of their raid and herds of cattle that would take years for Bingham's settlers to replace. They brought back, too, the body of the fierce old Phelim McCaffrey to rest, at last in peace, not on the flat plains of Connacht, but in the Maguire graveyard of Aghalurcher among the rounded hills of Fermanagh. Peace had never been much of a goal of McCaffrey, but perhaps his soul would rest more peacefully knowing that he had died in a Maguire battle, as had generations of his forefathers.

They rode north for hours in silence. Silence was unusual for Maguire. At last he spoke. "We've stung Bingham. I owe him that and more for his raids into Fermanagh. He'll be marching north to avenge himself as soon as he can muster a force."

Another long silence.

"You know, Turlough, old Phelim would never have forgiven himself, us either, had he died in his bed. Can you imagine being haunted by the ghost of Phelim McCaffrey with blood in his eye? His brother's son fell, too."

"And some of your own family, Cathal Maguire and the Abbot Maguire."

"And Cathal and the Abbot," Maguire said, lapsing again into silence.

It did not take a prophet to predict a response from Bingham, and Maguire's "prophesy" would not have gained him much fame as one. In the autumn of that same year MacRory stood on the north bank of the Erne at the Ford of Culainn, near Belleek, at the head of one hundred gallowglass. The English responded in force. Massed across the river were not only Bingham's Connacht forces, but also those of the English governor of the Pale.

From somewhere up ahead of the gallowglass, the skirl of war pipes echoed along the riverbank. This was the first time the gallowglass had seen the great Earl of Tyrone. O'Neill and his brother-in-law, Sir Henry Bagenal, led Queen's O'Neills and English troops across the ford. O'Neill was renowned, hated, feared, and admired. He had seen much war and was a brave and able soldier. He was renowned and admired for his skill in charting the hazardous course between being an English earl and an Irish chieftain. Many of the Irish in Ireland feared and hated him, but he had many enemies among the English in Ireland also. The Englishman crossing the ford by his side – his wife's brother, Sir Henry Bagenal – bitterly hated and distrusted him. O'Neill, some years earlier, had taken an active and willing part in the savaging of those Irish who had been unfortunate enough to follow the rebel Earl of Desmond. When Henry O'Neill, who had accompanied Red Hugh in his escape from Dublin Castle, had unexpectedly made his way back to the north, Hugh O'Neill had him imprisoned. O'Neill, to rid himself of a contender to the chieftainship of the O'Neills, had hanged his brother's son at Dungannon. But at Dungannon he had also given sanctuary to his son-in-law, Red Hugh O'Donnell, risking English wrath

O'Neill, recognizable by his red beard and by the red hand emblazoned on his corselet, sat astride a great black horse as he led his forces through the ford and through a hail of arrows, which were mostly ineffective against the armoured horsemen. A riderless horse plunged and reared behind him in the river. On his right, an English rider came abreast of him and looked as if he might pass him until O'Neill reminded the mailed horseman of his place by striking him a ringing blow across the chest with the flat of his sword. The man redoubled his efforts to curb his horse.

Downstream in a shallow eddy lay the debris of battle, partially submerged bodies oozing red blood into the amber water, bodies of mere soldiers, unhonoured in life, nameless and unburied in death – Irish kerns or English settlers, following their masters, who knew little of them. Days later, gas-filled intestines would perhaps float a bloated, nameless body ashore farther downstream and a cawing raven would be its only keener. Some of these nameless bodies might even plunge over Assaroe to drift for a few days in the Atlantic before finally reaching their graves on the ocean floor. Later, a mother or a sister, in a sad, little, mud-walled cabin in Connacht, or perhaps in nearby Tyrone, and remembering his face as a child, might say, "He fell at Atha Culainn."

In the middle of the ford, the water was belly deep on the horses and now Maguire's cavalry charged. Each prior attempt at crossing had been thrown back by the shock of his cavalry hurtling down on the slow-moving horsemen in the ford. If Maguire could not hold the enemy at the ford, the vastly greater numbers across the river would overwhelm his force, and Fermanagh would be at Bingham's mercy. Enemy soldiers, massed across the river, discharged volleys from their arabesques. A haze of blue smoke rose and slowly dissipated into the air with each volley, to be augmented a minute later by another rising cloud of smoke and the sound of another crackling volley.

Slowly, by virtue of the tenacity of O'Neill's armoured horsemen and the steady inexorable advance of the massed foot soldiers behind, the enemy gained the bank in front of the gallowglass. Maguire signalled his cavalry to fall back to either side and galloped his horse over to where MacRory stood ready at the head of his gallowglass. Maguire nodded to the gallowglass and pointed his sword at the enemy swarming across the river. The gallowglass moved forward with grim purpose and swaying steel against the horsemen and foot soldiers. They loped forward in four ranks – the first two with sheathed swords and armed with halberds, the last two with swords only.

The gallowglass busied himself with the intense and focused work he knew well – warding off the arching sword with the halberd's metal blade, stabbing up and under the mail or hooking the horseman's armour to unseat him from his horse, and once fallen, either leaving the mailed horseman to drown in the fast flowing ford or slicing for the unprotected groin or face. He was focused, but also aware of each potential surrounding adversary; unthinking and unafraid; afraid to think of the fearful death that might befall him, the death he steadily dealt to others; concentrated and remote from the noise and confusion of the battle; images registering briefly and gone; an open-mouthed unheard scream; a long deep wound and red thick blood on a horse's neck. Poor innocent brute, MacRory thought, involved by man in man's brutality; a gallowglass a fraction late in warding off the sword that bit deeply into his arm; O'Neill with blood streaming from his leg; Maguire's cavalry charging the flanks; masses of men coming up out of the ford; the battle moving uphill and pushing Maguire's forces back; his gallowglass being pushed back, at first slowly and then falling back, fighting, retreating, disciplined, and desperate; massed men surging up from the ford; Maguire and his horsemen charging and charging again to protect the retreat; the sudden silence of the war pipes.

CHAPTER 14

Enniskillen

Two Enniskillen gurriers[1] lounged against the railing of the East Bridge of the town. They had been drawn to each other from early school days where they were known collectively as "The Numb Nuts". It was uncertain whether the strangely appropriate name was acquired by a process of natural selection, or was the result of a misadventure at a football match in Kinawley. Dominic and Billy were spectators at the match and were engaged in heckling the Kinawley team, jeeringly referring to them as "yous bogmen". As a result of this way with words they found themselves impaled in the glower of a sullen-looking youth from that unsophisticated part of the country. Tensions heightened and Dominic felt obliged to remind their antagonist that he himself had some expertise in Kung Fu. He then adopted a strange arthritic looking stance, and uttered a high pitched sound reminiscent of a chicken in the clutches of a fox. An uncivil and unheralded kick to his privates – the manoeuvre known colloquially as a "Kinawley uppercut" – brought his keening to a pitch that many an operatic diva might have envied and himself to his knees. This unorthodox low blow was accompanied by a terse and enigmatic "Yous bog men yerself – numb nuts." Billy, aghast at this rather louche interpretation of the rules of engagement, opted not to engage.

Early on, each had developed a mutual aversion to the drudgery of work. Billy was on the dole[2] and Dominic was awaiting a settlement for whiplash. Dominic had never worked and now never would. On occasion he wore a soft cervical collar which he described as a "chick magnet" However, considering his lack of success in that field, someone more grounded in reality might have considered the probability of reversed polarity. His imagination was sufficiently feverish to envision the chicks thinking. "A pile up at Le Mans? A fall repelling off the Eiger?

Billy had once tried work but soon realized that work was not for him. He had persisted for as long as a month and a half working in the linen factory at Lisnaskea, up at half seven each morning and not back home until half four each evening, commuting the four miles to Lisnaskea, working five days a week,

---

[1] Urban "Red-necks".
[2] Unemployment payments.

eight hours a day. He still shuddered at the memory of that soul-destroying toil. He had made his decision early in life and had had the tenacity to stick by it. For him now the free untrammelled life of the rapparee on the dole.

The whiplash victim had hit a farmer's cow on the road out by Letterbreen. As Dominic saw the incident: "I may have had a few jars in me at the time but the cow oughtn't 'av been there" The farmer was claiming compensation for injury to his livestock and Dominic was claiming compensation for whiplash. As the farmer saw the incident, "It's him that hit the cow from behind. It's the cow should be having whiplash"

When the doctor was having difficulty with a definitive diagnosis and was suggesting "maybe a soft tissue injury?" Dominic, who knew his own body, made the diagnosis for him. "Whiplash" had a more snappily severe sound to it and could possibly be more lucrative. His legal-aid lawyer had been a disappointment and far from being the hoped for barracuda, had told Dominic that his insurance was not under any obligation to cover him as he had been impaired. Not only might he get no settlement for his neck, but most likely he'd be liable for the injury to the cow, and there was still the possibility that criminal charges could be laid. Not one to suffer fools gladly and recognizing this as a ploy by the lawyer to boost his fees, he was now representing himself. He was going with a two-pronged strategy, suing the farmer for allowing his cow on the road and thus causing an accident that resulted in a neck injury and mental anguish and demanding a fitting settlement from the insurance company for a neck injury and untold mental anguish. He felt it was a win/win approach.

Under "Occupation" on a court document he had entered "Unemployed" and lest this label him as some idle nonentity he had added "fighting the Insurance". This hinted of the warrior spirit, someone not to be trifled with, something like the whispered "He's in the paramilitaries."

Once he'd been heard to state "I'm a fighter and as long as this whiplash lasts I'll fight them till I die, and never look back."

The pitying gaze of the two young men followed two students who exited the gate of the old Saint Michael's school and walked off up Belmore Street

"Poor wee studious shit heads."

The words were spoken loudly enough to make it look as if he didn't care if the "wee studious shit heads" heard him, but not quite loudly enough to be heard by the students, for the brave men holding up the wall were well aware that the students outnumbered them two to two. They were not aware nor would their intellects have allowed them to contemplate that the objects of their pity might perhaps one day make decisions regarding disbursement of the dole and insurance settlements

Having reached early manhood with little accomplishment in his wake, each had manufactured in his mind a gallant persona – that of a bit of a wit, a man of the world, yet a man a little world weary, and a man of some intellect. Who could tell what fame might lie ahead for the late bloomer! A lacklustre past did not preclude a glorious future.

In one recurring fantasy, Dominic of the feverish imagination could see himself at Buckingham Palace receiving the military cross, his celebrated disregard for military regulations apparent in the jaunty non-regulation rakish tilt of his Special Forces beret. The event had passed into military lore and would be a topic of conversation in many an officers' mess by future generations of British Army Officers. Had the camera captured a roguish wink in acknowledgement of her majesty's "A grateful country will be forever in your debt, Captain?" Would any man dare to wink at the Queen! But Captain Dominic Carty was not just any man.

His lot forbade - by a farmer's cow!

Two girls, students of Mount Lourdes Convent School, walked down from the convent, schoolbooks beneath their arms. The girls fell silent as they became aware of the gauntlet to be run on the bridge ahead. One of the duo holding up the parapet of the bridge nudged his friend to insure his full attention and both smiled at the girls, who staring fixedly ahead, walked past.

"Get them orf ye," the wit growled to the retreating girls' backs, and the sally was greeted with an appreciative gale of laughter from his friend.

Some years earlier, a doctor on a popular medical television program had turned to a pretty nurse with the unfortunate demand, "Get the Morphia." A variation of the words had passed into the language and was popular with some who favoured the terse no-nonsense approach to the gentler sex. Such was the popularity of the phrase that it was even shouted at football matches with exuberant irrelevance. The witty one doubled over gasping, as his friend dealt him an appreciative and playful punch to the stomach with the words, "You wanker!"

Enniskillen was a bastion of Unionist rule in Northern Ireland. When the native Irish, led by Owen Roe O'Neill the nephew of Hugh O'Neill, had rebelled in 1641, Enniskillen held out against the rebels. A monument to Sir William Cole, an English planter of the early 1600s dominated Fort Hill above Belmore Street. Belmore Street was named after Lord Belmore, scion of another prominent planter family. Two of the British Army's oldest Regiments – the Enniskillen Dragoons and the Enniskillen Fusiliers, whose home base was the old Maguire Castle in Enniskillen, and who had fought bravely at the Somme and in many other engagements – were formed at the time of the planter's defence of Enniskillen later in the 1600s. Their swords,-and their reputations, were first bloodied at the battle of Newtownbutler when they pursued and massacred a defeated enemy, but the heroic defence of the town by those first Enniskilleners was also the inspiration for the celebrated élan and valour of the two famous regiments down the centuries.

Opposite the two young men stood the war memorial to the dead of two World Wars. In the first of these wars, another 140,000 Irish Volunteers joined the 100,000 Irish already fighting for Britain. In response to this Irish contribution to King George's dispute with his cousin the Kaiser, the British Government had promised that at war's end Ireland would be granted Home Rule, with special provision to be made for Ulster. At war's end, King and Kaiser patched up their differences, and the bodies of young men of Ireland and of many nations fertilized the rich earth of France and the arid soil of Gallipoli. Countless others returned, maimed and broken, to relive their glorious nightmare from time to time. The elderly soldiers and statesmen, who marshalled armies and sent these young men to die, and who themselves had fought with bravery in earlier conflicts, did not wish to deny to another generation the same opportunity for glory.

Any measure of Home Rule for Ireland was not popular with Unionists in the northern part of Ireland. In 1886 the Liberal Prime Minister, Gladstone, introduced a Home Rule bill for Ireland. Lord Randolf Churchhill, father of Winston, and a Conservative M.P., travelled to Belfast where, preaching to the converted, he made fiery speeches urging the Ulster unionists to join with the Conservatives to defeat the bill. The bill was defeated. Some Nationalists in the south of Ireland wanted complete independence from England and were prepared to use force to obtain it. In this they faced daunting odds, for they were clashing not only with the ruling elite of England, many of whom were Anglo/Irish, but with the might of an empire. In 1916 in the midst of the war, a small group of men in Dublin, led by Patrick Henry Pearse, took over the General Post Office and other buildings, and hung out a rebel flag. At the time, this was not a popular gesture with the people of Dublin or with some of the Irish in general, many of whom had fathers and sons in the British Army fighting in the trenches in Europe. The British military, even less impressed, easily suppressed the abortive rebellion, and in the usual manner dealt "sternly" with the rebels. They were summarily tried and shot at Dublin's Kilmainham Gaol. One of them, a wounded James Connolly, could not stand and was shot strapped to a chair. His body was buried without a coffin in a mass grave with the other rebels.

The malevolence of the English response, however, backfired, and the insurrection became generalized. Earlier a volunteer army called the Irish Volunteers under the Irish Nationalist Politician, John Redmond, had been formed, and an offshoot of these Volunteers, the I.R.A., inspired by the sacrifice of Pearce and his comrades, fought the British Army in Ireland. England terrorised the country by sending in irregulars known as "Black and Tans" and officers called "Auxiliaries," who further outraged the Irish with their brutal tactics. Irishmen returning from four years of horror in the trenches of Europe did not brag of their service in the British Army in a country now in open defiance of British rule. These Irishmen were looked on, not as returning heroes, but as recent comrades in arms of the Black and Tans.

An I.R.A. leader, Michael Collins, was sent to England to negotiate a treaty. Lloyd George the British Prime minister threatened Collins with "war and war in three days" if the Irish delegation did not agree to the terms of a proposed treaty that divided Ireland into a northern six counties under British rule and a virtually independent twenty-six counties in the south. Winston Churchill, a member of the negotiation team, added that it would be "real war and not mere bush ranging." It was perhaps not Churchill's finest hour when he threatened all-out war on a small, already terrorized country, one in four of whose quarter million contribution to England's recent war had given their lives in that war, a war fought ostensibly to free small nations from tyranny.

> *'Twas England bade our wild geese go, that small nations might be free.*
> *Their lonely graves are by Suvla's waves, and the fringe of the grey North Sea.*
> *But had they died by Pearse's side, or fought with Cathal Brugha,*
> *Their graves we'd keep where the Fenians sleep,*
> *'Neath the shroud of the Foggy Dew.*

Collins, signing the treaty, said, "I fear I am signing my own death warrant." He was. His erstwhile comrades shot him.

Some of the I.R.A., refusing to accept the treaty, fought on in an Irish civil war, and now their former comrades, known as Free Staters, opposed them using armoured cars and weapons supplied by England. In the Irish Civil War of 1920-1922, both the I.R.A. and Free Staters proved themselves the equal of any English "Black and Tans" in atrocities against each other.

The northern part of the island, planted centuries earlier with English and border Scots, was predominantly British in sentiment. These descendants of the Ulster planters, who had taken over Ulster after the defeat of the old Gaelic chieftains, vehemently rejected any possible union in a united Ireland. Some of these Northern Irish families had been in Ireland for three hundred years, yet never regarded themselves as Irish. The Irish, used to seducing their conquerors to Irish ways, found this unforgivable.

The Normans, who had invaded Ireland in 1169, had begun to adopt Irish ways within a few centuries. They spoke Irish, married the Irish, and engaged in the Irish penchant for rebellion. Cromwell and his army came to Ireland in 1649, and after a campaign lasting only nine months, left such an imprint on the Irish psyche that ever after the name Beelzebub took second place to Cromwell in the pantheon of Irish antichrists. Yet a few generations later in the 1798 Rebellion, descendants of Cromwell's "adventurers" featured among the Irish rebels. However, these Northern Irish now were a different breed.

The officer corps of the British Army was traditionally Unionist in its sympathies. Many of the senior officers were Anglo-Irish and had family ties with Ulster. In 1893 a second Home Rule Bill for Ireland had been passed in the Commons but vetoed in the House of Lords. A third Home Rule bill for Ireland was introduced in 1912 under the Liberal Prime Minister, H.H.Asquith. The implementation of this third Home Rule Bill was militantly opposed by Ulster Unionists, 500,000 of whom signed a covenant, some in their own blood, vowing to oppose Home Rule. An army of 100,000 – the Ulster Volunteers – was formed to resist Home Rule by force if necessary. Arms were smuggled into Ulster from Germany, and the British Government feared that British military bases in Ulster could be raided for weapons.

In March 1914, an incident known as "The Curragh Mutiny" occurred. General Hubert Gough was in charge of a cavalry brigade at the Curragh which was a British army camp close to Dublin. Gough, born in Wexford, Ireland, was Anglo-Irish and a Unionist. His family had come to Ireland from England in the 1600s and subsequently became an illustrious military family; his father, his uncle, and his brother had all won the Victoria Cross. He threatened to resign his commission if the British Government ordered him north to disarm the Ulster Volunteers. Over fifty of his officers followed suit. He had the tacit backing of other British army generals of Anglo-Irish descent, including the Chief of the Imperial General Staff, General French.

The commander of the sprawling Aldershot military complex in southern England which was known as the "Home of the British Army" was General Haig, of World War 1 fame. Haig's Chief of Staff was John Gough, who wore on his uniform the wine-red ribbon of the Victoria Cross, and was the brother of Hubert Gough. Haig warned Prime Minister Asquith that if Hubert Gough was forced to resign, most of the officers at Aldershot were also prepared to resign their commissions.

Haig was destined to be one of England's most controversial generals. When he became commander of the British Expeditionary Force in World War 1, Field Marshal Haig, K.T., G.C.B., O.M., G.C.V.O., K.C.I.E., 1st Earl Haig, fought his war surrounded by his staff officers, from a French chateau, *above a well-stocked wine cellar and well behind the front line. These senior officers cloned in the Public School system and honed in Sandhurst, and Woolwich, were all eerily alike, all looked well-bred and well fed, most had look-alike moustaches; the manner of their speech at once bespoke their social status. Their tailored uniforms bristled with ribbons won fighting Dervishes in the Sudan and Dutch farmers in the Transvaal – not really top drawer warfare, but the best to be had at the time; spurs gleamed on cavalry boots polished to a sheen by a batman proud to serve so far up the chain of command – and happy to serve so far back from the front. While this was the accepted life of the senior officers, quite different was the life of a junior officer. The life expectancy of the lieutenants and captains who lived with their men in the mud-filled, rat-infested trenches and led them "over the top" was short. Three such junior officers, Clement Atlee, Anthony Eden and Harold Macmillan, survived the odds, and went on to become future Prime Ministers of England. During the war Prime Minister Asquith lost a son at the Somme, and a future Prime Minster, Bonar Law, lost two sons and a nephew in the war. Rudyard Kipling's son had twice been rejected for army service due to poor eyesight. His father, who was an enthusiastic propagandist for the war, had then used his influence to secure for his son a commission in the Irish Guards. His son, John, soon after arriving in France joined the ranks of those, "Known unto God". The last man to see him alive told of the eighteen year old lieutenant staggering back from the front lines, crying in pain and horror having had the lower part of his face torn away by a shell fragment. The father who had seen the war as an opportunity for "one crowded hour of glorious life" for his son, and perhaps, by vicarious association, for himself, now wrote, in poignant remorse, his son's epitaph: "If any question why we died, tell them because our fathers lied" – words that could serve as the epitaph for all the young men of all nations who died.*

The men doing the dying lived and died facing an enemy similarly entrenched a few hundred yards away. The thunderous bombardments that screamed overhead drowned out all else, but when the guns fell silent, the screams of mutilated men and horses could then be heard. They died, their dismembered bodies entangled in barbed wire, or their convulsing bodies inhaling mud among the bloated bodies of unburied dead in a shell crater – 50,000 of them in the first few hours of the Battle of the Somme, total casualties at the end of that battle, 1.3 million. With the young men of the colonies and dominions at his disposal Haig felt that he could fight a war of attrition. He prosecuted the war, remote from the battlefield and remote from his men, many of whom saw him as a passionless robotic figure, profligate with their lives, moving divisions, brigades and regiments around like pieces on a chess board – "Let's throw in this Newfoundland Regiment. It's time these Colonials got blooded. We'll see what they're made of." They were made of flesh and blood and their blood flowed freely. In the first few hours of the Somme the Regiment ceased to exist, suffering 781 casualties out of a complement of 800 men. Opinion after the war swung to regarding Haig as a dangerous fossil, a tunnel-visioned relic of the Victorian era who had squandered the youth of an empire. Sharing his vision on the conduct of war with any who cared to listen he made the unfortunate prediction: "I believe that the value of the horse and the opportunities for the horse in the future are likely to be as great as ever. Aeroplanes and tanks are only accessories to the men and the horse." Only living creatures could be the appropriate sacrifice to the god of war, and to a Field Marshal's glory.

The Treaty of Versailles silenced the guns, but the peace of Whitehall was now shattered by the rattle of typewriter keys as the battle of the memoirs commenced. Rolling barrages of recrimination rumbled forth. Withering salvoes of retort and reprisal shredded reputations. Masses of unassailable facts were marshalled to be thrown against entrenched impregnable conviction. Huddled in their club, men lived in daily fear of opening their copy of "The Times" lest they find themselves skewered by invective or their characters ripped apart. The savagery of the attacks stripped away all normal conventions of discourse. In a world of everyman for himself, and no prisoners taken, lifelong friendships perished amid groans of, "Et tu Brute".

Much vilified after the war Haig, whatever his faults as a leader – and on this opinions differed vehemently – remained true to his own code of duty and devoted his retirement to improving the lot of veterans. He lobbied the government to provide assistance to veterans and he involved himself in the British Legion, an institution to help veterans, He was president of that organization from its origin in 1921 until his death, but he was not the sole founder as is often suggested. If that honour were to go to any one man it would be to Tom Lister, an enlisted man and one of the "lions led by donkeys" who had been invalided out of the trenches. Despite the opprobrium that attached to Haig's wartime leadership, his untiring post-war work to improve the lives of those who survived the war belied the label of an uncaring commander, but whether the countless dead would have agreed, only they may say. If, when Haig's body lay in state, those whom he had sent to their deaths could have arisen and marched single file past his coffin, this spectral procession would have stretched for twice the length of England, as in silent reproach this army of the dead paraded before their former commander to receive him into their ranks. At the time of his death in 1928 thousands of veterans who had served under him did march past his coffin to pay their last respects to their wartime commander. Such is the military ethos, and such was the man whose lot it was to send his fellow man marching across a blighted no-man's-land to bayonet other men, and to do so in parade-ground order in the face of a hail of machine gun bullets, or to send someone's broken and shame-tormented son, to be tied, trembling, to a post in the early dawn and shot by his comrades.

Haig was A.D.C. to and a personal friend of King George V, who also put pressure on Asquith's government to reconsider any move against the Ulster Volunteers. Gough, summoned to London to explain his conduct, returned to the Curragh, not with a reprimand, but with an assurance from General French, the commander-in-chief of the British Army, that the army would not be used against the Ulster Volunteers. While the incident was the muttering of a mutiny rather than an actual one it had some significant and far-ranging consequences. Senior officers in the British Army had colluded in the actions of an illegal army that was raised to prevent the implementation of a proposed British act of Parliament. The army could not be relied on to carry out the orders of the civilian government. The unthinkable, a civil war in the British Isles while Britain was on the brink of a European war, loomed as a possibility. The king and the army had meddled in politics. The incident had given encouragement to Germany. In Ulster, the Unionists felt vindicated and were encouraged to continue arming. The Nationalists in the south, in an attempt to safeguard Home Rule, and as a bulwark against the Ulster Volunteers, formed and armed their own army – The Irish Volunteers – a minority of which would later become the I.R.A. The crisis was averted for the time being by the outbreak of war in Europe. The actual implementation of Home Rule was suspended for the duration of the war.

Blandly ignoring any irony, Redmond of the Irish Volunteers and Carson of the Ulster Volunteers made the requisite ringing speeches urging their young men to immolate themselves for King and Country and to free small nations from tyranny. The king for whom they fought belonged to that race now demonized as the Boche and the Hun, and was the head of a country that had for centuries tyrannized another small nation. Similarly, in many a country the cant of old men filled graveyards with the corpses of millions of their young.

Members of both the Ulster Volunteers and the Irish Volunteers swelled the ranks of the British Army. Edward Carson, who had co-ordinated Ulster's opposition to Home Rule, hoped that his show of loyalty would prevent the implementation of Home Rule for Ireland at war's end; Redmond of the Irish Volunteers hoped that his show of loyalty would ensure the implementation of Home Rule for Ireland at war's end.

After the war the British Government found itself in a difficult position. In any event the Easter Rebellion of 1916, whereby some Irishmen had effectively fought for more than just Home Rule, had radically changed the political landscape. Ireland eventually became divided into a northern six counties, which were part of Britain, and a southern twenty-six counties known as the Irish Free State. Fermanagh of the Maguires was one of the six counties, Donegal of the O'Donnells one of the twenty-six. The Ulster Volunteers were largely wiped out on the battlefields of Europe, most notably, the Somme, but Ulster had successfully resisted Home Rule. The Royal Ulster Constabulary, a paramilitary police force augmented by an armed part-time Special Constabulary, the "B" Specials, was formed in 1920, and effectively replaced the Ulster Volunteers. These forces, drawn almost exclusively from the Protestant Unionist population safeguarded the new statelet, now established in the north-east of the country. The anti-treaty faction of the I.R.A, who had not accepted the division of Ireland, donned balaclavas and stalked in the shadows; a force never to be discounted.

During the Second World War, the six northern counties contributed strongly to the British war effort. Despite the neutrality of the new Irish Free State to the south, equal numbers from the south enlisted and fought for the Allies. In a telegram to De Valera, "It's now or never, 'A nation once again'," Churchill had offered the possibility of a post war united Ireland, if Ireland joined the Allies. This offer, when it became known to the Ulster Unionists, was regarded as a betrayal. Sir Basil Brooke, a staunch unionist, was Prime Minister of N. Ireland and the nephew of General Alanbrooke. Alanbrooke, Chief of the Imperial General Staff, was Churchill's chief adviser and confidant. No doubt these considerations influenced De Valera's decision in turning down the overture. Ireland had reacted favourably to a similar overture in the First World War only to see the promise thwarted by Ulster Unionists at war's end. Perhaps with this in mind De Valera would have construed the words of Thomas Davis, "A nation once again," on the lips of an Englishman as "A betrayal once again."

From their base in Castle Archdale on Lower Lough Erne, Catalina and Sunderland flying boats flew west over neutral Free State territory to reach the Atlantic four miles away. This tacit violation of neutral territory gained for the flying boats a quicker access to their patrol area and a longer time on station. It was a Catalina from Lough Erne that sighted the Bismarck.

A roaring explosion filled the air, followed by a blast as chunks of concrete rose upward. The war memorial on Belmore Street was engulfed in dust and smoke. Large slabs of concrete fell through nearby roofs and on the street. People stood still, staring, and as the dust settled, some ran toward the war memorial. Others walked slowly with dazed expressions away from the settling cloud of debris. Then amidst the debris, the toll of the blast became apparent, the wounded —

some standing or walking around, some sitting or lying stunned and shocked, and some crumpled bodies that would never again arise. Among those who would die was a young twenty-year-old girl named Marie Wilson. A few minutes later the wail of an ambulance siren was heard, approaching from the direction of the Erne Hospital.

Later the B.B.C. announced that "a spokesman for the outlawed I.R.A". had confirmed that the I.R.A. was responsible for the bombing of the war memorial in Enniskillen.

Not only in Enniskillen and throughout Northern Ireland, but also in the Republic and throughout the world, a shock wave of revulsion followed the blast. The killed and wounded had been attending a memorial service in memory of the dead of two World Wars. The bomb had been placed behind the wall of the old Saint Michael's school close to the war memorial and had apparently been intended for the security forces.

Gordon Wilson, a draper in the town, and his daughter, Marie, a nurse, had been standing by the wall when the bomb exploded. They were both buried under the rubble, and the twenty-year-old nurse, who sustained multiple injuries, died later that day in the Erne Hospital. Eleven people died and sixty were wounded in the blast. Many people suffered anguish and bereavement as a result of the bomb in Enniskillen, but no one event in the dreary history of violence in Northern Ireland had more impact on the minds of people than did Gordon Wilson's words spoken when interviewed within hours of his daughter's death.

"… And our friends have been great, but I have lost my daughter and we shall miss her. But I bear no ill will, I bear no grudge. Dirty sort of talk is not going to bring her back to life. She's in heaven and we'll meet again."

In Northern Ireland's atmosphere of reprisal and counter reprisal, the simple pathos and Christian forgiveness of the man – who some hours earlier had lain beneath the rubble, holding the hand of his dying child – reverberated with a force greater than that of a hundred bombs, and echoed across all political boundaries. His daughter was dead, but his words prevented the otherwise inevitable reprisals from loyalist paramilitaries and further loss of innocent lives. The people of Enniskillen of all political creeds, chastened and inspired by his example, became united rather than further divided by the horrible event.

On 27 June 1995, eight years after his daughter's death, Gordon Wilson and Marie were reunited.

CHAPTER 15

Dunvegan in Skye

Red Hugh rode ahead of three of his sub-chieftains, Turlough MacSweeney, Owen O'Gallagher, and Conor O'Boyle. He now rode easily, his feet finally healed after a year of his physician's careful, continuous attention. Red Hugh turned to the gallowglass at his side.

"As soon as you return to the Swilly, send a messenger and I'll come to meet Rory Mór and his Scots. Urge him to sail soon. Bingham will be back and Maguire may not be safe anywhere in Fermanagh. Winter and the fact that Bingham could not provision his army in Fermanagh saved him this time. Maguire could only shelter in one of his castles while Bingham's men looted the country around him."

"Aye, O'Donnell. I'll urge him to come at once."

"You were with Maguire at Atha Culainn. It's said that O'Neill helped Bingham plunder Fermanagh after the battle, but that he was a somewhat reluctant associate."

"He displayed little reluctance either at Atha Culainn or afterwards. Some do say, however, that he and his horsemen were planning to ride off before the battle, but Bagenal prevented them from doing so."

O'Donnell laid his hand on his friend's shoulder. "You'll be seeing again your home in the Hebrides, Turlough. It often seems like many lifetimes since as boys we sailed from there with MacSweeney. Killing brutalises us and we have had time for little else lately. We've both done our share of killing."

"You are The O'Donnell, and killing is often necessary. I'm a gallowglass and it's my trade," MacRory replied, and then uncomfortable with the direction the conversation had taken, continued, "Rory Mór McLeod's castle at Dunvegan is on what we call *Oilean a Cheo* (The Misty Isle). You call it by its old Norse name, the Isle of Skye."

"Be sure to get the right island, Turlough! It's somewhere off the coast of Scotland – the West Coast!"

The two gallowglass – MacSweeney still liked to think of himself as one – retraced their voyage of ten years ago, and relived their friendship. As their boat left the shelter of Sheephaven, they were exposed to the full force of the northwest wind. The boat lifted on huge green swells that rolled on with sullen force to thunder in white foam at the foot of Malin Head to starboard. MacSweeney pointed beyond the headland toward the east.

"There's an ocean graveyard over there. It's five years now since a storm drove the *Girona* of Spain's Armada ashore over there on the Antrim coast. The people along the coast call the place where she foundered, Port na Spaniagh. She was under the command of Don Alonzo Martinez, or to give him his full title, Don Alonzo Martinez, Señor de la Casa de Levia de Rioja.

Don Alonzo was second in command of the Armada, and when his own ship, the *Encronada*, was driven ashore in Blacksod Bay off the coast of Mayo, he salvaged his ships' cannon, burned the ship, and fortified a nearby castle, intending to show the English that a Spaniard sold his life dearly. To the Spaniard honour is all and to a Spanish captain like Don Alonso, who had faced death many times, it was not death, but the manner of death that was of importance. But then another ship of the Armada limped into the bay, and taking his men and his cannon aboard her, he put to sea again, only to be driven back north by the gales and shipwrecked again in Donegal Bay. He and his men, now said to number one thousand and still in possession of their cannon, made their way to Killybegs Harbour where they had heard that the *Girona* sheltered to repair a damaged rudder."

"What a pity," MacRory interjected, "that we do not have those Spaniards with us now, for 1,000 well-trained Spanish soldiers with their weapons, and their cannon would be a formidable force."

"A pity all right, a pity too that the bones of those brave men who had already survived two shipwrecks now lie on the sea bottom off the Antrim coast. The *Girona* was a galleass, a sailing ship augmented with oars for greater manoeuvrability. Don Alonzo decided to take the ship back north to a safer haven in western Scotland and at a later date attempt the homeward voyage to Spain. But the *Girona's* rudder again failed. Can you imagine, Turlough, the frantic efforts of her two hundred oarsmen in that storm as the wind drove the galleass inexorably toward the waiting rocks beneath the cliffs over there on the Antrim coast? On that grim winter's evening in an Atlantic gale, those brave Spaniards met their deaths. The crying wind their requiem, over one thousand thrashing bodies tumbled in the cold grey waves before slowly sinking to the ooze on the ocean bottom. Luck had run out for the heroic Don Alonzo Martinez and his countrymen, who would never again see their native land, never see again the sunlit vineyards and neat white houses of Spain that Fr. O'Mulconry speaks about. Another courageous Spaniard, however, a Captain Francisco de Cuellar who was shipwrecked in Breffney-O'Rourke, did, after many adventures, escape back to his native land."

"I've heard that Sorley Boy managed to salvage some of the *Girona's* cannon, and they now adorn the battlements of Dunluce Castle. I wonder if he hoisted the cannon up to the castle walls in baskets, as he did his men when he stormed the castle nine years ago. I was with you at Doe at the time, and I well remember the story of how he infiltrated some of his men into the castle to masquerade as servants. These men then lowered baskets by which their comrades were hoisted up to the battlements."

MacSweeney nodded. "One way or another it was only a matter of time before Sorley Boy became master of Dunluce. It was far too enticing a morsel to be left within reach of that insatiable Scot. The English have now accepted his occupation of the castle, and bestowed on him the title of Constable of Dunluce, but with or without their title, Dunluce would have ended up a McDonnell stronghold."

The two gallowglass remained on deck as the boat ploughed into the heavy Atlantic swells. The conversation turned to Donel O'Donnell's rebellion and the division it had fostered among the O'Donnells. MacSweeney's opinions agreed with Hugh Maguire's.

"Donel was an able leader. At Derryleathin he led like an O'Donnell, but he was no Red Hugh. The O'Donnell chieftains have always commanded attention, but not for centuries, if ever, has Donegal had a chieftain like Red Hugh. Like an Alexander, the aura of destiny surrounds him, and like Alexander, he leads from the front and is found where the battle is fiercest." MacSweeney looked sideways at his companion "This you yourself must well know for you are usually there by his side. He's followed and loved as if he were a messiah. In his life he's a legend; his name spoken with awe. The loyalty of the MacSweeneys of Fanad has always been to Hugh

O'Donnell and his chosen heir, Red Hugh. Niall Garve wanted the chieftainship too and now follows Red Hugh, but only reluctantly. Red Hugh deprived him of his castle at Lifford and occupies it himself. I have heard that Niall Garve may even go over to the English."

"He may, but no O'Donnell crosses Red Hugh unless he's ready to meet his maker. Niall Garve had better have powerful friends and the devil among them if he decides to do so, for Red Hugh would hound him to the very gates of hell."

"And Ineen Duive would not forgive her son for stopping there." MacSweeney smiled. "Maguire too is threatened by his own kin. Conor Roe's son, Conor Óg, is with the English. I remember that Conor Roe of the senior line contested the inauguration of Hugh. Hugh is of the junior line, the line of Philip, and the O'Donnells have always supported that line. Maguire and Red Hugh have a useful ally in Brian Óg O'Rourke in their war with Bingham. O'Rourke will never forget how the English took his father to Tyburn Tree to be hanged like a criminal."

When his friend did not answer, MacSweeney looked toward him. MacRory, bracing himself on the pitching deck, stared off to his left to where Tory Island lay on the horizon. The dull ache in his heart contorted his face, the same ache that was with him since word had reached Fermanagh that bits of wreckage and pieces of ship's timbers had floated ashore on Donegal beaches. One piece of wreckage with the name *Inish Saimer* had come ashore on MacSweeney of Doe's Tory Island. MacRory wiped the sea spray from his eyes.

Knowing something of what was in his friend's mind and not being an insensitive man, MacSweeney turned away, gazing ahead, and left his friend to his thoughts.

The long twilight of the northern latitudes was fading into darkness as the boat entered the narrow channel between Iona and the Isle of Mull. They found an anchorage sheltered from the Northwest winds in a small inlet around the point of Mull. They would continue up along the Inner Hebrides to the Isle of Skye the next day. Iona, the fabled island lay small, lonely, and sombre in the gathering darkness.

One thousand years had passed, MacRory thought, since Columcille and his monks had lived their lives of prayer and contemplation on this remote sea-girdled rock on the Atlantic's verge. What passion and ardour inspired those early saints, only a few generations removed from their pagan fathers, to leave home and hearth to live and die on this windswept ocean rock? What chance or fate or design led Columcille to this islet? What momentous events had been the result?

MacRory knew of the warrior saint that both Irish and Scots revered. Columcille, born Crimthann O'Donnell at lonely Gartan in *Tir Conaill*, was of royal blood and in line for the High Kingship of Ireland. Instead, he chose the ascetic life of a Celtic monk. At Derry he became involved in a dispute regarding the ownership of a manuscript; this manuscript called the "Cathath" became a cherished relic of the O'Donnells and was for centuries carried by them into battle. Columcille's considerable influence and fiery temperament resulted in a battle and the loss of 3,000 lives. He left Ireland in remorse, taking with him twelve monks, and sailed for Iona. From this small island and from the zeal of this saint, Christianity had spread to Scotland and northern England. From this small island, the saint had sailed to found monasteries throughout Scotland and England and to anoint kings of Scotland and England.

Columcille, the monk, had changed history in a way that Crimthann O'Donnell, the king, could never have. Because Columcille had walked ashore on this rock – a little over three miles long and a little over one mile wide – the dust of forty kings of Scotland, eight kings of Norway, and four kings of Ireland now rested there. Yet in God's scheme of the universe was this of any more consequence than if some lone exhausted sea bird, driven ashore by an Atlantic storm, had perished on the island and its dust too rested in Iona's soil?

Columcille and his monks had seen the same golden flair on the rounded heather-clad hills of Mull as the sun sank into the darkening western ocean. They had awakened to the same wailing cry of the gulls and to the same surge and roar of surf on rocky shore. In the intervening millennia, Norse had raided, reformists had torn down churches and men of God had perpetrated godless acts in the names of their deities. One thousand years, yet nothing of essence had changed.

When Columcille left his beloved Derry to search for a place of solitude, he had chosen the place well. The gallowglass pondered as he gazed on Iona. What had dictated the path of holiness Columcille followed? What dictated the soldier's life of violence he himself followed? Could he too, like Columcille, redeem himself? Was he driven? Was he led? Was all preordained since the world began?

Next day they continued north, passing among the islands of the Hebrides. Long before they reached Skye, the filmy veil of morning mist lifted to reveal the far jagged outline of the Cuillin Hills rising in the southern part of that island. The hills were named after Cuchulainn, a Celtic second century hero that both the people of Ireland and of these Western Isles claimed as their own.

MacRory and MacSweeney stood gazing on sea and misty islands, on sky and ever-changing clouds. The wind-driven sea spume blew in their faces as it had in the faces of generations of their ancestors sailing these western seas. Did the Celtic soul of each man sense that the wind and the sea carrying him back to the ancient land of his ancestors ahead carried him away from the even more ancient homeland of his ancestors astern?

It was late afternoon before they rounded a promontory on the northwest of the island of Skye and turned into Lough Dunvegan. Dunvegan Castle lay at the head of the sea lough. Any eager invader, sailing up the lough intent on easy plunder, would have turned homeward in despair on seeing the castle. It was built high on a rock and steep cliffs surrounded its three seaward sides. The sea almost encircled the rock completely, and may have encircled it completely at one time. A deep rocky ravine isolated the castle on the landward side. Its only entrance was by a sea gate. A MacLeod Norse ancestor had built the castle in the twelfth century, and it had been added to in the intervening centuries. The MacLeod castle appeared to be, was, and always had been, impregnable.

The portcullis creaked up, and they sailed into a rocky cavern. MacRory could not help thinking that had Brian O'Rourke remained here at Dunvegan instead of crossing over to Argyle on the mainland, he would still be alive. His daughter, Maeve, would have been safe here. MacRory's heart ached and he could not allow himself to think his thoughts.

Rory Mór Macleod met them at the top of a series of stone steps hewn out of the rock. The "*Mór*"[1] was apt, for he was a big man whose presence brought to mind his warrior Norse ancestors who, erupting from their forbidding northern lands had brought centuries of terror to the world, and change, too, change that still echoed down the centuries. Rory led them to a hall in a large bastion, which comprised the east wing of the castle.

In answer to MacSweeney's appreciative comment on the imposing siting and structure of the castle, Rory Mór told him, "Aye, the walls of the great keep in which we stand are ten feet thick, thick enough to keep the MacDonalds on the outside."

He turned to the gallowglass. "I knew your father. His murderer – Alistair MacDonald, as foul a fiend as ever drew breath – no longer walks the earth. Your uncle came over from Ireland and sought him out in Argyle. In the fight, Donagh severed MacDonald's sword hand at the wrist. He then made his way back to Ireland, leaving a few more MacDonalds dead behind him. It may have been that your uncle, after severing Alistair's right hand, refused to kill an unarmed man, or he may have had other motives, for a swordsman with the reputation of Donagh MacRory could as easily have killed him as severed his hand. It would seem to me, too, that Donagh, as a soldier, would have known that letting him live was no mercy. In any event, unable to defend himself, MacDonald, for close to a year, skulked like a pariah from one hiding place to another until one of his many enemies found and skewered him.

Rory Mór stared at his guest. The Scot reached out his huge hand to steady MacRory, whose face had paled, and who swayed as if he might fall. "Forgive me. I can see the memory of your family's death is still with you."

But it was another memory that assailed MacRory's mind and chilled his blood. He shuddered involuntarily at the memory of a vision on the hill of Aileach, a vision that he now knew had parted the veil between the living and the dead.

---

[1] Big.

"Donagh too I have heard is dead. I knew him before he and his father went to the Maguires in Ireland. As a boy he had the makings of a soldier, or a priest, for he had a strange streak of compassion in him.

"But Alistair MacDonald was devil's spawn, like all of the name." Then remembering himself, he added, "But some of the name," and crossed himself. "May your mother's gentle soul rest in heaven.

"There's many like Alistair in these isles, but now that he roasts in hell, there's one less. I trust Alistair will find the heat to his liking in his new home. Burning people in their homes is a MacDonald specialty. Fifteen years ago on a May morning, the MacDonalds came over from Uist and fired the church of Conan in which my kinsmen worshipped. All burned alive except for one girl who, though injured, escaped and raised the alarm. We caught up with the foul bastards before they got their boats out of Ardmore Bay, and no MacDonald escaped the island that day."

Rory Mór had not seen fit to mention that the MacDonalds had screamed, "Remember the cave of Eigg" as they had barred the door and fired the thatch of the church. A year earlier the MacLeods had suffocated by smoke a party of MacDonalds whom they found sheltering in a cave on the island of Eigg. In these isles memories of past atrocities provided fuel for future ones. An eye for an eye and a people blinded by their madness, MacRory thought.

As they were seated and offered food and drink, MacLeod went on to tell them the Great Keep was the central castle structure containing the great hall, bed chambers, and dungeons. In another part of the castle was kept the "Fairy Flag," a flag which had been in the possession of the MacLeods for centuries, and was reputed to have magical qualities that protected the MacLeods in time of extreme danger.

"But where are my manners? I talk too much and you'll be tired after your voyage. I'll have the servants show you to your quarters, and we'll discuss matters relating to your visit after you have rested."

Rory Mór's huge hands rested on the table. "O'Neill, then, will allow us to march through Tír Eoghan. Derry at the head of the Foyle would be our best landing place. O'Neill will not contest it?"

"O'Neill has intimated to Red Hugh that he intends to be busy elsewhere when you land in the Foyle. The English no longer fully trust the earl. By agreement, he is allowed to train and maintain six hundred soldiers. He has trained many times that number by the expedient of disbanding each group and training another. He's rumoured to have at least four thousand well-trained troops. It's said he may be more interested in being the O'Neill at the head of an Irish army than being an English earl. He was once a favourite of the English, but has fallen out of favour of late."

"The Sassenach's favours are in the Sassenach's interest. *Timeo Sassenachos et dona ferentes[1].*"

Rory Mór looked around, smiling broadly, unabashed by his mutilation of Virgil. "English beliefs, customs, and thinking are different to ours. The Irish will find themselves hewers of wood and carriers of water for their English masters if Irish leaders continue accepting such favours. If you are defeated in this present struggle, your conquerors will write your history, and your past way of life will be unknown to your future generations. Do you think that history, if recorded by your English conquerors, will speak kindly of you? Such is not the way of the conqueror; such is not the way of mankind. The Celt will be seen as a crude barbarian, whose decaying culture was inevitably swept aside by the more enlightened vision of the noble Saxon.

"I hear that Bingham and his settlers, with the aid of the O'Connors, control Connacht. If, however, O'Neill were ever to join Red Hugh and Maguire, all the north would come over to them, and the English would be hard pressed to hold the country."

"Red Hugh told us to inform you that the Spanish have an envoy with him and they offer aid. They already supply arms, armour, and gold, and promise an armed invasion if all of the north unites," MacRory said.

"I have heard that O'Donnell's kerns and bonnaghts look a lot like Spanish cuirassiers." Rory Mór smiled. "I have also heard

---

[1] "I fear the English bearing gifts."

that Donegal has a worthy young chieftain in Red Hugh. His fame has spread to these isles."

He turned to MacRory.

"News of your coming here seems to have reached Uist. The son of Alistair MacDonald sends you an invitation to meet him with swords on neutral ground in Uist." He smiled. "You'll no doubt do us the favour of ridding the isles of another MacDonald. The whelp is no more than seventeen years old, but he seems to have more honour than did his father, and courage too, for your reputation with the sword precedes you."

MacRory answered immediately. "Tell MacDonald I'll gladly accommodate – ", he paused and sat staring at the table. An eye for an eye! Rory Mór continued to look at him expectantly, and after a long interval, the gallowglass said quietly, "Tell him – tell MacDonald that I also have heard of his reputation, and will not be visiting Uist."

The smile faded from MacLeod's face. "His reputation! He is a mere boy, inexperienced with the sword. If you feel this is a trap, my men will accompany you to Uist. If you refuse this challenge, what will men say of your courage?"

MacSweeney had been staring at MacRory and he answered for him. "If Turlough wished to go to Uist, he would go alone. If he chooses to decline MacDonald's challenge, it is not because of a lack of courage. There are many kinds of courage."

Rory Mór shrugged his massive shoulders in a gesture of incomprehension. He rose from the table, his huge bulk dwarfing even MacSweeney and MacRory. "Donel Gorm McDonnell, Sorley Boy's brother, already has two hundred men waiting. Tell Red Hugh and Maguire that Donel Gorm and I will have five hundred men at the Foyle in two weeks."

The gallowglass stood on a headland where steep cliffs fell hundreds of feet to the sea below. He looked across the water toward Uist where he had been born. Here fifteen sea miles separated the Island of Skye in the Inner Hebrides from the Island of Uist in the Outer Hebrides. Here on this headland, eight hundred years before, the leaping flames of a watch fire would have thrown a beacon of dread into the night sky to warn of the approach of Norse longships, to be answered by winking fires on distant islands.

Here among these sea loughs and on many an island shore, Gael had met Gall and spilled each other's blood.

> *"The bloody blade of the Gall, has filled the shores of the Gael*
> *With many a floating corpse and many a mother's wail."*

Over the centuries their blood also mingled in marriage and now, the Gall/Gael fought each other with equal savagery. Turbulent seas girdled storm-tossed isles, for centuries isles of discord, peopled by turbulent clans who had fought each other to near extinction.

Today, however, the sea and the islands lay in peace. To seaward the blue vault of the sky met the far blue ocean horizon. Behind him, soft white clouds floated gently over the jagged peaks of the Cuillin Hills of Skye. Skye, a Norse word for cloud or heaven, not the Christian heaven nor yet the warrior Valhalla of the Norse, but a word more closely resembling the ethereal essence of nature – beauty and peace, horror and violence.

Only the strong sea wind blowing in from the outer islands and the uneasy, heaving swell of the ocean gave hint of the fury that lay hidden in that ocean. Hidden in MacRory's mind were memories of the destructive island fury that had destroyed his family. Over there on Uist, a boy, who was related to him through his mother's blood, sought to continue the mindless bloodshed. In a tribute to his mother's memory, he would not set foot on Uist. He would not take the life of the boy and continue the blood feuds his mother abhorred. If he himself ever had a son, he would not bequeath to that son this unholy burden of vengeance. He thought of the life of violence he himself had chosen. But had he chosen this life or had he unconsciously slipped into it? He was employed to kill because he was an able killer. Well it was that the mother, who had tried to nurture his gentler nature, was dead. He thought of his family, mother, father, and brothers now part of the earth of Uist, Donagh, body mouldering in a beech grove on the shore of an Irish lake. He thought of Maeve O'Rourke, bones whitening in the quiet Atlantic depths, undisturbed by the turbulent waves above. Why did he himself, the last of his family, still live when so many he had loved were dead?

He turned his back on Uist and his thoughts, and walked the six miles back along the west shore of Lough Dunvegan to the castle.

CHAPTER 16

The Spanish Armada

Returning to Sheephaven, MacSweeney, and the gallowglass learned that Bingham had taken Maguire's Enniskillen Castle, and now in turn, Maguire and O'Donnell besieged the English warden holding the castle. MacRory immediately set out for Fermanagh and found the two chieftains at the stronghold of Tempo, while their forces encircled Enniskillen Castle with the intent of starving out the English garrison. Their united forces were managing to hold at bay any relief from reaching the castle.

Red Hugh shook his friend's hand. "Welcome home and welcome, too, are the Scots you bring with you, for their help we surely need. The arrival of Rory Mór and Donel Gorm is timely. Bingham and his O'Connors with O'Reilly of Breffney are like wolves on our flanks, but so far no supplies have gotten through to the English. There's word from one of our agents in Dublin that the Lord Justice is sending a large armed relief. I'll meet Rory Mór myself at Derry and bring him and his men south."

He looked at Maguire.

"We'll only take a small escort, Hugh. You'll be needing every man. You'll come with me, Turlough."

The gallowglass travelled back thorough Donegal with O'Donnell and his twelve-man escort, spending two nights at Donegal Castle and one at Lifford Castle. At the Franciscan monastery at Donegal, the gallowglass again met Father O'Mulconry. The priest, thirty-five years of age, had now, more than ever, that assurance and air of scholarship that had struck MacRory at their earlier meeting at Ballyshannon, and that contrasted strangely with his less worldly brethren of the order. The Franciscan monk, who five years earlier had sailed with Spain's Armada, was embroiled in Spanish politics, and functioned as a link between O'Donnell and Spain. In O'Donnell's castle was a Spanish envoy, and also stockpiled in the castle were Spanish muskets, Spanish pikes, and Spanish armour. There were similar stockpiles of Spanish armament in castles throughout Donegal.

The despoliation of the monastery at Donegal that had occurred earlier by the troops of Willis and Conwell had occurred in monasteries elsewhere in Ireland. The faith embraced so ardently by the early Irish monks had been embraced by all of Ireland. The new English in Ireland embraced a different faith. In Connacht, the Irish saw church lands, monasteries, chalices, and vestments for the celebration of mass – donated by the devout faith of their ancestors – in the hands of a people of a different faith, a people anxious only to root out the ancestral faith and customs of the Irish, a people who showed an increasing intolerance, derision, and contempt for the faith, beliefs, and customs of the Irish.

In the Friary, Father O'Mulconry, Turlough MacSweeney, and the gallowglass sat, while Red Hugh paced with a restless energy.

"Rory Mór and Donel Gorm were lucky to evade English patrols in the North Channel," the priest remarked. "Since the defeat of the Armada, the English have been more successful in interdicting the supply of gallowglass from Scotland."

Red Hugh stopped his pacing and turned to the priest. "Tell us about that battle, Father. What is it like to fight a battle at sea?

"The defeat of Spain's Armada is already being described as a great sea battle, but it was no great battle that defeated Spain's Armada. The weather defeated Spain. The English were responsible for the destruction of less than ten ships out of a fleet of one hundred and thirty. Seventeen years before the Armada, when the cross faced the crescent at Lepanto, that was a sea battle, some say the greatest sea battle since Actium. At Lepanto the Muslims lost 25,000 men to the Christians 8,000. Philip of Spain also was the guiding hand in that battle, for he supplied many of the ships and Philip's brother, Prince John of Austria, commanded the Christian forces.

"While Spain's Armada was being prepared for the invasion of England, Spain's great admiral, Santa Cruz, died, and Philip gave the command of the Armada to the Duke of Medina Sidonia, a man who had never before commanded a fleet. The duke's only qualifications for such a tremendous responsibility were that he was a gentleman and Spain's foremost nobleman. This availed him little, facing the pirates Hawkins and Drake, who were seamen, and to give them due credit, the English had better ships and better sailors, and the better luck.

"I myself was aboard Sidonia's flagship, the *San Martin* when on May the 20th, 1588, the mighty Armada of one hundred and thirty ships stood out from Lisbon and turned north to rendezvous with the Prince of Parma's army off the Spanish Netherlands[1].

"Can you feel the excitement, Hugh? Can you sense the power? Squadron upon squadron of Spain's naval might stretching from horizon to horizon. An ocean of ships and sail and power and might. Look in any direction and the ocean is covered with the billowing sails of mighty ships. The plan was that the fleet would embark Parma's invading army at Calais and ferry it across the Straits of Dover to England.

But from the beginning, ill winds hung over the Armada and storms forced the ships to seek shelter and refit at Corunna. The Duke of Medina Sidonia, who had accepted his post with reluctance, pleaded with Philip to cancel the invasion. Communication with Parma in the Low Countries was poor and the English seemed better informed regarding the movements of the mighty force than was Parma.

"Approaching England, but while still out of sight of land, we passed through an English fishing fleet. I can still see the shock and disbelief on the faces of those fishermen as they stared up at the mighty galleons, the colours of Spain fluttering high above their heads from burnished flag staffs while the wind bore the Armada inexorably on toward the south coast of England.

"On July 19th, we sighted the Lizard off Cornwall and turned east up the English Channel. What a sight to stand on the deck of the *San Martin* and see that great Armada, with its towering masts and billowing sails, sweep majestically up the English Channel! No force on earth could prevail against us. At night we watched the beacon fires blazing from the hilltops ashore to warn of our approach. We imagined the horsemen galloping through the night, beyond that dark shore, to spread the dread news of the Spanish invasion.

"The English came out from Plymouth and followed us, but dared not close on the more powerful Spanish galleons. When we arrived at Calais, Parma had not yet assembled his army, but worse

---

[1] Present-day Netherlands, then a Spanish possession.

still, we found the shallow anchorage at Calais would not accommodate the draft of the Spanish ships. As we lay at anchor, exposed, off Calais, the English sent fire ships among us, scattering our formations, and several of our ships were driven aground. The next day when the wind favoured the English, and our whole fleet was in danger of being driven aground off Gravelines, the English ships stood off and engaged us with their cannon. Four Spanish galleons stood out against them and fought a heroic rearguard action against ten times that number of English ships, allowing the Armada to claw off the lee shore, and giving Sidonia time to regroup his ships and take them into the North Sea. Of those four ships, one was captured and the other three sunk".

"Four against forty, a modern day Thermopylae! Three hundred Spartans against the Persian host, and like Thermopylae, the sacrifice in vain. But perhaps no sacrifice is in vain if it sets a glorious example," O'Donnell mused.

"Or if it is the supreme sacrifice that redeems mankind," the priest said, thinking on a more spiritual plane. "The Spanish tactic was to close and board, knowing the English sailor would be no match for the Spanish soldier. The English, however, with their faster and better-handled ships, refused to allow the Spanish to close, and pounded them from a distance with well-directed cannon fire. On some Spanish ships, the shot supplied for the cannon did not even match the gun's calibre.

"Having failed to embark Parma's army, the Duke of Medina Sidonia decided to abandon the invasion. To conserve the Armada, he elected not to fight his way back through Howard's squadrons in the channel astern. Since the wind was already driving him into the North Sea, he made the fateful decision to return to Spain by continuing up the east coast of England and rounding the north coast of Scotland. But now the weather became an even more merciless enemy than the English, and we lost ship after ship to the incessant storms and rockbound coasts of Scotland and Ireland. We had no charts or pilots with knowledge of the northern route. On September the 13th, having lost half our ships and three quarters of our men, the shattered remnants of our proud Armada straggled back to Spain. The weather and the fortunes of war had favoured the English."

O'Donnell vigorously shook his head.

"Spain can blame neither the weather nor the fortunes of war for the loss of her Armada. One often hears of the 'fortunes of war' as an excuse for the loss of a battle. It would seem to me that fortune, in a sea battle, would favour men with experience of the sea, and men experienced in manoeuvring ships. Sidonia had no knowledge of warfare at sea, went to sea with the wrong shot for his guns, and was unaware that the anchorage where he was to pick up the invading army was too shallow for his ships. Nor can he blame the weather. I am no seaman, but I know that the weather in the North Sea and North Atlantic is always predictable. It is either bad or very bad. I think, Father O'Mulconry, that having sailed with such a man, you are fortunate to have ever reached shore again!"

"The Duke of Medina Sidonia was no seaman," the priest admitted, "but when, like a true nobleman, he took sole responsibility for the loss of the Armada and went on his knees before his king, Philip did not blame him as so many others did. I was present at the palace of El Escorial when the king raised his contrite admiral to his feet with the words, 'I sent you out to war with man, not with the wind and waves.'

Elizabeth, however, seems to have seen the breath of God in the gales that scattered the Armada, for she had a medal struck that reads, 'God blew and they were scattered.'"

"Now there's presumption". MacSweeney muttered. "Surely the God who brings all things into existence, who causes a red rose to spring up from the dirt of the earth, has better things to do than to manipulate the weather in the English Channel to Elizabeth's advantage, But no doubt, in the centuries to come, as in the centuries that have gone, countries successful in battle will see the hand of God in their victories."

"Don't you believe that God can intervene? Don't you believe in miracles? Where is your faith MacSweeney?" the priest commented. "We are told to have faith, even though we don't understand".

"I believe in miracles," replied MacSweeney somewhat heatedly. "But the miracle in which I believe is the ongoing miracle of the world that surrounds me every day of my life and not solely in some occurrence that, like a magician's act, seems to defy the order of that world, My miracle is the growth of a child in its mother's womb, the cycle of life that is changeless and unending, the miracle of our minds that can bring into being images and thoughts that exist without substance, the miracle of the soul within me that began life's journey with me, but has no end. I believe all existence is a miracle and that we walk among miracles.

You ask me 'Where is my faith? My faith is that the God who gave me my immortal soul also gave me my mind and when I use that mind to seek the truth, I am seeking God." My faith is the faith that springs from my God-given soul. Those who tell us to have blind faith are really saying, 'We will tell you what to believe and have faith in what we tell you.' They are afraid that our minds, un-shepherded, will lead us down a path different to that which they would have us follow. If you control how people think you control them utterly.

"I have heard of another island nation that saw divine intervention in a storm that scattered an invading fleet," O'Donnell interjected. "On the far side of the world a small country known as Japan called the typhoon that scattered Kublai Khan's invading Mongol fleet in the thirteenth century, the 'Kamikaze' or the 'Divine Wind'."

"Personally I do not think it was a divine wind that scattered the Armada,

But do not underestimate the Spanish," the priest continued. "Philip the Second is still the most powerful monarch in the world. In Europe he controls Spain and Portugal, as well as the Spanish Netherlands, Austria, Switzerland, southern Italy, Sicily, and Sardinia. In the New World, he is master of the vast territory and immense resources of Brazil, Peru, Mexico, and Honduras. The Spanish are still a sea power, as great as any in the world, and their soldiers are surpassed by none in the world. They are hardened by war. For them, for centuries, war has been a never-ending reality."

"Indeed for us, too, war has been a never-ending reality," Red Hugh remarked, "but never before has it been a war of annihilation. In the past, war was used as a leverage to gain an advantage or to readjust alliances."

The priest smiled, "Or to give the bard the opportunity to sing sad songs of the death of his chieftain. There's no more glory in war."

"There has been no glory in this war for some time. The war the English now wage is to change the character of Ireland. It's a war with a new bitterness, a different purpose, and we are becoming aware it's a war we must not lose."

Listening to Red Hugh, MacRory was reminded of the words of Rory Mór in Dunvegan.

Of O'Donnell's twelve-man escort, five were Donegal chieftains – his brother Rory, his cousin Niall Garve, MacSweeney of Doe, Owen O'Gallagher, and Cahir O'Doherty. The rank of the chieftains was a remark of respect to their Scottish allies. It occurred to MacRory that Maguire could well have used these leaders, and that in this instance, protocol seemed of as much importance as retaking Enniskillen Castle.

As they passed through a miserable little hamlet, O'Donnell and his retinue came upon a small group of soldiers, who surrounded a prisoner. The prisoner, a one-armed man whose head was covered with a black hood, stood beneath a scaffold from which dangled a noose. The captain of the soldiers brutally kicked the man.

MacSweeney rode over and with one foot pushed the captain away from his victim. As the captain staggered back, MacSweeney said quietly, "Do not brutalize a man who is about to die. What was his crime?"

The captain, recognizing Red Hugh, addressed his reply to the O'Donnell chieftain. "He killed one of my soldiers, Lord O'Donnell. The killing was unprovoked."

"And the circumstances?" O'Donnell asked.

"I'm only sorry that I must go to my death without killing the captain also." The hood muffled the words.

"Remove the hood," Red Hugh commanded, then addressed himself to the prisoner. "Why did you kill the man?"

"He and the captain raped my daughter. I lost an arm at Atha Culainn, but I thank God it was not my sword arm. When they ignored the 'eric' levied by the Brehon, I sent one of the cowards to hell. When the brave captain here saw that the loss of an arm hadn't affected my swordsmanship, he preferred to have me hanged rather than face me with a sword."

"You lost an arm at Atha Culainn, but what you do not say is that you lost it fighting for the English," the captain sneered. "A man about to die in the noose should speak the truth. Your English friends are not here to help you now. While you fought their battles, we amused ourselves with your daughter, and I will do so again while you swing in that noose."

The captain, whose face was a well-written page testifying to a lifetime of indulgence in his every passion, turned to look in the direction of a cabin where a young girl's pale and tearful face peeped from an open doorway. The one armed man spoke resignedly,

"Yes, I fought for the English. In battle men fight on one side or the other. Brave men died in that battle on both banks of the Erne, while you skulked in garrison duty and ravaged innocent women."

He stretched his one good arm toward his daughter, who stumbled toward him. As he held her beneath the swinging noose, he spoke slowly, his eyes boring into the captain's, and eyes and voice conveyed a frightening conviction.

"Since I am to hang, hear then the last words of a dying man. If any force exists by which I can reach you from beyond the grave, I will repay you for what you have done to my child"

"He admits, Lord O'Donnell that he fought for the English." The captain seemed to have difficulty tearing his eyes away from his victim, and his voice betrayed his unease.

Red Hugh stared speculatively at the captain.

"So, the killing was unprovoked you say! By your own admission, you and one of your men violated this man's daughter, and now, once you hang her father, you brag that you will violate the girl again. You have ignored the judgement of the Brehons. That noose is surely better fitted to your own neck. Indeed, I have seldom heard a man so eloquently talk his neck into a noose. Today this girl and her father will have justice.

He turned to the one-armed man and unsheathed his own sword handing it to him. "Do you wish a sword with which to avenge your daughter? You will find this one is nicely balanced. We'll insure a fair fight. Fight well, and you need not worry for your daughter's safety, for if he bests you, we will hang him."

At Derry, a small settlement at the head of the Foyle, Red Hugh met and welcomed his Scottish allies. The five hundred armed Scots, piped onto the quay by a MacCrimmon piper, presented an impressive martial display.

Red Hugh sat his horse in front of the Scots, and his clear voice carried out across the assembled army.

"Men of Scotland, we asked for your help and you came with your bravest and best, MacLeods and MacDonnells, whose prowess in battle is a story of courage and glory repeated in your every generation. Kindred Scots, you have left your island homes to come to our aid against another race that has crossed those same seas to enslave us. You come as our allies. You come as our friends. You come as our kinsmen, for we are the same people. The same memories awaken our spirit. The same music stirs our souls. The blood of a common ancestry binds us. The memories of a common heritage bind us. Our love of freedom binds us. Our determination to be free binds us. We were not born to be slaves."

O'Donnell drew his sword and held it aloft. "With the help of our God, with the help of our swords, with the help of you men of Scotland, we will drive the Saxon from these shores."

The words of the young chieftain struck a resonant chord in the Scots, whose cheers echoed across the waters of the Foyle.

Donel Gorm MacDonnell turned to Rory Mór MacLeod. "That is a man whom men will follow. He plucks the right strings."

Rory Mór nodded. "The O'Donnells, like yourselves, have always been fortunate in their chieftains, but the mantle of leadership seems particularly suited to this one's shoulders. Even as a youth the English feared and sought to neutralize him. He has courage and heart and vision. His name may yet stand in Ireland with that of Malachy and Brian."[1]

"Aye, if he lives," Donel Gorm rejoined. "Courage can lead to a glorious life but a short one, and equally dangerous for any chieftain, his fame in Ireland has not gone unnoticed by those in power in England."

Within two days half the Scottish force was under Maguire's command in Fermanagh and the remainder under O'Donnell's in Donegal.

Maguire and a dozen armed men stood around a table in a large tent. Outside the tent a considerable force of cavalry and foot

---

[1] The last High Kings of Ireland; King Brian won the Battle of Clontarf against the Vikings.

soldiers waited. Maguire, suited in armour, addressed the men at the table.

"Bingham's brother, George, and Miles O'Reilly are with the relief column. It is led by Captain Fuller. They are being provisioned in Cavan, and I estimate that with their supplies they will travel slowly. They left Cavan last night, travelling down the west side of the lough. It will take them at least twelve hours to reach Enniskillen. We'll meet them at the pass of the Arney. They'll have scouts out ahead, and we must avoid being seen if we are to surprise them. We'll engage them on my signal, waiting till most of their force is into the pass, and then MacLeod's men will attack from the front and the cavalry from both sides."

A young chieftain, Manus MacManus, interjected, "How come MacLeod and his mercenaries –"

Maguire's mailed fist struck the table. "Rory MacLeod is no mercenary."

"I meant no offence to MacLeod but surely the place of honour, the frontal –"

"They have a large armed escort and surprise is all important. Good luck to all of you," MacManus looked as if he were about to speak again but Maguire rose and walked from the tent. As MacManus came out, Maguire turned to him. "You'll not engage in the first attack, but keep your men to the rear in reserve."

He stared at MacManus waiting for his acknowledgement and it finally came as curt and impolite "Aye." Maguire continued to stare at the man, who stared back. Maguire's face reddened.

"By God!" He stepped back and his sword rasped from its sheath. Eamonn MacCaffrey leaped between the two men. MacManus stood, face pale with his hand on his sword hilt.

"Hugh! Manus! For God's sake!"

"It was a gratuitous insult to call MacLeod a mercenary." Maguire's sword was still in his hand.

"A gratuitous insult! I never referred to MacLeod himself as a mercenary. Do not blame me if your hearing is defective."

MacManus cleared his sword from its sheath. "I'm not so ill bred as to give accidental insult, nor have the MacManuses ever taken up the rear in any fight."

More men intervened between the two. Eventually both men, neither happy with the outcome, sheathed their swords and joined the men outside.

Maguire turned to the gallowglass before mounting his horse. "Turlough, gallowglass mercenaries have been in Ireland for three hundred years, and it's an honourable profession, but The Macleod of Dunvegan is the chieftain of the MacLeods and is not a mercenary and should never have been referred to as one."

MacRory was about to point out, as MacManus had done, that the reference to mercenaries had been to MacLeod's men and not to MacLeod himself when Maguire continued.

"These Highland Scots have always been our allies. MacLeod's men will be paid in gold, but Rory Mór himself will take with him to Scotland a gift befitting a chieftain. He will take with him to Dunvegan the Maguire Chalice."[1] MacRory, aware of what a treasured heirloom the chalice was to generations of Maguires, thought it indeed a princely gift.

Mounting his horse, Maguire, with half the cavalry and all of the foot soldiers, took a path diagonally away from the river. MacCaffrey and MacManus, with the remainder of the cavalry, rode off to the left more closely paralleling the west bank of the Erne. Both parties approached the Arney Pass by a circuitous path so as to give no signs of the passage of the force to the enemy scouts who would be out ahead. Both converged on the pass, but from opposite sides. MacCaffrey's men positioned themselves in the woods about half a mile to the left of the narrow pass, and Maguire, with the rest of his force, took up their positions hidden in the wooded hills opposite him. Scouts would be out well ahead of the enemy, and Maguire did not wish them to see any evidence of his force. MacManus and his mounted men took up their positions behind MacCaffrey. The narrow defile was a natural site for an ambush, and Maguire hoped that his enemy, aware of this, would not try to take a different route to Enniskillen.

After three hours of waiting, Maguire, lying behind a knoll, began to think the enemy had indeed followed a different route. Then he saw a lone horseman riding quietly through the trees below him. The rider continued toward Enniskillen, glancing frequently up

---

[1] Today exhibited at Dunvegan Castle and known as the "Dunvegan Cup"; Walter Scott makes reference to it in *Lord of the Isles*.

the slope to where Maguire's men were hidden well back in the trees. Another rider was seen on the opposite slope, moving among the trees. Another half-hour passed, and a group of twelve horsemen appeared in the pass. They wore mail armour and were followed by the main force of some sixty horsemen. As they proceeded along the pass, a troop of foot soldiers followed, then came the baggage train of supplies on packhorses.

Maguire knew there would also be soldiers at the rear, but if he waited any longer, the leading horsemen would be through the pass. He stood, walked back to his horse, and mounted. Pointing the way with his sword, he galloped through the trees. On emerging into the open, he screamed his war cry as he and his horsemen swept down on the pass. His cry was echoed opposite as MacCaffrey's men poured into the pass, fanning out to engage the enemy along its flank

There was confusion in the narrow valley below. Horses reared and hoarse voices shouted orders as the soldiers in the pass prepared to face an enemy charging them from both sides. Pack horses plunged and whinnied as armed horsemen galloped to and fro, attempting to form a defence to right and left.

In order to ensure surprise, Maguire had positioned his forces well back from the pass, but this now gave the English some time to prepare a defence. By the time Maguire and MacCaffrey reached the baggage train, they faced an uninviting line of steel to either side of the column as the foot soldiers knelt with halberds. The enemy horsemen galloped to take up positions on the flanks of the baggage train. To block the enemy's advance, MacLeod's Scots poured into the pass. MacLeod's piper stood exposed on a rocky outcrop, piping the Scots into battle.

The battle was bloody and despite the element of surprise in Maguire's favour, the outcome was in doubt. As horses reared and swords slashed and stabbed men fell wounded or dead from the saddle. MacLeod's and Maguire's foot soldiers entered the fray. Men groaned and died and others took their place. The rearguard came forward and joined their comrades. Maguire was outnumbered.

Without waiting for any orders, MacManus and his men thundered down the hillside and changed the tide of battle. Maguire had lost the advantage of his initial surprise, and the English, now somewhat organized, fought with tenacity, and the battle promised to be a bloody one. The sudden appearance of this new group of horsemen, however, demoralized the English.

MacManus leaped his horse into a melee of men and steel. He singled out Captain Fuller and raged towards him. The ferocity with which he and his men fought reflected the perceived affront to their name.

As enemy foot soldiers backed into those behind only to find themselves with nowhere to go, they were no longer fighting or listening to the shouted orders of their leaders. Some tried to surrender, some fled in whatever direction seemed to offer some degree of protection. Horsemen disengaged and galloped for safety. Among the first to do so was George Bingham who was last seen bent low over his horse's neck, fleeing desperately back toward Cavan. With the leader of the baggage train fleeing for safety the battle became a rout. Here and there a few groups of men refused to join in their comrade's disgrace and fought on alone and isolated, knowing they could not win and knowing they would likely die, but scorning to seek safety in reckless flight. Miles O'Reilly and his McCabe gallowglass fought a stubborn rearguard action to save the men of the supply train from total annihilation.

Hugh Maguire rode along the pass and surveyed the aftermath of battle. Provisions destined for the relief of the castle were strewn in the pass. The encounter had not lasted long, but the death toll on both sides was high. Some of the wounded sat dazed and silent, some limped or staggered among the dead. The dead lay stilled forever. Among the dead were Manus MacManus and many other MacManuses. Maguire dismounted and stood over the dead chieftain, whose body bore many wounds, and whose bloody sword lay some feet away by the dead body of Captain Fuller. Maguire picked up the sword and carrying it to MacManus's body, knelt and laid the sword by MacManus' side. He closed the lids over the dead staring eyes. His lips moved in a silent prayer. He turned to one of his own men.

"Cover his body and take it back to Aghalurcher[1] for burial."

At the castle, Bingham's garrison knew they could no longer hold out. They had been in desperate need of the supplies the

---

[1] Ancient burial ground close to Maguire's castle of Lisnaskea.

ambushed relief column had been carrying, and felt their only course now was to send an emissary to Maguire asking for terms. Maguire's terms were surprisingly generous in view of the fact he now had time on his side and had merely to bide his time to starve the warden and his men out. However, as a gesture to the bravery with which the warden had held the castle, Maguire and O'Donnell allowed him and his men to march from the castle, to retain their arms, and return unmolested to Connacht. The Lord Deputy in Dublin however reported to England's Privy Council that the rebels, having promised safe passage to the warden and his men had then slaughtered them.

CHAPTER 17

Plotting rebellion

In March of 1595 the three most powerful of Ireland's northern chieftains came together to plan rebellion. Red Hugh O'Donnell and his cousin, Hugh Maguire, met with Hugh O'Neill at his castle in Dungannon. The three chieftains had other things in common, apart from their unity of purpose in hoping to rid Ulster of the English. O'Donnell was married to one of O'Neill's daughters, Maguire to another. All three had come to the conclusion that no further accommodation with the English was possible, and alone, no one of them could prevail.

For three years Maguire and O'Donnell had waged a war with the English. During those three years, O'Neill had watched and weighed the chances, biding his time. That time had come.

O'Neill was forty-five years of age and had engaged in war for most of his adult life. He had led many campaigns, usually as an English commander. Over the years, he had become familiar with all the aspects of waging war: the cautious, careful planning of the campaign, the remorseless brutal savagery of the battle, and, too often, after the battle, the casual, senseless slaughter of the helpless vanquished. He had been prominent in the suppression of the Earl of Desmond's rebellion in Munster, and had shown himself the equal of any Englishman in exterminating Irish rebels and their families. He had led his own and English troops on their rampage through Fermanagh, He was a man of contradictions, indeed of so many bewildering contradictions as to cast doubt on whether he aspired to be the Irish O'Neill or the English Earl of Tyrone. In 1588 he risked the displeasure of the English by succouring the Spanish when two of their ships came ashore in Donegal. A lesser chieftain, Brian O'Rourke, had suffered death and his people a fearsome retribution at the hands of Bingham, for offering similar assistance to the Spanish.

This was the same O'Neill who assisted the First Earl of Essex in suppressing Sorley Boy and his Antrim Scots with a ferocity unprecedented even for those savage times. He came close to treason in courting England's enemy Spain. Yet at the command of England's Lord Deputy, he had joined forces with Bingham and Bagenal against his own son-in-law, Hugh Maguire. It was said his participation at the Ford of Culainn was half-hearted, yet to those opposing him in that battle; his performance had seemed heartily full-blooded.

O'Neill was the bearer of a name that reverberated down the centuries of Irish history. He was a man who understood power, and a man who, unlike many of the other Irish chieftains, understood that with unity came power. He understood that unity made England powerful and that unity made Spain powerful. He came to understand that if unity could make Ireland powerful, Hugh O'Neill would be the most powerful man in Ireland.

"You are aware that I offered no resistance to the Scots when they landed in the Foyle," he reminded his sons-in-law. "The Lord Lieutenant will order me to suppress your excursions, Red Hugh, into Connacht against Bingham's settlers. I am not as yet prepared to show open defiance, and I will seem to comply with these orders. When you know of my movements in advance, it should not prove too difficult for you to evade me."

"Will I in Fermanagh also be forewarned of your movements? Such a small courtesy from one's father-in-law would have been helpful at Atha Culainn and afterward." The memory of O'Neill's depredations in Fermanagh still rankled with Maguire and he was quite willing to escalate the conversation and follow wherever it led. He had killed a kinsman of O'Neill's in a sword fight some years earlier and would not hesitate to settle matters similarly with the Earl.

O'Neill stared at him a few moments before speaking. O'Neill's intent was to form a coalition with these two chieftains, and he was too disciplined to allow himself to be distracted from his purpose. When he at last spoke, it was in a remarkably conciliatory tone.

"Our families, Maguire, yours and mine, have done what we had to do. Now let the past be the past. Many regard the O'Neills as a nest of venomous vipers, and my uncle Shane would have shamed the Borgias of Italy, but if we cannot put old grievances behind us, we will live to wish we had. We have all had our Shane O'Neills; one of your own Maguires pursued a kinsman and murdered him on the very steps of the altar where he sought sanctuary at your

Aghalurcher burial church. We have all had men with few redeeming qualities in our families."

Neither O'Donnell nor Maguire disagreed with O'Neill's assessment of his own family, but both perhaps would have given the present O'Neill equal status with Shane or with any viper or Borgia. Shane O'Neill's excesses were legendary. He had captured, imprisoned, and tortured O'Donnell's Uncle, Calvagh. He had kept Calvagh's wife, the Duchess of Argyll, imprisoned as his mistress, and treated her shamefully. Shane had murdered his half-brother, Matthew, and Matthew's son, Brian, brother of Hugh O'Neill.

Maguire, kept his eyes fixed steadily on O'Neill.

"To equate your uncle Shane with a Borgia brings no credit on the Borgias. A more apt comparison would have been Caligula. And your mention of men with few redeeming qualities reminds me of an occurrence at a funeral. The officiating priest could not find a single redeeming thing to say over the body of a dead man. In desperation the priest appealed to the congregation, asking if anyone could stand up and say something good about the deceased. One man stood up and volunteered, 'His uncle was worse.'"

O'Neill and Maguire continued to stare at each other, but O'Neill refused to be baited. After some moments, he smiled a thin smile and murmured. "Possibly a case of *Nil nisi mortuii bonum*[1]. I have come to realize that further cooperation with the English is not in any of our interests. They feign friendship, they play us skilfully against each other, and their ultimate aim is our destruction. When we look back, we see we have already lost much and gained nothing. We ourselves, to our own discredit and to our own destruction, assist them in their purpose. If we cannot unite against them, we cannot win against them.

"In the past three years, both of you have caused them considerable damage in Connacht. I do not mean to minimize the damage you have done to the English or the renown these raids have brought on yourselves, but raids only they may be called. The English are constantly pouring more armies into Ireland, and we will need a united strategy and our united forces to stand against them. We must forget our past quarrels and unite. We will start here

---

[1] 'Speak no ill of the dead."

in the north, and we will start now. You yourselves have seen how your successes in Connacht brought the chieftains over to you. For the past, I offer you any reconciliation that is within my power to offer. I also offer you six thousand trained men to join yours."

Both men were startled to learn of the size of the army at O'Neill's command. To build up such forces he must have been preparing for years, for all those years when he was a "loyal" English Earl! In the past year, the English had become increasingly uncertain of his intentions, and indeed O'Neill himself had seemed uncertain, vacillating between acts of open rebellion and abject pleas for pardon. When he had been suspected of having his cousin, Hugh Gavelock, hanged, O'Neill had rushed to England to plead his innocence. While there, he had taken the opportunity to purchase a large quantity of lead, ostensibly for the roof of his castle. On returning to Ireland, he melted down the lead to make bullets. When ordered to send his son as a pledge to Dublin Castle, O'Neill, ruler of Ulster, offered the strange excuse that those fostering his son would not yield him up.

He was late in joining their campaign against the English, but neither Red Hugh nor Hugh Maguire doubted he was now with them. O'Neill's value to them was immense. His prestige, his leadership, his influence, and his army would change the nature of the conflict. He was the one man powerful enough to enforce the allegiance of the northern chieftains. The addition of O'Neill to the Irish side would weigh heavily in attracting further Spanish aid. However, O'Neill's declaration of rebellion would also galvanize the English to gain complete control of Ireland.

While the three chieftains discussed their new accord, their three wives discussed other matters in another part of the Dungannon stronghold. Mabel Bagenal was O'Neill's third wife, his first wife having died and his second been divorced. It was now three years since Mabel had eloped with her father's bitter enemy. The bishop, who had hurriedly married them, had made the ungallant remark that he had done so "for the lady's honour." Mabel Bagenal was no older than O'Neill's two daughters, one of whom, Rose, was the wife of O'Donnell, the other, Nuala, the wife of Maguire. But this closeness in age did not result in any affection between O'Neill's delicate and refined wife and his haughty spirited daughters.

Red Hugh's wife spoke in English to Mabel Bagenal. "I have heard you do not enjoy our land or our climate. I've been to London and found that rivers of filth run in its streets and England's climate is quite similar to ours. Perhaps it's the winds here that are not to your liking. I've heard it said that something in the winds blowing in from the Atlantic makes us Irish wild and savage."

"Little in Ireland is to my liking" Mabel sighed, "and 'wild and savage' is an apt enough description of your country and its people."

Maguire's wife laughed. "You must then become more like us, inured to the savage elements. Wild storms can blow the petals off a delicate English rose, and what is a rose when deflowered of its petals?"

Mabel Bagenal's pale face flushed, knowing the choice of words had not been accidental, but she was not giving in. "Your priests seem able to tame you by playing on your superstitions. My father speaks of the Irish as a priest-ridden people. These servants of Rome seem to exert considerable influence here."

"They do tame and legitimize our … our unbridal passions," O'Donnell's wife admitted.

"Unbridal indeed," her sister laughed. "What can have been on your mind, Rose? Your English is faulty. The word is 'unbridled,' wilful, unrestrained."

"You must have many words to express the concept in your Irish language," Mabel suggested, outnumbered but fighting on, "since the Irish so exemplify those distasteful qualities."

O'Donnell's wife turned to her sister. "Nuala, would you rather be distastefully 'wilful and unrestrained' or tastefully dull and insipid?" Then with deliberate rudeness, she switched to Irish. "But perhaps insipid is an impolite word to use in the present company."

Mabel spoke no Irish, but reddened at the laughter.

Again in English, Rose O'Donnell continued, "Forgive us, when we wish to be explicit, we are more comfortable in the old language"

Mabel, whose delicate exterior hid the fire within, was not about to let the insult pass. "Yes indeed, no doubt you are more comfortable in Irish, that soft, gentle language of the dissembler, so apt on the Irish tongue, the language of traitors who conspire with Spain against England."

"Traitors! Conspiring with Spain!" Rose O'Donnell's eyebrows arched upward in mock horror at the mere thought of such wickedness. "If you have knowledge of such treason, you must at once inform your husband. It is your duty as a wife, and as an Englishwoman. I myself this day will certainly make Red Hugh aware of the perfidy that is afoot in Ireland."

"As for the Irish language," Nuala Maguire smiled and her fine eyes fixed Mabel Bagenal in their steady gaze, "it is the venerated language of a race that kept civilization alive when your Hun ancestors, grunting, chortling, and scratching themselves, destroyed all that was worthwhile and beautiful in Europe."

"The language of barbarians, who decapitate the dead on the battlefield," came Mabel Bagenal's reply.

"When you succeed in civilizing us, perhaps we'll follow your Tudor example and include the decapitation of women," came Rose O'Donnell's response.

Mabel blanched, unsure if this was a reference to Henry the Eight's decapitation of two wives and Elizabeth's similar treatment of Mary of Scotland, or a threat to her own neck. Realizing they had far exceeded the bounds of decorum, all parties fell silent.

Nuala Maguire called for a servant. "Look to our mother, she appears somewhat pale. Perhaps a glass of red Spanish wine will bring some colour to her cheeks."

CHAPTER 18

Desecration of Rathmullen and Tory monasteries

The combined forces of O'Donnell and Maguire drove the English out of north Connacht, and their successes saw many proud chieftains bend the knee and bow their heads in submission to the princes of the north. Sir Henry Bagenal's suspicions that O'Neill was "a traitorous, dissembling Irishman" were confirmed, at least to that Englishman's satisfaction. Bagenal's opinion of O'Neill's trustworthiness was in agreement with that of his queen, who on hearing that Essex in Ireland had accepted O'Neill's oath on a temporary truce had fumed. "To trust this traitor on oath is to trust the devil on his religion." O'Neill, now in open rebellion, continued to insist that circumstances had forced him into rebellion, and indeed there was some truth in his insistence. He built up his army, conspired with the Spanish, intermittently sought peace with the English, while successfully ambushing the armies of the Lord Lieutenant sent to subdue him in Tyrone. He used diplomacy and war with equal skill to gain his objectives. While O'Neill engaged the English in the east, O'Donnell and Maguire controlled the western approaches to Ulster.

In the next three years, Turlough MacRory crossed and re-crossed the Erne's fords in raid after raid into Connacht. He slept with his armour by his side, marched, and fought, leading the gallowglass of Maguire and O'Donnell. The tall gallowglass, who fought by O'Donnell's side, became as well known to O'Donnell's enemies as the red-haired chieftain himself. He was wounded and wounded again and again.

Red Hugh's army would advance to take an enemy stronghold, regroup, and advance to the next castle. Behind him, he placed his own wardens in the captured castles.

Richard Bingham governed Connacht for the English. Connacht was inhabited by lawless tribes and ruled by a lawless governor. Richard Bingham hanged Irishmen for no other reason than that they were Irish and thus deserved hanging. George Bingham, who held Sligo Castle, was cast in the same mould as his brother. Sligo was one of the few castles in north Connacht still in English hands. It was a strategic stronghold guarding the approaches to Connacht and providing a refuge from which English troops sallied forth on raids into O'Donnell's Donegal and Maguire's Fermanagh.

Red Hugh bypassed Sligo and ranged far south, dealing merciless war to those who resisted, granting generous terms to those who came over to his side. Ruthless in his determination to rid his territory of the English, he put to the sword anyone who could not speak Irish on the not unreasonable assumption that they must be English colonists. His chieftaincy was no longer confined to Donegal; he was now overlord of a large part of Connacht. This over-lordship of north Connacht, the traditional territory of the O'Rourkes, did not always sit well with Brian Óg O'Rourke. Indeed, O'Rourke's resentment was so great that he briefly went over to the English. The English sent larger armies to face O'Donnell, but Red Hugh now also had more and better equipped men, and repeatedly bettered his adversaries. Experienced English captains, who had gained renown in England's wars against Spain in the Low Countries, suffered signal defeats at the hands of the young Irish chieftain.

As had always been so, the common people of the land suffered most and endured most in the to-and-fro sway of the fortunes of war. Advancing armies raided and retreating armies despoiled the small patches of land on which the common people depended to raise and feed their families. These people, peremptorily torn from their families, were the nameless inglorious units of the battle, to be used either with care or with profligacy at the whims of their leaders, and of what consequence to those leaders the personal toll? A fresh mound of earth in some graveyard, a raw ache in some heart. For these humble and often unwilling participants, the grand scheme of the conflict was often blurred in the more immediate daily battle for mere survival. They saw no further than the hollow eyes of their starving children. Dreams of conquest and glory were for those who could see beyond.

Elizabeth had told her Lord Deputy in Ireland that she wished, "The people to be trained from the inordinate tyranny of the Irish captains and to taste of the sweets of civil order." When Sir John Norris and Sir Richard Bingham were touring their territories in 1584 as newly appointed governors, a chronicler described the "sweets of civil order" accorded to one such Irish captain.

"Hanged from a cart and his bones were broken with the back of a large and heavy axe; and his limbs thus mangled and half dead, was placed fastened with hard and tough hempen ropes on the top of Cloccas Cuinnche, under the talons of birds and fowls of the air to the end that the sight of him in that state might serve as a warning and an example to evildoers."

From England's shires and England's towns came the Devereuxs, the Raleighs, the Drakes, and the Spensers, Renaissance men all, poet-warriors some, all eager to acquaint rude Irish chieftains with the sweets of English civilization.

The union of O'Neill, O'Donnell, and Maguire was the most serious, concerted Irish effort that had ever challenged England, and the English now realized they stood the risk of losing Ireland. They effectively controlled only the Pale, a shrinking few miles of land around Dublin. O'Neill had 6,000 trained soldiers, 1,000 of them cavalry, and these forces, combined with those of O'Donnell and Maguire, seriously threatened England's hold on Ireland. The stakes were further heightened by the Northern chieftains' open collusion with England's enemy, Spain.

Off to the right in the darkness, the sound of breaking waves had been heard for the past half-hour, but now the muted roar of the breakers faded astern. A disembodied voice came out of the darkness on deck.

"That will have been Tory Island. We can now head due east. With a following wind, we'll be off the Swilly at dawn"

The ship's movements smoothed from the violent pitching to a more gentle yawing as she turned eastward and sailed before the wind toward Malin Head, hidden somewhere in the darkness ahead. The ship was a large one, and eighty armed men sheltered beneath her deck.

Two men, wrapped in heavy cloaks, sat in a cabin beneath the aft deck. A small fire glowed in a protected grate. The cabin was a warm and cozy haven insulating the two men from the biting cold of the night air. Timbers groaned rhythmically and the cold dark waves without slapped menacingly along the hull. Like grotesque puppets, the shadows of the two men, projected in the yellow light of a swaying lantern, loomed back and forth across a bulkhead. One of the men was George Bingham, brother of the English governor of Connacht, and the other Ulick Burke, an Irish nobleman allied to the English. An hour passed with neither man speaking.

Finally, George Bingham spoke without looking at his companion. "O'Donnell is with O'Neill in Tyrone. The Lord Justice has raised another army against them. MacSweeney of Fanad will be with O'Donnell."

"Conor O'Brien, the Earl of Thomond, has added his army to that of the Lord Justice," Burke said.

Bingham sneered contemptuously. "These O'Briens and O'Neills, who pride themselves on their kingly lineage, are nothing more than crude barbarians. This is the same O'Brien who helped O'Neill suppress the Earl of Desmond's rebellion in Munster. How easily they are induced to turn on their own kind. Such people cannot be trusted, and will as readily, when opportunity presents, turn on us English. Sir William Russell will have to watch his back, lest the Earl of Thomond join the Earl of Tyrone in rebellion. We will show O'Neill and his Irish rabble the price of rebellion. We'll teach them to lick the boot that grinds their face in the dirt. We will teach these Irish dogs to whimper, as we did when we suppressed Desmond's rebellion in Munster, but here in Ulster we intend to leave behind us a people so cowed and mutilated as to make our work in Munster look like the work of children. Those left alive will pass on to their breed the memory of how a race such as ours deals with rebels. We'll teach them to fear their masters."

Listening to the vindictive diatribe and seeing the distorted face in the yellow lamplight Burke for a moment wondered what he was doing in this man's company. He also had an uncharacteristic moment of sympathy for any man woman or child of Ireland who came within the power of this man. An inventive mind polluted by past atrocities dreaming up future ones.

"My brother governs these natives in the only manner they understand; those who do not submit and serve, he hangs. He would hang all the Irish in Connacht, but he must allow some to stay alive and breed to serve us. All these Irish and Norman Irish should be hanged before they can turn traitor."

Burke stiffened. His family had come to Ireland with the Normans in 1169 and he had both Norman and Irish blood. He qualified for hanging on all counts except, for the moment, that of being a "traitor".

"Traitor is a facile word that seems to be used by all sides with little meaning. One man's traitor is another man's patriot. The Irish, who ally themselves with the English, or indeed with the Spanish, may feel that as free men in their own country they are entitled to ally themselves with whom they see fit. You describe the Irish as barbarians because their culture is different to yours. Many, sir, might consider the sentiments you just expressed to be quite barbarous and unworthy of a civilized man. Indeed, though, as you say, their pretensions to kingly lineage can be galling. If they look with condescension on a De Burgh such as myself whose ancestors were Norman Earls that came to England with William the Conqueror in 1066, can you imagine how they must look on someone such as yourself?"

Burke paused to allow Bingham time to digest the insult before continuing. "Your brother's tactics for pacifying Connacht may not be as effective in Ulster. O'Neill is a powerful opponent and has easily outmanoeuvred any force sent against him. The Lord Justice should beware he does not lose his army. These Irish traitors are masters of ambush, as both you and your brother must well know."

A sword thrust would have been kinder.

George Bingham had led the relief column that Maguire had ambushed at the pass of the Arney, and in that encounter Bingham had fled the battlefield somewhat ingloriously. O'Donnell in Connacht had repeatedly ambushed George Bingham's brother, Richard Bingham.

Cold night air blasted into the cabin as the hatch cover slid back and a man shouted down the gangway.

"You may wish to come on deck, sir."

Bingham brushed past Burke and climbed through the hatch to the deck. The man on deck pointed to the outline of Malin Head off ahead and barely distinguishable in the dawn sea.

The ship sailed down Lough Swilly and anchored off the strand in front of the Carmelite friary at Rathmullan. The friary looked peaceful in the early dawn. Seagulls wheeled and cried around the shore. The dim grey hills behind the friary rose, wreathed in wisps of morning mist, blurred and indistinct. The rocky outline of the Inishowen Peninsula was faintly discernable across the sea lough.

Bingham went ashore first and his men were rowed to the beach in relays. He spoke to one of his captains.

"Guard the beach against any horsemen from Fanad. Our business should not take long." While the remainder were ferried ashore, Bingham took twenty of his men and strode toward the friary. An elderly abbot walked hesitantly from a door to meet him. The abbot bowed. "I am Father John O'Donnell. Our brothers are in chapel at matins, but I can show you to the refectory[1] and offer you what hospitality we can. Whose men are you?" The abbot's voice betrayed a note of apprehension. Bingham bowed to the Abbot and smiled: "Queen's men on the Queen's business, Father O'Donnell."

He drew his sword and still smiling; thrust it through the old man's body. To remove the sword from his gasping victim, he placed his foot against the body and pushed. He paused over the dying monk to wipe some of the blood from his sword on the man's white wool habit. Bingham straightened, and reddened sword in hand, entered the friary followed by his men. The monks within, gentle men dedicated to God and prayer, died, their screams and shrieks echoing across the still lough.

The wheeling seagulls now cried a shrill reproach around the ship as she sailed back up Lough Swilly. The Queen's men had conducted the Queen's business with some haste, as Rathmullan was close to MacSweeney's Fanad castle.

On shore the Carmelite friary again looked peaceful, as it had before the arrival of the ship. Without, the small, crumpled, white bundle with dark red bloodstain lay half way to the beach. An errant gust of wind stirred the white habit and gave a momentary false impression of life. Within, in the small chapel, similar bundles, each in its pool of dark blood, lay crumpled among the disarrayed, bare, wooden pews. The chapel altar was uprooted and lay against one wall. Spread-eagled, a monk lay clasping the blood-streaked altar, in mute supplication in death to his God, who had deserted him in life. By the altar, a silver chalice, its cup crushed, lay tossed aside

---

[1] Dining area.

among some blood-stained Mass vestments, neither crushed chalice nor vestments of any value to the slayers.

No part of the friary had escaped the malignant attention of the visitors. The tables of the refectory, where the monks had eaten their simple meals in silence, were smashed and hacked, as if the swords of the invaders had not been sufficiently sated by flesh alone. Each small cell where each monk had slept, kept clean and orderly as a duty to God, looked now as if some evil force had swept through it. An occasional crucifix or some monk's small personal item not of sufficient value to be taken with the raiders lay broken or discarded. Tables and benches had been piled and set alight, but the fire had gone out and now a partially charred heap of debris lay still smoking in the entrance hallway.

When they reached the open ocean at the mouth of Lough Swilly, Bingham and his men sailed west along the northern coast of Donegal.

Before turning south for Sligo, they put ashore at Tory Island where there was a monastery dedicated to Saint Columcille.

"You spoke earlier of ambushes."

George Bingham sat in Sligo Castle; thigh-booted legs resting on a wooden table, and drank from a pure gold chalice. The O'Donnells had donated the chalice two centuries earlier to the priests in the church of Columcille on Tory Island.

Bingham's voice was slightly slurred as he continued.

"You Irish seem to fight best from ambush. Well, I have taught O'Donnell something of ambush. I hear he rushed back to Donegal in time to bury the stinking carcasses at Rathmullan and Tory."

"Indeed your heroism will be long remembered. You and your men fought bravely against O'Donnell's monks." Burke's irony barely reached Bingham.

"They were Irish vermin; some of them were of O'Donnell's family. I noticed you seemed to have little stomach for the work."

"I hope never to develop a stomach for such work as you did at Rathmullan and Tory. I would not stain my sword or my honour by such work. My men are soldiers, and I brought them north to fight soldiers. We understood that the fight was to be with MacSweeney's men and not with some unarmed monks."

"When the time for fighting soldiers comes, I expect you and your men will be hiding in ambush. You remained aboard ship at Rathmullan and Tory. Were you afraid of O'Donnell's monks?"

"You yourself certainly showed less fear facing unarmed monks in Donegal than you did Maguire's gallowglass at the Arney Pass. It's said your horse outdistanced all others in the retreat." Burke's hand was on his sword.

Bingham rose unsteadily to his feet.

"I need no lessons in courage from a coward, who sheltered aboard ship when there was work to be done."

His judgement was clouded with wine, and the reference to his flight at the Arney ford rankled, or he would not have given the insult. Burke's sword was out.

"Withdraw those words."

"I withdraw nothing." George Bingham's defiant words were his last. The chalice fell from his hand as Burke's sword passed through his chest. Burke withdrew his sword and watched dispassionately as Bingham's body, convulsing in death, lay on the floor. Dark red blood oozed to mingle with the lighter red wine. He strode to the doorway and called down a flight of stairs. "Conor, Conor Burke."

A young man of seventeen or so entered the room and stared in dismay at the body on the floor.

"We hold this castle for O'Donnell. Send a messenger north. Red Hugh's at Tory Island, either there or campaigning with O'Neill. Have our men guard the armoury. Say nothing of Bingham's death. When you have dispatched a messenger to O'Donnell, come back here with ten of our men. I'll look after Bingham's body. What are you staring at? Have you never seen an Englishman's blood before? Get used to the sight, for they have just become our enemy. We have sufficient men to hold the castle if O'Donnell can get here in a few days. Move! Now!"

Conor Burke hastened from the room after one further look at Bingham's body. Three days later Red Hugh himself marched his men into Sligo Castle.

CHAPTER 19

Battle of the Yellow Ford

At Ballyshannon in the midst of a battle, an apprentice physician who was O'Cassidy's nephew applied a bandage to a wound on the gallowglass's arm while the elderly O'Cassidy and Maguire watched. The apprentice had a strange deformity of the little finger of his right hand. The finger was bent almost at a right angle and caused him some difficulty with the bandaging.

"In my experience as a doctor, Hugh, such a deformity of the hand is often found in those who are overly fond of *uisce beatha*."

The apprentice, who rarely drank alcohol, looked up somewhat aggrieved.

"I doubt any connection to alcohol, O'Cassidy." Maguire's gaze fell lazily to the physician's surprisingly delicate hands. "There's no sign of any such condition with your fingers.

The apprentice smiled gratefully at Maguire.

"I'm no physician," Maguire continued, "but I do fancy myself a keen observer of the human animal. While I cannot say with certainty that the condition is caused by him picking his nose, I can certainly see how the condition would facilitate that disgusting habit."

O'Cassidy's nephew looked up startled, then unconsciously in his own defence, held up his left hand to show that it, too, was similarly deformed.

"By God! He's ambidextrous! A finger for each nostril! I'm telling you, O'Cassidy, if this young man is ever to be of any use to you as an assistant you'll have to cure him of that habit. It spreads disease I've heard. Ah well, he'll keep the O'Cassidys in business for another generation."

The young man had not developed his uncle's skill in jousting with Maguire. His only tactic was, with deliberate rudeness, to keep his back turned on his tormentor, as he sullenly continued to dress the gallowglass's wound. Maguire watched his manoeuvring with delighted amusement.

The gallowglass was among the forces of Hugh Maguire and Brian O'Rourke that hastened to cut off the retreat of Sir Conyers Clifford, the new Governor of Connacht. He had recaptured Sligo Castle, and with a large army of twenty infantry regiments and ten of foot, had marched on O'Donnell's Ballyshannon Castle. Clifford had forded the Erne at Ballyshannon and making Abbey Assaroe on the north bank his headquarters, besieged the castle with artillery ferried by sea from Galway. However, he found himself trapped on the north side of the Erne when Cormac O'Neill, brother of Hugh, led an army of one thousand men to assist O'Donnell. Isolated on the wrong side of the Erne, the Englishman was dismayed to see a large force of Irish led by Maguire and Cormac O'Neill assembling to his rear across the river. O'Donnell, thus reinforced by Cormac O'Neill and Maguire, was able to sally from his besieged castle and engage Clifford's army. The newly arrived Irish were massing in ever increasing numbers on the south side of the Erne to cut off Clifford's retreat back to the safety of Sligo castle. Their derisive cheers floating across the river could not have been reassuring to Clifford and his men.

Maguire and the gallowglass returned to assist Red Hugh and Brian O'Rourke in the running battle between Clifford's retreating army and the Irish. Red Hugh engaged Clifford, who lost many men at a ford above Ballyshannon in his retreat across the Erne. He finally got most of his men across to the south side of the river, but he now faced Maguire's men, who attacked the contingent of musketeers set up to prevent O'Donnell's men from following Clifford across the ford. The musketeers vigorously and successfully prevented the Irish from closely following and annihilating Clifford's men. They fought stubbornly, some continuing to fire across the ford while others turned to face Maguire's attack.

Red Hugh in the ford was engaged with a mailed horseman whose shield carried three gold lions on a red background, the coat of arms of the O'Brien of Thomond. Each man had difficulty controlling his horse in the treacherous footing of the ford. The adversary's sword was not the only danger, for to become unhorsed wearing mail in the fast flowing water was to risk drowning. Perhaps because the fords of the Erne were well trodden paths to Red Hugh or perhaps because he was the better horseman he was able to manoeuvre to better advantage. He lunged, and his sword entered the unprotected area beneath the upper arm. The wound was not a mortal one but O'Brien leaning over to avoid the thrust lost a stirrup and his balance and fell from his horse. He struggled gasping in the water and O'Donnell changed his sword to his left hand and reached down with his right to aid his adversary. But O'Brien was swept flailing into deeper water and Eoghan MacSweeney rode over to aid O'Donnell who was now defending himself left handed against a new adversary. Red Hugh left this new antagonist to MacSweeney and sitting his horse in the ford shouted across to Maguire. "This will never do, Hugh. Clifford will be behind the walls of Sligo before I get my men across."

Maguire turned to the gallowglass. "Form your men. The cavalry is not effective against their muskets. They have learned to fire in relays and they aim for the horses. If your gallowglass can disorganize them, we'll sweep them aside with the cavalry."

The gallowglass swarmed forward and were within feet of the muskets when a first volley, then a second, thinned their ranks, but by then they were among the enemy. The English, with no time to reload, used their muskets as clubs then threw them aside, and the battle became one of swords and halberds. The fight raged by the ford while the main English army was escaping south toward Connacht.

Maguire waited impatiently, then unable to wait longer waved his sword as he and O'Rourke and the cavalry charged into the battle. Clifford's rearguard refused to yield, but now besieged from front and rear, they could only fight hopelessly on, isolated in their bloody battle that bought valuable time for their comrades' retreat toward Sligo. It took nearly an hour of fierce fighting before Red Hugh could cross with his men and join Maguire in the pursuit.

Red Hugh looked back across the ford of carnage. "He must be an exceptional man, this Clifford, who can inspire men to fight so bravely. This ford should be known as the Ford of Heroes. Now let us destroy those heroes before they reach Sligo and safety."

One of the heroes who fell in the battle had an illustrious ancestry. He was Murrough O'Brien, 4th Baron of Inchiquin, a direct descendant of the great King Brian Boru, who in 1014 at the battle of Clontarf drove the Norsemen from Ireland. The first Baron of Inchiquin had also been created Earl of Thomond in 1543 in the reign of Henry V111. According to the terms of "Surrender and Regrant" some Irish chieftains accepted English titles in exchange for accepting English law, English customs, and renouncing the Catholic faith in exchange for the Anglican. The O'Briens of Thomond, since the reign of Henry V111, were thus allied with the English and Murrough O'Brien had been fighting on the English side when he met O'Donnell in the ford. The Cistercian monks at Assaroe found and buried the body with all due honours at Assaroe. But the Franciscans in Donegal felt the body should have been interred at the Franciscan monastery in Donegal, the O'Briens of Thomond having traditionally been buried in a Franciscan cemetery. Was there some incongruity in Catholic Irish monks disputing who should have the honour of interring the body of an apostate Irish noble who was killed fighting against the monks own benefactor! Was there some incongruity in a descendant of Ireland's most famous king, fighting on the side of an English queen against Ireland! The warring monks appealed to O'Donnell for a judgement and the body of Murrough O'Brien was disinterred at Assaroe and its final resting place was the Franciscan cemetery by Donegal castle.

Clifford fought a determined rearguard action all the way to Sligo. The combined forces of Red Hugh, Maguire, O'Rourke, and Cormac O'Neill soon came in contact with the rear of Clifford's army, and a running battle ensued. Initially, muskets kept the pursuers at a distance, but then it became apparent the retreating army had either run out of powder, or the rain, which was falling heavily, had dampened whatever powder they had. The fight closed to pike and sword. Clifford himself took up the post of danger in the rear and charged with his cavalry to prevent the Irish cavalry from outflanking his army. The wake of the retreating army was strewn with dead, but not all the dead were English. Night overtook the battle and the Irish continued to assail the retreating army while the English continued as orderly a retreat as possible. Confusion increased in the rain and the darkness. It became difficult to distinguish friend from foe. Horsemen charged out of the darkness, huge menacing shapes, more fearsome in the dark night than in the light of day. Groups of men with pikes thrust forward materialized, screaming from the blackness. Continuing throughout the night to suffer casualties, the retreating army fought the enemy and its own terror. Clifford kept his station in the *Bearna baoil* at the rear of his retreating army.

As dawn approached and the running battle approached Sligo, the Irish broke off. O'Donnell turned to his cousin as Clifford herded his bruised army into the shelter of Sligo's walls.

"There is a true nobleman and a gallant soldier. This new governor is no low mongrel like Bingham. Hugh, do you think you could use your charm to entice the man over to our side?"

"I doubt if even my undeniable charm could accomplish that," was Maguire's modest answer.

In this year of 1597, both O'Donnell and Maguire were so steeped in rebellion that from the English viewpoint there could be no redemption. From the viewpoint of the two chieftains the actions of the invader had long ago ordained their own course of action. Unlike many of the other Irish chieftains, these two remained single-minded in their opposition to the English incursions into Ireland. Maguire was conscious of the fate of his neighbour, Hugh MacMahon, who had recently been hanged by an English sheriff who coveted his lands. Maguire knew also that if he gave up the fight, Fermanagh, the ancestral home of the Maguires, would become the new home of English colonists.

O'Donnell was equally determined to maintain Donegal for the O'Donnells. He also had a larger vision of driving the English from Connacht first, then from Ireland. Red Hugh would never forget the dark wasted years of his youth spent in Dublin Castle. Nor could he forget the recent fate of another rebel, the man who had sheltered him in the Wicklow Mountains, Fiach MacHugh O'Byrne, 'The great firebrand of the mountains' whose head was now impaled on the South Gate of Dublin City.

The English had set up a fort on the Blackwater River in the middle of O'Neill's country, but its commander, Captain Thomas Williams, was in desperate straits. He was low on provisions and daily under attack. For months he and his men had held out against every attempt of O'Neill to take the fort. Reinforcements from England had arrived at Dublin and O'Neill's brother-in-law and lifelong enemy, Richard Bagenal, eagerly offered to lead the relief expedition into Tyrone. Bagenal was England's most experienced commander in Ireland—and the man destined to lead the English to the worst defeat their army was ever to suffer in Ireland. He had under his command as he marched north four thousand foot soldiers and three hundred cavalry. It could not be called an English army, as at least half of the army was Irish.

The forces of O'Neill, O'Donnell, Maguire, and the northern chieftains were about equal to those of Bagenal's, but the Irish commanded more cavalry.

Bagenal had arranged his men in regiments of five hundred men interspaced with his cavalry and cannon. The serpentine column like a gaily coloured centipede stretched out for over a mile as it wound through the small wooded hills toward the fort on the Blackwater.

Hugh O'Neill in the company of his northern chieftains sat his horse on a hill and watched the English army approach. O'Neill wore no armour and his only weapon was a light sword. Beside him on horseback and in battle armour were Red Hugh O'Donnell, Hugh Maguire, Sorley Boy MacDonnell, and O'Neill's brother, Cormac MacArt O'Neill. The vanguard was close enough for O'Neill to recognize its commander, an old friend, Sir Richard Percy, clad in black armour. O'Neill turned to his companions. "Let us welcome our friends of the Pale to the land of the O'Neills. Red Hugh, take their right flank. Cormac and Sorley Boy take the left. Harass their flanks, but avoid any frontal assault until we separate their formations."

O'Neill, from his vantage point, watched the Irish skirmish and withdraw. English cavalry pursued, but soon found themselves floundering in the marshy ground. Puffs of smoke appeared from muskets hidden in the woods and horses reared and fell. The Irish continued to attack and retreat, attempting to draw the English within range of the men hidden in the woods. Red Hugh and Maguire, each readily recognisable by his distinctive plumed *cathbarr*[1], cantered back and forth close to the English line, directing their men, both horse and foot, in the attack.

The clamour of the battle became louder as more Irish engaged Percy's vanguard. Light cavalry whirled in on the English flank, each horseman accompanied by a swift and surefooted runner hanging on to a stirrup leather.

---

[1] The traditional battle helmet of the Irish chieftain.

Horseman and runner discharged their javelins and wheeled away for fresh weapons. Foot soldiers, armed with muskets and pikes, shrieked like banshees as they ran forward from the woods on either side and joined in the battle. Maguire and O'Donnell, riding with stirrups in the English manner, led armoured horsemen that charged into the English ranks, attempting to break up their formations.

Percy, rallying his men, was struck in the chest with a musket ball the force of which lifted him back in the saddle and he fell over his horse's rump to the ground. His Irish aide dismounted and dragged him aside while his men formed a protective cordon around him. Percy's cuirass saved him from what otherwise would have been a fatal wound and showed a large dent where the ball had struck. He lay gasping for some moments, then, still breathing with difficulty and unable to speak, gestured toward his horse, which was led over to him, and he remounted.

Percy and the English vanguard pressed on under continuous attack as the Irish wedged a gap between him and the rest of the army to his rear. Percy, now separated from the main army, finally came within sight of the Blackwater fort, and a distant cheer drifted across to him from the fort. A troop of Captain William's men sallied out, but were immediately surrounded on all sides by about five hundred Irish. Bagenal, at the head of the main army, was prevented from reaching Percy, and now shouts and musket fire from behind told him the rear of his army, commanded by Sir Richard Billings, was also under attack.

Sir Thomas Wingfield, Bagenal's second-in-command galloped up, and spoke accusingly to his commander.

"The Irish are driving a wedge between our columns. The saker[1] is bogged down and we are invested on all sides. They have cut off Billings, and I cannot get back to support him. Our regiments are being separated. Our columns are too far apart. We must regroup; we are fighting as three separate units."

Musket balls sang around the men as they sat their horses. Bagenal turned to an aide. "Get to Percy and tell him to retreat

---

[1] Cannon.

toward me and the main force. Tell him I'll push on ahead to join up with him."

And then turning to Wingfield, "You'll have to do the best you can. Try to hold them off till Billings comes up to you."

The aide galloped off ahead to find Percy, and Wingfield, with a curt reproachful nod, galloped back in the other direction.

His limited view of the battle hampered Bagenal, but he had a sense that things were not going well. He had expected that O'Neill would engage him somewhere along the route, but O'Neill had chosen and prepared his ground well. The Irish, familiar with the areas of boggy ground, made better use of their cavalry and had also prepared pits covered with bracken as traps for the English cavalry. The dense woods had been plashed[1] to herd the English into predetermined ambush routes. Bagenal found himself fighting well-trained, disciplined soldiers skilfully deployed by experienced leaders. He himself was also an experienced soldier. Slowly and in the face of spirited attack, he struggled forward to meet up with Percy, who was trying to prevent his own retreat from becoming a rout. To get a better view of the battlefield, Bagenal lifted his visor and a musket ball struck him in the face, killing him instantly.

The gallowglass fought on foot, commanding his mercenaries, who were attempting to widen the wedge between the regiments of Wingfield and Billings. A large cannon had sunk in marshy ground, and the English tried to extricate it while under incessant musket fire and repeated assault by the Irish. A mailed horseman rode a white horse back and forth, encouraging and protecting his men attempting to free the cannon. He seemed impervious to the musket balls that zipped and whined around him. A group of Irish ran forward and knelt, firing their muskets at the unfortunate team of oxen straining to pull the cannon from the bog. Muskets were inaccurate at any but the closest range, but following the fusillade, two oxen fell kicking and dying. The mailed horseman, well out in front of his men who followed with pikes, charged the group of Irish musket men, and the battle became fiercer as more gallowglass ran to join the fray.

---

[1] Branches interwoven.

In the midst of the battle, MacRory became aware that the English were being besieged on all sides. Large forces of cavalry were entering the battle and the English were falling back. They had abandoned the cannon and its now dead team of oxen. MacRory and his gallowglass pushed forward steadily, moving the English back before their pikes the armoured man on the white horse coolly directed his men in the retreat, which was still disciplined and orderly. When it looked as if they might falter and run, he rallied them with an act of reckless bravery. He single-handedly charged the line of approaching gallowglass, and MacRory found himself in a desperate struggle with this determined antagonist.

As the English retreated their musketeers knelt and discharged their weapons, then ran back to reload behind the line of their retreating pike men. MacRory, engaged with the horseman, was aware of the flash of the muskets and suddenly felt as if a horse had kicked him as a heavy ball struck him in the right groin. He spun around and the force of the ball carried him backward before he fell to the ground unable to rise. Helpless, he stared up at the mailed horseman. The horseman leaned down from the saddle and swept his broadsword upward. MacRory, who had often wondered what might be his thoughts at the moment of death, now only wondered why this man, who bore the emblem of a severed right hand on his corselet, the emblem of the O'Neills, should fight for the English. The horseman seemed to hover thus for long moments, then he straightened, touched the hilt of his sword to his visor, and, wheeling his horse, galloped back to direct the retreat of his men.

O'Neill, directing the battle from his vantage point on the hilltop, was aware that the tide of battle turned in his favour. A huge sheet of fire flamed amid a rising cloud of smoke, and then the dull roar of an explosion reached him. An English soldier had accidentally ignited some powder kegs, causing further confusion and dismay among the English. Percy fought to prevent his bloody and costly retreat from degenerating into a rout. A grunt of admiration escaped O'Neill as one of Percy's officers wrapped the colours of his regiment around his body and continued fighting until he fell in death, enshrouded in the bloodstained emblem.

"A gallant act, but gallantry will not save you now," O'Neil muttered. Presently it became apparent that the whole of the English army was in retreat, and O'Neill ordered all his forces into the battle. The English had been under unrelenting skirmish and assault for four hours since the first engagement, but now they came under the full fury of the Irish forces as O'Neill ordered an all-out onslaught in an attempt to cut off their retreat. Cavalry swept in from all sides.

"*Lamh Dhearg na hUlaidh*![1] *O'Donnell Abú*![2] The war cries shrilled from the throats of O'Neills and O'Donnells as the English vanguard came under attack from right and left. Pike men and musketeers rushed in, cheering to the wail of war pipes as they attempted to overwhelm the retreating English.

Only the angry courage of Wingfield, who himself fought like a madman, kept the English fighting as an army, while the English cavalry, commanded by Sir Calasthenes Brooke, met and blunted the onslaught of the Irish cavalry and prevented annihilation.

The English commanders held the remainder of their army together and took their dreadful punishment in a gory rearguard action as about two thousand of their exhausted and demoralized troops staggered back to Armagh. They left behind one thousand three hundred dead, twenty eight of them officers, four hundred wounded, the large saker cannon, supplies of arms and ammunition, but took with them Bagenal's body. Behind them also they left the fort on the Blackwater and its garrison. The defeated remnants of the English army huddled that night in Armagh while the hills around the town blazed ominously with the campfires of O'Neill's victorious forces.

O'Neill, with the virtually defenceless fort at his mercy and a victorious army at his command, offered amazingly generous terms to the isolated Blackwater garrison. When his attempts to storm the fort on several occasions in the past had been beaten off, he had attempted to starve out the garrison. The fort and its garrison in the heart of Tyrone had been a constant irritant to O'Neill, who had vowed to obliterate this symbol of English arrogance. Yet in a gesture of respect to a brave foe that had held out against his every assault, he allowed Captain Williams and his men to march unmolested from the fort to join the English at Armagh.

---

[1] Red Hand of Ulster.
[2] "O'Donnell to victory".

Inexplicably he did not pursue his victory, but allowed the defeated army to retreat from Armagh back to Dublin.

The fiercest fighting had taken place at a marshy crossing of a tributary of the Callan River called the Yellow Ford and the battle became known as the Battle of the Yellow Ford.

CHAPTER 20

Bloody Sunday

Joe Daly entered a bar in Derry's Bogside[1] and asked for "A pint." A pint anywhere in Ireland, whether north or south, meant a pint of Guinness and usually needed no further qualification although some verbose customer might ask for a "pint of porthur." While the pint was being pulled, he lit one cigarette from another and asked the barmaid if Sean was around.

On being told "My brother's out the back," he first took a critical draught of his drink, then, offering no payment, carried it with him through a door that led to a back yard. He found Sean noisily stacking aluminium Guinness kegs on top of each other.

Joe Daly was a small, wiry-looking man of about fifty with a sallow complexion, who chain-smoked. He had been a member of the official I.R.A. in the 1950s and since 1968, a member of the Provisional I.R.A. or "Provos." British Intelligence had turned him one year earlier, and the I.R.A. had known for the past eleven months. Squadron 22 of the Special Air Services regarded Joe Daly as a valuable asset and, unknown to Joe Daly, the I.R.A. regarded him as an invaluable one. The I.R.A. fed Joe Daly selected information, which he faithfully reported to his masters in the S.A.S. As a result of such information on several occasions the "executive action" group of Squadron 22 had helpfully and unwittingly performed executions for the I.R.A.

Looking at the kegs, Joe commented, "God, Sean, your dad must be doing a roaring trade."

Sean, a hard-working, young man, who neither drank nor smoked and who wore a pioneer pin, continued working as he replied, "If he got paid for all the drink he sells, he'd probably own the brewery."

"Well, Sean, at least you won't be drinking up the profits yourself, having taken the pledge."

Some Irishmen, but by no means all, took what was called "the pledge," a commitment to foreswear all alcoholic drink, and in token of this, they wore a small shield-shaped pin in the lapel called a pioneer pin. A Father Cullen, knowing the Irish propensity for alcohol combined with the Irish inability to handle it, had started the movement in 1898. When Sean took the pledge at

---

[1] A Nationalist area in Derry City.

sixteen, his mother was happy to know her son would not be getting into trouble because of drink. Actually, her son was engaged in another rather dangerous activity. At twenty-one years of age, Sean was the deputy commander of the I.R.A. in Derry.

Sean Harvey stopped work and rested both hands on an empty keg. "Joe, we're having a meeting tonight to discuss the march. We'll meet at seven at Kelly's. We know the place is being watched, but our boys will cordon it off."

"I'll be there at seven." Joe Daly finished his pint, lit another cigarette, and walked off.

At six o'clock Harvey's Bar was crowded and Sean Harvey spoke to a man who had sat with an untouched pint of Guinness in front of him for an hour. "Get hold of Joe and tell him we have changed the meeting place. We'll meet here in half an hour."

Joe walked into the meeting late, but the commandant of the Derry I.R.A. abruptly brought him up to speed.

"You're late, Joe. We're taking on the Army on Sunday. We expect a crowd of somewhere around five thousand, maybe twice that at the march. There'll be a lot of media coverage. This time it will be an all-out firefight between the Brits and us. You and your men will be under Sean's command. I will brief each brigade commander separately, but this must be a coordinated attack, and each of you must know the overall strategy." He unfolded a map. "As usual we will have some of our men among the marchers, but our main force will be here in the Rossville Flats and here in William Street. We expect the Brits will have lookouts in the flats, but we've made plans, which you need not concern yourselves about, to deal with that. For security reasons the brigade commanders will not conduct a final briefing until twelve hours before the march."

"Are we ready, Martin, to take on the Brits in an open battle?" Sean Harvey asked with an admirable pretence of concern.

"No better time than now, Sean, and no better place than Derry. But we want the element of surprise, so pass the word that there'll be no I.R.A. presence at the march."

When the others left, Sean Harvey and Kevin Martin remained behind.

"When the Brits realize they have been duped, he'll be of no further use to us. He'll be your responsibility, Sean."

In Northern Ireland it was a fair statement to say that the words Nationalist, Republican, and Catholic were synonymous, as were the words Unionist, Orangeman, and Protestant. The rare exceptions were rare indeed. For accuracy as a working hypothesis, the statement would fall somewhere between the marine weather forecast and Newton's law of gravity with a bias towards Newton.

Few Unionists called the city at the head of Lough Foyle "Derry" and few Nationalists called it "Londonderry." "I'm from Derry and a member of the Orange Order" was as impossible a combination as "I'm Cardinal so and so and this is my wife."

"Danny Boy" was the "Londonderry Air" to those schooled at Portora Royal School in Enniskillen and the "Derry Air" to those who went to St. Columb's in Derry/Londonderry. In the latter instance, however, the Unionists/ Protestants/ Orangemen had the upper hand as even the most fervent Nationalist /Republican/ Catholic might choose to refer to the famous song simply as "Danny Boy" in order to avoid any unfortunate French Connection.

To the Unionists, the history of Londonderry began in 1690 when thirteen Apprentice Boys closed the gates of the city and held it for William of Orange and denied access to the Irish forces that supported the Jacobite King James. The ensuing siege lasted one hundred five days until a relief ship the "Mountjoy" broke through the barricade on the Foyle and relieved the city. The defenders had endured daily shelling, famine, and death.

The Nationalists had an older memory of Derry that related to Saint Columcille and the O'Neills and O'Donnells. In more recent times events in Derry had brought the British Army to Ireland. Commencing in the 1960s, and under the auspices of the Northern Ireland Civil Rights Association, Civil Rights marches had taken place in Derry and the marchers frequently came into conflict with the authorities. Civil Rights for the Nationalist minority had never been a priority of the Stormont government in Belfast, and now to their embarrassment, these marches focused media attention on decades of abuse. Of the ten thousand employed at the large shipbuilding works of Harland and Wolff in Belfast less than one hundred were Catholics. The Northern Ireland Prime Minister, Terence O'Neill, tried to persuade his fellow Unionists that reforms were necessary, but this "lack of bottom" cost him his job. The Nationalists availed themselves of the media attention to embarrass the Stormont government and indeed that government had much about which to be embarrassed.

In 1933 Basil Brooke, later to become "Sir Basil" and Prime Minister of Northern Ireland, spoke to his fellow Unionists. "I can speak freely on this subject as I have not a Roman Catholic about my own place. I appreciate the great difficulty experienced by some in procuring suitable Protestant labour, but I would point out that Roman Catholics are endeavouring to get in everywhere. I appeal to Loyalists therefore whenever possible to employ good Protestant lads and lassies."

At about the same time De Valera to the south also spoke freely on the subject. "If I had a vote on a local body and if there were two qualified people who had to deal with a Catholic community, and if one was a Catholic and the other was a Protestant, I would unhesitatingly vote for the Catholic."

Only after the discriminatory practices became widely known as a result of media coverage that showed authorities baton charging and attacking peaceful protestors, did England, too, react with astonishment that such amazing practices could occur in Ulster. A self-serving astonishment that many regarded as strange considering these practices had existed for more than forty years since the formation of the state in 1921. The marchers were well aware of the visual impact of these pictures shown on TV and in newspapers around the world and used such media coverage to their advantage.

The Stormont government feared also, and with reason, that subversive elements – the I.R.A. – had infiltrated the Civil Rights Movement.

Remnants of Derry's walls still stood and from their heights the Unionists looked down on the Bogside, an underprivileged Nationalist enclave. The annual traditional Apprentice Boys' march took place on 12 August at the end of the "Marching Season." From Derry's walls the parade proceeded close by the Bogside. On August 12, 1969, the march met a counter parade in the Bogside. The Nationalists regarded the Unionist parade as "Triumphalism." To the Unionists their traditional parades honouring their celebrated victories of the late 1600s at Derry, Aughrim, Enniskillen, and the Boyne were sacrosanct. Rioting on a serious scale in Derry and Belfast with many deaths ensued over the next two days. The authorities unleashed the "B Specials," who joined Unionists mobs rampaging throughout Nationalist areas in scenes reminiscent of Unionist pogroms at the formation of the state in 1921. Unionists and Nationalists fled back behind tribal barriers.

The Irish Army in the south moved up to the border in nearby Donegal and casualties were treated in Irish army field hospitals across the border and in Derry's Altnagelvin Hospital. Barricades went up in Derry and Belfast, and "No Go" areas, where the R.U.C. were denied access, were declared, and held by militant Nationalists.

Northern Ireland's Prime Minister, Terence O'Neill, bearer of an illustrious Irish name, was more English than the English themselves. His Anglo-Irish ancestry included both the O'Neills of Tyrone and the Chichesters of the Plantation of Ulster days.

O'Neill had been born in England but had holidayed in Northern Ireland where he had relatives among the ruling establishment. He was the product of Eton, Sandhurst, and the Irish Guards. He had served in the Second World War in which both his older brothers had been killed. His father, a captain in the Irish Guards, had died in the First World War. O'Neill was that rarity in N. Ireland's politics, a moderate, and his efforts to find a solution to the sectarian strife alienated him from many of his fellow Unionists at Stormont.[1] O'Neill adopted the tricky stratagem of being all things to all men, while at the same time being more things to all Orangemen. One fellow Unionist who did support O'Neill was made to understand that his stance was an unpopular one. He was dragged from the platform at a 12th of July Orange Lodge rally in Coagh, County Tyrone, and kicked into a coma by other Orangemen. This may have hinted to O'Neill, a decent man and a visionary, -- albeit a man at times afflicted with tunnel vision, -- that he was out of touch with elements of his own party. He resigned. Earlier O'Neill had made the hilariously naïve comment:

> "It is frightfully hard to explain to Protestants that if you give Roman Catholics a good job and a good house they will live like Protestants because they will see neighbors with cars and television sets; they will refuse to have 18 children,....If you treat Roman Catholics with due consideration and kindness, they will live like Protestants."

This statement showed that O'Neil was also "frightfully" out of touch with the reality of conditions in N. Ireland. Despite the deliberate economic bias that adversely affected Catholics, their children, thanks to the dedicated efforts of the Catholic Church, were at least as well educated as were Protestant children. More Catholics than Protestants now attended institutions of higher education, Few Catholics looked with envy at their Protestant neighbor's Morris Minors, and 12 inch television sets. As for the families with 18 children, he may have had in mind a Punch Caricature from the 1800's

It would have been fitting had O'Neill, the descendant of Plantation stock and of Irish chieftains, been able to bring together the Orange and the Green! O'Neill's successor was James Chichester-Clark, of plantation stock, a relative, also an Etonian, and also an Irish Guards officer who had served in the war. He too tried to introduce reforms, came under fire from his fellow Unionists and he too resigned.

Decades of injustice came home to roost in the unsympathetic lap of the Minister for Home Affairs, William Craig. Craig, a "hold the line" Unionist was not the man to right these wrongs. When O'Neill fired him he formed the Vanguard Party with ties to Protestant paramilitaries. Those who voted with their boots at Coagh would have found a home in the Vanguard Party. The

---

[1] Seat of government for Northern Ireland.

Party favoured fascist style monster rallies to pump up the faithful with motor cycle outriders and distinctive regalia. Hitler-like, Craig proposed compiling a dossier on malcontents, men and women, who might one day need to be liquidated. This ex war-time R.A.F. tail gunner informed the British Government that he could mobilize 80,000 armed men under his command and informed his followers at a rally. "We are prepared to come out and shoot and kill. I am prepared to come out and shoot and kill, let's put the bluff aside. I am prepared to kill, and those behind me will have my full support." There is no record that the I.R.A. ever acknowledged their indebtedness to William Craig for the thousands of recruits he sent their way.

The British Army came to Northern Ireland on 14 August 1969 to restore and maintain order. Initially the British were welcomed, but not for long. Further serious sectarian rioting broke out in Belfast and across Northern Ireland, and the I.R.A. fragmented into two groups, both of which took on the task of protecting Nationalist areas.

During the next two years, the Provisional I.R.A., or "Provos", gained recruits and strength, and went on the offensive against the security forces. In August 1971 at the insistence of the Stormont government, internment without trial was introduced. The police and army rounded up over three hundred people, and again an immediate upsurge of protest and violence occurred. In the space of forty-eight hours the British Army shot seventeen people, all of them Nationalists. A march was scheduled for 30 January, 1972, in Derry to protest internment without trial. The authorities banned the march.

The largest crowd yet to assemble at a Civil Rights march in Northern Ireland gathered in the Creggan Nationalist area of Derry. Some estimated the gathering at twenty thousand. The British Army commander in Derry, Brigadier Andrew McLennan commanding the Eighth Infantry Brigade, erected twenty-six barricades around the city to contain the march to Nationalist Derry. Lieutenant Colonel Derek Wilford commanded the First Battalion of the Parachute Regiment. The presence of the tough "Paras" was an indication that the British Army expected trouble.

The march formed up in the Creggan and proceeded up William Street to confront an army barricade. The organizers directed the march down Rossville Street away from the barricade and toward what was known as Free Derry Corner some five hundred yards away where one of the march organizers, Bernadette Devlin, would address the crowd. Some two hundred marchers, however, continued up Williams Street to the barricade and commenced the rite of passage ritual of harassing the British soldiers with stones and bottles. The army used a water cannon to spray purple water by which the rioters could later be recognized and arrested. C.S. gas and rubber bullets were also used to disperse the protestors.

A sniper on a roof sighted through the scope of his Drugonov sniper rifle. The S.A.S. favoured the Russian-made weapon. He sighted his electronic distance-finding device on a soldier's head, which confirmed his distance as one thousand plus or minus three feet, moved his aim four feet above the soldier's head, and gently squeezed the trigger. The bullet hit its target, a drainpipe on a building above the army barricade on Williams Street. The sniper removed the small tripod used for steadying the rifle barrel, and, as he unhurriedly disassembled the rifle, muttered, "That should get the ball rolling."

From the barricade on James Street, Major Ted Loden led his paras forward for the arrest operation, some in Saracen armoured cars, some running in pursuit of the now fleeing protestors. The events of the next thirty minutes, during which Loden's men shot to death thirteen unarmed civilians and wounded another fifteen, were the subject of much investigation and re-examination. The British Government ordered an immediate investigation into what became known as "Bloody Sunday". The tribunal of investigation was under the sole chair of Lord Widgery, an ex-British Army officer, and it soon became apparent that another casualty of "Bloody Sunday" was British justice. It was subsequently revealed that Edward Heath, the British Prime Minister, had reminded Lord Widgery that the British were also fighting a propaganda war in Northern Ireland. Lord Widgery's disregard for any semblance of truth or justice was so blatant as to be almost unbelievable.

A storm of protest broke over the British Government at what was perceived to be a political whitewash. When Reginald Maudling, who as British Home Secretary was responsible for security in N. Ireland, stated in the House of Commons that the paratroopers had been justified in their actions Bernadette Devlin, a twenty-one year old Irish M.P. for Mid-Ulster called him a liar and walked across the floor and slapped him in the face. When asked later if she felt she should apologize to the Home Secretary she said: "I'm only sorry I didn't get him by the throat." Devlin had taken part in the march and had witnessed the events but was denied the opportunity to speak of it in the House of Commons. She was unsuccessful in bringing the incident before the International Court of Justice at The Hague.

Essentially, the Widgery Report accepted the army's contention that the paras had come under sustained attack from gunfire and bombs, and had been justified in their response, while ignoring evidence from civilians and journalists at the scene denying any such attack. No photographic evidence was produced showing any gunman or bomber, despite the fact that there were many journalists and photographers, including at least two army photographers present and helicopters overhead. No soldier was injured. None of the deceased or wounded, with one exception, was proved to have been shot while handling a firearm or bombs. The one exception, seventeen-year-old Gerald Donaghy, was found later with a nail bomb in his pocket, and there were grounds for suspicion that it had been planted there after he had been shot. Seven of those shot were seventeen years of age.

Ignoring evidence to the contrary, Lord Widgery reported: "There is no clear reason to suppose that the soldiers would have opened fire if they had not been fired upon first. Soldiers who identified armed gunmen fired upon them in accordance with the standing orders in the yellow card. There was no general breakdown in discipline." As a sop to reality he did comment that the soldier's firing had "bordered on the reckless".

The Lord Chief Justice's report was received with some short-lived relief by the British Government and with incredulity by anyone who had any knowledge of the events. To this latter group Lord Widgery's attitude relating to the evidence had seemed to be, "My mind is made up, don't confuse me with facts."

A subsequent British Government, embarrassed by the obvious subjugation of truth to expediency, ordered another investigation by Lord Saville and when his report was made public it was a direct contradiction of Lord Widgery's. Lord Saville concluded that soldiers had lied in their earlier testimony further reported:

> Firing by soldiers of 1 Para on Bloody Sunday caused the deaths of 13 people and injury to a similar number, none of whom was posing a threat of causing death or serious injury. What happened on Bloody Sunday strengthened the Provisional IRA, increased Nationalist resentment and hostility towards the Army and exacerbated the violent conflict of the years that followed. Bloody Sunday was a tragedy for the bereaved and the wounded, and a catastrophe for the people of Northern Ireland.

When Lord Saville's report was made public, the British Prime Minister, David Cameron apologized for the events of Bloody Sunday saying that the shootings had been "Unjustified and unjustifiable". This honest admission went a long way towards furthering the peace process in Northern Ireland. As a result of Lord Saville's findings, soldiers of the Parachute Regiment who shot civilians in Derry could face murder charges.

There was the perception among the Nationalists, reinforced by the army's use of the aggressive paratroop regiment, that those who entertained facile solutions to complex problems had had their way. "It was an illegal march. Shoot the bastards and teach them a lesson they won't forget."

The ghosts of General Dyer and Rudyard Kipling would have nodded approval from Derry's walls.

Joe Daly, sitting in the backseat of a car with Sean Harvey, spoke hesitantly, "Where were our people today, Sean? The Brits had it all their own way."

Harvey didn't look at him as he replied, "Our people, Joe? Only your people were active today."

He spoke to the driver as the car drove down a deserted street between two rows of slate-roofed tenement houses, "Take the road to Magilligan Beach."

"Sean ...", Joe Daly's voice had an edge of unease.

"Hold your tongue!"

It was the driver who spoke, looking at Daly through the rear-view mirror, and Sean Harvey gazed unseeingly out the window as the tenement houses slid past. All four drove in silence, and after five minutes, Joe Daly lit another cigarette and asked:

"Can I have a priest, Sean?"

He got no answer. Nearing the beach, Harvey signalled the driver to turn into a lane way. The car stopped by a barn and all three got out. Harvey motioned to the other man, who followed Joe Daly through the door. As Harvey spoke to the driver, a farmer approached the barn from a nearby house. After a short conversation, the farmer walked quickly back to the house and the car drove off. A half hour passed and Harvey opened the barn door and was followed inside by a priest.

"You have fifteen minutes." Harvey stood by a window looking out, but the other man kept careful watch from a distance as Daly knelt and blessed himself.

At the end of his confession, Daly blessed himself again and stood. He looked toward Harvey. "Could I have one more cigarette?"

Harvey still refused to look at him, but the other man nodded. "You smoke too much, Joe, those things will kill you."

Before he had finished his cigarette, Harvey turned from the window and nodded to Daly, who stubbed out the cigarette and turned around and again knelt.

213

CHAPTER 21

Capture

The ball that struck MacRory at the Yellow Ford shattered his right hip. He was carried in a litter to Enniskillen Castle escorted by Hugh Maguire himself. When they arrived at Enniskillen, O'Cassidy's examination and manipulation caused the gallowglass more pain than the initial injury. The physician was kindly by nature and both by nature and duty, kind and solicitous to those in his care, but when his ministrations demanded it, he could be brutally detached.

MacRory lay with a traction device attached to his leg for the first week, but thereafter during the day was allowed to hobble around using a crutch, and with his right heel flexed up to his buttock, suspending a weight at the knee. After a few days O'Cassidy seemed more satisfied and ceased comparing the colour and warmth of the gallowglass' two feet. The red-faced old man sat by MacRory.

"If the ball had struck a little more to the centre, Turlough, you'd have sought employment as a mercenary in some sultan's harem. I've heard your Norse ancestors were once mercenaries for the Sultan of Constantinople, although I doubt the sultan would have been so foolish as to let them near his harem. I think the leg will heal, although it will be a little shorter than the other, and I'm afraid you'll walk with a limp."

The gallowglass, who initially had accepted the possibility that he could lose his leg and possibly his life, was now perturbed by the lesser disability of a limp. He smiled bleakly. "So long as I'm left with a leg to stand on."

"I'll guarantee at least a leg and a half to stand on. Actually it's best to be on your feet, or at least on one, as much as possible, as the weight will pull the bone into a better alignment. Use these crutches as much as possible. You can try chewing on these leaves and it might lessen the pain. They are leaves of a plant called the coca plant. A Spaniard gave me some and said the natives in the New World chew them for pain relief. In a few months the bone will be set anyhow and we can then allow you to bear some weight on the leg."

The physician gave him some leaves from a pouch.

Over the next few months the gallowglass found that not only did the leaves work well for pain relief, but chewing them also relaxed him and enabled him to endure the boredom of his forced inactivity. He became less inhibited and restrained, and seemed to have lost something of his usual serious nature. The physician was delighted with the beneficial effect of his new medicine. The two spent much time together. Maguire had not returned to Enniskillen, but campaigned with Red Hugh and O'Neill. The elderly physician, now nearing fifty, no longer accompanied him in the field, leaving that dangerous duty to a younger assistant.

"The leg looks wasted and I don't think it will bear my weight." MacRory laughed and did not seem particularly perturbed as he tried to support himself on both legs. For a man accustomed to the active eventful life of a soldier, he had borne his months of disability with remarkable equanimity and seemed more amused than dismayed by his clumsiness as he attempted to walk. The old man supported him.

"It will, at first, feel weak and strange, but each day will get stronger. The muscles and tissues have weakened and now you must work at exercising daily to get back on your feet so to speak. In no time you'll be leaping about, brisk as a bee. There should be little or no pain by now, and in any event, you have exhausted my supply of leaves"

In subsequent days the lack of motivation his patient exhibited in "getting back on his feet" surprised the physician. MacRory, habitually even-tempered and cheerful, became listless, moody, and depressed. His own unaccountable behaviour appalled even him at times. He occasionally exhibited a short-tempered irritability and found himself frequently having to apologize for this and for his uncharacteristic surliness. When he thought how those around him, who had shown such kindness, perceived his ungrateful behaviour, he at times sank into a state of depressed guilt.

The old physician, who knew his craft and treated mind and body, paid as much attention to the mental state of his patient as the physical. He allowed his patient little time for introspection and kept him physically active to the point of exhaustion. O'Cassidy, familiar with the symptoms of opiate withdrawal, began to suspect the withdrawal of the leaves caused the change in MacRory's behaviour. He would have to reassess the medicinal value of his new medicine.

The patient sometimes hated but at all times trusted his physician. Gradually over a month, the gallowglass's mood improved and he became more like his normal self. He did initially limp, but with Cassidy's continuous insistence that he take steps of equal length and put equal weight on each foot, he eventually walked with only a barely discernable limp.

Throughout his convalescence, Maguire's wife and her household also treated him with kindness and solicitude. When he was able to walk, she, her friends, and the old doctor frequently accompanied him for walks along the banks of the Erne. Later on horseback, they travelled farther afield. After the Yellow Ford, O'Neill, and his alliance had undisputed control in the north, and no danger threatened these expeditions in the area of Enniskillen.

Long after he was able to walk without pain, riding horseback still induced a dull ache in his hip joint. His doctor insisted his patient sit whenever possible with ankles crossed in the posture of some Eastern mystic, and told him this posture would make horseback riding eventually less painful also. In matters of health, the old man ministered to all at the castle and while in many ways he was treated with an affectionate disrespect, in matters of health he was obeyed.

The gallowglass had always had a real affection for the old man, but the constant constraints and impositions became wearisome. MacRory one evening announced his intention of going off by himself for a few days, and the next morning he saddled his horse and did so.

He set out heading in a southerly direction but with no particular destination in mind. In his saddlebags he carried enough food for several days. He wore a light sword but no armour. His earlier dark mood had left him, and on this particular morning, it was difficult to entertain any morose or gloomy thought. His horse's hooves crunched the brown leaves beneath trees still clad in yellow and gold. The light breeze floated errant leaves gently to the ground around him. In a month the less languid October gales would lay these branches stark and bare, swirling and rustling the dead brown leaves around the denuded titans of the forest. On this day the mellow autumn sun slanted its still warm rays through the foliage, dappling the pathway ahead with patches of soft gloom and pale light. As he rode the only sounds were the soft clump of his horse's hooves, the musical jingle of the bridle, and the sigh of the wind through the trees, murmuring a soft lament for the dying year.

He rode through the morning and when the sun was high in the sky, stopped and dismounted to allow his horse to rest. Stretching out in the cool grass beneath the shade of some willows, he gazed up through the trembling leaves to the sky, his senses soothed by the murmur of the rustling leaves and the rhythmic crunch of his horse cropping the grass. Small clouds drifted across the sky briefly blotting out the sun. His mind drifted back to his childhood. More than two decades had slipped by since an eight-year-old boy had lain in a hay field in North Uist, watching white clouds move in slowly from the ocean, pass on overhead, their shadows darkening the waters of the Little Minch, as they drifted on across the sky toward the Inner Hebrides. How imperceptibly, he thought, do the innocence of a child and the peace of a mind likewise drift away from us.

After half an hour he remounted and again slipped into an unthinking reverie, slumped and swaying to his horse's gait, scarcely conscious of the passage of time, until his horse stopped to drink from a stream. He recognized the stream as the Claddagh River and when his horse finished drinking, he turned its head up along the course of the stream. The wild and lonely Claddagh Glen, a remote solitude seldom disturbed by man, bordered on Breffney-O'Reilly lands. Here, before memory of man, the cycles of nature had pulsed in undying rhythm to the eternal heartbeat of the living earth. The seasons of death and renewal, unnamed and unknown, had passed timelessly on. The river, unheard and unseen, had flowed ceaselessly on to the sea, an eternal cycle of renewal.

He rode up the stream, sometimes in the riverbed, sometimes along a fern-bordered path on its left bank. Limestone cliffs rose up across the river on his right, while to his left the glen, clothed with ash, oak, and sycamore, inclined more gently in terraced slopes. Some way up a wooded slope, a wild sow and her litter, emitting a series of eager grunts and snorts, rooted for acorns in a shadowed glade beneath the whispering canopy of an oak. Brown-leafed hazelnut trees arched out over the hurrying river, and chattering red squirrels harvested nuts among their branches. The amber waters tumbled down, hastening on with the endless urgent murmur that had forever announced their arrival to the flat meadowland below.

Here in the steeps of the glen, the stream slid smoothly over rounded rocks and frothed in the pools beneath small cataracts. The eager waters rushed swiftly around the larger mossy rocks in the streambed. A busy dipper, displaying flashes of white and chestnut-coloured, breast feathers, bobbed up and down as it fed in the current, its feathers dry despite its repeated immersions. In eddies where the water flowed more gently, shimmering images of horse and rider reflected back from the liquid depths. Some way up the glen a silvery veil of water erupted from the limestone cliff. The underground stream, bursting free from its dank stygian passage through the cold grave of the earth, cascaded joyfully into the sunshine to splash into the river below.

His horse shied violently in response to a guttural roar that startled the peace of the glen. The strange sound in this lonely place gave even the gallowglass a moment of superstitious fear. The roar was repeated and then a movement on the cliff top across the river caught his attention. A red stag walked out on to a rocky promontory and stood like a sentinel on a rampart. The antlered head was thrown back and the great rack of burnished antlers lay along the thick red mane on its neck. The neck and mouth were flecked with frothy saliva. Again the stag echoed its deep-throated challenge across the Claddagh Glen.

MacRory sat thrilled by the sight of the majestic animal, lord of its wild haunts, thrilled to hear it roar out its challenge to the world, thrilled to be privileged to witness this sight in this remote place. Man was now the stag's main predator, as wolves, which for millennia had tested and strengthened the great stag's ancestors, while still present in Ireland were not as numerous as in the past. In Munster however there was a significant population of the predators, due to the number of unburied corpses that littered the land following the suppression of the Desmond Rebellion. The great monarch remained standing on the cliff top for minutes after the last dying echo faded into silence. He then turned and disappeared back into the trees.

Near the top of the glen the Claddagh River itself issued forth from an underground cave among a jumble of rocks beneath an arch of white limestone. MacRory tethered his horse to a sapling and walked along the stream into the mouth of the cave. Some prior visitor had left a blackened pitch torch at the entrance. After a few attempts he lit the torch with a flint and steel retrieved from one of his saddlebags, and holding it out in front of him, he waded into the cave.

Inside, the smooth limestone in places formed a walkway along the side of the slowly moving, almost still water. The flickering torch cast a circle of eerie light on the dark water and the white, marble-like limestone walls. Here in the silent tomb of the earth, walking by an underground river, he was reminded of what he had learned in tedious hours of Latin study under the tutelage of a Carmelite priest at Sheephaven. In Virgil's *Aeneid* he had read of the belief of the Ancient Greeks that only those who were properly buried, and their passage prepaid with a silver coin placed under the tongue of the corpse, were rowed across the River Styx to the underworld by Charon. The grim ferryman accepted the silver obolus as payment for his service.

The sibilant swish of the water by his feet as he waded into the cave whispered a sinister echo in the dark recesses of the cavern. The vaulted roof of the cave was just discernable in the yellow torchlight and from the limestone in places, a white dampness oozed down the smooth walls. Maguire had once told him that three underground rivers converged in this cave to form the Claddagh River. He could only remember the names of two, the "Owenbrean" and the "Aghinrawn." He came to a smooth rock platform where he sat looking down at his torch's reflected light in the menacing-looking dark water. He wondered if many others had visited this dark subterranean void. Not many, as the Celts, though brave in battle, might have had a superstitious fear of this dark underground world, for surely here spirits might dwell, but the Celts had not been the only inhabitants of this land.

Tiny drops of water over slowly evolving eons of time had oozed along tiny limestone cracks in the rock above and over further immeasurable eons these vast vaulted caves had formed from this infinitesimal beginning. What was a human life span in this eternity of eternities!? Like that tiny drop of water, it was an indivisible and indestructible part of the whole!

Somewhere along these past creeping reaches of time other generations, long before the Celts, would have trod the earth above, their decayed bodies now mouldered for millennia into the timeless soil that clothed the still more timeless rock. Had they loved and laughed and dreamed? What long dead eyes had gazed on this dark water? Perhaps here others had huddled and hidden in darkness, seeking shelter in some long ago conflict. Would they have quaked in terror for themselves and for their families, their hiding place betrayed, as torches similar to his cast a yellow foreboding light on looming grotesque approaching shadows? Would those long dead hearts have raced with fear as harsh voices echoed down the vaulted cavern?

Perhaps, in some rude shelter in the glen without, a mother feeding a gurgling infant had looked with astonishment and with loving eyes on the miracle her body had produced. Perhaps some lone hermit, lost in thoughts of the mysteries of life, had sat on the leaf-strewn ground resting his back against an oak on the terraced slope, an oak now hundreds of generations of decay removed from its present massive progeny.

Or perhaps some primitive nomadic family group clad in animal skins, weary and with gnawing hunger their constant attendant, seeking shelter, had trudged barefooted by on the moorland above, unaware of the sheltered glen that was hidden in the mist below, savage uncouth creatures, each with an immortal soul, a soul that now floated in the timeless void of eternity. Would he live now, had they not lived then? Did all living things have an immortal soul? Was the earth itself a living thing, the sun the moon and the night sky that rotated around the earth? Was the creator creation itself, the creator, and creation one and the same?

Would Druids have worshipped here? Certainly one would expect that such a place as this, with mouths of caves opening into underground worlds and underground streams gushing from openings in cliff walls, would have more than a passing interest to those learned priests with their consuming fascination with portals.

The Druids had seen great significance in portals, gateways that stood between two worlds, in both and yet in neither. In common with all cultures they treated the portals of birth and death with reverential awe. They believed in an immortal soul, but believed that after death and a period in the underworld, a person was reborn. When they celebrated a birth, they also mourned the death in the underworld that had made the new life on earth possible. They celebrated the feast of Beltane that marked the birth of spring, and they observed the solemn ceremonies of Samhain that marked the death of summer. Samhain was the time when the shield of Scathach[1] was lowered and the souls of the dead, and souls of the yet unborn, mingled with the living.

Perhaps as recently as a thousand years ago those white-robed priests had gathered around an oak on the hillside without to invoke the spirit of their sacred tree to combat the power of a new god that had come to their land, threatening their old beliefs and threatening their mystic power.

MacRory was brought back to the present as his torch dimmed and the flame threatened to go out. Hastily he arose and started back along the smooth rock toward the unseen entrance. As he made his way back, the light from the torch became progressively dimmer until finally he was in total darkness. It took him a long time to reach the entrance to the cave; at intervals he struck his flint to obtain a momentary view of the way ahead before being again engulfed in darkness. Finally he groped his way back and stood blinking in the bright sunlight.

One man held his horse's bridle and closely examined the saddlebags and accoutrements. Another sat a white horse close by. The man on horseback spoke to him. "You'll come with us, Captain."

The man on horseback wore a saffron riding cloak with an embroidered crest, which depicted two rampant lions, one on either side of a severed red hand. MacRory by now knew that the Red Hand of Ulster belonged also on the crest of the O'Reillys. He walked toward his horse, drawing his sword, and the young man who had spoken smiled and gestured to his right with a slight movement of his head. MacRory looked in that direction and saw what his dark-adapted eyes had earlier failed to see. Farther up the glen was a troupe of some twenty mounted men. The man holding his horse's bridle continued to hold the bridle while MacRory mounted, then the other man brought his horse alongside and reached out his hand.

"Miles O'Reilly. You may not know me but we have met, at the Yellow Ford."

---

[1] Celtic goddess of the shadow world.

Miles O'Reilly! The name brought memories other than of the Yellow Ford. Maeve O'Rourke had been betrothed to a Miles O'Reilly! MacRory also knew that O'Reillys had fought in Bagenal's army, and were unfriendly neighbours to Maguire.

"I had thought you would never walk again after that musket ball, but am glad to see you can." O'Reilly smiled, still holding out his hand. MacRory felt it would be ill mannered to refuse the proffered hand, but his handshake was less than warm.

"My apologies for the inconvenience, MacRory, but the friend of Red Hugh and Maguire may prove a valuable hostage. We'll send word to Maguire that you are now our guest. We were passing above and saw a horseman make his way up the glen. Not many people pass this way, and you piqued our curiosity. We'll attempt to make your stay at Tollymongan as comfortable as possible. Will it be your word or your sword?"

MacRory took his light sword from its sheath and wordlessly passed it across.

"I thought so. Still, I hope to show you hospitality rather than swordplay. We're aware of the captain's reputation and will attempt to keep any weapons out of your reach. My father killed your father's father, and it would have been a regret had I killed you at the Yellow Ford. Besides, I owe you a debt for an incident ten years ago in Glencar."

The horsemen and their captive continued up the glen until they reached the flat moorland above. They then turned southeast toward the O'Reilly's stronghold of Tullymongan. Their route took them initially across high boggy moorland interspersed with small loughs. They skirted O'Rourke lands on their right, before again descending toward Lough Oughter.

O'Reilly chatted to his captive in an easy, friendly manner, but MacRory was in no doubt that he was a hostage and would have been cut down without hesitation had he attempted to escape. O'Reilly wanted to know about the Western Isles and the gallowglass's home. He showed a keen interest in and knowledge of the gallowglass families of the Isles. Generations of MacCabe gallowglass had been in the employ of the O'Reillys since the late 1300s. He was knowledgeable also regarding the history of the Isles and their association with the Norse.

"This plateau with its scattered small loughs, which we now traverse, lies between the headwaters of the Shannon and the headwaters of the Erne. Our storytellers say that it was used in the times of the Norse to transport their ships from the Shannon to the Erne. What a feat for those men to drag their ships from lough to lough across such a distance! Do you think it's just another Irish legend or would it have been possible? Perhaps it's merely conjecture and they abandoned their ships in the Shannon and rebuilt others on the Erne?"

Listening to him, the gallowglass was reminded of Maguire, who had told him similar story years ago in a boat on the Erne. How alike were all these men – Maguire, Red Hugh, Brian O'Rourke, and Miles O'Reilly! It seemed they were all bred to the same manner, thought, and character and each wore the mantle of leadership with an easy casual arrogance. All were born to lead, but more was required, for each must prove to those who marched behind him that he was also the fittest to lead. In wisdom, in cunning, in battle, he must, like the Celtic chieftain of Caesar's time, be superior to those he led. Was it the system of choosing a leader from among the Derbfine, offering as it did a choice from among the best, which resulted in such natural leaders, essential in a warrior society? The man who rode by his side could as well have been a cultured, brave, and dangerous Hugh Maguire, or a Brian O'Rourke, able, gracious, and ruthless.

"Like many a legend, it probably had a foundation in fact," MacRory replied.

"I agree," O'Reilly continued.

"It's unlikely the Norse would have abandoned their good boats on the Shannon. These ships had also to be seaworthy to take them back to their homeland, and without shipyard facilities they would not have been able to build a seaworthy ship in the wilderness. The same stories are told of the Swedish Vikings who navigated from the Baltic by way of the Dnieper River down to Kiev and beyond. The Viking galley was a shallow draft boat, lightweight so that she could be beached easily. It's said that as they went, they enslaved the local people to transport their ships by land from one waterway to the next. What an interesting time to have lived! To sail across oceans and conquer new lands!" The way O'Reilly spoke sounded as if he had more admiration for the Norse invaders than sympathy for their Irish victims.

"It was maybe not all fun." MacRory commented. "The Chinese have a curse: 'May you live in interesting times'"

"Oh, come on, MacRory. Any man who regards that as much of a curse deserves to die of boredom."

CHAPTER 22

The O'Reilly fortress

The O'Reilly fortress of Tullymongan was situated on a hill near a small hamlet called Cavan. East Breffney, or Breffney-O'Reilly as it was called, had been shired fourteen years earlier in 1584, and was now known sometimes as County Cavan. Miles O'Reilly was a fairly constant and genial companion, more host than jailer, and if it had not been for the fact that he was denied access to some places within the stronghold, the gallowglass would have had trouble reminding himself that he was not among his friends, the Maguires. O'Reilly and MacRory were frequently alone together and typically at such times O'Reilly regarded any other guard as unnecessary, whether he felt that it was out of the question that MacRory would attempt to overpower him, or whether, with an unconscious self-assurance, he felt that such an attempt would in any case be unsuccessful. MacRory noticed that at all other times two armed men were always close by. Later an incident occurred that forcibly brought home to him the fact that he was first and foremost a hostage.

O'Reilly was as eager as Maguire had been to utilise the expertise of the gallowglass in sword practice. O'Reilly and the gallowglass practiced often with the broadsword and after each practice session, MacRory was required to surrender his weapon to a man named MacGowan, O'Reilly's armourer. After one such session in the castle courtyard, MacRory handed his sword to MacGowan. At the same time a soldier came up to O'Reilly and spoke to him, then O'Reilly strode off with the man. After O'Reilly had gone, MacRory followed McGowan down several flights of stone stairs to a dungeon which served as the castle armoury. Here his sword was placed on a rack with a few hundred others. As a soldier, the gallowglass took an interest in the array of weapons in the armoury and MacGowan, the custodian of the armoury, was equally interested in showing a soldier the range of stored weapons.

The stout, stonewalled dungeon contained quite an arsenal. There were several hundred broadswords, a similar number of the heavier two handed claymores. Hundreds of halberds were stacked against one wall, and kegs of powder, muskets, and harquebuses against another. Several large casks contained musket balls. The walls were hung with helmets and cuirasses and horses' armour. There were four small cannons and one larger four-pounder in the room. MacGowan, in addition to serving as custodian of the armoury, also forged and repaired some of the weapons.

When O'Reilly and another man clattered down the stone steps, MacRory was examining a beautiful sword with an ornate guard, testing its perfect balance. O'Reilly walked over and removed the sword from his hand, and at the same time gestured with the other hand toward the stairs. In the courtyard above were several men, one of whom MacRory recognized as Owen MacCabe, the captain of the O'Reilly gallowglass. At a curt command from MacCabe, two of the men descended to the dungeon. When these two men returned leading MacGowan up into the courtyard and across to O'Reilly, who was in conversation with the leader of his gallowglass, MacRory became alarmed. The MacCabe captain and O'Reilly spent some moments in discussion, then a decision of some sort seemed to have been reached, and the McCabe captain turned and spoke briefly to MacGowan. When after some further minutes of conversation, McGowan was led over to the courtyard wall while another gallowglass, at a nod from the captain, primed his musket, MacRory's alarm increased

He hurried over to O'Reilly. "What goes on here?"

"He's to be shot," was O'Reilly's startling reply.

"Why? What has the man done?" And then with dawning understanding, "He cannot, any fault here was mine."

"It's a matter of discipline for my captain to decide. You yourself know of these things. The man is lucky he's not to be hanged." O'Reilly turned away to signify an end to the conversation.

The two men who had escorted MacGowan to the wall walked away, leaving him standing alone against the wall neither blindfolded nor restrained and apparently awaiting the last event of his life. He gazed back at his executioners, eyes wide in terror.

MacRory turned to the captain. "You must hear me. I take responsibility for entering the armoury and putting this man's life in danger. Neither he nor I knew of the consequences."

"He knew, or should have known," the captain replied shortly.

"He will not be shot for some minor lapse when the fault is mine," MacRory said, still addressing Owen McCabe, and then he turned in desperation to O'Reilly. "Where is the justice here? What of Brehon Law? How can – "

"This is a matter of military discipline. Please stand aside. You need not concern yourself in this. Your interference is inappropriate." O'Reilly's face was pale and his voice quivered with anger. He was not accustomed to discussion once a decision had been made.

MacRory looked from one to the other and when, at a word from the captain, the musketeer raised his weapon; he turned and rapidly strode over to the wall to stand facing the musket in front of MacGowan. The musketeer remained for a moment sighting along his musket, then not knowing what to do, turned his head toward the captain while keeping his musket to his shoulder. Three long strides and O'Reilly ripped the musket from the man's grasp and, shaking with rage, sighted quickly along the barrel and fired. The musket ball tore through the gallowglass' tunic and chips flew from the stone wall beside MacGowan's chest as the heavy, lead ball flattened itself against the stone. O'Reilly remained for a moment, sighting along the barrel, then lowering the musket, slowly exhaled his pent up breath.

"A brave act, gallowglass, and a rash one. My aim is usually better. I and my men decide matters here and will still decide whether this man is to live or die."

MacRory had come close to death before and was familiar with that dazed state of languor that now came over him and that occurs when the angel of death has whispered a warning but passed on. He vaguely heard the words "live or die" and thought that at least an option seemed to have crept into the situation and that MacGowan's chances were slightly more favourable than they had been a moment earlier. He also knew these chieftains respected and rewarded bravery, and he hoped that the sparing of MacGowan's life would reward his own rash act.

MacGowan lived, and surprisingly, was even reinstated as custodian of the armoury. Perhaps not so surprisingly, as surely no better guardian could have been found than one who had been taught so salutary a lesson.

In the following days, O'Reilly seemed to have forgotten the event in the courtyard and was as friendly and courteous as before.

The day following the incident O'Reilly again asked the gallowglass if he might consider accepting his sword back in return for the gallowglass' word that he would not attempt to escape. MacRory once more refused, and O'Reilly seemed saddened, but the offer was never again repeated. Only once afterward did O'Reilly make reference to the fact that he had attempted to kill MacRory.

O'Reilly and MacRory continued their almost daily sword practice. O'Reilly was a proficient swordsman, but few could match MacRory's expertise with either the lighter claybeg or the heavier, two-handed claymore. On one occasion practicing with the light dress swords, O'Reilly's guard was completely overwhelmed and he stood defenceless and at MacRory's mercy. The two stood, O'Reilly's sword parried aside and MacRory's at his opponent's throat.

O'Reilly looked along the sword to the eyes above it. "What are your thoughts, MacRory, with your sword at the throat of the man who would have put a musket ball through your heart? If a lunge now is to finish the life of Miles O'Reilly, let it be by the hand of a brave man such as yourself."

MacRory dropped his sword to his side and O'Reilly laughed. "Well, I see you won't accommodate me today. I had never before missed with a musket at that range. I wonder if something deflected my aim. I myself do not know the answer to that question, MacRory."

MacRory, the hostage, was treated as much as a member of the O'Reilly household as was O'Reilly's own family, and he came in frequent contact with them. His first introduction to Fiona O'Reilly, a spirited nineteen-year-old girl, who was Miles O'Reilly's sister, was an interesting one. MacRory and Miles O'Reilly walked by a wall, some six feet high and three feet wide and part of the outer fortifications of the stronghold, when they heard the thunder of hooves and an impatient shout.

"*Faugh an ballagh*"![1]

MacRory turned in time to see a young woman vigorously urging her horse at the wall. He barely had time to follow the example of O'Reilly and throw himself flat at the foot of the wall as

---

[1] (Irish) "Get out of the way"!

horse and rider soared over the wall and the prostrate forms beneath it. O'Reilly leaped to his feet, shouting *"amadhaun"*[1] after the retreating form of his sister. From beyond the wall, laughter and drumming hooves faded away across the field.

Fiona O'Reilly, with long dark hair and direct dark eyes that challenged any man to be her equal, would not have seemed out of place in Boadicea's[2] chariot, scourging the Romans, or striding through a palace courtyard in Grenada. When her wilful nature was thwarted, as when her horse refused some outrageously dangerous jump, she cursed with equal fluency in Irish, English, or Spanish.

MacRory ate in the hall with the large extended family and had the freedom of the castle, if freedom was the right word, considering the discrete but constant presence of his two armed guardians. He slept in a room in an upstairs tower above the main castle guardroom.

Two days after he had interposed his body between MacGowan and a musket ball, a young girl of about eighteen approached him and introduced herself shyly. "I'm Sheila MacGowan. MacGowan is my father, and I thank you from my heart. You saved his life."

MacRory had seen the girl before and, although never having been introduced to her, was certainly not unaware of her presence. She seemed to function in a capacity somewhere between companion and servant to Fiona O'Reilly. Her eyes did more than her words to convey a look of grateful thanks as they looked up at the gallowglass, who was happy to have risked his life. Her face blushed slightly as he reached out his hand. "Turlough MacRory, ma'am. I've seen you with Fiona O'Reilly."

"I'm her companion, but really I'm only a servant," she replied with simple honesty. A profusion of heavy dark-red hair cascaded over her shoulders and framed a startlingly beautiful face He saw she was shy in his presence and her wide green eyes gave her a look of frightened innocence that instantly invoked a protective urge in MacRory. The blush on her face heightened as he unconsciously remained holding her hand. He became aware that he

---

[1] "Reckless fool".
[2] Celtic queen in Britain.

still held her hand, then he too flushed with embarrassment and suddenly pulled his own away. As he did so, he became aware also that the hand he held was in some way deformed, and he had the awful thought that perhaps she might have misconstrued his sudden embarrassment.

That night he lay awake and thought of Sheila MacGowan.

"I'm only a servant." The daughter of a man who, like himself, was only a soldier. To reinforce a point of discipline and on not much more than his commander's whim, the soldier, who often risked his life for his master's glory, came close to losing that life, and the beautiful, innocent daughter, despite her relationship with Fiona O'Reilly, had come close to losing her father. MacRory himself as a captain had on occasion sent some of his men to their deaths. How many others had he killed in battle? Did these men leave behind daughters and children who grieved for them? In this male, warrior-oriented world when the sword unleashed its rivers of blood, what rivers of tears did the innocent shed?

Sept wars in Ireland had always left their share of bereaved. In the past, however, there had been long interludes of peace. For the last seven years, the country had known continuous war as Elizabeth's generals sought to bring Ireland to heel. The powerful monarchs in neighbouring England required their ever-growing power and glory be regularly watered with tears. The scale of slaughter and grief for the Irish had escalated. Half of England's army in Ireland was composed of Irish soldiers. While lessons of discipline were taught to individual soldiers, lessons designed to teach the Irish who was master were taught to the country.

He knew that England was not unique in this respect. Spain, France, and Portugal had discovered new fertile fields across the seas where a harvest of grief might be sown. What poisonous fruit might such a harvest yield? Dynasties were being built in the New World on the rotten edifice of slavery. Slavery indeed was as old as humanity, but a new pernicious and specious reasoning was now being used to justify the perfidious practise. Ignoring the countless millions of attributes that all humanity had in common, these men who would rule other men focussed on some inconsequential difference, such as skin pigment or facial features, as proof that these slaves were an inferior race and could never aspire to any higher function than to serve those ordained to rule them. Those possessed of the better weapons were evolving the concept of a master race with white skin and European features.

The gallowglass mused on the oft-heard concept of "glory." Who was more glorious? A belted earl in shining armour seated on a caparisoned war horse, leading a victorious army with proud banners fluttering, and defiling the land in his wake with the stench of rotting corpses, or a Columcille of Iona clad in rough-spun garments converting, by example alone, a people to a god of humility and peace? The red hand of war or the dove of peace! More heed had better be given to the latter, thought the gallowglass, as the former will lead us into mass graves.

Why can we so readily accept the concept of war and yet be appalled at the obscene atrocities that accompany war, when war itself is the obscenity, the periodic descent of man back into some depraved bestial abyss, the weapons of war – pikes and swords, muskets and cannon – designed by humans for the sole purpose of rending human flesh and extinguishing human life?

The sword and pike were still efficient killing weapons, but new and better firearms allowed their users to kill more people from a greater distance. The merest pressure of a finger on a trigger extinguished lives. Where would it end? Would better devices be perfected that would eliminate whole populations? The gallowglass wondered whether one day people would kill each other merely with a thought, and dozing off, reflected, that's how we kill each other now. It starts as a thought.

MacGowan approached MacRory and asked with some diffidence, "Sheila and my wife asked me to ask you if you would come to our house and meet our family."

MacRory was glad to know Sheila had been involved in the invitation and from MacGowan's wording of the invitation, he hoped she had perhaps initiated it. He readily accepted. Prior to leaving the fortress, however, MacRory told O'Reilly of the invitation and gave his word that he would make no escape attempt.

The single-roomed, mud-walled house in the hamlet of Cavan held a family of five and was similar to others used to house married soldiers. A curtain partitioned the living space from the sleeping quarters.

MacGowan himself was a squat, square man, fifty years of age, whose red hair was gathered and tied at the back, and in front fell over his forehead in the traditional gleebe. MacRory had earlier noticed that he had large callused hands and a powerful upper body that were no doubt the result of his occupation of blacksmith. Looking at the eyes which peered through this fringe of hair, the gallowglass had no doubt either as to where Sheila came by her green eyes. Sheila's two sisters, Eileen and Bridie, were twelve and fourteen. Her red-haired, little brother, Eamonn, gazed solemnly out on the world, also through green eyes.

MacGowan's wife, Kathleen Brady, a careworn woman from adjacent Leitrim, shook MacRory's hand and expressed her gratitude. "We owe you so much, and we have so little to offer."

The hospitality and generosity of the MacGowans was no less instinctive and genuine for being on a much humbler scale than that of the O'Reillys in the castle above. Sheila strove to overcome, and to help her parents do likewise, the initial awkwardness inevitable in hosting their guest. MacRory, although a soldier like MacGowan, was far above MacGowan in station. Their guest was not only a captain of gallowglass, but also the friend of O'Donnell and Maguire, and indeed, despite the event that had come close to ending MacGowan's and his own life, the friend of O'Reilly.

At dinner the two younger girls, hair neatly braided and tied with a bow at the back, sat looking down at the rough, well-scrubbed table except for occasional inquisitive, sidelong looks from doe eyes. Soon MacRory and MacGowan had slipped into a relaxed discussion as they had many common interests and gradually the tension eased. The two younger girls, shy but conscious of what good manners dictated, bravely attempted to relay each other in speaking with MacRory. Presently they found it was not such an unpleasant duty and by the end of the meal, each had to wait impatiently for the other to finish before engaging the gallowglass in conversation. MacRory found the younger girls charming but not as devastatingly so as their older sister.

Sheila and her mother served the meal and Sheila, now more relaxed, spoke to the gallowglass whenever her two younger sisters left her an opening to do so. MacRory noticed her right hand was held cupped with the thumb flexed across the palm, and that this deformity made it difficult for her to grip objects.

Seven-year-old Eamonn had to vacate his place at the table and sat on a small stool by himself and ate his portion from a plate balanced on his knees. The small boy intently observed the family's guest and patiently waited for a lull in the conversation. At last his chance came and he informed the gallowglass,

"My sister says you're a brave man. I'm learning to be a *gowhan*[1] like my father. I work the bellows. If O'Reilly had killed my father, I'd be the only one to work the forge and support our family"

"And a great help you are, too, Eamonn," his father smiled. "What would I do without you? But you mustn't forget your sisters. Everyone helps out." He turned to the gallowglass. "Sheila wasn't even Eamonn's age when she used to come to me to help out in the forge."

MacGowan's weathered face softened as he looked toward his eldest daughter. "From the day she could walk, it was her nature to be trying to help. She was leading a horse through the half-door of the forge when the horse reared, and her hand, still holding the reins, got jammed between the door and the frame. She was left with a deformed hand, but all I can say is thank God her arm wasn't pulled out of its socket."

The gallowglass, looking at Sheila, saw only perfection, but he noticed she unconsciously tended to keep her right hand hidden from sight whenever possible.

Sitting in their small home, he sensed the love and closeness that existed among the MacGowans and sensed too in all of them, even in the adults, an aching innocence. He was appalled to think of the sorrow and devastation that might have visited this happy family, and glad to have been the instrument that averted it.

MacGowan was speaking and MacRory inclined his head politely to the father while at the same time taking advantage of the opportunity to observe the pleasing figure of the daughter.

"Even the common people like us are now learning some English. Eileen and Bridie speak only Irish, but Sheila speaks a little English. I myself have picked up a little, but could not carry on a conversation in the language."

---

[1] Blacksmith.

"I learned the language at Sheephaven and speak it occasionally, but am more at ease in Irish," MacRory replied, then glancing at Sheila, "Do you find it a difficult language?"

"I do indeed," she said, " but scarcely speak enough of it as yet to even know whether it's a difficult language or not. A Spaniard speaks it with Fiona O'Reilly and I pick up bits and pieces. It's difficult to pick up English from a Spaniard. I'm sure it would be easier for an Irish person to have it taught through Irish."

MacRory willingly took the bait. "I'd be glad to teach you," then feeling that he had sounded as overeager as he had felt, "I have little else to do here."

He wished he had omitted the last sentence, which made it look as if he would perform the onerous task only to relieve his own boredom. He hoped he had not offended. He was glad at least that he was not under the sardonic eyes of Hugh Maguire.

"It would be a pleasure," he finished lamely.

The tutor and his pupil spent long, arduous hours in study. Sheila worked hard at pleasing her tutor and mastering the new language. English was not the gallowglass's native tongue either, and his literal translation of Irish to English meant Sheila's English was liberally sprinkled with Irish idiom.

"Have you eaten?" translated as "Would you be after eating?" "It's a fine day" became "It's a fine day that's in it." Sheila's pronunciation had a guttural, strangely exotic quality that MacRory found pleasing, and indeed he found all things about her pleasing. He wondered if being the oldest of the McGowan children had made her unselfish by nature. She seemed to feel her role in life was to help others and, seeing good in everyone, she brought out what was good in everyone. He knew her life could not have been free of hardship, nor could she have been totally shielded from the brutality of military garrison life, yet she still looked on life with the joyful innocence of a child. To her smitten tutor, she was the unexpected and glorious enchantment of a beloved melody that resonated in the soul, more beautiful with each repetition. Commendably neither teacher nor pupil volunteered to shorten the study sessions. As time went on they spent long, ardent hours with little thought of study. MacRory, who earlier had spent much time devising plans for escape, now gave little thought to anything other than Sheila

McGowan. On occasion he felt a vague guilt that he was not considering some means of escape. When they were together, however, his guilt melted away in the flame of love.

They frequently reverted to speaking in Irish, the language in which they best expressed their love for each other. MacRory, with increasing frequency, gave his parole to O'Reilly and wandered with Sheila around the hamlet of Cavan and the surrounding countryside. On his repeated visits to the McGowan household, Sheila had to compete with her two sisters for his attention, and she suspected her sister Bridie at fourteen was also secretly in love with him.

Fiona O'Reilly aided the couple by making few demands on her servant's time. Fiona, a healthy and spirited young woman, knew something of these matters of the heart as she herself fell in love on an average of once every few months. This attrition rate should have daunted the most ardent suitor, but a steady stream of lovesick young men was always on hand vying for her attention. Her current suitor was a young man named Brian Dillon, scion of a neighbouring Anglo-Irish family. Since becoming smitten, he had discovered in himself a gift for poetry and spent much time agonizing over the just correct words to describe Fiona's dark eyes and dark hair. He was as yet unaware of the fact, but he was soon to go the way of the others. Fiona was no less susceptible to poetic blandishments than any other nineteen year old girl, but she liked her poets to also be men of action. Besides, his affectionate shortening of her name to "Fi" was becoming an irritation to her.

One poem, in his opinion his best, but to be delivered to his love only after his death in battle, ended with:

> *I will see your face in heaven,*
> *I cannot speak the words Good Bye.*
> *But forever and forever,*
> *May God be with you, Fi.*

He was proud of his effort and it required only his death to have Fi's tears stain the page.

Sheila initially learned some English, and some of what she learned got them both in trouble. MacRory had taught her an English expression which he informed her was a slang form of greeting and was the expression of the day. She delighted in greeting him with her new English expression. He, in turn, delighted in hearing it, but she was occasionally somewhat puzzled by his reaction to the greeting. A simple greeting should not make someone react as if they might choke with suppressed laughter? Perhaps it was her accent. Once when she was summoned to Fiona's presence, she decided to try the greeting on Brian Dillon. "Would you like a roll in the hay?"

The wide, innocent eyes looked into the startled face of Fiona's suitor. Fiona O'Reilly, who was proficient in English and proficient enough in English idiom, looked at her servant/companion with a new interest.

"MacRory is teaching me English." Sheila now reverted to Irish and felt that some form of explanation was necessary, as the greeting had not been met with the expected response.

"Indeed."

Fiona O'Reilly's tone and look told Sheila that something was wrong.

"It's a common form of greeting," Sheila plaintively explained.

"That it may well be among some," was the cool response, "but usually in polite society some small talk over a glass of wine takes place first." Fiona cast a sidelong glance at the still bewildered Brian Dillon, and now there was the hint of a smile at the corners of her mouth. "Even someone with the earthy passions of a poet might pause long enough to dash off a quick sonnet first. Would you not agree, Brian Dillon?"

Then she too responded somewhat as MacRory had done, but ending with a gale of unsuppressed laughter. She took Sheila aside and explained as delicately as possible the expression.

"Excuse me, ma'am." Crimson-faced, Sheila MacGowan hastened from the room, unable to look at Brian Dillon in passing, and went in search of MacRory.

MacRory defended himself with much desperation and little skill. "Ah, *asthore*,[1] I never meant you to greet anyone else with the expression. It was just something between you and me and – "

"Something between you and me? And every time I greeted you! Oh how humiliating! It wasn't a greeting at all. I will never

---

[1] (Irish) "Darling".

again trust a thing you tell me. Oh you reprobate, you ... you ... you villain! Dear God, what will Brian Dillon think of me? Oh, that was cruel!" She burst out crying.

A contrite MacRory embraced her. "Fiona O'Reilly will explain to Dillon and I will also. I'm so sorry. It was only a joke and I'd have told you later."

She sobbed on and he held her more tightly, becoming alarmed as the sobs took on a hysterical note. What was happening, was she crying or laughing? She was doing both, but finally mostly laughing uncontrollably into his chest as he held her.

"You should have seen Brian Dillon's face," she gasped, convulsed with laughter. "You will have to explain to him, though. You will, won't you? And soon? How can I ever look him in the face again? Fiona O'Reilly said some small talk and wine should ..." Again she went into convulsive laughter.

She wiped tears from her face and looked up at him. "I'll never, ever forgive you."

He kissed her tear stained face and was forgiven a thousand times.

The day after MacRory told Miles O'Reilly that he and Sheila MacGowan intended to be married, O'Reilly came up to him carrying a sword in his left hand.

"You're no longer a prisoner. O'Donnell is camped in the Curlews and you may rejoin him there. Consider this sword a wedding present from your former jailer."

MacRory looked at the beautiful Toledo blade with intricately woven guard. It had a silver boss inlaid with an ivory five pointed star within the horns of a crescent. It was the same sword he had earlier admired in the castle armoury.

"An ancestor brought it back from Spain. The star and crescent on the boss is a Moorish emblem."

O'Reilly spoke casually but MacRory had no doubt as to the value of this family heirloom.

This was the armoured man with sword raised to deliver the deathblow, who had stayed his hand and instead delivered a salute. This was the jailer who had sent a musket ball speeding at the chest of his hostage. This was the man who was now offering that hostage a beautiful Toledo blade, and his freedom.

A month later he and Sheila married at a Franciscan abbey restored after it had been burned down twenty years earlier.

Following their wedding MacRory was free to go wherever he wished and he took his wife to the Claddagh Glen. They wandered the woods of the glen, the flatlands below and the moors above. No destination guided their footsteps. The late summer sun brought warmth to the body and joy to the soul. At night they lay in their cloaks on a bed of pine boughs with the leafy canopy above for a roof. They followed the paths of the stars in the sky, those thousands of eyes, forever remote, peering down from the heavens. The night wind that blew down the valley brought the fragrance of heather and gorse from the uplands. In their nest in the bracken they were lulled to sleep by the voice of the nearby stream murmuring its ageless refrain. The animals they encountered seemed strangely tame and unfearful, perhaps because of a lack of acquaintance with man. Once, a fox emerged from a mossy bank and on parting some ferns they found a den with three small cubs. Three pairs of unblinking, unafraid eyes stared back. The mother remained quite close by nervously licking her snout. One morning Sheila awoke to a gentle nudge and a "don't move" A doe stood looking down on them with a male fawn a few months old by her side. It was now the turn of the humans to be the object of curiosity. "Look, son, what I've found in our glen!"

MacRory had spent many a night under the stars, but in this still valley no sentry stood guard, no sword hilt lay within easy reach of his hand, no vigilant breath held awareness of each sound in the night. In captivity he had found freedom, happiness, and peace. But he knew that peace was an illusion. The hoot of the owl and the call of the wolf in the darkness were reminders that here too the hunter and hunted were partnered in the age old dance of death. How long before the human predator, earlier sated with blood in Munster and now prowling the borders of Ulster, brought the stillness of death to this wild and beautiful place that now knew the stillness of peace!

MacRory gave little thought to his former life and now merely wished for the freedom to be able to flee from the unending violence to some peaceful spot with his wife, but where was there peace anywhere in Ireland?

Red Hugh and Maguire had carried the war to the English far south in Connacht around Galway. O'Neill threatened the Pale, the only safe English enclave in Ireland, and Elizabeth had sent her new favourite, Robert Devereux, the Second Earl of Essex, with a massive army to Ireland. Devereux was the son of the First Earl of Essex, of Rathlin Island fame.

MacRory and his wife lived their brief idyll of peace, but the war that raged around them in this last year of the sixteenth century spread to all of the country and was reaching a climax. The war surged on with its own momentum, and they were mere flotsam tossed on a turbulent ocean with no will of their own.

CHAPTER 23

Battle of the Curlews

The gallowglass rode alone, passing along the southern shore of Lough Oughter. A year had passed since he had ridden reluctantly along this shore toward Tullymongan as O'Reilly's captive. Now with even more reluctance, he left Cavan and his wife behind and rode to join Red Hugh at Sligo. He reflected on how the powerful emotion of love always seemed to result in momentous changes in one's life: Love of man for a woman, love of family, the strange love, deep in the soul, for the familiar earth of the homeland, the love of power and fame. The emotion of love itself that was so easily perverted to the equally powerful emotion of hatred.

He looked across to an island crannog reflected in the smooth waters of the lake. The stronghold was similar to many such scattered throughout Ireland, a fortified structure on either a natural or man-made island which was easily defended. In some instances a submerged causeway followed an erratic course, connecting the crannog to the mainland, making any enemy approach difficult. O'Neill had torn down his Dungannon fortress and distributed its contents among more easily defended crannogs scattered throughout Tyrone. A crannog on this site in Lough Oughter had been the original O'Reilly stronghold until they moved to their present site at Tullymongan some centuries ago. The O'Reillys usually allied themselves with the English and in the present war had come under attack from O'Neill and Maguire. MacRory wondered how O'Reilly would fare at the hands of O'Neill, O'Donnell, and Maguire should these northern chieftains be successful, but then he reflected that these were all practical men and that allegiances were constantly shifting. The O'Reillys would survive as they had for centuries. The gallowglass, remembering O'Reilly's words, hoped the man's usually accurate estimate of events was in this case also accurate.

"It will soon be settled in some decisive battle. Whoever wins, we O'Reillys have always survived. Indeed we are considering throwing in our lot with O'Neill and Red Hugh as have so many others and you may say as much to O'Donnell. If you must join your friends, Sheila is as safe with the O'Reillys as anywhere in Ireland."

He was probably right. Certainly MacRory's friendship with Maguire and O'Donnell guaranteed her safety if these chieftains won, and O'Reilly's friendship with the English would be useful if they did not.

MacRory had learned something of the O'Reilly history while in Tullymongan, and they were indeed survivors. They had been overlords of East Breffney ever since the late twelfth century when they sided with the Norman knight, Hugh De Lacy, against their traditional enemy to the west, the O'Rourkes. They had protected their lands by war when necessary and by guile when possible.

Riding west toward Sligo, the gallowglass crossed the headwaters of two of Ireland's rivers. He crossed the Erne as it flowed between Lough Gowna and Lough Oughter. The Erne had its source in Lough Gowna and from there flowed north through Lough Oughter, then northwest as Upper Lough Erne before curving to the west as Lower Lough Erne and disgorging the waters of all four loughs into the Atlantic below Ballyshannon.

Continuing on to the west, some four hours later he crossed the Shannon as it issued from Lough Allen. The Shannon flowed south from its source in the Cuilcagh Mountains above Lough Allen. Here, where he crossed the river close to its source, the Shannon was still a small stream and gave no promise of the mighty river that, draining Ireland's heartland, entered the Atlantic at Limerick.

Before reaching Lough Allen his attention was drawn to two rounded hills off to his right, Sheemore and Sheebeg, each surmounted by a rath[1]. There were many of these hilltop fortifications in Ireland, standing as mute testimony to the work of some long-forgotten people. For the people who built these raths to have been forgotten in Ireland, they must have been lived long ago indeed thought the gallowglass.

---

[1] Circular earthen fortification.

O'Donnell had returned from his foray into southern Connacht to lay siege to a small but well-defended castle at Collooney a few miles south of Sligo, and was intent on winkling out the O'Connor occupant. Conyers Clifford, the new English Governor of Connacht, hurried supplies by sea from Galway to Sligo to raise the siege, while he himself led an army north to face O'Donnell. The castle at Collooney was no longer of any great strategic importance, but it was one of the last to hold out against O'Donnell in North Connacht, and he was as determined to take it as Clifford was to prevent him from doing so.

It was late in the evening before the gallowglass reached Collooney, where to his delight Eoghan MacSweeney greeted him and accompanied him to where O'Donnell camped with his main army at Dunavaragh in the Curlew Mountains some miles away. Darkness was falling by the time they reached the encampment and made their way to a tent flying a banner that depicted a right hand clasping a red cross.

If there was truth in the legend that St. Columcille had given this emblem to the O'Donnells, then the banner of the O'Donnells had borne the red cross for over a thousand years.

Without any introduction, MacSweeney pulled aside the opening to O'Donnell's tent. "See who has deigned to visit us, Hugh! While you and I were living in tents in the hills campaigning against Clifford, our comrade here was romancing the enemy in Cavan."

O'Donnell leaped to his feet. "Turlough! You have come back to us." He reached for both his friend's hands and held them in his. "How long is it since we parted? Close to a year, it must be. That battle seems like such a long, long time ago now. Thank God you have recovered. The Maguires kept me informed. And now you have a wife! You were not idle in captivity!"

"He's a sly dog, Hugh. He's lucky he didn't set his cap for the fiery Fiona. You'll learn, though, my brave gallowglass, that sword's play is child's play compared to defending yourself against a woman, any woman." MacSweeney gave the gallowglass a friendly slap on the back that would have sent a lesser man reeling.

MacRory had already learned there was wisdom in MacSweeney's statement, for shortly after their marriage he had replied honestly to Sheila's apparently innocent query, "Did you love Maeve O'Rourke?" He was now aware that while honesty is essential between a man and the wife he loves, there are some thoughts better not voiced.

Red Hugh released his friend's hands, but stood gazing on him. "Ireland is your home now, Turlough, and indeed you have fought as hard as any of us for it. When this is over, Maguire and I have decided you will be *Erenagh*[1] of lands in either Fermanagh or Donegal. However, if in the end we lose – but I do not think we will – we have lost everything. The English will take to themselves the church lands as they have already done in many areas."

"I cannot find the words, O'Donnell. I do not deserve this truly generous offer." MacRory was astounded at his friend's generosity, as he had been at O'Reilly's.

Generosity and selflessness was as much a part of the nature of these men as was pride and ruthlessness. He knew the value of the gift bestowed. An Erenagh administered the often extensive lands throughout the territories of the chieftains, lands which had been donated to the church. It was not only a gift to himself but to his posterity, for an Erenagh was a hereditary position.

"But will it ever be over? Will we ever again live in peace? I long to live in peace, to live simply and in peace with my wife and, if God grants it, my children."

Red Hugh looked at his friend for moments without replying, forming his thoughts.

"We all long for peace, Turlough. This war has devastated our country, and I myself have caused some of that devastation. This country is ours and has been the country of our fathers and our forefathers' fathers stretching back in time. We have not brought armies to England to devastate their land, to spread famine, and to subject their people to our ways and laws. I grant you we Irish have had our own history of bloody sept warfare, but we have never waged war on a scale such as this. We have never used famine to cause death on such a scale. The English tell us our ways are savage and our laws unjust. Have they really come here to civilize us and to bring us a new and better justice? I do not profess to be a seer, Turlough, but from what I have seen of these English, if they rule Ireland, I do not foresee more justice.

---

[1] (Irish) A hereditary office managing church lands.

"When a captive in Dublin Castle I was introduced to their justice. They cloak their designs in lofty motives while they dominate our people from our own castles. Base and shameful motives can be transformed into honourable and lofty ideals on the tongues of eloquent liars. Having to endure their hypocrisy is more galling than dealing with their armies. Our Brehon Law has more justice than their English law and long preceded it. Our sept system is better suited to our people than their feudal rule. I grant indeed that their feudal system is efficient for war, and for war and conquest it was evolved. The sept however functions for the good of all of its people. They elect the chieftain and he rules with the permission of the members of that sept and for the welfare of the sept.

"Do you think that their queen, having dug into her purse, sends these English to Ireland to improve the lot of our people? Elizabeth sits in pomp and finery at the centre of her web of power, delicate white hands steeped in Irish blood. Their poets are stirred to write paeans of praise to their virgin queen, but would they be so eloquent in praise of the woman were she not queen and in a position to grant favours and patronage? Where are the verses to the careworn face and callused hands of a selfless mother struggling to protect her family from the privations and horrors that their great queen inflicts daily on the women of our country? When the English poet, Spencer, sat at his ease in his Irish castle at Kilcolman[1], was he struggling to find the right words to evoke raging indignation for the humiliations imposed hourly on the women of our land by that noble and just queen of his land? This is the man who speaks so volubly of the barbarism of the Irish, yet is silent when his patron, Lord Grey, aided by another poet, Walter Raleigh, hangs Irish women from a gallows at Smerwick."

MacSweeney interrupted.

"No, Hugh, Spencer was not silent regarding Lord Grey's work at Smerwick. The poet was Grey's secretary at the time, and he wrote condoning his master's actions, bemoaning the fact that, 'the noble Lord was blamed, the wretched people pitied'. What a

---

[1] Spencer's Irish castle, burned down in the general rebellion that followed O'Neill's victory at the Yellow Ford; Spencer's young child died in the flames.

mockery to refer to such a beast as 'noble'! Perhaps the 'noble lord' was avenging himself on Irish women for his defeat by Fiach MacHugh in Glenmalure, when he fled back to the safety of the Pale leaving eight hundred of his men behind him."

Red Hugh, who paced the tent, now stopped and stood in front of MacSweeney nodding his head.

"Indeed what a mockery! And a poet as ignoble as his patron! Should a poet not have compassion? Should a poet not be a voice for truth? A poet without compassion is a harp without chords, a cock crowing on a dunghill, a voice as meaningful as the babbling of a fool. And what voice speaks the truth that must first weigh the cost? Are we to them creatures so far removed from humanity's form as to be beyond the pale of pity? Would truth be wasted on such worthless beings as us? Do these English think of their own mothers, sisters, and children when they subject ours to such degradation and horror? Are our women, our children, and our people so much less than theirs?"

The young chieftain resumed his pacing.

"They revile our faith, the faith of their own fathers. They slaughter our priests and desecrate our churches. Their contempt for us and for our culture is such that they regard us as less than human and so can assuage their consciences for their deeds. Our cultures will never merge, for their arrogance will never conquer our pride. We, too, will always hold them in contempt, judging them, not by their words, but by their deeds and by their values.

"We cannot have peace, Turlough, as peace is not their aim. Their aim is to destroy us, to destroy our way of life, and to rule our land. I know these English of Elizabeth from my time of captivity in Dublin. Their veneer of civilization is polished but thin. The pirate and the barbarian lurk not far beneath. They have come to take our land and to rule our lives and while we may have contempt for the values of such men we must not underestimate their capabilities."

"Yet some you admire", again MacSweeney interrupted, "I have heard you speak well of Clifford, the new Governor of Connacht."

"This Clifford, whom we will soon meet in battle, is a true nobleman. He serves his country according to his conscience and to the best of his ability, and in doing so does nothing to dishonour his name. Docwra at Derry is also such a man. But the Binghams, the

Raleighs, and the Drakes are low marauders, men without honour, and it is men such as these, who seek to make their fortunes in Ireland. Others like Walter Devereux, the First Earl of Essex, although high born, by their actions dishonour their names and indeed dishonour the name of all humanity Elizabeth praises and rewards Walter Raleigh and Francis Drake for their atrocities in suppressing the Desmond rebellion. Twenty years later Munster is still a desert. The memory of the raw savagery these noble men unleashed on the land is still branded on the memory of what's left of its people. From his grateful English queen, Raleigh is given twenty thousand hectares of Irish land, and Drake money to outfit his pirate and slaving ships. From such men and from such a monarch we can expect no mercy. The only peace they'll allow us will be the peace of the grave.

"What will future generations think of us if, for peace now, we bequeath them a legacy of slavery? And make no mistake, slaves we would be, and slaves to merciless masters. Will some future O'Donnell, knowing that his people once ruled this land, bow like a slave to the people who took it from him? Such peace is for cattle. I do not intend to be the O'Donnell who settled for such peace."

"But the common people bear the brunt of the hardship," the gallowglass said when O'Donnell paused. "People like my wife's family, who have little to gain either way."

"You are wrong." O'Donnell's voice resonated with vehemence. "They may seem to have little to gain, but they have surely much to lose. They lose their freedom. You will hear that no matter who wins the common man will always lose, but this need not be so. The Irish fight on both sides and so suffer in both defeat and victory. The English have perfected the "divide and conquer" concept. If we continue to allow ourselves to be divided, we deserve to be conquered. If our Irish chieftains are not willing to give up some of their freedom to unite under a strong leader, they will lose all of their freedom. O'Rourke is less than pleased to be my sub-chieftain in Connacht, even though he himself cannot protect his territory.

"Elizabeth's soldiers are loyal to their queen. The loyalty of these ruthless men may be self-serving, but loyal they are, and land grants, carved from the birthright of our people, reward their loyalty.

"Our victory at the Yellow Ford brought many of the chieftains to our side. They at last show a willingness to suffer some loss of personal freedom in a common cause. Believe me, the common people, and all of us if the English win this struggle, will be made to know what it is to be a conquered people."

O'Donnell's army waited for two weeks in the Curlews. Each morning, Red Hugh rose early and attended Mass. He prayed each day at noon and ended each day in prayer. When, during his captivity in Dublin, his captors had mocked his faith and attempted to induce their young captive to renounce his beliefs, Red Hugh had only become more strengthened in his faith.

The gallowglass, as before, was his constant companion as O'Donnell supervised his captains in the training and readying of the men for the coming encounter. No detail was so insignificant as to be beneath his notice. Niall Garve, commanding the troops investing O'Connor/Sligo's castle, chafed under Red Hugh's frequent interventions.

Only a small part of Red Hugh's army besieged Collooney Castle; the bulk of the army was encamped some miles away in the Curlew Mountains.

MacRory was in temporary command of the mountaintop camp when Niall Garve rode in accompanied by his brother, Con O'Donnell. Red Hugh and MacSweeney had left earlier to confer for a few days with the McDermot chieftain below. Niall Garve dismounted and accompanied by his brother strode over to Red Hugh's empty tent. MacRory was summoned to report to Niall Garve. As he entered the tent Niall Garve was speaking to his brother.

"... Of course the casualties could be enormous with a frontal assault, but what of that if it can be done, and it can, it can be done. By tomorrow the castle could be ours."

Niall Garve looked up and coldly addressed MacRory who was standing uncertainly inside the entrance to the tent.

"I have a job for you, gallowglass. You are now under my command. You and your men will accompany me back to Colloony."

MacRory looked from Niall Garve to his brother and spoke with unease.

"To Colloony? For what reason? Is this by O'Donnell's order?"

Niall Garve looked at his brother and laughed.

"Yes, gallowglass. Consider it an O'Donnell order. As to why, that is no concern of your's."

MacRory, by now was beginning to suspect that his men's lives were to be squandered in front of Colloony castle so that Neill Garve and not Red Hugh could take the credit for capturing the castle. The gallowglass valued his men's lives as much as had his uncle. He walked over and placing both hands on the table stared down at Niall Garve O'Donnell.

"My question was, is this by the order of Red Hugh O'Donnell, the chieftain of the O'Donnells?"

He was well aware of Niall Garve's aspirations to be chieftain and his choice of words was no accident, for he had neither liking nor respect for this man whom he regarded as Red Hugh's enemy rather than his ally. He was also aware of what a dangerous opponent the man before him could be.

"You have your orders and they come from me. Do you question those orders?

"I do. O'Donnell's orders were that I remain here."

Niall Garve leaped to his feet his face paling with anger. He had difficulty controlling his voice.

"Both your words and your manner are insolent. Despite your position you are still a mercenary. Remember to whom you speak. Do you defy me gallowglass? You and your men will do as I order."

"Neither I nor my men will do as you order, and if my words and my manner are insolent it is not by accident."

Niall Garve drew his sword, and MacRory who was unarmed stared back at him across the table.

Con O'Donnell rose to his feet.

"I assume gallowglass that we all fight on the same side here. You will do as my brother commands."

MacRory kept his eyes on Niall Garve as he replied.

"Your brother's assumption as to where his allegiance lies from day to day is his own affair. My allegiance is to Red Hugh O'Donnell. I take orders from him and from no other man"

Blood was flowing back into Niall Garve's face giving it a mottled appearance.

"Arm yourself."

Con O'Donnell knowing that his brother's intemperate nature was about to result in his death put a hand on his arm and spoke quietly.

"Sheath your sword. We will not prevail here."

Niall Garve stared at MacRory with manifest hatred as he slowly returned his sword to its sheath.

"Another time, gallowglass. Another time."

MacRory turned abruptly and walked from the tent. Aware of the tension between the two chieftains, he thought it best to make no reference to the incident on Red Hugh's return.

"Clifford will be lured north to raise the siege of Collooney Castle. O'Connor, in the castle down there, is the bait. I plan to wait for the English here at Dunavaragh in the Curlews. O'Rourke declines to place his men under my command, but he and MacDermott are across their path below. O'Rourke fights on our side. Although he resents my intrusion into his territory, he resents that of the English more. The English have sent a fleet from Galway to Sligo and their ships are presently lying off Erris Head. Theobald na Long[1], the son of Grace O'Malley and Richard Burke, commands the ships from Galway, and as soon as he has word that Clifford is on the march, Theobald na Long will sail into Sligo. You will of course, Turlough, remember Grace O'Malley, the pirate queen of Connacht? She is not someone easily forgotten! You met her years ago at Donegal castle when she sailed into Donegal Bay with a proposition for my father. My family frequently shipped fish to France and sometimes even Spain. Grace O'Malley mentioned to him that pirates from the Barbary Coast were plying their trade out into the Atlantic on occasion and offered to protect my father's shipping trade from these pirates - for a price.

My father, a practical man, who had heard stories of ships being intercepted by "Barbary Pirates" who spoke Irish with a Mayo accent, felt it better to receive the Pirate Queen with all due hospitality – and to agree to her price.

She married two of the greatest chieftains in the west. Her first husband, Donal O'Flaherty, whom she married when she was fifteen, was killed, and Sir Richard Burke, heir to the Macwilliam

---

[1] ("Theobald) of the ships".

title, was her second husband. To gain complete control of Clew Bay she needed control of Rockfleet Castle, which was one of those in the hands of Sir Richard 'Iron' Burke. He was so called because he was usually clad in armour, always being at war with someone. The story is told that she went to the castle and knocked on Sir Richard's door and suggested they get married according to the old Irish custom, 'for a year, for certain.'

"You know the custom, in Brehon Law, Turlough, whereby either partner after a year can dissolve the marriage by dismissing the other. It seems she was as persuasive as she was beautiful, for she and her entourage moved in. A year later, Sir Richard, returning from a foray, was greeted with locked gates and a cry from the battlements. 'I dismiss you.' Despite this unpromising anniversary greeting, they remained together until Richard Burke's death about fifteen years ago, and their son, Theobold na Long, is legitimate heir to all the vast Clanwilliam lands in Connacht. He is said to have been born in the midst of a sea battle. At the height of her fame, the pirate queen commanded six castles in Connacht and had a fleet of twenty ships, many of them well armed, three-masted caravels.

"Between husbands she fell in love with a Norman named Hugh de Lacy, whom she rescued from a shipwreck. The MacMahons later murdered De Lacy. Grace O'Malley stormed the MacMahon castle at Doorna in Blacksod Bay and personally slew her lover's murderer. After this she was often known as the 'Dark lady of Doorna'."

"I've never heard of her by that name," MacRory remarked, "but I do know how she became known as 'Granuaile.' As a young girl she was forbidden to go to sea aboard her father's ships, so she cropped her long hair and stole aboard as a boy. Her brothers teasingly called her, 'Gráinne Maoile Ni Maille'."[1]

"Aye, that's possible. The sea would have been in her blood. The O'Malleys have been seafaring people for as long as the sea has been salt. From her base on Clare Island at the entrance to Clew Bay her ships trade with France and Spain and have fought sea battles with the English. Twice the English captured her and she once narrowly escaped the gallows Bingham had prepared for her.

---

[1] (Irish) "Bald Grace O'Malley".

Bingham curses her as 'The nurse of all rebellions in Connacht for the last forty years.'

"When she was denied trade with Galway, her ships patrolled the waters off the town and exacted tribute from any who traded with the port. Six years ago when Bingham imprisoned her brother and her son Theobold, Granuaile sailed to England and announced herself at the English court. She demanded – and secured – their release from the English queen. For good measure while there, she also attempted to discredit Bingham with his queen. On her way back from England, she stopped to visit Lord Howth at his castle outside Dublin, but Lord Howth was reluctant to entertain the controversial pirate queen and kept his castle gates barred. His son, however, happened to be on the wrong side of the castle gate and to rebuke the Lord for his lack of manners, she sailed back to Connacht holding his son a hostage.

The terms for the release of Lord Howth's son were that the gates of Howth Castle must always remain open and there must always be an extra place setting at the dining table in the event that Grace O'Malley should ever pass that way again!"

"Not someone to snub," the gallowglass observed.

"A formidable lady," O'Donnell agreed. "Some years ago six hundred Scots innocently sailed into Clew Bay in search of plunder. It was a case of the cat biting the tail of the tiger. 'Righteous indignation' does not begin to describe Granuaile's reaction to the effrontery of these Scottish thieves in attempting to violate the Holy Grail of Irish thieves. The decimated Scots hastened back to Scotland scorched by shrill Gaelic invective and the wrath of the O'Malleys. The stories these Scots told, themselves not noted for timidity, only added to the legend of Grace O'Malley. It's quite likely that Granuaile, the pirate queen of Connacht, will one day stand in legend beside Maeve, the warrior queen of Connacht."

"I have certainly heard of some of her exploits, who hasn't? But I have heard little of her of late. Is Granuaile still living?"

"She still lives but she no longer goes to sea. Bingham has greatly curtailed her freedom. Bingham's iron rule has finally shackled the spirit of Connacht, and Theobold na Long, brave son of a brave mother, now fights for the English and holds title to all the Burke lands in Connacht. Apart from the castles and lands he controls, any man in whose veins flows the blood of Richard "Iron" Burke and Grace O'Malley is a man to be reckoned with."

Red Hugh rested his hand on his sword hilt. "I plan to unshackle the spirit of Connacht."

Early on the morning of August 15, a hoblilar scout galloped up and saluted Red Hugh. "Lord O'Donnell, Clifford marched from Boyle last night and approaches from the south."

O'Donnell's men, well prepared and practiced for the encounter, had little now to do but await the vanguard of Clifford's army. An hour passed and the sounds of a distant battle alarmed O'Donnell, who feared O'Rourke and MacDermott had engaged the approaching enemy prematurely. O'Donnell turned to MacRory. "Take half the men. Leave the rest here under MacSweeney. Assist O'Rourke or MacDermott as you see fit, wherever you are needed."

Throughout the day scouts galloped up and down the mountain to keep O'Donnell informed about the approaching enemy. A scout reined his horse in front of Red Hugh. "Lord O'Donnell, Clifford tries to rally his men. Some are fleeing back towards Boyle."

From below distant cheers drifted up to O'Donnell and his men, guarding the pass, then the sounds of battle receded. An hour later Brian Óg O'Rourke, bloodied from his wounds and from the grisly trophy which he carried, rode up and tossed the head of Conyers Clifford at O'Donnell's feet.

A lone horseman galloped up to Collooney Castle and dismounted. In front of the castle he stuck a stake in the ground. Impaled on top of the stake was the head of Sir Conyers Clifford. The horseman remounted and sat for some time looking up at the castle before reining his horse around and galloping away. O'Connor Sligo recognized the head as that of the Governor of Connacht. He surrendered his castle to O'Donnell.

Red Hugh ordered the body of the governor to be buried with all due honours in holy ground at Trinity Island in Lough Key and sent a message in Latin to Richard Bingham, offering to send him the head for burial, but the offer was refused. Clifford had last been seen in the battle furiously lashing about him with his sword, attempting to stop his fleeing men. He was reputed to have killed several of them as he raged at their cowardice. As he wheeled his horse and galloped into the enemy he had been heard to cry, "I shall not outlive the dishonour of this day."

Later he met Brian O'Rourke on the battlefield.

CHAPTER 24

The Orange and the Green

Staunch Protestants and devout Roman Catholics – the adjectives invariably used to qualify the two main denominations – populated Northern Ireland. However, the fight was never merely a religious struggle between Catholics and Protestants. Those doing the fighting were not particularly religious nor were there many noted theologians among them. The Reverend Ian Paisley might have regarded himself as the exception to this statement on both counts, but few others would have agreed with him. To regard it as a religious conflict would make equal sense to regarding the American Civil War as having been fought because one side wore blue and the other grey. It did, however, perhaps suit some interests to obscure the reason for the conflict and to propagate the concept that this was a struggle between two atavistic groups of religious fanatics.

The struggle was a political one. The overwhelming majority of Catholics were Nationalists seeking union in a united Ireland; the overwhelming majority of Protestants were Unionists seeking to maintain Northern Ireland within Britain. Catholic Nationalists and Protestant Unionists knew their history, knew it well, but knew it from differing perspectives. There was a large section of people of both religions who, struggling to make a living and raise their children, lived in the present and did not much involve themselves in the political struggle.

The village of Pomeroy in Tyrone was almost wholly Nationalist. The village of Lisbellaw in Fermanagh was almost wholly Unionist. In Pomeroy the I.R.A. slogan, "Tiocfaidh ár lá"[1], painted beneath the Irish flag, was an ominous reminder to the Unionists that they were still not secure after three hundred years of supremacy.

In Lisbellaw "No surrender" beneath the British Union Jack reminded the Nationalists of the Unionist defence of Derry in 1690 and that any accommodation with the enemy was anathema to the Unionists.

In Lisbellaw the Unionists sang of a glorious victory:

> *It was old but it was beautiful and the colours they were fine,*
> *It was worn at Derry, Aughrim, Enniskillen, and the Boyne."*

---

[1] (Irish) "Our day will come."

In Pomeroy the Nationalists sang of a glorious defeat:

*"Who fears to speak of '98? Who blushes at the name?
When cowards mock the patriot's fate who hangs his head in shame?*

Nationalists and Unionists went to different schools, attended different social functions, bought their groceries along sectarian lines, and attended different sporting events. They lived side by side in different worlds.

One of the few places where the young of both sides came together in a wary standoff was Queen's University in Belfast. Here the student body was mostly Nationalist, the faculty mostly Unionist. The emotional element, so strident in Northern Ireland politics, here was muted, but still not far below the surface.

Teresa O'Neill from Pomeroy instructed a group of fellow climbers from the Outdoors Club of Queen's University: "Rappelling is the most exhilarating aspect of rock work and the most dangerous if not done with care and attention. You must check each link in your attachment to a secure anchor – the runner, the rope, your harness, and your attachments. We use an eleven millimetre rope and we have already checked that."

The group listened attentively to the soft voice. The three males in the group tried to focus on the work at hand and not to appear too obvious in their appreciation of the lithe figure of their instructress. She bent down and attempted to brush some blue climbing chalk from the legs of her well-fitting climbing gear and the male contingent became dangerously unfocused.

She walked over and checked the water knot that secured the loop of the runner. "We're using a figure eight rappelling device, and it should be secured to your harness by a locking carabiner. Some of you are using two non-locking caribiners instead, which is fine, but you must be sure that the gates on your carabiners are not only opposite each other, but also form an "X" as they cross. In this way the rope cannot work its way out."

She checked one climber's harness.

"You might get away with it, but why risk your neck. The gates are opposite each other alright, but as you see are parallel when open and not forming an "X." She smiled up at him. "It's not all that likely, but if the rope worked itself out of the carabiners and gravity had its way with you, we'd have what we call a 'screamer." Telfy Armstrong from Lisbellaw undid one of the carabiners with his large hands, turned it around to form the proper configuration, and said with a shy formality, "Thanks, Miss."

"*I think you placed those carabiners in the wrong configuration just to get my attention that day at Tollymore in the Mournes,*" she said accusingly, arms linked around his neck, looking small beside him on the couch.

"*Yes, but I had a back-up plan. If you missed the carabiner, I figured falling to my death would have got your attention.*"

"*That would have made an impression of sorts, as well as ruining my reputation as a guide.*"

"*Ah well, both our reputations are ruined anyhow, mine for consorting with a Fenian, yours for being seen with an Orangeman.*"

She cuddled closer. "*I've heard that one difference between apples and oranges is that you never hear of an apple bastard.*"

"*I'll not have my ancestors maligned. We Armstrongs are solid Ulstermen, who crossed the Boyne with King William of Orange in hot pursuit of your King James, who, I understand, was hiding up a tree somewhere.*"

"*We may have had the wrong king on the Irish side that time,*" she admitted. "*I understand Sarsfield said, 'Change kings and we'll fight you again'. Telfy Armstrong—what kind of a name is Telfy anyhow? Are you sure it shouldn't be Telly? Perhaps you were conceived in front of a T.V. set?*"

"*The name in all its historic grandeur is Telford. It was a common – I should say a frequently recurring – name in our family in the border area between Scotland and England and still is to this day. The Armstrongs, together with the Grahams, the Scotts, the Elliots, and the Johnstons came to Ireland in the 1600s at the time of the Plantation of Ulster. Did you know that Neil Armstrong's ancestors came from Fermanagh?*"

Many of the name were eminent reivers, some would say bandits, on the border in the late 1500s until subdued by King James the Sixth of Scotland and sent to Ireland at the time of the Plantation of Ulster to teach the Irish how to be blackguards.

"*And did you find us apt pupils, Telfy?*"

"*That you were. None more apt in the entire world – zealous and eager to learn, picked up the art as if born to it.*"

"*I've given my heart to Telfy, the rollicking reiver,*" she sighed, "*so now the descendant of a lawless reiver is on a leave of absence from the R.U.C. in order to study law and to bring justice to the land.*"

"*My child, are you so naïve? Even as a second year student I already know enough law to know that the law has little to do with justice. Justice is to found only with God. When you qualify as a doctor and start playing God, we'll look to you for justice.*"

"*I can't wait to play God and make some money doing it,*" she sighed. "*They say 'God heals and the physician takes the fee.' If God persists, though,* in practising medicine without a license, He'd better have his malpractice insurance paid up. I'm permanently broke and my father supports me. He farms a small patch of bog and heather up in the mountains near Pomeroy, not like your prosperous farm in Fermanagh."

"The Armstrongs got the land and the O'Neills got the view," Telfy said, summing it up admirably.

Telfy Armstrong and Teresa O'Neill shared a small apartment off Malone Road in Belfast. In the anonymity of the city, they were no different from any other couple in love. Indeed, Teresa told Telfy that to look at him one would never know he was a Protestant! They walked to the Ormeau Cinema where they sat in a back seat, the large man with his arm around the pretty girl with the long flowing, red hair. They were lucky enough to get tickets to the U2 concert and danced with wild abandon among a crowd of five hundred equally uninhibited young people.

Telfy played in the scrum for Queen's, and Teresa cheered him on from the sidelines. When Telfy was not playing rugby, they spent their weekends in the Mourne Mountains, climbing and hiking and relishing the surging vigour of youth, taking their exuberant health for granted with the thankless acceptance of youth. They discussed marriage; they studied with guilt and feverish concentration before exams, and Telfy, a bright student, failed his oral.

It is never safe to generalize, but safe enough to say that all professors, by virtue of the fact that they stand on an elevated platform talking down to their students, consider themselves superior people. Professor Simon Smythe-Jones, LLB, Q.C., stood on a dais, his elevator shoes adding minimally to his height, his glasses peeping from the pocket of his yellow waistcoat. One day, when practising a pose in front of his mirror, he had noticed that the thick lenses magnified his protruding eyes, so now he only wore the glasses when it was absolutely necessary to see. They were however useful props for his famous and well rehearsed courtroom mannerisms. His abdomen protruded also, and as a result of a sway back, his plaid coat-tails rode out rearward over a prominent rump. His appearance struck Telfy as that of a small, bug-eyed rooster, a rooster conscious of his place at the top of the pecking order. In court he liked to try to bewilder opposing council with a litany of Latin phrases which he had committed to memory. Once, facing a small-town lawyer from Ballycastle, he found himself finessed.

"Is my learned colleague not familiar with that dictum in law: 'Cuius est solum eius est usque ad coelum et ad inferos'?

"I am indeed, for after a few pints, the farmers in the pubs in Ballycastle speak of little else."

The law professor informed the thirty or so faces beneath him that only the "best and the brightest" among them would one day graduate as lawyers. He mentioned that a good lawyer uses his tongue with the precision of a scalpel, and he spoke of the pen being mightier than the sword. He said that in the practice of law practice makes perfect. He also said something to the effect that brains will always best brawn. Some of the eager, upturned faces, being young, were committing this litany of clichés to their notebooks. When he used the phrase "the brightest and the best" a second time in the lecture, a rugby friend on Telfy's left raised his hand and asked why it was that the brightest were always assumed to be the best. Were, for instance, the brawniest ever the best?

Those at the front of the hall suppressed any urge to mirth. A few at a safer distance in the back tittered, while another rugby friend on Telfy's right gave vent to a cretinous guffaw and brayed like a donkey.

The question set in motion a practised ritual. S.J. took his glasses from his waistcoat pocket, and holding them in his left hand between finger and thumb, thoughtfully polished the lenses with a red handkerchief retrieved from a jacket pocket. The glasses were then placed well down on his nose. His head went back and he peered down his nose. "Ah yes! One of our brawny brethren. Armstrong, isn't it?"

Telfy manfully sat in silence and awaited the lethal riposte, but the head merely nodded, the glasses reflecting little malignant shafts of light and the question remained unanswered.

Had Telfy known of an incident six weeks earlier in which Professor Smythe-Jones – considered by some, and by S.J. himself, to be the brightest of all – had been bested by one not at all bright, he might have understood the startlingly venomous look cast in his direction. The professor, mildly paranoid at the best of times, wrongly assumed that knowledge of the incident had prompted the sly question. He also assumed wrongly that the question had come from Telfy.

Professor Smythe-Jones was pleased as he drove home. His well rehearsed speech to the law society had been well received. He saw himself again standing by the lectern accepting the applause, as he slowly and pensively removed his glasses with his left hand holding them just so between forefinger and thumb, the other three fingers fanned evenly outward. He held the famous courtroom mannerism until it was captured by the photographer's flash. It would appear in tomorrow's "Belfast Telegraph".

But no harm in a preview. Professor Smythe-Jones turned his rear view mirror inwards so he could see himself in it. He reached up and with thumb and *forefinger of his left hand slowly and pensively removed his glasses - and ran into the back of a shabby looking Volkswagen. The heavier Mercedes suffered only minor injuries, but had ridden up on and mashed the left rear of the Volkswagen which had been innocently making a right hand turn onto the Ormeau Road. The professor, getting out of his Mercedes, put on his glasses as he approached the other driver, and drawing on years of courtroom experience, managed in two short sentences, to accomplish three things:*

- *convey a civilized regret for the incident;*
- *without telling a direct lie, shift the blame from himself;*
- *administer a mild rebuke, thereby automatically establishing his own moral superiority.*

"*Sorry about this, young man, but your signal light is out. You really should keep your vehicle in a roadworthy condition.*"

The muscular young man was joined by his passenger, a pretty girl in a miniskirt, and in silence they both inspected the damage to the rear of the Volkswagen. With the appearance of the girl, S.J. shifted into charm mode.

"*You know, my dear, your friend should be more careful, but since there's only slight damage to my Mercedes, and in deference to, may I say, such a charming member of the gentler sex, we won't need to get our insurance companies invol —*"

A cuff to the side of his head interrupted his sentence and his train of thought. It was more of a gesture delivered with the heel of the hand than a blow, but it knocked his glasses to the pavement and his hairpiece askew.

"*Ye baldy auld bollocks, of course my signal light is out. Look what ye've done to it!*"

"*Y-You lout. How dare you! This is an assault — an assault, I say.*" *Professor Smythe-Jones peered, blinking, attempting to read the number plate of the Volkswagen.* "*Do you know with whom you're dealing? When I'm finished —*"

His speech was cut off, with his air, by a large hand closing around his throat.

"*Ye huoor ye. An' afther it's you that ran into the back of me. One more word outta ye and I'll squeeze your scrawny neck till shit comes out your ears.*"

His lower denture was in danger of following his glasses to the pavement as the young man, holding him by the neck with one hand, attempted, unsuccessfully as he was wearing sneakers, to even the score by kicking in one of the headlights of the Mercedes.

A crowd gathered, and the girl put a hand on her man's arm. "Put him down, Hughie. It's only a scrape. You'd have to be looking at it to see it. You can fix it yourself in the garage in no time. There'll be a line up for the pictures and now we're late. "The Commitments" is on, and everybody says the first part is the best."

S.J.'s most vivid memory of the ugly scene was its last act, when the charming member of the gentler sex reached out and straightened his hair piece, patting it down into place and, smiling down at him with perfect white teeth, stood on his glasses.

"Didn't yer mammy never teach ye not to tell lies, ye wee shite. C'mon, Hughie."

Telfy was still unaware of having offended when he presented himself for his oral.

"Ah yes, Armstrong, isn't it?"

"How about a trip on the Shannon-Erne Waterway? It's just been opened. You can now travel by boat from above Limerick on the Shannon to Belleek on the Erne."

"Oh, Telfy, wouldn't it be brilliant, but I could never afford the time. I'll be needed to help out at home. How long would it take?"

"Probably a few weeks taking our time, it's well over two hundred miles. You know what we could do, though, is start at Carrick-on-Shannon and cruise to Belleek, which would only take a few days."

"I'll ask Daddy. What'll we do for a boat?"

"I suppose we'll be needing one of those. Leave it to me."

On a Saturday morning in early August, they left Carrick-on-Shannon in a small, single-berth, motor cruiser. The boat-hire company had equipped them with maps, a full tank of diesel, a comprehensive handbook covering all aspects of their cruise, and a plastic card to operate the sixteen locks along the waterway. A mile above Carrick-on-Shannon the river forked, the left fork leading to Lough Key and the town of Boyle, the right to the small town of Leitrim and the beginning of the Shannon-Erne Waterway. At Leitrim they turned right out of the River Shannon to enter the canal system.

In 1846, during the famine in Ireland, work had commenced on the waterway as a famine relief project, but the link had never been completed and had afterwards fallen into disrepair. In the 1990s the project had been resurrected and in three years, as a result of exemplary cooperation between the governments of Northern Ireland and the Republic, and assisted by funds from the European Union the Shannon-Erne link was completed. Some of the stone of the earlier attempt was still to be seen in the present-day lock construction. How many tourists lounging on the deck of a cabin cruiser and throwing morsels of food to ducks and swans would have been aware of the men who died of starvation and exhaustion in that earlier attempt to link the Shannon to the Erne? But then, how many travelers in Canada and America, being transported in comfort by train through the Rockies, gave much thought to the thousands of Chinese workers who lost their lives in the construction of that railway?

"According to our guidebook, that smaller hill two miles away there is called Skeebeg." Telfy Armstrong sat in warm sunshine on top of Sheemore, overlooking Lough Scur and the town of Keshcarrigan, population forty-five.

The previous day they had navigated eight locks, gained forty-five vertical metres, and four hours after leaving Carrick-on-Shannon, had cruised into the peaceful little Lough at the top of the Shannon-Erne Waterway. From Lough Scur the Waterway descended twenty-one meters through another eight locks to enter Upper Lough Erne at Belturbet.

Teresa sat with arms grasping her knees and smiled up with a sideways glance at Telfy Armstrong.

"Sheebeg, Telfy, not Skeebeg. Sheemor and Sheebeg, the big fairy mountain and the little fairy mountain. Mór is 'big' in Irish and beg is 'small.' Shee is Irish for a supernatural being - a sorcerer or a fairy, one of the little people".

"I think I got it, Teresa. Sheemor, the big little people mountain and Sheebeg the little little people mountain"

"Oh very witty! Or half witty anyhow! I suppose they didn't teach you Irish at Portora Royal School? Why don't I teach you Irish? Just imagine what a hit you'll be, walking into a pub full of Orangemen in Lisbellaw and shouting, 'Beannacht Dé oraibh go léir". ("God bless all here.").

"All right, I take your silence for consent. First lesson: 'Póg' is Irish for 'kiss', and my tuition fee will be a kiss and/or a hug for each bridge we pass under along our route."

"Póg! Sounds like a strange word for a kiss to me. Are you sure you're not taking the mickey out of me?"

"I'm not. Now that the matter of payment is settled, let's get to work. Those blue mountains you see away in the distance to the west of us are the Curlews – Corrshlievthe – Irish for 'rounded hills'. There in 1599 Red Hugh O'Donnell defeated Conyers Clifford, and today on the top of the Curlews is a sculpted horseman commemorating the victory. The O'Rourkes and the MacDermotts were also involved in that victory, indeed they were mainly responsible for it, and the sculpture is called 'The Gaelic Chieftain,' although most Irish people seeing it think of Red Hugh. To the Irish, the name Red Hugh rings like a clarion call. He is to us what Charlemagne is to the French, Richard the Lionheart to the English, and Robert the Bruce to the Scots. He's our hero and our saint. His name is almost sacred in our memory.

"Over in that direction also General Humbert's French army, together with the Irish, won the Battle of Carrignagat in the United Irishmen Rebellion of 1798. Humbert then marched his French and Irish army through Keshcarrigan, that little town below us, on his way to their final battle, and defeat south of here in Longford. Any Irish who survived being bayoneted by Cornwallis's vastly superior force were hanged. The French were supplied with ships and returned to France. One of the leaders of that rebellion was Wolfe Tone, the 'Father of Irish Republicanism', and sadly, that was also the last time the native Irish and the Northern Irish fought for the same cause.

"The majority of place names in Ireland are still Irish language names. Tara, the seat of the High Kings of Ireland before the days of the Norman invaders – incidentally a post the O'Neills occupied for seven hundred years – is probably the most famous place-name in all of Ireland. The name derives from the goddess Tea, the wife of Eremon, the first Milesian High King. But our legends speak of the place long before the coming of the Celts. Tara stood in the days of Troy.

"The music of the Celt echoed from the halls of Tara five centuries before the Romans established a palisade in Britain, which they called Londinium. As an embryo lawyer, you'll also want to know that laws were promulgated in the great hall of Tara, and the High King there was the court of last appeal. A poet of those days speaks of an unsuccessful litigant and the summary justice of the king. 'Gold was not received as retribution from him, but his soul in one hour'."

"Uhm, that man could have done with a good lawyer. I must say, though, that the poet nicely conveys both the power of kings and the finality of death."

"The place-names along the waterway ahead are all from the Irish: Ballinamore, 'the mouth of the big ford', Aghalane, 'the wide fields', Belturbet, 'the mouth to Tairbairt Island', Enniskillen, 'the island of Kathleen', Belleek, 'mouth of the flagstones'.

"As for the hill on which we sit, a blind harper, Turlough O' Carolan, composed a well-known melody, with lyrics in Irish, called Sheebeg-Sheemore. His music is popular nowadays, and as a matter of fact, they played it the other night in the pub in Carrick-on-Shannon. He was born close to here in 1670 and became blind at the age of eighteen as a result of smallpox. It's said that if you lose one sense, the others are heightened, and actually, quite a few of the Irish harpists of old were blind. Another was the Galway poet, Raftery. The harp has always been associated with Ireland. The Irish poet, Thomas Moore, wrote of the harp and the Ireland that's gone."

"I'll sing you a song about the harp, Telfy." A beautiful contralto voice caressed the lyrics, and Thomas Moore's evocative melody floated out to beguile the evening stillness.

> The Harp that once through Tara's halls the soul of music shed,
> Now hangs as mute on Tara's walls as if that soul were fled.
> So sleeps the pride of former days, so glory's thrill is o'er,
> And hearts that once beat high for praise now feel that pulse no more.
> No more to chiefs and ladies bright the harp of Tara swells,
> The chord alone that breaks at night its tale of ruin tells
> Thus freedom now so seldom wakes the only throb she gives
> Is when some heart indignant breaks, to show that still she lives.

He reached over and put his arm around her. "Beautiful, Teresa, a beautiful song, sung by a beautiful girl! The Irish so love their sad songs. Only a poet could get away with talking of a heart breaking of indignation. Someone, I don't know who, spoke of 'The great Gaels the men whom God made mad, all their wars are merry, and all their songs are sad'?"

"Our songs reflect our history, and many of them indeed have a poignant sadness. Our songs, our music, and our poetry stir us deeply. Like a genetic code, they pass on our memories and aspirations from one generation to the next.

"Padraig Pearse, in an oration at the graveside of the Fenian, O'Donovan Rossa, called the English fools for having left us the graves of our patriot dead, saying that while Ireland held those graves, Ireland unfree would never be at rest. He might well have said also that the English were fools for having left us our songs and our music, for these keep alive our memories. Music is embedded in the soul. If I had not known from history that we share a common ancestry with the people of the Scottish Highlands, I would have guessed it because their songs and their music strike a chord in my soul."

"You can teach me your songs and your history, Teresa, and I'll teach you mine. My knowledge of Irish history begins with the Plantation of Ulster in the early 1600s, when we came over to civilize you natives. Actually, we were taught more about Wellington of Waterloo and Gordon of Khartoum than about Irish place names and Irish harpists. I'm willing to learn, though. Continue the lesson."

"Well then, if your Irish history begins in the 1600s, you won't be aware that Finn, our mythical pre-Christian warrior and his men, the Fianna, fought a battle right here between Sheemore and Sheebeg, and some say that he's buried *over there on top of Sheebeg. When you Unionists use the epithet "Fenian," referring to us Nationalists, you should know that the word derives from our legends of the Fianna, and to us the word has no pejorative connotation. Your friends in the Shankill*[1] *will have to come up with something a bit more spiteful, Telfy."*

"I'll have them work on it, honey."

"The past, the distant past, reminds us of other days and of past glories. All our glories are in the past. Not many recent ones."

"And who is buried under this cairn here on top of Sheemore?"

"Oh, that's some old pre-Christian fortification, so long lost in time that the builders are forgotten, forgotten even in Ireland, but there's a legend that down below us on that island in Lough Oughter is buried Owen Roe O'Neill."

"Hold yo hosses! Now you're getting into modern history and I can hold my own. Owen Roe, nephew of the traitor earl, Hugh O'Neill, returned from Spain to lead the Irish rebels in 1641 when they tried to murder us planters, and would have succeeded, too, had we not held out in our walled towns such as Enniskillen and Londonderry. Then Cromwell came over from England in 1649 and suppressed the rebellion and dealt very harshly with the Irish and any who supported them. He was only in Ireland for a short time. The population of native Irish on his arrival was one and one half million, and nine months later on his departure was reduced to half a million. I've also heard it said by some Unionists that it's a pity he hadn't stayed another six months!"

In response to Teresa's indignant look, he put two protective arms around her. "Not my sentiments, Teresa. Cromwell also captured the stronghold on Lough Oughter, which I believe was the last to hold out against him."

Teresa took over. "Philip MacHugh O'Reilly, grandson of the last O'Reilly chieftain of Breffney, defended Cloughoughter against Cromwell. Philip O'Reilly was also married to Owen Roe's sister. I don't know how O'Reilly managed to escape Cromwell's vengeance but I do know that he died in Rome. Owen Roe would have succeeded in regaining our land if Cromwell had not had him poisoned at Lough Oughter. Actually it's not certain that he was poisoned but he may well have been. Poison seems to have been a favourite method of disposing of enemies in those days. An English agent poisoned Red Hugh in Spain. They attempted to poison Shane O'Neill, but thanks to his robust constitution he survived the attempt. However, not even his robust constitution enabled him to survive his decapitation by the MacDonnells! It's a wonder the

---

[1] A Unionist enclave in Belfast.

English didn't try to poison our patriot chieftain, Hugh O'Neill, but were so negligent as to allow him also to die peacefully in exile in Rome. In his poem, 'Lament for the death of Owen Roe O'Neill,' Thomas Davis speaks of poison as the 'Weapon of the Sassenach.' I suppose they wouldn't have taught you that poem in Portora."

"No, but I have a feeling I'm about to hear of it. Another sad one, Teresa?"

"You are, and it is, Telfy."

> Though it break my heart to hear, say again the bitter words,
> From Derry against Cromwell he marched to measure swords,
> But the weapon of the Sassenach, met him on his way
> And he died at Clough Oughter upon St. Leonard's day.

"It seems to be a day for poetry. Maybe it's the place. No, Teresa, we didn't learn that one. Our poem to a tragic hero would have been Charles Wolfe's, 'The Burial of Sir John Moore.' Sir John Moore, a British general – as I'm sure every school girl in Pomeroy well knows – fought a gallant rearguard action against Napoleon and died at Corunna, in Spain."

"Am I about to hear of it, Telfy?"

"You are, Teresa."

> Slowly and sadly we laid him down
> From the field of his fame fresh and gory
> We carved not a line and we raised not a stone
> But we left him alone in his glory.

"Actually, Telfy, I have heard of that English general and Corunna was not his only 'field of fame fresh and gory.' Sir John Moore commanded the British troops that suppressed the 1798 rebellion in Wexford. Although it's said that he himself was a humane man, he failed to control the atrocities of the yeomen and Hessian mercenaries under his command. But then both sides committed atrocities at Wexford. War seems to breed atrocity. And it wasn't as a schoolgirl in Pomeroy that I learned about Sir John Moore and the rebellion of '98, but as a child in my father's house. You knew of Sir John Moore as a hero and I knew of him as the commander of troops that committed atrocities in an Irish Rebellion. We learned different histories, Telfy"

"All right, Teresa, time out." He kissed her. "Then we'll continue teaching each other our history."

"Do you think this would work for Jerry Adams and Ian Paisley," Telfy asked after a few moments.

"Nah. Ian would complain that Gerry's beard tickled. Also their picture in the 'Belfast Telegraph' under the headline, "ADAMS AND PAISLEY NECK 'N NECK" would ruin them both.

On Sheemore by the age-levelled rath of a long forgotten people, they sat together above the winding blue waterway interspersed with small blue loughs. Telfy took her hand, and for the rest of the day Teresa admired her new engagement ring.

The next morning, leaving Lough Scur, they cruised slowly along the waterway, Sometimes the canal threaded through a land of brown moor and reeds; at other times lush greenery threatened to choke their passage. Now and then they cruised into green bordered loughs, with views of rounded hills rising up blue in the distance. The entire sixty-nine kilometres of waterway from Leitrim to Belturbet was remote from any major centre of population, and up on this plateau of reedy grassland and loughs, there was little habitation of any kind visible from the waterway. They drifted slowly, reluctant for the idyll to end, along grassy riverbanks, which in places opened to give glimpses of little green fields reclaimed from heather and rushes. They passed by a neat whitewashed cabin with honeysuckle framing the windows, surrounded by a low whitewashed stone wall, but nowhere could they see any road or laneway connecting the dwelling to the outside world. A black-and-white sheep dog stood on the river's bank and, tail wagging eagerly, barked a welcome. As the boat drifted down the canal, the sheepdog trotted back to the shade of the stone wall to be ready for the next guest with his dutiful greeting.

Small, hilly meadows with neatly winnowed swathes of newly mown hay slid past. Clusters of golden whins[1] and clumps of rushes marked marginal land that was useful only for grazing. Drifting on the warm breeze, the hypnotic scent of the whins mingled with the fresh fragrance of new-mown hay. Cattle, chewing placidly, gazed with dumb indifference at the passing boat. Clumps of reeds grew to the water's edge, in places bunching out into stream and lough, providing hiding places for pike, perch, brown trout, and bream. Willows and white hawthorn overflowed banks and trailed in the slowly moving water. Occasionally, where the waterway narrowed their leafy branches whispered along the hull of the boat. A slender willow bounced gently as a kingfisher alighted to scan a pool beneath. A snipe rose and skimmed the water in swift erratic flight.

---

[1] Furze.

Overhead a hawk floated on wavering wings, a pitiless predator with the advantage of the high ground. The sun shone steadily and only on two occasions, both on the same day, did it become eclipsed by clouds that disgorged soft apologetic showers.

Ballinamore, a small town in County Leitrim, enjoyed a new lease on life from its fortuitous location on the waterway. Since the opening of the waterway in 1990, German, Swiss, French, English, and Australian could now be heard spoken in its pubs, alongside County Leitrim vernacular. Rows of gaily painted houses lined either side of the town's main street and anyone, tourist or local, thirsting for a pint would not have thirsted for long. The Singing Pub had become a tradition in Ireland, and in Ballinamore, in the countryside of the blind bard, it would have been difficult to find any other kind of pub.

A babble of voices greeted Teresa and Telfy as they entered the crowded pub. Telfie leaned forward between the heads of two customers at the crowded bar and shouted his order to the bartender. Finally armed with a pint and a glass of white wine, he looked around and in vain for a seat for himself and Teresa. At a bench by the wall, a man of about sixty gestured to Teresa, and then poked an elbow into the ribs of the young man beside him.

"Get up outa that and let her sit down."

The young man, thus peremptorily ousted from his seat, got up with good grace, smiled to Teresa, and wandered off. However, the evicted young man landed on his feet, for soon he was in smiling conversation with a couple of Australian girls at the bar.

The elderly man pushed his neighbour further along the bench and a seat for two opened up.

"The band will be here any minute now," their benefactor mentioned and from his accent they deduced that he had not come from afar.

The band walked in with their instruments and sat, placing their drinks by their feet. The foursome consisted of an accordion, a fiddle, a tin whistle, and a bodhrán or small, hand-held, open-faced drum.

The fiddler gave a few warming-up scrapes, and then nodded to his companions and with no further preamble; they burst into their first number. They were good. Some of the locals, who would not have tolerated musical mediocrity, nodded appreciatively, and the night proceeded pleasantly with music, singing, calls for pints, and a background hum of continuous chat. Those in the bar, brave enough to attempt a song, were encouraged to get up, and were politely greeted with loud enthusiastic applause when they finished. The man beside Teresa shouted "Eamon, give us the 'Dawning of the Day'". The young man who had yielded his seat to Teresa, at first demurred, but then taking a long draught on his pint, rested his elbow on the bar and obliged with:

God rest you Robert Emmet, and God rest you brave Wolfe Tone,
God rest you Hugh O'Donnell and O'Neil of old Tyrone.
God rest you Patrick Sarsfield in your grave far, far away,
God rest you all who strove to speed the dawning of the day.

Teresa's neighbor informed her in a whisper, "There's another Dawning of the Day with a different air. This one's to the air of 'The Rising of the Moon'". After each verse he himself joined in, sotto voce, in the chorus.

Freedom's bright and blessed day, free from Saxon sway"
Lift your hearts and pray God speed us, to the Dawning of the Day.

Some others of the locals expecting to be asked, made the requisite protestations on being asked, "Me! Arah, no! Sure I can't sing a note," put down their pints, stood up and sang like larks.

Between Ballinamore in County Leitrim and Belturbet at the head of the Erne in County Cavan the countryside looked more prosperous with larger fields and new bungalow dwellings. Teresa continued to instruct Telfy in Irish and received her instalment payments by each bridge. At Aghalane, the bridge that linked Fermanagh in Northern Ireland to Cavan in the Irish Republic had been blown up in 1974 by either the British Army or by a Loyalist paramilitary group. The bridge was now in the process of being rebuilt. In any event Teresa received payment here, too, for the bridge that once was and might again be.

At Belturbet, in County Cavan, they decided to explore Turbet Island, but finding little of interest returned to the boat only to find that their diesel engine wouldn't start. A man on the quay told them it was probably the filter and pedalled off on his bike to find a man from Smith's garage, who he had assured them, was "the man for the job."

Eamonn Smith stood in grease-soaked coveralls, green eyes looking accusingly at the engine, and even before any examination voiced his opinion.

"With a diesel it's the filter."

He took apart the two in-line filters and found them to be pristine.

"Then it's probably the injectors, but don't worry, we'll have you back on the water in no time."

He was as good as his word and in an hour he stood, pressed the starter, and they were "back on the water." Eamonn smiled broadly, his teeth looking startlingly white in a grease-blackened face. He ran a grease-blackened hand through his grease-blackened red hair and informed them. "It wasn't the *injectors either. The wire to the ignition had become loose. And did you enjoy the band the other night?"*

It took a moment before they recognized, beneath the grease, the young man who had been evicted from his seat in the pub.

"Some of us go up to Ballinamore. It's a good spot to meet the girls," he added by way of explanation with another gleam of white teeth.

Telfy made the comment that there seemed to be many by the name of Smith in County Cavan.

"It's a common Cavan name right enough," the boy admitted. "There's always been Smiths in Cavan. Not as common a name as Reilly, though. You've heard of John Joe O'Reilly?" Telfy looked blank.

"The famous Cavan footballer."

The question was asked with such eager innocence that Telfy wished he had, but had to admit he hadn't. Admittedly Ireland was a small country, but it would still have been highly improbable that Telfy Armstrong would have heard of a Gaelic football hero. Apart from the fact that John Joe O'Reilly had died in 1952, before Telfy was born, Gaelic football, a game somewhat akin to Australian Rules football, was a game played exclusively by Nationalists.

They spent the night on board at Belturbet and entered Upper Lough Erne the next day,

"A few of the name may actually be Smiths, but the vast majority are really MacGowans. The boy back there does not know the origin of his own name. In the sixteen, seventeen and eighteen hundreds most of the Irish were illiterate and a lot of Irish names became Anglicized to some English or some English sounding equivalent. The "Mac" and the "O" prefixes disappeared. Their new English masters were not interested in trying to pronounce outlandish Irish names. They also regarded any pride in lineage among the conquered Irish as an impertinence. 'Gowan' is Irish for a blacksmith and the MacGowans became Smiths. The MacGowans were an Irish sept in what was then known as Breffney-O'Reilly and in adjacent Breffney-O'Rourke. Some names that sound totally English may be quite Irish. Most with the English-sounding name of Judge are really O'Brehonys, derived from the old hereditary judges or Brehons who interpreted the Brehon Law. Many with the name Ward are descendents of the bards of old. In this part of Ireland the name Ro —"

Telfy waggled a finger.

"We have now crossed into Northern Ireland, Teresa, and it's my turn to take over the history lesson. To the best of my knowledge there are four more bridges between here and Belleek, and I think it only fair that I be awarded the same tuition fee for my services as you got for yours.

"The castle on your right, resplendent in turret and gable, Crom Castle, is the home of the Earl of Erne, and the miniature tower on the island to your left is called a 'Folly.' Yes, you guessed it. If you have time on your hands and money in your pocket, you build a 'Folly.' I think those ruins over there are part of the original castle built by a Scottish Planter, Michael Balfour. The castle is now owned by the Creighton family. A Colonel Creighton led an Enniskillen regiment in the defeat of the Jacobites at the Battle of Aughrim in 1691. The Creightons became Earls of Erne. I know this, Teresa, because we did a project in Portora on the history of the Planter families in Fermanagh.

"Until 1914 and the outbreak of the First World War, the castle was the centre of social life in Fermanagh with regattas on the Erne and receptions and balls in the castle. Many young men of the Anglo-Irish Ascendancy in Fermanagh went off to that war and never came back, many too of the common people. You're familiar with the word "boycott." Well, it was the Third Earl who earned a vicarious reputation by employing a man called Captain Boycott as his estate agent on his Mayo estates, and it is from this captain that the word "boycott" has passed into the language. Boycott was so unpopular that the locals would have nothing to do with him. The Fourth Earl of Erne, who was also Grand Master of the Orange Lodge for all of Ireland, was killed in the First World War, and the Fifth Earl lost his life at Dunkirk in the Second World War. Like many other Planter families a Creighton fought in all of England's wars. With privilege came responsibility."

They drifted on down the Erne and Crom Castle faded into the landscape behind them. Its days of glory and bright youth were gone, gone with the lives of the many young men of the loughside who had gone off to war in 1914, never to return.

Telfy opened his mouth to continue, but Teresa interrupted.

"The Battle of Aughrim that you mentioned was the decisive battle in the Jacobite war in Ireland. The Battle of the Boyne in 1690 that you Orangemen celebrate was only a skirmish. After the Irish defeat at Aughrim, Sarsfield surrendered at Limerick. When he and the Wild Geese sailed away to the continent, Ireland was left defenceless."

"I thought it was my turn to teach history. We may have to penalize you a bridge or two here. What's this 'Wild Geese'?"

"Don't be peevish now. I'm coming to that. Just because you Unionists now own Ulster doesn't mean that only you can recite our history. As you know the Irish sided with James, the Stuart king, in the Williamite – or Jacobite – war. As you also know, the Irish lost battles at the Boyne, at Aughrim, and at Limerick. Patrick Sarsfield, the Red Hugh of the late sixteen hundreds, and the commander of the Irish forces, signed the Treaty of Limerick, which *stipulated that in return for the just treatment of his countrymen he would leave Ireland with his army. Before Sarsfield and his army were out of sight of the Irish coast, England broke the Treaty of Limerick and subjected the Irish to a repressive code of Penal Laws. The start of the 1700s was the start of a century of repression for the now defenceless native Irish. Sarsfield took 20,000 men to the continent and the banished Irish soldiers who fought abroad became known as the 'Wild Geese.' They formed an Irish Brigade in the French Army and indeed for the next hundred years there was always an Irish Brigade in the French Army. Over the following century around 500,000 emigrant Irishmen died fighting for France. Others fought for Spain, Austria, and other European countries. The Wild Geese fought for any country that was England's enemy and for over a hundred years went into battle with the cry 'Cuimhnígí ar Luimneach agus ar feall na Sassenach'.*[1]

"All this because the Irish fought on the losing side when two English kings decided to duke it out in Ireland. When kings make war, the aftershock affects the lives of common folk for generations."

"I won't ask now about the Penal Laws you mention," Telfy said, manoeuvring through the traffic at Carrrybridge, "as I'm too busy trying not to hit one of these boats."

Carrybridge was a narrow busy bottleneck on the Erne. As they emerged from under the bridge, Telfy desperately grasped for the wheel just in time to avoid a collision with a large floating palace. A man on the deck above them with a flat Belfast accent shouted down in mock reproof.

"Get a room the pair of ye. If ye can't conthrol yourself fella, how'd y'expect tae conthrol the wee boat?"

After lunch ashore, they moved on into the open lough below the bridge, and approaching Enniskillen, Telfy turned to Teresa.

"Actually I do know something of the Penal Laws of eighteenth-century Ireland as they also affected the Presbyterians of Ulster. Among other things Ulster Presbyterians had to pay a tithe to the established Anglican Church of Ireland. It was a time when many Scotch/Irish emigrated from Ulster to the colonies in America."

"The impoverished Catholics also were required to support the established Protestant Church to which, like the Presbyterians, they did not belong. Yes, the Penal Laws did affect the Ulster Presbyterians too, but to a far lesser extent than the native Irish. The Treaty that Sarsfield signed pledged that Irish

---

[1] (Irish) "Remember Limerick and the Saxon faith, (perfidy)."

Catholics were to be 'protected in the free and unfettered exercise of their religion.' Before the ink had dried on the Treaty of Limerick, the Penal Laws were enacted. The English, who in earlier centuries had expressed contempt for our Brehon Laws, now introduced us to a new code of law.

Irish Catholics were forbidden to exercise their religion, to receive an education, to enter a profession, to vote, to keep arms, to own a horse of greater value than five pounds, to live within five miles ..."

"My God, Teresa! Have you learned those off by heart?"

"That's only some of the "forbiddens". There are lots more of them. It was an event in our past that has had much influence on the present. These laws, by creating an impoverished peasantry, were responsible for the enormous death toll later in the Great Famine. Only in the last few generations are we emerging from the servitude and ignorance engendered by those Penal Laws."

"I understand, though, that those Penal Laws gradually fell into disuse, and as time went on, humane people refused to enforce them."

"I understand that humane people in Europe occasionally thwarted Hitler's policies for the extermination of the Jewish race," Teresa retorted. "That such laws against a people were ever promulgated can only be answered by a sad silence. Every once in a while some revisionist historian, eager to reveal a unique insightfulness that had evaded others, tells us that the centuries of oppression were our own fault; the Plantation of Ulster; Cromwell's genocide; the failed rebellions; the penal laws and the great famine were the result of a flaw in the Irish character. Can you imagine what a flawed race the Jews would have turned out to be if Hitler had won the war?"

"If it was forbidden to exercise your religion and forbidden to attend Catholic worship how come that Ireland remained Catholic?"

"The majority remained Catholic although there were inducements to relinquish our faith. For instance if an eldest son converted to Protestantism he alone would inherit his father's land rather than have it divided among all the male children as mandated by the Penal Laws. Our priests in those days dared not wear a Roman collar and were indistinguishable from the rest of the people. They were educated and ordained abroad in other Catholic countries. They returned to Ireland, at risk to their lives, to minister to their people and to celebrate the Mass, which they had to do in hidden remote places. There are many of these "Mass Rocks" around Ireland; three that I know of were not far from us in Leitrim. Of course nowhere is far from anywhere in County Leitrim which is the smallest county in Ireland. There's one near the old O'Rourke stronghold of Dromahaire, one at Carrigallen and one over on a mountain called "Sleive an Iarainn".

"The love and respect of past generations of Irish Catholics for their priests dates back to those days when our priests shared our hardships with us. The example of sacrifice set by our priests in those days of the Penal Laws kept us faithful to our faith when it would have been advantageous to desert that faith. But it's strange how these things go. Many now have deserted that faith, partly because of the arrogance of later generations of priests who came out of the seminaries expecting and demanding as their right the adulation of their flock, while having done nothing to earn it. An arrogant priest, like an uncaring doctor, is an affront to God and man. I have heard one priest say: "From the day of my ordination in Ireland I will never hear a harsh word nor miss a meal." Actually it was said tongue in cheek and that particular priest was neither arrogant nor fat but I can see how this feeding of the ego with no feedback, could result in a fat and self satisfied clergy, a far cry from the priests of the Penal Law days.

"While the priests toiled among the people, the Catholic hierarchy of those days frequently sided with the English in power. These prelates, unlike Dermot O'Hurley and Oliver Plunkett of earlier centuries, sought accommodation with the rulers. What would be the thoughts of a Father Murphy in '98, burning to death on the rack surrounded by jeering Wexford yeomen, knowing that the Catholic hierarchy had excommunicated him? Was he now doomed to burn forever in a hell that they had ordained? I would hope that his faith in God, and indeed his intelligence, would, in his final agony, have been of a higher order than that of those bishops who had relegated his soul to hell. More recently the Catholic Church that had excommunicated De Valera in 1922 was quick to cosy up to the Free State Government that he formed in 1932. Indeed, in the present day, the insistence of the Catholic bishops in the Republic in having a say in government is a stumbling block to any accommodation with your Northern Unionists. Some of these powerful Irish Catholic bishops came from humble beginnings, as did the first bishop of Ireland and indeed the first bishop of Rome. Saint Patrick and Saint Peter retained the virtue of humility. In the past in Ireland, we were whipped into obedience by both church and state; If the pastoral shepherd failed to bring us gently back into the fold with the crook end of the crosier, there was always the other pointy end and the threat of a hell, hot and eternal. If we entertained thoughts of rebellion against unjust rulers we heard the words of dread: "high treason"; the punishment; "hanged, drawn and quartered.

"That said, it was the Catholic Church and the Catholic hierarchy that provided education for us and lifted us out of centuries of ignorance. They were paternalistic but wise and farsighted. They knew the value of education and many priests, nuns, and brothers dedicated their lives to educating us, and now that they have succeeded we in our own arrogance can criticise them.

"We have always, too, held our teachers in high regard, and this also dates back to the time of the Penal Laws. Again as with the "Mass Rock" we had the "hedge school"

"The teacher taught his pupils under hedges or anywhere else they could find safety and shelter. Education has always been of great importance to us, for its own sake as well as a means of climbing out of generations of servitude. Those pupils, shivering under some hedge and fearful of discovery, would have listened respectfully and treasured their little scraps of hard earned knowledge, while you and I, Telfy, on paid scholarships, give no thought to skipping lectures if we've been out partying the night before.

"I remember my mother, God have mercy on her, being less than thrilled when I told her I wanted to be a doctor. She'd have preferred I be a nun or a teacher. Her generation didn't have much to do with doctors. They couldn't afford them."

Below Enniskillen on the Lower Lough, they anchored for the night off Devenish Island. In the quiet summer evening, Teresa and Telfy sat on the deck of their small craft enveloped in the stillness. The distant barking of a dog on the mainland seemed only to accentuate the silence. The occasional "plop" of a rising trout rippled the quiet surface of the lough. Like a protective stone giant, an eight hundred-year-old round tower stood guard over some small sad ruins of even earlier times. The tower, the island's mute sentinel, cast its lengthening shadow toward the lough. As the sun sank below the hills and the waters of the lough darkened, the guardian tower retrieved its shadow, and tower and ruins faded back into the darkening gloom of the island.

Next morning, just before the lough narrowed into a river above Belleek, Telfy steered to the right toward a peninsula of land indented by three small, sheltered bays. They went ashore by the ruins of an old castle. Unlike Crom Castle on the upper lough, which was still inhabited, Castle Caldwell was in ruins, but like Crom Castle this ruined relic had once too seen its days of glory.

Assured and confident ladies had floated down wide, gently curved stairways in Parisian satins to take the arms of titled gentlemen who, with heads bowed attentively, guided them to the dining room. Over tables draped in immaculate white Irish linen, Shelley and Wordsworth vied with Wellington and Nelson as topics of conversation. The diners sipped the finest of French wines while discussing the upstart Bonaparte. Perhaps the Irish Rebellion of '98 may have been touched upon.

"Old Lake[1] cut loose the yeomanry in Wexford and taught the Croppies[2] a lesson they will not soon forget. Paid them back in spades for Oulart Hollow. Mind you, I don't condone the pitch cap and the burning of priests on the rack, but it's hard to control yeomen once they get the bit between their teeth. Sad how these atrocities get out of hand, but the Irish need some such lesson every few generations. This would be their fourth trouncing if one goes back to the Traitor Earl's rebellion. Lessons sink in slowly through a thick Irish skull."

Well-trained Irish servants stood along the walls behind each guest's chair while others moved quietly from kitchen to dining table. Carriages rolled up a curved driveway to the front entrance of what was more mansion than castle. Tall windows looked out on green lawns sloping down to the lough. Fine horses champed in the courtyards. A discreetly unseen army of servants and labourers dutifully toiled to achieve a proper level of serene elegance. Occasionally some menial, unnoticed – perhaps a Maguire or an O'Donnell – stood aside in the ditch, doffing his cap as a cavalcade of gentry cantered past.

By the loughside there had been boathouses and wharfs, mahogany-decked pleasure boats and vessels of commerce. In those days the Erne had been a busy thoroughfare for traffic, both for commerce and pleasure boating. Gentle hills, sloping down to the loughside, now reforested in conifers, had then been clothed in stately beech, ash, and giant oak, and among these wooded hills had been pleasant bridle paths and shelter for deer, pheasant, and grouse.

Telfy and Teresa stepped through a hole in a crumbling wall, a gaping breach overgrown with foliage and ivy that had once been a window. Here, in other days, some house-guest might have sat in the window nook of the library, reading a book of Byron's poetry. A sad silence now pervaded the place, a silence broken only by cawing crows winging homeward overhead to a nearby rookery. As the couple stumbled over damp grass-covered stones and masonry, exploring the roofless ivy-covered ruins, Telfy explained the castle's history.

"The once extensive grounds of the old castle are now a bird and nature refuge. The Blennerhasset family built the original stronghold in 1615 in Plantation times and fifty years later, it came into the possession of the Caldwells, who were the owners for the next two hundred years. These

---

[1] General Lake, English commander during the 1798 Rebellion.
[2] Rebels.

Plantation families were known in those days as "undertakers" in that they undertook, in exchange for land grants in Ireland, to build fortified strongholds and maintain armed men to defend the territory for England. Many of these undertakers were English knights, but at that time the practise of selling knighthoods and other honours had tarnished the title."

"Somewhat like the earlier practise in the Catholic Church of selling indulgences to which Martin Luther objected, and which led to the Reformation," Teresa observed.

"Quite so. King James, Elizabeth's successor, found himself in debt to the incredible amount, for those days, of one million pounds, while the entire revenue of the crown was less than seventy thousand pounds a year. To augment his personal income he sold titles. A knighthood for fifty pounds; a baron was worth ten thousand pounds; a viscount, fifteen thousand; and an earl, twenty thousand. He also created the new title of baronet – one thousand and ninety five pounds – which applied initially only to Ulster. A baronet was required to assist in the building of towns and to maintain thirty foot- soldiers to contribute to the defence of Ulster."

"I can see how this ersatz nobility would scorn an Irish name that only dated back a thousand years or so." Teresa O'Neill laughed.

"I'll ignore these irreverent interruptions from the peasantry. Come to think of it, Teresa, you should claim to be a direct descendant of the last O'Neill chieftain, that would have been Hugh O'Neill, wouldn't it, and petition the Stormont Government to divvy up the ancestral O'Neill lands among those who still bear the name; it would make a nice dowry for when we get married."

"Interesting thought. Hugh O'Neill has had some illustrious descendants. Both the present Queen of England and the Duke of Wellington have O'Neills in their ancestry. But it wouldn't help me. Apart from the unbridled enthusiasm with which the Northern Ireland government might be expected to greet such a petition, women in Celtic society weren't allowed to be chieftains."

"Excuse me ma'am. Wasn't there a Celtic chieftain lady in early England called Boadicea who tried to send the Romans packing "

"Boadicea was a queen and queens can do as they wish. Even if I were a man, it would be impossible to claim the O'Neill title. Under Brehon Law the chieftain was selected from among the males in the Derbfine. Since any male descendant of a common great-grandfather of the ruling family was eligible, who can say centuries later, with all these possibilities, that he is the lawful heir to a chieftain? When the English abolished this old system of tanistry, it disappeared forever. Under the English system of primogeniture you could perhaps trace back and make such a claim. The Heraldic Office in the Republic has recognized some people as 'Courtesy chieftains.' These courtesy chieftains had better not let it go to their heads, though, as I can't imagine many of today's Irish having much time for aristocratic titles. I can still hear my father tell the story of a Co. Cork politician who was running for the new Irish Parliament in the 1920s. Among the benefits of breaking ties with England he told the assembled farmers "and we'll have our own gentry" Perhaps the politician already fancied himself in the role of the neighbourhood squire.

"Our own gentry me arse" was the crude response from one unimpressed listener who didn't relish the idea of exchanging one 'm'lord' for another. Also, ironically enough, the claim of these courtesy chieftains can only be supported by the English convention of primogeniture. The current courtesy chieftain of the O'Donnells is a Franciscan Priest."

"There goes the farm. He'd be a brave and barefaced O'Donnell who'd claim to be the next courtesy chieftain succeeding that priest on the basis of primogeniture. He might look back with nostalgia to the good old days of that Derbfine thing you mentioned, when he could perhaps have done an end run around the priest. But as Ian Paisley said, 'Nostalgia ain't what it used to be'!"

"Did Ian Paisley say that? It doesn't sound like something he'd say."

"Actually I think it was Mark Twain, Between Mark Twain Yogi Berra and Churchill, they've said everything worth saying. But couldn't we grant poor old Ian the occasional 'bon mot'? He might well have said it, though, thinking on how Civil Rights activists cramped his style. Gone the glory days of Burntollet Bridge.[1]

"Anyway, the Caldwells, like the Creightons of Crom, came to Ireland from Scotland. All the north side of the lower lough was settled with plantation families – the Archdales, the Irvines, the Bartons, the Caldwells, and Blennerhassets."

"What families settled the other side?"

"Oh, the land over there was not quite as good and was left to those who preferred the view. Actually from up there on top of the Bar of Whealt there's a great view northward across the Erne to Donegal, and westward to Lough Melvin and the Atlantic.

"In the 1641 rebellion, the rebels took Francis Blennerhasset to Ballyshannon and shot him. In Fermanagh when the Irish in that rebellion temporarily reclaimed most of the plantation settlements, they murdered many of

---

[1] Where an angry mob of Unionists attacked a Civil Rights march.

the Planters. Some fled to Enniskillen and formed a militia under Sir William Cole. The siege mentality so often attributed to Ulster Unionists dates back to those times. To use another Paisley 'bon mot': 'We are not prepared to stand idly by and be murdered in our beds!'"

"Isn't that a somewhat ambiguous stance?" Teresa murmured.

"Cromwell's brutality when he suppressed that rebellion was in retaliation for the treatment the rebels meted out to the Planters,"

Teresa interjected heatedly,

"Cromwell was a monster who attempted to annihilate the Irish race. He massacred the entire garrison, together with many women and children at Drogheda. For months afterward no one could approach the city because of the stench of rotting bodies. He repeated his atrocities at Wexford. He offered the Irish the option of going to 'Hell or to Connacht', and those reluctant to avail themselves of either option he shipped to the West Indies as slaves. Admittedly, the Irish committed atrocities against the settlers in the 1641 rebellion, but while figures of the alleged Irish massacre of 1641 vary, depending on whose ox is being gored, no one has ever claimed the Irish deliberately killed women and children. The exaggerated claims of deaths of English settlers attributed to the rebels often exceeded the number of settlers in Ulster at the time."

"We have obviously been taught from different history books. On to modern times. A Caldwell descendant founded the pottery in Belleek in 1853. They and the Blennerhassets also started iron smelting in this part of Fermanagh and transported the iron down the Erne to Ballyhannon where it was shipped to England and elsewhere. At that time Ireland was wooded and the trees provided fuel for the smelters, or did, until demand outstripped supply and the countryside became denuded of trees."

"You know, Telfy, it must sound as if we Irish hate the English but personally I'd have to work hard at it. I can't think of any that I've met that I don't like. They seem like decent people, although their record in Ireland has been abysmal, but that is not the fault of the everyday Englishman of today. Politicians, of course, are a different breed, although I think Tony Blair is sincere in his efforts to find a solution to the problems here. Now, Margaret Thatcher I don't think I'd care for, although I'm not ever likely to meet her. I hear she took elocution lessons to sound like the queen. We should not forget our past, but we should forgive and learn from it. It would be the best remembrance. To forget would be to betray those past generations of our own blood who, for centuries suffering poverty and degradation in their own land, kept their faith and their humanity. Living and dying in abject poverty they had no material possessions to pass on to us but instead they left us the examples of courage and honour in adversity.

Nevertheless when we look back, we'd do as well to forget the recriminations and be sure that we ourselves have learned something worthwhile. Did the Irish experience with oppression at home make the Irish in the New World more compassionate to the plight of indigenous and oppressed people there? I don't know, Telfy. I'd hope so, but I've never heard that it was so."

Their trip ended at Belleek where Telfy's brother, Willie, met them. Telfy was preoccupied driving back to Belfast. Passing through a small town, on a road he had driven a hundred times, he drove down a one way street, and was forced to reverse back to an intersection in front of a large, angry lorry, emitting loud horn blasts.

The driver of the lorry took his hand off the horn long enough to lean out the window and point to his right and the correct route with the one word. "Y'eegit."

Telfy, who like his father was somewhat economical with words, confined his thanks for the directions to a simple gesture. The lorry driver, enraged and at a loss for a response to the terse gesture, looked like he might have a fit and responded with a sustained horn blast.

Telfy continued to be preoccupied all the way to Belfast, but did not share the reason for his preoccupation with Teresa.

The Armstrongs farmed one hundred acres of good land near the village of Lisbellaw. They were a solid and stolid family, respectable and respected, in no way foolish or rash. They saved their money and planned carefully. Over the centuries they had become so far removed from the ways of their wild borderer ancestors that they had not even engaged in the wartime smuggling so prevalent in many areas of Fermanagh close to the Free State border.

During the war, smuggling, especially of cattle, was widespread along the border between the Free State and "The North." Customs men manning the border posts, officious and important in their uniforms, thoroughly searched the rare vehicle, cyclists, and pedestrians while herds of cattle were smuggled across the moors behind them. Later, with increased I.R.A. activity, a series of bombed-out blackened and abandoned customs buildings – each one at a "safer" distance from the border and each off in a field at a "safer" distance from the road – marked the approach to the border. Eventually, the motorist approaching the border found a prefab a mile or so back from the border and off in a field well away from the road. A small head would appear in the window of the prefab and an arm would anxiously wave the motorist on. One jokester was reputed to keep a supply of pineapples in his car and would now and then lob one in their direction. Customs officers were no more beloved in Ireland than elsewhere. People delighted in telling the somewhat unlikely story of the man who weekly crossed the border, balancing a burlap sack of sand on his bicycle, and weekly was made to empty out the sand by the custom's officer, who was certain the sand concealed contraband. The customs officer never found any contraband and the man continued smuggling bicycles.

Neither of the two Armstrong sons was interested in taking over the family farm; Willie was a sergeant in the R.U.C. and Telfy, on a leave of absence from the R.U.C., was studying to be a lawyer. Their father was a large, kindly man, who spoke only after careful deliberation, and then with an economy of words. Their mother, a small woman with bright eyes, ran most things in the household, managed the finances, and did all the worrying for the household. Both had welcomed Teresa O'Neill into their family; neither she nor they felt any awkwardness.

Willie's conversation at the farm in Lisbellaw, when he had taken Telfy aside, had been extremely disturbing. "Telfy, would there be much involved if you and Teresa were to continue university in Dublin or in England?"

"What's wrong, Bill?" Both the question and the seriousness of his brother's face immediately worried him.

"I can't be certain but I believe there's some danger to both of you."

"From which side, the I.R.A.? The U.D.A.?"

"The way things are now in the North, from both. You know how things are these days in Ulster, Telfy. In addition to the O.D.C., we now also have to deal with the I.R.A., the I.N.L.A., the U.D.A., and the U.F.F."

"The O.D.C.? What the hell is the O.D.C.? Another bloody paramilitary outfit?

"Don't they teach you anything in University? Have you forgotten all your police work? Telfy! The O.D.C., the Ordinary Decent Criminal." Willie smiled. The man who makes a bank withdrawal wearing a mask. Nowadays most of the crimes we deal with are politically motivated. God be with the days when policing was pulling over a motorist to demand, 'And where would you be going with one tail light out?'"

Telfy lost his habitual composure.

"What a Goddamned country! Neither of us is involved in any of this political crap. We just want to get on with our lives. I can't see how we could change to another university just now. What kind of danger?"

"The County Inspector came to Dungannon to talk to me. A liaison with the Gardai in the South had told him that a possible attempt on your lives had been made at Belturbet. It seems someone may have been attempting to wire a bomb to your boat's ignition but was interrupted in the act. The informant couldn't be certain of it but he'd heard the rumour. What'll you do, will you tell, Teresa?"

"No, I don't think I will, not yet anyhow."

Telfy spoke little on the drive to Belfast, and Teresa, gazing out at the peaceful countryside in the fading dusk, left him to his pensive mood. It was dark by the time they passed the Maze Prison on their left, which housed many I.R.A. and U.D.A. prisoners, and reached the outskirts of Belfast.

"Did you ever think of emigrating to Canada or Australia?"

Teresa laughed. "What brought that on? Actually I have. I often thought of it before we met. It would be exciting, but maybe only for a few years and not forever. I have a friend in British Columbia in Western Canada, and she says it's lovely there. Wouldn't it be great to climb in the Rockies?"

"I wonder if we could ever go somewhere like that as exchange students," he said.

"We could never afford it. We're both at Queens on university scholarships, but abroad, we'd have to pay tuition and find a place to stay. Anyhow, I couldn't leave Ireland just yet. I help Daddy with the children in the summer. Fiona's sixteen and helps at home, but she'll be going away to nursing school next year. Nuala and Kathleen are too young to be much help, and the twins are only four."

"Cormac and Shane, the twin terrors of Tyrone." Telfy laughed. "It would take an army to look after those two." He reached over and put his right arm around her and by the time they reached their apartment she was dozing with her head on his shoulder.

In Lisbellaw a man and a woman stared in anguish at each other across the kitchen table as they listened to the morning news.

"A man and a woman were found shot to death in their car off the Malone Road last night. The names of the victims have not yet been released. It is believed to be another sectarian killing."

The man and the woman in the kitchen knew the names of the victims. The R.U.C. Inspector in the black Humber car that was now turning out of their driveway onto the Enniskillen road had just told them.

In Pomeroy two small children still clad in their night clothing were oblivious to the morning news as they combined their efforts to extract a fiercely resisting cat from beneath a kitchen dresser.

Teresa O'Neill was buried beside her mother in Pomeroy's Roman Catholic graveyard. Telfy Armstrong was laid to rest in the graveyard of the Anglican Church in Lisbellaw.

CHAPTER 25

Death of Maguire

In January 1600, Hugh O'Neill, in the manner of the Irish kings of old, took an army the length of Ireland, accepting the voluntary obeisance of some while enforcing the homage of the reluctant. He swept through the lands of the O'Carrolls and the Dillons, who had refused their support, leaving some of their castles in the hands of O'Neill wardens and others in smoking ruins.

Some Dillons lived to regret Sir Theobald Dillon's haughty reply to O'Neill's overtures, some did not. "Do you think that I would forsake so loyal a mistress and my natural Prince for your sudden coming to Dillon's country, assuring myself that I shall never see you there again?"

O'Neill passed by the Pale and no English army came out to dispute his passage to the south. He continued to the far south of Ireland and accepted the homage of the Lords of Munster. In all but name Hugh O'Neill in the year 1600 was High King of Ireland. O'Neill passed through a land prostrated by years of protracted war. The armies, both English and Irish had advanced and retreated across the war-ravaged land and now death from famine and disease was as readily available throughout the land as was death from war.

Elizabeth of England had been displeased with her one time favourite Robert Devereux, the second Earl of Essex, who unlike his father had not been sufficiently zealous in waging war on the rebels. The second Earl of Essex came to Ireland with a retinue of dandies and sycophants and an army of twenty thousand soldiers. He squandered this large army in pointless expeditions into mostly pacified Munster while making specious excuses to Elizabeth for his failure to face O'Neill in the north. Essex postured in Dublin in regal splendour, and even usurped the royal prerogative by elevating some of his friends to knighthood. Elizabeth had scathingly remarked of her one time favourite that he only drew his sword in Ireland to dub knights.

After the defeat of the Spanish Armada twelve years before, England had control of the seas and had largely cut off the supply of gallowglass from Western Scotland to the Irish chieftains. The Spanish, however, managed to continue to supply Ireland with arms and there was the ever present promise of more tangible support by way of landing Spanish troops in Ireland. Several such attempts had been made already. The involvement of the Spanish raised the stakes for England and made that country pour more and more men and arms into the fight. The Irish war was costly to England, and the English merchants and others who had contributed to the cost of the war would expect repayment and rewards of land grants at the successful conclusion of the war. After the Irish victory at the Yellow Ford, however, it seemed doubtful these English merchants would realise a return on their investment.

A new Lord Deputy, the Lord Mountjoy, replaced Essex, and his Queen had no complaints regarding the vigour of the warfare that her new favourite waged in Ireland. At the same time O'Neill passed inland on his triumphant romp down the length of Ireland, the man in whom Elizabeth reposed her hopes for the rebel earl's defeat — thirty-six-year-old Charles Blount – sailed into Dublin with another large army. Mountjoy advocated, and was to pursue with zest, a scorched earth policy in a country already exhausted from war, famine, and disease. He believed the only way to root out the rebels was to burn the crops and induce a famine that rendered the people incapable of resistance. Mountjoy believed in fighting in the winter when the populace would most feel the effects of this policy, and on his arrival in January, he lost no time in enlisting what was left of the winter on the side of the English.

Hugh Maguire commanded the Irish cavalry in O'Neill's march south. When the Fermanagh chieftain had expelled their sheriff, Willis, from Fermanagh in 1592, he was the first to defy the English and since that time, had either led his men in forays against Bingham in Connacht or defended Fermanagh against Bingham's enraged reprisals. Maguire was a natural commander of cavalry. Aggressive and recklessly brave, he believed in carrying the fight to the enemy. He led from the front and was usually well out in front of his charging squadron, screaming the war cry that for four centuries had drifted back to Maguires galloping eagerly behind. The Maguire graveyard of Aghalurcher near Lisnaskea and the Franciscan burial vault in Donegal bore mute testimony to many a chieftain of the family who had fallen while thus leading his sept.

As MacRory and Maguire rode at the head of a small company of mounted men that included Maguire's son, they were as far away from Fermanagh as it was possible to be in Ireland. They were within a few miles of their main body of cavalry camped some miles ahead in a fold of the West Cork hills.

Maguire, returning from a reconnoitre, was lightly armed and rode with only a small company of his cavalry. He observed to the gallowglass who rode by his side:

"The Spanish are landing arms in Donegal and if they also send a Spanish army as promised, the new Lord Deputy will not be eager to again venture into Ulster. Red Hugh rules Donegal and most of Connacht from Ballymote."

"Red Hugh didn't even have to lay siege to Ballymote Castle, but 'captured' it by buying it from the O'Connors," the gallowglass said.

"The O'Connors are practical people." Maguire laughed. "They knew they could not hold out against Red Hugh and struck what they thought was the best possible bargain. I wonder what the English would offer me for Enniskillen! But there are other ways into Ulster than through Connacht in the west or the Moyry Pass in the east. Before O'Neill bought us time with a short-lived peace, Essex contemplated landing an army to O'Neill's rear at the Foyle. England controls the seas since the disastrous defeat of the Spanish Armada. The Spanish are still a sea power to be reckoned with, but the English can largely do as they wish around these isles. If any sizable English force could be landed in the Foyle or the Swilly, both O'Neill and Red Hugh would be threatened."

"They say the new Lord Deputy is a sickly man and plagued by headaches," the gallowglass commented.

"We'll attempt to give him ample cause for headaches here in Ireland. And Ireland right now in the grip of an epidemic of spotted fever is no place for a sickly man."

"No place either for our child. Sheila is pregnant and the baby expected soon. Are we cursed, Hugh, to continue forever this war that breeds disease, famine, and devastation, this brutality that escalates daily and deadens our souls? Will the cycle continue forever? Will the innocent eyes of our children, looking eagerly out at their new world, become dulled also, reflecting neither hope nor compassion?"

Maguire looked curiously at his companion. "Strange sentiments for a soldier, Turlough. Perhaps like Philip the Second of Spain and Hugh Duv O'Donnell you'll be exchanging your armour for a monk's habit. Indeed though, I myself have often thought as you do. We profess a Christian faith, but stray far from its tenets. Our Saviour gave us an example of how to live that faith, but few among us have the courage to follow that path. Yet if courage fails us, our intellect should not, for when we look back; we see that life is merely a fast gallop towards death. From birth we are shadowed by death. *Pulvis et umbra sumus"* – We are but dust and shadows.

Seeing the almost startled look on his friend's face at such unaccustomed introspection, Maguire continued. "No, Turlough, don't be alarmed. I am not yet so close to death that I am preparing to forsake the sinning ways of my ancestors and enter the cloister."

Maguire paused and reined in his horse, staring ahead. A group of horsemen had appeared on the path about a quarter of a mile away and after a few moments of intense scrutiny, Maguire put spurs to his horse and was in a flat gallop before MacRory and the others could follow. MacRory saw the flash of a musket. The man, who had fired the weapon, threw it aside and had his sword at the ready by the time Maguire reached him.

The two fought, thrusting, and parrying, while manoeuvring their horses with reins and knees. Both men were skilled swordsmen, but Maguire was the better, and his sword passed through his opponent, but not before he himself was wounded. As the man fell, Maguire turned to face another adversary. He was too late to save himself from a thrust that found its mark beneath his right armpit.

MacRory and the other men entered the fray and MacRory, seeing Maguire wounded, engaged Maguire's assailant. Despite his wound, Maguire dispatched his assailant, but was himself again wounded. Furious at the injury to their leader, the enemy horsemen now swarmed around the wounded Maguire, intent on his death. Maguire bled from several wounds and it was obvious he would not survive the sustained onslaught. MacRory dispatched his own opponent and shouting to the others, charged his horse into the crowd of men around Maguire. Maguire's men followed and the battle encircled the wounded chieftain. With his left hand, MacRory seized one rein of Maguire's horse and holding it, galloped through the melee of fighting men, slashing to left and right with his sword. A troop of cavalry made its appearance, galloping from the direction of Maguire's camp.

The Fermanagh chieftain, pale and gasping for breath, was barely able to sit in his saddle. "Help me dismount, Turlough. I don't want it said that the leader of Tyrone's cavalry fell off his horse. How did my son conduct himself in the skirmish? The man I killed was Warham St. Leger, a noble gentleman. Ensure his body suffers no indignity."

MacRory helped Maguire to the ground. Even at this moment, and especially at this moment, he could not tell his friend a lie.

"Your son fought bravely as you'd expect him to, and died with his wounds in front."

He stood with sword in hand over his dying friend, but the battle was over and St. Leger's men disengaged.

Maguire's death cast despondency through the Irish that the loss of a battle could scarcely have done. On hearing of the death, O'Neill first took Maguire's body and that of Maguire's son, to Cork for burial, then made preparations for returning north. The death of his friend, son in law and comrade now devastated O'Neill, who in earlier years had campaigned with the English against Maguire. The coalition of northern chieftains had suffered a severe loss. O'Neill and the army marched back to the north in a pall of sadness.

MacRory rode north with an aching grief for his dead friend. As always the suddenness of death shocked and numbed. The vibrant life was gone — and forever. After MacRory's recovery from his illness, the buoyant young chieftain had been his constant companion at Enniskillen. The thoughts of those earlier days brought with them now a crushing sadness. His friend remained behind, laid to rest far from the Erne. MacRory had known Maguire to be quick-tempered and rash, but also compassionate and generous with no meanness in his nature. The magnitude of his loss was on a scale with the loss of his family, with the loss of his uncle.

Hugh O'Neill sat in his tent with Cormac, his brother, and Turlough O'Hagan, his foster-brother. All three sat in a sombre silence. Apart from the personal loss of his friend, O'Neill had other reasons to mourn the death of Maguire. O'Neill at last broke the long silence.

"He was the first to throw down the gauntlet in this struggle with the English, and once committed, he followed his path, straight as an arrow released from a bow. Indeed I look back with remorse to when I myself imprisoned him. At the time when Brian Óg O'Rourke defected to the English and knowing of Maguire's friendship with O'Rourke, I feared Maguire might follow O'Rourke's example. I need not have worried. Maguire, noblest of his noble line, remained true even in the face of that indignity. He knew only loyalty and brought no dishonour on his name. He was the most honourable of us all. His son, as brave as his father, died by his side. His noble nature knew no baseness. His example shames us and points out that higher path to us who follow. He followed his destined path and never strayed, and now he rests with God."

Turlough O'Hagan pondered on how specious talk of God, and honour, and destiny, fell so easily from the lips of the mighty. He thought, too, on how all memory of the profane path to power was so easily lost in the heedless labyrinth of the conscience. Both Cormac O'Neill and Turlough O'Hagan knew well what dark byways Hugh O'Neill had trod in his path to power. Did the mighty O'Neill now envy the dead Maguire his nobler idealism? O'Neill, whose faith had previously been the faith of expediency, after the Yellow Ford had assumed the holy mantle of defender of the old faith, a title held by Henry VIII before that monarch declared himself head of the new faith. Yet a chastened O'Neill had indeed emerged from the grim travail of war. His imperfect metal, refined in the heat of that furnace that he himself had kindled, had become the bright sword that would avenge his wounded and bleeding race.

When O'Neill continued, he spoke of more pragmatic considerations. "Our dead friend was an effective leader whose raids into Connacht tied down English troops. The Maguires have always been a powerful and influential family, and Hugh Maguire's example influenced other chieftains, who came over in increasing numbers to our northern alliance. He was the only Maguire powerful enough to unite his people in our common cause. O'Donnell now supports Hugh's half-brother, the young Cuconnaght, for the chieftaincy, and the English will take the opportunity to support Conor Roe of the senior branch to divide the Maguires. If it would unite the Maguires to our cause, I myself would support Conor Roe, but for the sake of the alliance, I dare not antagonize O'Donnell."

By the time O'Neill reached the north, his fears were confirmed. The Maguires were divided; the senior branch in Lisnaskea refused to acknowledge the new chieftain Cuconnaght, and Conor Roe left the northern alliance and went again over to the English.

O'Neill also had other matters of concern on which to brood. Elizabeth had given Lord Mountjoy, the new Lord Deputy, an army as large as that which Essex had previously squandered in his fruitless campaigns in Munster. Mountjoy sent part of this army to prevent O'Neill's return north, but O'Neill avoided a confrontation as he hurried homeward. There were rumours again of a landing of English troops in the Foyle, and if this happened, O'Neill and O'Donnell would be besieged from two sides. The steady stream of successes of the past few years, of which the Yellow Ford and the Curlews were the most notable, had brought many chieftains to their side, but O'Neill was realistic enough to know that if his northern alliance suffered one major defeat, those same chieftains would hurry with feigned repentance to make their submissions to Mountjoy.

The momentum had to be maintained. If a Spanish force were now to land in Ireland, it would give renewed life to the rebellion. Well before the Armada had sailed twelve years ago, there had been the promise of such a force. The English were at some disadvantage in having to supply their army from a distance, but the English controlled these northern seas. The Irish had the advantage of fighting on their own ground, but that ground was being terribly devastated.

To the eternal disgrace of the Irish, the English made good use of the concept of divide and conquer. A good half of English troops in Ireland were Irish. Without these Irish, the English could never have held Ireland. Unknown to those Irish they fought for their own destruction and for the total destruction of all they believed in and all their countless generations before them had believed in – the destruction of their freedom in their own generation and in their future generations. With eager ignorance, they shed their blood for their new masters to ensure their own slavery.

CHAPTER 26

A Birth

As they passed through the territory of the O'Farrells, MacRory parted from O'Neill's army and rode alone toward Cavan. Now that he was close to seeing Sheila, his sorrow at the memory of Hugh Maguire's death was tempered with the anticipated joy of again being with his wife. Earlier, he had deliberately tried not to dwell too much on thoughts of the beautiful woman who was his wife, as his separation from her was too painful, but now as the miles shortened, he was in an ecstasy of expectation.

Sheila was to be found neither in the hamlet of Cavan nor the nearby O'Reilly stronghold of Tullymongan. Much had changed in the country of the O'Reillys in recent months. The O'Reillys had finally thrown in their lot with the other northern chieftains and had suffered the retribution of all rebels as evidenced by the burnt-out hamlets and ruined cabins. In addition, an epidemic of spotted fever had ravaged the hamlet of Cavan and there had been deaths also at the nearby stronghold of Tullymongan.

The O'Reillys had cared for Sheila and her family who had fared better than most. Miles O'Reilly had sent Fiona, together with Sheila and her two sisters and little brother, to the safety of Ballyshannon. MacRory, more grateful for the kindness than any words could convey, hoped that the O'Reilly capacity for survival would see his friend through these turbulent times. The gallowglass spent one night with Sheila's mother and father in Cavan before hurrying on to O'Donnell's castle at Ballyshannon.

MacRory often relived the joy of that reunion. Later, after a torrent of words and questions, they sat quietly, replete with happiness, and exhausted by the joyful emotions of the reunion.

"Will the baby arrive soon?" MacRory placed a tentative hand on his wife's belly.

Sheila looked down at her belly. "Very soon, and Thank God you're here for the baby's due any time now. I feel secure now that you are back with us. Fiona O'Reilly has been very good. Her physician and the midwife for the O'Reillys look after me. Others in Cavan have not been so lucky, Turlough, but I thank God my mother and father are well. We are close to a famine. There have been lots of deaths from spotted fever."

"I know, Famine and disease come with war, and now spotted fever is a plague throughout Ireland."

"Will there ever be peace again? Will our child, too, live in a country doomed to this eternal warfare?"

He wanted with all his heart to grant the craving expressed in the lovely eyes, to grant peace by merely wishing for it. His mind wandered off in thought and it looked as if he was not going to reply, but at last he said, "This is not a minor sept war. This is full-scale war between Ireland and England with much to be gained and much to be lost. England, if she wins, gains a country which will be moulded to England's laws and England's ways, and ruled for England's benefit. Ireland, if she loses, loses everything: her culture, her faith, and her language. Ireland loses all that is Ireland.

"O'Donnell and O'Neill are aware of this; Maguire was, too; so was Fiach MacHugh O'Byrne. There are too many, however, who for greed ally themselves with the English, and it is those Irish, feeding at the English trough, who could destroy us all. Red Hugh said the only peace the English would allow us would be the peace of the grave, and if we do not soon defeat them in war, famine and disease will grant us that other peace. I'm afraid that for us there is no peace. Like a man struggling against death in a storm, it would be pleasant and tempting to rest, but it would be fatal. England comes to Ireland and makes war on our people and when we resist, calls us rebels and traitors. How can a man fighting in his own country and for his own country be either, and by what name are a people called who impose such deprivations on another?"

Sheila shuddered and moved even closer. "Let's talk of other things. Have you thought of a name yet?"

"Oh, I've had time to think of a hundred." Turlough laughed, happy to return to this more joyful consideration. "After all, it's now several minutes since I've become aware that the baby's birth is imminent."

Sheila said to her husband with some seriousness, "Fiona O'Reilly says it's going to be a girl. Fiona has an infallible method of predicting. She ties your wedding ring on a length of string and dangles it above your belly. If the ring starts circling clockwise, it's a boy, if counter clockwise, it's a girl. Will we try it?"

"Yes, we must certainly determine what we're dealing with here before rashly picking out names," Turlough replied with amused scepticism as they got ready the necessary prediction apparatus.

For the first ten or so seconds, the ring hung motionless, but then slight oscillations became apparent. Gradually, and to Turlough's amazement, the ring at the end of the string began describing a definite clockwise circle. "It's a boy."

"Let me try now," Sheila said. They both concentrated fiercely on the ring, which began ever so slightly at first, then very definitely to rotate counter clockwise.

"We're either dealing with twins here or a baby who even at this late stage hasn't yet decided," MacRory remarked. "Let me try again."

Again the ring rotated clockwise. Turlough looked thoughtful for a moment before trying one more time, but this time the ring rotated counter clockwise.

"I've got it!" he said, almost yelling in his enthusiasm. "The ring will rotate in whatever direction you wish it to. If you imagine it is going to go counter clockwise, it will. Here try it, Sheila, but this time think of it rotating clockwise."

They laughed like children as the ring described a definite clockwise circle.

"Don't tell Fiona, Turlough. She has a half and half chance, and she'll be so proud of herself if she's right. Anyway what choice have we in the naming of it. If it's a boy the first child has to be named after the father's father, if a girl after the mother's mother.

Fiona was right, and in any event she would never have accepted such a mundane explanation of her powers as a seer. The baby was called Kathleen after Sheila's mother.

O'Donnell's castle at Ballyshannon was a safe refuge near which no enemy dared to venture, but another enemy, no less deadly for being unseen, stalked the castle. Spotted fever spread through the castle garrison. One of the first to succumb was an elderly soldier, a man Sheila remembered for his kindness. A week earlier, as she had sat with her baby on a bench outside the castle in the sunshine, he had approached and placed his sheepskin cloak over her knees, shyly murmuring that there was not much warmth as yet in the winter sun. This man was the first of many, who over the next few weeks, died. The victims first complained of feeling vaguely unwell with a headache and a cough, then an abrupt onset of a high fever and an ague with severe intractable headache, progressing to delirium and prostration. Four days after the onset of the illness, a rash appeared on the body. Some of the younger, healthier victims recovered after two weeks, but many others died.

A week after the first death, Sheila herself developed a headache and a cough, and a day later, Fiona O'Reilly also developed the same symptoms. Turlough MacRory's heart could not accept the dread possibility that his mind told him he must. When the fever and ague confirmed his worst fears, he was torn between staying with Sheila or leaving her long enough to reach Enniskillen and the Maguire physician. Knowing he could do nothing in Ballyshannon, he set out for Enniskillen, praying that the man who had once saved his life might now be able to save a life infinitely more precious to him than his own. The old physician returned with him to Ballyshannon and immediately took over the castle and commenced issuing orders as if he were the O'Donnell warden.

"This disease has been known in Ireland since the last century. It is a plague that accompanies war and famine and goes by the name of 'War Fever' and sometimes is called 'Spotted Fever' because of the rash that goes with it. Soldiers spread it, but men, women, and children are affected. Fresh air and sunlight seem to be beneficial. A monk once told me that bathing in the holy well at Ballyshannon can prevent the disease."

O'Cassidy first ordered all clothing, including the soldiers' sheepskin cloaks to be washed and then, hung out each day in the sun. The healthy were paraded down to the holy well where they took their turn shivering in the cold water. All the victims were placed on clean pallets in the large central hall with curtains providing privacy for the females. During the day, the large doors were opened, allowing fresh air to blow through. These measures seemed to be effective as after two weeks, no new cases occurred, but deaths continued despite the physician's best efforts.

The Maguire physician spent every day with his patients and seemed equally concerned and solicitous for the state of the lowest soldier as he was for that of Fiona O'Reilly. The one-month-old baby, Kathleen MacRory, was a special source of concern, as she, too, had contacted spotted fever. The baby's mother lay delirious, shaking with ague and unable to feed her newborn. The baby's cry was strident and demanding at first, but each day the cry became weaker and more piteous. At first, the baby failed to gain any weight, and then began to lose weight. The skin hung loose on her little body except for the abdomen, which became bloated. O'Cassidy found a wet nurse, but the baby fed poorly. The portly old physician every day spent time with the scrawny baby, attempting to feed it small amounts of water with dissolved honey and salt. Gradually, the baby became less lethargic and its cry became again more strident. It fed more readily at the breast of the wet nurse. The baby stopped losing weight and actually started to gain.

The baby's mother and Fiona O'Reilly wavered between life and death. Neither was conscious of her surroundings, tossing, and turning, shaking with fever. O'Cassidy hourly spooned a liquid into the mouths of his patients. The old man was perpetually cheerful; attempting to buoy up the spirits of those around him, and with two exceptions never seemed to lose hope for his patients. The two exceptions were men who developed a purple rash. O'Cassidy had these men removed, saying there was no hope of recovery and each man did indeed die within twelve hours.

MacRory sat beside his wife, his lips moving in silent prayer, sponging her face with a damp cloth. She occasionally opened bloodshot eyes in a flushed face to stare unseeingly, muttering fragments of meaningless sentences. His heart ached when one fragment was spoken with startling clarity. "It's difficult to pick up English from a Spaniard."

MacRory slept in a chair beside his wife's bedside. Two weeks after the onset of her illness, he awoke one morning to find Sheila looking at him. Her face was no longer flushed, and she smiled at him and asked, "Was I talking about a Spaniard? How is Fiona O'Reilly?"

With equal suddenness, Fiona O'Reilly recovered the next day. Later, O'Cassidy told MacRory that he had in fact expected the recovery of Sheila and Fiona as both were young and healthy.

MacRory, uncertain whether to thank or to strangle the physician, asked him why he had not seen fit to relay this information earlier.

"Even with young healthy people, one in ten die after contacting war fever. It was no harm having your prayers assisting my treatment. Perhaps it's why Sheila is not that one in ten. Even we physicians sometimes need God's help."

MacRory shook his head, thinking with a pang of sadness, that the old man had been too long around Maguire.

MacRory and Sheila strolled by the woods of Camlin on the banks of the Erne above Ballyshannon in the spring of 1600. Looking at his wife and child, MacRory's heart thrilled with joy, immensely grateful for the gift of the lives that had been given back. New life was all around them, glorying in its vitality. A thrush trilled spring's renewal melody in the hazelnut trees by the river below. The sun gave welcome warmth to body and spirit.

Below them in the gorge the deep flood of the river rushed swirling to the sea. The Erne, that fabled river whose fords had for centuries guarded the gateways to Ulster and whose waters had been reddened with the blood of battles! Over the centuries how many eyes had gazed on the unchanging river, in the future how many more? Many things in Ireland are changing, MacRory thought, but this fabled river that has flowed on through eons of Ireland's history will remain unchanged as it has since the dawn of time. As the sun and all heavenly bodies have always rotated around the earth so will the tumbling roar of the falls forever herald the Erne's boisterous entrance to the sea.

He thought how his daughter, Kathleen, secure in her mother's arms, was too young to retain any conscious memory of this happy day, yet perhaps the love and security surrounding the child was felt at some as yet unknown level, perceived as surely as was the warmth of the sun on her skin. Perhaps the memory of these happy childhood moments, though lost in childhood's memory were stored somewhere in the baby's mind, and would be part of what the child would become.

Sitting on a rock, they gazed down into the swirling waters of the river. Sheila felt as if she were encased in a fragile cocoon of safety. As a child when she could not sleep, she had often imagined herself secure in a large nest in a tree out of reach of wild animals prowling beneath. She had something of the same feeling now, a feeling of security that she knew was nebulous.

"Do you think Kathleen will live in a land at peace?" There was a wealth of yearning in the mother's question.

"I don't know. We can hope for it. We can pray for it. These things have a life of their own like the river below us, which here is constrained and always turbulent, never peaceful like the loughs above. Maybe it's a matter of location, Ireland too close to a powerful neighbour."

"O'Donnell promised that after this war he would endow us as *Erenagh* of some church lands. Yes, I pray for our child to live in a peaceful spot in a peaceful land."

"God grant it."

CHAPTER 27

A Hostage

The baby, Kathleen, had fully recovered and her parents took her everywhere. The baby, secure in her mother's lap with only a plump face peeking from beneath warm blankets, slumbered and dreaming whatever dreams babies dream. MacRory's heart swelled with love as he watched Sheila clumsily tuck the clothing around their child, no longer conscious of her deformed hand.

The father pulled on the oars as they explored among the islands of the lower lough. They were accustomed to leaving Ballyshannon early in the morning and only returning as the sun set out over the Atlantic. Often they drifted silently on the lake for hours, happy in each other's company with verbal communication unnecessary. The gallowglass always took his sword along with him, although they seldom encountered anyone on the lough or the islands. Red Hugh had firm control of Donegal to the north, but since Maguire's death, Fermanagh, through which the Erne flowed, was in turmoil.

As the gallowglass rowed toward a projection of land on the north shore of the lough and one of three small bays he heard the sharp crack of a musket echo across the water. Some men stood on a spit of land and another man was fifty yards out in the water, swimming toward an island. Again the musket flashed and barked and echoed, and now the gallowglass was close enough to see a gout of water rise where the ball hit the surface well behind the swimmer. The man in the water was out of effective range of the musket, but it also looked as if he would never make the island. His strokes became uncoordinated and jerky, and his head sank beneath the water for long periods. MacRory pulled hard toward where he had last seen the swimmer's body and, looking down into the dark water; saw a vague shape, which became more distinct as the swimmer surfaced close to the boat, weakly treading water in an attempt to stay afloat. MacRory grasped the man's clothing and with difficulty hauled him over the gunwale into the boat.

A voice hailed him from the shore. "That man is Red Hugh O'Donnell's prisoner. Bring him ashore"

The man lay gasping in the bottom of the boat, bleeding from a bullet hole in his back. "If you do, you deliver me to my death. I may die from this musket ball anyhow. I'd rather not die by hanging. I'm Rory Maguire, Conor Roe's pledge to O'Donnell. Conor Roe has gone back to the English."

The young man, no more than seventeen years of age, gasped out the short sentences, and then was overtaken by a paroxysm of coughing. He apologized to Sheila, "I'm sorry, ma'am," as he attempted to wipe away the blood, which flowed from his mouth.

Another impatient hail from the shore: "You there in the boat, whoever you are, you endanger yourself and the woman by your delay. Bring that man ashore at once."

"I'm O'Donnell's gallowglass and I expect no threat to my wife from O'Donnell's soldiers."

The answer came immediately. "Our apologies, captain, we did not know. The man in the boat with you is Conor Roe Maguire's pledge to Red Hugh. He is to hang, but I think he took a musket ball and may not live to hang."

"He is now in my custody." The gallowglass did not wait for an answer, but seizing both oars, rowed rapidly down the lough.

A week later, O'Cassidy gazed down at the young man and marvelled at the resilience of youth. When MacRory had again summoned him back from Enniskillen, the physician had given a pessimistic prognosis.

"Pray hard this time, gallowglass, but I fear neither your prayers nor my own undoubted skill will bring this one back to life. The musket ball has penetrated deep into his back and he has lost a great deal of blood. It's amazing he was able to swim at all and did not sink like a stone."

O'Cassidy had fortified himself well before starting on the challenging case. Mercifully, the young man was unconscious and beyond any pain. With little to lose except a life that was already forfeited, O'Cassidy made a curved incision between two ribs commencing at the entrance point of the musket ball. He extended the incision following the path of the bullet along the course of a rib. He probed for and eventually removed a musket ball from where it had lodged anteriorly close to the heart. He ligatured a large freely bleeding artery. He sterilized the incision with a hot iron and then sewed up the incision with a gut suture. MacRory, who had indeed prayed for the young man, developed an awesome respect for both the power of prayer and the skill of O'Cassidy. Once it became apparent, however, that Rory Maguire would live, O'Cassidy, who earlier had seemed happy enough to enlist the help of God, now with an unseemly lack of modesty took sole credit for the miracle. O'Cassidy was no shy shrinking violet willing to let his deeds speak for themselves, but rather one who embellished the rose to an extent that would have made the rose itself blush. MacRory, who had come to revere the old man, however, readily overlooked this minor flaw of character. Three weeks after the removal of the musket ball, Rory Maguire, face still waxen, walked around the castle under the supervision of O'Donnell's guards.

As MacRory accompanied O'Cassidy back to Enniskillen, the physician lamented, "It's certainly a pity that all my fine work will merely ensure that the young man is in good shape for hanging."

"Surely he will not now be hanged," but even as he said the words, MacRory knew the fate that awaited Rory Maguire.

"O'Donnell has no choice; it's Conor Roe who's putting the rope around the man's neck," O'Cassidy murmured sadly. "It is sad, though, to have escaped captivity, to have escaped drowning, to have escaped one death only to die another. But you know the law relating to pledges."

By the time MacRory returned to Ballyshannon, he had made up his mind. Early the next morning, he arranged for two horses to be made available and rode out from the castle with Rory Maguire. They rode in silence the three miles to Belleek where they crossed into Fermanagh. Here the gallowglass reined in his horse and Maguire looked at him questioningly.

"I cannot see you hang," the gallowglass said.

The pale young face stared back at him.

"You will find a sword under my bed at the castle. I would most likely have died, but I would not have gone willingly to hang. You told O'Donnell's men I was in your custody. How will you yourself fare with O'Donnell in this?"

"I will take my chances," he replied, though a nagging anxiety surfaced in his mind.

Maguire looked at him steadily for a few moments more before saying simply, 'The debt I owe you is my life. You risk your own."

He reined his horse around and trotted off.

Within a week Red Hugh himself arrived at Ballyshannon with an army and a large retinue of sub-chieftains. O'Donnell was on his way to his Connacht headquarters in Ballymote Castle. Here he would rendezvous with the Connacht chieftains. Red Hugh then intended to lead them against two Irish earls to the south, O'Brien, Earl of Thomond, and Burke, Earl of Clanrickard, who were allied with the English.

Red Hugh O'Donnell cantered into the courtyard of Ballyshannon Castle at the head of a cavalcade of his chieftains. His host of gallowglass, bonnaghts, and kerns stretched back along the river for at least a mile. The young northern chieftain had made himself the undisputed ruler of the entire northwest of Ireland. He was master not only of Donegal, but also of a large part of Connacht. His name and prowess were known throughout Ireland. He had defeated some of England's best commanders. In the year 1600 such was the fame of Red Hugh O'Donnell that many in Ireland would gladly have hailed the Donegal Prince as *Ard Rí*. As he rode at the head of his men into his castle at Ballyshannon, he had the measured regal bearing of a king, that indefinable quality best described as the Roman virtue, "gravitas." If the Northern chieftains prevailed and rid Ireland of the English, would Ineen Duive accept anything less than *Ard Rí* for her son? Would Red Hugh himself accept less? But what man dare overshadow O'Neill's ambition?

The young chieftain, mounted in the manner of the Irish without saddle or stirrups, spoke briefly to the castle warden in the courtyard before dismounting and throwing the reins to a horse boy. Followed by his brother, Rory, Red Hugh, with a slight limp, walked over to MacRory and placed both hands on his friend's shoulders.

"God be praised, Turlough, that Sheila and your daughter are now well. Spend these weeks with your wife. I'll make no demands of you until I return from Connacht, but then you'll accompany me to Donegal. Henry Docwra has landed in the Foyle. I have left Niall Garve and O'Doherty to keep him pinned down while I deal with Thomond and Clanrickard. This Englishman, Docwra, may give us trouble. We have fought each other in Connacht. He is a determined and resourceful man."

MacRory raised his eyes to his friend's face. "O'Donnell, there's a matter –"

"We both mourn a friend, Turlough. Tell me about Hugh's death, you were with him."

The gallowglass gave an account of their friend's death, and in doing so reopened the wound of his own grief.

"Were his wounds so grievous?"

"Not even O'Cassidy could have saved him. He had many wounds."

O'Donnell stood with head bent for some moments before again speaking.

"Death shadows all of us throughout our lives, but his was not the soul that lives in fear of death. He lived as a man should live. He was the soul of honour. He died as he had lived, with honour, and he had the fortune to fall in battle at the hands of a worthy opponent. There are worse ways to die, Turlough. There are many worse ways to die. We ourselves, if we lose this fight for our way of life, may live to envy Hugh Maguire the manner of his death. May his brave spirit be long remembered. May his soul be with God."

O'Donnell crossed himself and paused before continuing. "Some say the death of our friend is an ill omen, and I am one who believes it is. Already there is dissension in Fermanagh. I have supported the young Cuconnaght as Hugh's successor, but Conor Roe has sought the help of the English to establish his own claim. Before I leave Ballyshannon, I must hang his pledge. Why would O'Cassidy have saved the poor boy's life so that he can live to hang?"

MacRory knew of no other way to say it, and no one had as yet dared to tell O'Donnell what his friend had done.

"Conor Roe's pledge is no longer at Ballyshannon. I gave him a horse and took him into Fermanagh."

It took a few moments for the impact of the gallowglass's words to register and when they did, the colour drained from Red Hugh's face as he stared at his friend. He asked for no explanation because there was no possible explanation that would have been acceptable. The gallowglass stared into his comrade's tormented face and dearly wished that this had not come between them, but he also knew he could have done no other than what he had done.

Moments passed and MacRory knew that his fate was being decided in those moments. The memory of an event that had occurred after the battle of the Curlews came to him. Brian Óg O'Rourke's son had murdered MacSweeney of Banagh. O'Donnell, despite the anguished protestations of his O'Rourke ally who offered recompense to the family in the form of all the gold he could collect, had insisted the law be followed. Brian Óg's son was hanged that same day from the walls of Sligo Castle. The father had to be restrained while his son died in the noose.

Memories of their bond of friendship struggled with the imperatives of duty; discipline and honour in the mind of the chieftain and the conflict were mirrored in his tortured face.

"No! No! There are some things no man can do. There are things no man can be asked to do."

The law should not be circumvented by any person, nor by any chieftain, or the law itself was diminished. To overlook his friend's action diminished also the chieftain's authority, admittedly by no more than a trickle diminishes the flood of the Erne, but by such a trickle is the mighty river itself first formed. O'Donnell, with the instincts of the consummate leader, knew that even the slightest erosion of his authority was a dangerous precedent. He reached a decision quickly enough, and it was a decision on this occasion dictated more by mercy and memories of a shared friendship than by a consideration of duty, discipline or honour.

"You lay a heavy burden on our friendship, gallowglass. Any other man, *any other*, I would order to the gibbet in place of the pledge, and the castle warden with him".

Either by design or unconscious accident O'Donnell's gaze was on his own brother as he spoke the words.

"I don't know your reasons for doing what you did, nor will I ask for them. You have been as a brother to me, aye, more than a brother, a comrade in my soul. I will not allow this to come between us. You have fought in my battles. You have fought by my side. I cannot take the life that you would willingly give for mine." O'Donnell turned to walk away, but stopped and turned to face the gallowglass.

"I know your compassion, Turlough, a commendable quality in those who can afford it. I know your compassion led you to risk your life in this matter. I also know that when you get your teeth into something, you do not let go."

The next day Red Hugh took his army south to Ballymote Castle. This fortress of Ballymote, O'Donnell had earlier "captured" by the simple expedient of buying it. A price of four hundred cattle together with the equivalent value in gold was negotiated with the O'Connor occupant. Such a tactic was more lucrative and appealing to all concerned than a costly and time-consuming siege. More lucrative certainly for O'Donnell who then raided into the surrounding O'Connor territory and rounded up the requisite price in cattle and gold. What O'Connor may have felt when he became aware that it was his own cattle he herded ahead of him is another matter.

Arriving in Ballymote Red Hugh summoned the O'Rourkes, the MacDermotts, the O'Connors, including his recent enemy O'Connor Roe of Sligo, and other Connacht chieftains. On his way south he was joined by the ever faithful Richard Tyrell, an Anglo Irish nobleman of Norman stock. O'Donnell led the combined forces south as far as the mouth of the Shannon into the territory of O'Brien, Earl of Thomond, returning by way of Loughrea and the Earl of Clanrickard's territory. The spoils were divided and O'Donnell returned to Donegal to deal with Henry Docwra.

CHAPTER 28

A Betrayal

On arriving in Dublin in January of 1600, Elizabeth's new Lord Deputy enacted his strategy for the winning of the long, drawn-out war in Ireland. He sent his able and ruthless assistant, Sir George Carew, south to war against the Munster chieftains who had submitted to O'Neill. The ablest of these O'Neill allies outside Ulster was Colonel Richard Tyrell who had some years earlier decimated an army of the Pale at a place called Tyrell's Pass in Co. Westmeath. He sent the equally capable Henry Docwra north by sea with four thousand men to dig in behind O'Neill at the head of the Foyle. Lord Mountjoy himself set about burning crops, inducing famine, and breaking into O'Neill's Ulster by way of the eastern Moyry Pass.

Throughout the summer, the stubborn Docwra maintained a tenuous toehold at Derry at the head of Lough Foyle despite all efforts by both O'Donnell and O'Neill to dislodge him. MacRory led O'Donnell's gallowglass in forays and skirmishes against Docwra who began to run short of supplies and was forced to make desperate sallies for provisions into the surrounding countryside.

O'Donnell himself expressed admiration for Docwra's tenacious resistance.

"I know him from Connacht. If I could have had such a resourceful soldier as Henry Docwra as my ally rather than my enemy we'd have driven Bingham and his settlers into the ocean long since."

Red Hugh sat on horseback on a plateau overlooking Docwra's camp and watched as a troop of fifty cavalry escorted a large herd of horses from the camp to a nearby meadow for forage and exercise. Behind the escorting cavalry marched about one hundred foot soldiers armed with muskets. On the plateau and hidden in the woods behind Red Hugh were two hundred of his horsemen. Another four hundred of his soldiers had taken up their positions in the darkness and now lay hidden beyond the meadow.

It was a daily routine for the horses to be taken each morning to the meadow for exercise, and as Docwra's encampment at Derry was under frequent attack, a substantial force of English cavalry and foot soldiers always accompanied the horses. Red Hugh made no attempt at concealment, and the English cavalry commander, Captain Basil Brooke, escorting the horses, rode with frequent glances up towards the lone horseman on the ridge above. Sir Henry Docwra's hostile neighbours kept his camp at the Foyle under constant surveillance, and the sight of a lone horseman observing the morning cavalcade aroused no great concern.

The horses scattered throughout the clearing, most to graze on the lush meadow grass, some to cavort and gallop and exult in their daily interval of freedom.

The commander of the escort looked again at the plateau above, but the lone horseman had gone. Gradually, Brooke became aware of a rumble as if the earth itself trembled. At once he shouted to his men to form up and prepare to receive a cavalry charge. He had served with Docwra's horse in Connacht and was unlikely to mistake the sound made by a large body of cavalry at the charge.

Two hundred throats roared "O'Donnell Abú" as O'Donnell's horsemen swept down on the English. Captain Brooke, one of Docwra's most seasoned campaigners, strove to keep his voice steady as he readied his men to face the wild onslaught of the Irish cavalry. At the same time, Red Hugh's foot soldiers rose from hiding beyond the meadow and swarmed forward. O'Donnell's chief objective was to capture the horses, and to this end, half of his cavalry commenced driving the horses before them while Red Hugh himself and the remainder of his cavalry, together with his foot soldiers, engaged Docwra's men. It soon became apparent that not all of Docwra's horses had been sent out for exercise. Another body of cavalry, about one hundred strong and headed by Docwra himself, galloped forth from Derry to support their hard-pressed comrades, and a large number of the Derry garrison followed these new horsemen.

In the initial shock of surprise, O'Donnell's men had secured their main objective and two hundred of Docwra's horses were herded at the gallop down the valley. Some of Docwra's cavalry shepherded a smaller group of about fifty horses back toward Derry. In the meadow, the English fought desperately to keep from being annihilated and to hold on until Docwra and the men from the camp reached them. After the initial discharge of muskets, there was no time to reload, and the fighting closed to hand to hand.

MacRory and his gallowglass ran forward from their hiding place in the meadow until they came in contact with the enemy. The disciplined gallowglass pressed steadily forward. The enemy retreated fighting.

Henry Docwra reached the field and his presence rallied and heartened his men. Docwra and O'Donnell, both distinctive in their armour, fought their way toward each other, but it was MacRory on foot in the vanguard of his gallowglass who found himself engaged by Docwra. MacRory warded off with his halberd a slashing sword sweep from the horseman. A young kinsman of O'Donnell's galloped screaming across the meadow and hurled a spear when within a few feet of the English knight. Docwra fell from his horse, hit on the forehead. MacRory leaping astride the fallen horseman, changed his grip on the huge sword, and raised it with both hands on the hilt to stab down on Docwra's exposed neck. He hesitated to deliver the death blow to a fallen man and again changing the grip on his sword turned aside and engaged in the melee around him. The pause gave Captain Brooke time to rally the English around their fallen leader and the battle now raged with renewed intensity around the man lying senseless on the ground. With the loss of Docwra, the disheartened English seemed only interested in retreating to the protection of their fortifications. This they managed to do, taking with them Docwra, fighting each bloody step with O'Donnell's men howling and attacking like wolves on the heels of an injured prey.

Over fifty Irish chieftains assembled in the Franciscan abbey by O'Donnell's Donegal castle. Red Hugh and Father O'Mulconry stood speaking with two Spaniards, Fray Mateo de Oviedo, and Don Martin de la Cerda. These two Spaniards had sailed into Donegal Bay, bringing with them one thousand harquebuses, powder and ball, and Philip III's promise of Spanish aid for Ireland. Neither Spaniard spoke Irish and neither was proficient in English.

Father O'Mulconry translated from the sonorous Spanish with its pleasing, thrumming "r"s to the Irish with its soft, throaty intonation. "Spain will certainly continue her help, but you must realize that Ireland is not Spain's foremost concern. The war in the

Netherlands stretches the resources of Spain, but she will continue to supply arms and equipment to Ireland as she has done in the past."

O'Donnell nodded and phrased his reply carefully. "For all of Spain's assistance in the past, Ireland will always be grateful, and whatever the outcome of the present conflict, Ireland and her future generations will never forget the assistance of Spain, our gracious and powerful ally. Because of your help we have been able to bear ourselves with honour in this struggle against a powerful adversary. No future generation can ever say that we, in this, brought dishonour to our name. If fate has decreed that the Saxon is to extinguish the light of our race, let it never be said that we crept away like cravens into the darkness. We are a small, divided country, fighting a war with a powerful, united nation. I say a divided country, and as yet we *are* divided, but our common enemy unites us. The war is no longer confined to the northern part of the country, but now involves all of Ireland. O'Neill has taken his army unopposed the length of Ireland in a show of force that has weakened the English and brought many to our side. However, we are well aware of what forces the English can bring against us. Mountjoy, the new Lord Deputy, is well supplied with men and the weapons of war. A year ago the Second Earl of Essex landed a vast army in Ireland, and –"

O'Donnell paused, aware of Father O'Mulconroy's steady gaze on him. When dealing with the touchy Spaniards, a certain delicacy was necessary. Red Hugh had been about to mention how O'Neill had outmanoeuvred Essex both militarily and diplomatically. However, it was perhaps better not to appear boastful regarding O'Neill's triumph over the Earl of Essex, the same earl who, with Drake, had defeated a Spanish fleet and burned Cadiz some years earlier.

O'Donnell continued, "And only his ineptitude as a commander saved us. He hastened back to England to explain his failure to Elizabeth, and it is rumoured that he has been beheaded. So far we have prevailed and our victories have drawn many to our side, but the English can afford to lose many battles and still win the war. We cannot afford to lose a single battle. We ask Spain to come to our aid with a Spanish army landed in Ireland, an army of experienced soldiers such as those who defeat England's army in the Netherlands. It is well known your nation breeds soldiers whose valour is unequalled throughout the world, and I do not fear to be thought a sycophant in saying so, for who can exaggerate the deeds of such men as Cortes and Pizarro! If you send us aid, it must be soon. The tide flows for Ireland now, but this war takes its toll. The common people of this country slide into an abyss of despair and ruin. This war shows them the face of hell."

Fray Ovido murmured, "*Facilis descensus Averno*".[1]

O'Donnell, usually disciplined in conversation, uncharacteristically slid into a digression.

"Indeed Father, in war the descent into hell is all too easy. Wars and great warriors leave behind widows, sorrow, and mass graves. Great poets like Virgil are a gift to all mankind and the enemy of no man. Great poets and great saints like Columba, enrich mankind with inspiration and exalted thought. Indeed the qualities that make great warriors are the same qualities that make great saints. Courage, passion, and vision are qualities found in Alexander of Macedonia and Columba of Iona. Perhaps it is the direction in which these qualities are channelled that makes the difference. The poet and the bard reach out and sound our souls, and with their art evoke wondrous and sublime emotions. Is the difference between the poet and the warrior the difference between good and evil? All countries have both their poets and their warriors, and indeed, there is something of each in all of us."

Fray Ovido listened politely while Father O'Mulconry translated O'Donnell's musings and when he had finished returned to the subject of Spanish aid.

"The Spanish people are aware of your gallant struggle. Our two earlier attempts to send soldiers to your aid were thwarted when storms scattered our ships. You will remember that in 1596 and again in 1597 gales scattered Spanish expeditions to Ireland. Fate and the elements seem to favour the English, as it did also in the case of our great Armada. Our new king, Philip III, is personally most anxious to help Ireland and has even offered to finance another expedition from his own purse. Such an expedition may be launched within the year."

O'Donnell nodded, and chose his words carefully.

---

[1] "Easy is the descent into hell." (Virgil).

"This, of course, is good news, and please do not think us ungrateful, but I must point out some further facts regarding the situation here. Our coalition of Irish chieftains under O'Neill and myself has held together because of a fortuitous string of Irish victories. Any setback and the situation may change. A grave setback has already occurred with the death of Hugh Maguire. Carew in the south hard presses our allies there, while Mountjoy advances on O'Neill's Tyrone. The English at Derry are being supplied by sea. The land is close to famine and starving men have little belly for war. Forgive me for being importunate but I must emphasize that if Spanish help is to be effective, it must reach us soon."

De Cerda, the soldier, spoke for the first time.

"You have convinced us of your extremity and we will convey the urgency of your need to his majesty. I am a soldier as are you, and we both know that fortune favours the bold. The Irish have boldly thrown down the gauntlet, and so far fortune favours your boldness, but we both also know that war is like chess. You can be within one move of checkmating your opponent, but you may never get the opportunity to make that move because he, too, is within one move of checkmating you."

Afterward, when they were alone, Father O'Mulconry spoke with Red Hugh. "Do you remember many years ago at Ballyshannon asking me, if by accepting Spanish aid, we would not be exchanging one tyrant for another?"

"We have no wish to fight a war with England in order to hand Ireland to Spain. If it were Spain's intention to send an army to Ireland for that reason, I think she would have great difficulty holding the country once we were united, and driving out the English would unite us as nothing has done since King Brian defeated the Danes at Clontarf. At the moment, the loyalty of many Irish chieftains to the northern alliance is tenuous. But the Spanish have repeatedly told us that conquest is not their aim in Ireland, and the Spanish are honourable with respect to their word." O'Donnell smiled slightly at the naiveté implied in his last sentence.

"I'm aware that where the interest of great countries is involved honour is often merely a word, the concept a tool in diplomacy. The honour of great nations lies in doing whatever is necessary to maintain their greatness. They tailor their honour to their needs. We in Ireland are desperate and Spain will tell us what we wish to hear."

Again O'Donnell smiled. "I'm sure, Father, you are enough of both a Latin scholar and man of the world to translate Catullus. *'Mulier cupido quod dicit, amanti in vento et rapida scribere oportet aqua.'*"

"It is not a phrase the Franciscans frequently quote, but I think it translates as, 'What a woman says to a panting lover should be written on the wind and flowing water.'"

"Quite. Ireland is desperately in need of help and if we do not get that help from Spain, and soon, we will lose the war and Ireland," O'Donnell replied.

Red Hugh took advantage of the gathering of Irish chieftains in Donegal Abbey to reinforce with them the need for unity. Red Hugh, on the battlefield or in the council, had considerable powers of persuasion. The form of persuasion these chieftains most readily understood, however, was a display of power and O'Donnell was soon again forced to take an army south.

Sir George Carew, appointed by the Lord Deputy to be President of Munster, used the point of the sword to drive a wedge between the northern chieftains and their allies in the south. Again leaving Niall Garve to guard Docwra, Red Hugh took most of his army south to Ballymote. He also left MacRory and his gallowglass behind under the command of Niall Garve.

MacRory's gallowglass were thrown repeatedly against Docwra's precarious encampment at the head of the Foyle and repeatedly repulsed. In each attempt some of his men died but MacRory ensured that his men's lives were not sacrificed needlessly. Niall Garve O'Donnell was a capable leader and in military matters treated the gallowglass with a cold professionalism, but MacRory sensed the underlying seething hatred. Niall Garve had no way of knowing whether or not Red Hugh had been made aware of the incident in the Curlews. The fact that Red Hugh had not as yet challenged him on it did not mean that he was unaware of it.

MacRory and his gallowglass were encamped about a mile from the main force commanded by Niall Garve, but the two men conferred daily. On returning from one such meeting MacRory found Fr. O'Mulconry awaiting him in his tent.

"You and your men are in imminent danger. Niall Garve is about to go over to the English. Your loyalty and that of your gallowglass to Red Hugh has assured your deaths. Be careful

MacRory. He has also been heard to speak of avenging a personal insult. Niall Garve is a powerful and a dangerous man"

Niall Garve's treachery appalled MacRory but it did not come as a complete surprise. Niall Garve, a resolute captain, had recently shown a lack of resolve in assailing Docwra. Indeed he had just that day told MacRory to stand his men down as he was considering a new strategy in the struggle to oust Docwra. With the warning from Fr. O'Mulconry and Niall Garve's now ominous suggestion that he stand his men down the gallowglass was certain that he and his men were indeed in imminent danger and decided that he would take his men south to Ballyshannon the next day.

The dawn sun's rays were just illuminating the landscape when Niall Garve O'Donnell and a large contingent of fully armed men thundered into the gallowglass camp. They trampled tents and leaning down from their horses slashed ropes and canvas. Many were armed with spears which they hurled into the tents. Niall Garve sat on a prancing horse in the center of the ravaged camp and shouted:

"I promised another time, gallowglass. Did you think I had forgotten? Now is that other time." He looked around the encampment but something was wrong. No awakening men staggered in disarray from tents to be slashed to death. No shouts of dismay. The only commotion was of their own making. The camp was empty.

Silhouetted in the morning sun fifty mailed and helmeted gallowglass materialized in a semicircle on a bank on the edge of the camp. Each had a musket to his shoulder and each musket was aimed at the man on the prancing horse. MacRory stood slightly to the right of his men and stared down at Niall Garve.

"Perhaps you have lost your way. Docwra's camp is in the other direction. But a traitor and a cur should be on his knees crawling if that is your destination."

The situation seemed to have deprived Niall Garve of speech. He jerked his horse around in circles, only to find that an equal number of armed gallowglass had appeared behind him.

When he was finally able to speak his voice was quiet but charged with rage. "There will be a day, gallowglass." His head nodded. There will, and perhaps it *is* today." He dismounted and drew his sword.

"You called an O'Donnell a cur and a traitor. You will answer for it."

Whatever Niall Garve O'Donnell's faults, lack of courage was not among them, for few would be so foolhardy as to challenge the gallowglass to a sword fight.

MacRory leaped down from the bank and drew his sword. In his profession he fought dispassionately with no hatred of his enemy, but the betrayal of Red Hugh and the attempted callous slaughter in their sleep of one hundred of his men who had recently fought alongside this man evoked a blind rage.

But he now found that this very rage hampered his swordsmanship. He rushed almost clumsily at his opponent who easily enough parried his charge. Niall Garve was an accomplished swordsman and his courage made him a dangerous one, how dangerous was soon demonstrated to MacRory when Niall Garve in a fearless lunge caught the gallowglass by surprise. A searing wound in his right arm reminded him that this man was no amateur. It had been an attempt, and an almost successful one, to disable his sword arm. But his wound also reminded him of lessons taught by his uncle, lessons hammered home with sword pricks. "The mind, the mind", he muttered to himself and became again the cold-blooded adversary that would not lose this fight. Niall Garve, encouraged by the wound he had inflicted, fought well and with a reckless courage that made him a formidable opponent, but now the gallowglass was again master of himself and of his profession.

Soon this change became apparent also to his antagonist, but MacRory saw no fear in the other's eyes. He saw only hatred, two eyes that were daggers of hatred, hatred that matched his own. MacRory relaxed and defended himself while allowing the other to waste energy in repeated futile attacks. He bided his time deliberately letting his opponent know that he was outmatched, and then coldly chose the moment and the method to end the fight. With precision he passed his sword through the muscles of Niall Garve's upper arm and the arm fell uselessly to his side. Niall Garve took the sword from his right hand and clumsily attempted to continue the fight left-handed. The gallowglass sent his opponent's sword flying and then walked close to the man he despised, stared into his eyes and struck him across the face with the back of his left hand. He knew as did each man watching, and as did Niall Garve O'Donnell that a sword thrust through the heart would have been less cruel. O'Donnell's head hung in shame on his chest but he raised his eyes to MacRory's. He spoke quietly.

"For this insult I will take revenge on you and any of yours who walk this earth."

The gallowglass chilled by the threat that could only be directed against his family stared at his opponent, and in that moment regretted that he had allowed revenge to cloud his judgement, regretted that he had chosen to humiliate rather than to kill a dangerous enemy. He sheathed his sword and turned to his men.

"Take their horses and their arms."

O'Donnell, carrying a white flag of truce, rode at the head of about one thousand of his kinsmen into Docwra's fortified camp at Derry. The indestructible Henry Docwra had survived his near fatal encounter with an Irish spear and now stood in front of his entire army to receive the submission of O'Donnell. O'Donnell dismounted, walked up to the Englishman, and bent head and knee before him.

Henry Docwra raised Niall Garve O'Donnell from his knees and warmly embraced him. Docwra, well aware of Niall Garve's ambition to be chieftain, seized O'Donnell's left hand, his right was bandaged to his body and, holding it up, shouted to the assembled men, his own and O'Donnell's, "Welcome to the chieftain of the O'Donnells."

Since his arrival in Derry, the patient Docwra had ceaselessly wooed Niall Garve, who harboured a smouldering resentment against his cousin, Red Hugh. Docwra intimated the English would support Niall Garve's contention for the chieftainship of the O'Donnells. The English had already attainted Red Hugh, of course, as a rebel and in the event of an English victory, he would be lucky to retain his life let alone the chieftainship. Ambition finally triumphed over loyalty to family, sept, and country. Niall Garve's three brothers, Hugh Bui.[1] Donnell, and Conn, as well as

---

[1] "Yellow-haired Hugh".

some other O'Donnell kinsmen, accompanied Niall Garve in his defection to the English.

The benefit to the English of this coup by Docwra was enormous; the harm to the Irish cause inestimable. The English at Derry, hitherto confined, assailed, and impotent within their fortress prison, were now freed, and provisioned by Niall Garve. His first service to his new master was to take with him one thousand men to rebuild and hold for the English the derelict O'Donnell castle at Lifford. Docwra, now no longer constrained at Derry, could penetrate from Lifford to the heart of Donegal through the Barnesmore Pass. From Lifford also he threatened O'Neill's Tyrone from the west.

MacRory took his gallowglass south to Ballyshannon before hastening on alone to overtake Red Hugh at Ballymote. Never before had the gallowglass seen despair so overwhelm O'Donnell as when he conveyed the news of Niall Garve's desertion. Red Hugh's body and spirit seemed to slump as he sat in silence for long moments. When at last he spoke, there was more sadness than anger in the barely audible words.

"My cousin, my ally, my kinsman! A betrayer of the O'Donnells and of *Tir Conaill*! A traitorous Queen's O'Donnell in our hour of greatest need! It's my shame to bear the same name."

The words brought to mind a story MacRory had heard of Red Hugh during his captivity. Irish chieftains were frequent visitors to Dublin Castle and would no doubt have stared curiously at the ill-treated hostages wandering in the courtyard. Red Hugh, in shackles and filthy clothes, had blackened his hair with charcoal so that he would not be recognised as the son of the O'Donnell chieftain and bring shame on his family. He had also constantly encouraged the other pledges, some as young as ten and twelve, to maintain their faith and honour in the face of destitute circumstances and English derision.

"This act, Turlough, could be a mortal wound to us all," Red Hugh said. "Niall Garve is an able leader and others will follow his example. We have lost Maguire, and Conor Roe is again an English ally. And now Niall Garve! Is our tide of fortune on the ebb? Ever since Dermot MacMurragh[1] these alliances with the English have been the downfall of our race. When our chieftains, for their own gain, betray our people, are not the English justified in looking on us with contempt? In the face of such shame can we ever aspire to be a nation?"

O'Donnell's despondency, however, did not last for long. He rose to his feet and shouted orders in preparation for getting his army on the march.

"I will leave at once for Lifford. All of the cavalry will come with me. The army will follow as quickly as possible." He turned again to the gallowglass. "Come with me. The fault is mine, for I should have foreseen this. It will not be allowed. He will be made to return to our side or he will not live to serve the English."

In the past such an alliance with the English, motivated as it was by self-interest, would have been commonplace enough, and no one attempting to gain such an advantage would have been regarded as much of a traitor. However, O'Neill, O'Donnell, and Maguire had been the first to become aware of how such alliances with the English eroded Gaelic Ireland to England's advantage.

With so much now at stake, Niall Garve's defection was an act of perfidy that could spell disaster for the Irish. O'Donnell was too much of a pragmatist to allow himself to be motivated by reasons of revenge. He did not relish the idea of Irish O'Donnells fighting Queen's O'Donnells, but he also knew that he had no choice in the matter. He knew he must exert his authority and do so quickly. Within two days he was at Lifford with MacRory's gallowglass threatening Niall Garve with his cavalry and awaiting the arrival of the rest of his army before launching a full-scale attack

---

[1] King of Leinster, who brought the Normans to Ireland in 1169.

CHAPTER 29

A Peace Proposal

When people spoke of senseless sectarian hatred the Middle East and Northern Ireland came first to mind – the carnage of bombs in Enniskillen and Omagh, the obscenity of three young children burned to death in their home, the ceaseless retaliatory murders. What kind of barbaric people inhabited Northern Ireland who could allow such things to happen? No different from the people asking the question. The evil and the obscenity had happened before in the world, and continued to happen again and again, and again and again, with the predictability of the seasons. Burns was an optimist when he wrote, "Man's inhumanity to man makes countless thousands mourn." Perhaps had he lived post First and Second World War, he would have been more of a realist and his "thousands" would have been "millions." Ireland was a small country and the carnage, while spectacular, was not such as some larger and more powerful countries could boast of.

The antidote formula was known but too little practised in Northern Ireland as elsewhere throughout the world. Some of the best people in the world lived in Northern Ireland alongside some of the worst, much as might be said for Uzbekistan, Uraguay, or Denmark. Gordon Wilson, a draper who refused to seek revenge for his daughter's death, lived in Northern Ireland.

When three children walking on a Belfast street were killed by a runaway I.R.A. car, their aunt joined forces with Mairead Corrigan, who had witnessed the children's deaths. The two women founded an interdenominational organization to promote peace. Courageously and at risk to their lives, they denounced the violence of the paramilitaries. Their efforts were credited with reducing the death toll in Nothern Ireland by half.

The majority of the ordinary people of Northern Ireland continued with their daily lives throughout the long years of the conflict, submitting with dignity and patience to searches at checkpoints and the many other disruptions of daily life. These were kind, decent, and hardworking people. In Northern Ireland in 1994 for every four men between the ages of sixteen and forty-four, there was one army or police presence.

As the conflict approached thirty years of bitter communal strife, another proposed peace agreement was presented.

As part of the peace agreement the Republic of Ireland surrendered its long-held territorial claim to the six northern counties. This, for the Republic *was no small matter; no small thing to close its mind to those haunting, accusing voices of past generations; those guardian ghosts of the rebel past, watching from the shrouded shadows of history: the Wild Geese, the United Irishmen, the Fenians, the Republican Brotherhood, and their successors, the Irish Republican Army; those who had fought for centuries for a united Ireland and passed the torch to each succeeding generation. No small thing to forget Ireland's centuries old imperative that demanded of each new generation a blood sacrifice to the memory of the rebel dead of the last. The age old sacrifice, willingly embraced, to ones father's faith:*

> *And how can man die better than facing fearful odds*
> *For the ashes of his fathers and the temples of his gods!*

But many in Ireland, North and South, welcomed the concept the Peace Accord embraced and now had a different vision. They longed to emerge into sunlight after thirty years of wading in an underworld of sordid atrocities; "Romper rooms" in which eager sadists plied their trade; Callous executions performed in the presence of mothers, fathers, and children; children burned to death; Security forces by day, death squads by night; And the perpetrators walked among us, and looked no different from us. They longed to live in peace and saw an Ireland at peace. They saw an Ireland where Ulster Unionists with a four hundred year history binding them to Ireland would at last call themselves Irish, and where all of Ireland would accept and welcome the undoubted contribution of these Ulstermen over the centuries to the culture and character of the country. Their vision was an Ireland where both Unionists and Nationalists would see both the Battle of the Boyne and the Easter Rebellion as part of "our" history.

The new nation of the peace accord would be neither the exclusive Gaelic nation of the Gaelic Revivalists nor the embattled Ireland of the eternally entrenched Ulster enclave of the Orange Order. Their Ireland would embrace all who lived on the island, and would recognize and cherish all of their cultures by all of the people, an Ireland where an Armstrong or an Elliot was as Irish as a Fitzgerald or a Burke, as Irish as a McCarthy or an O'Brien. The biblical welcome accorded the prodigal son would seem a chintzy affair compared to the welcome awaiting the Scotch/Irish of the north if they choose to participate in the dream of Thomas Davis. The return of the Protestant son, alienated since the time of Wolfe Tone, would indeed make Ireland whole again "a nation once again."

Those who voted for the peace accord and the new nation seemed heedful of the sentiments expressed in the poem by Thomas Davis:

> *It whispered too that freedom's ark and service high and holy,*
> *Would be profaned by feelings dark and passions vain or lowly,*
> *For freedom comes from God's right hand and needs a godly train.*
> *And righteous men must make us then, A Nation once again.*

Those who would rebuild a new Ireland were challenged to replace self righteous rhetoric with righteous deeds. The proponents of the accord accepted a geographical division, which they hoped in time, would fade away in the dawning recognition of a common humanity and an honest acceptance of each other's traditions and aspirations. High hopes for the future, indeed, in view of the debacle of the present and the deeds of the past, but nothing less would work; nothing at all had worked in the past.

People saw more truth and hope in the words of a Gordon Wilson than in all the cant and rhetoric of the politicians. No matter which side eventually claimed to be "victorious" in the present struggle, the fight would not end there. Both sides would remain locked in a convulsive dance of death, now fox-trotting to the tune of "The Protestant Boys", now waltzing to the tune of "The Bold Fenian Men," both sides the loser as for decade after decade their only victories would be measured in mutual defeat. Logic and the lessons of history decreed there must be another solution, but in Northern Ireland emotion had always triumphed over logic, and the lessons of history only fuelled the flames.

In an all-Ireland referendum over 94% of the people of the Republic of Ireland to the south and over 71% of the people of Northern Ireland accepted the proposals of the peace agreement. However, while the referendum in Northern Ireland passed by a substantial majority of 71% of the population – Unionists and Nationalists – only a bare majority among the Unionists passed it. Another stumbling block was that according to the terms of the agreement the I.R.A. must decommission its weapons. The I.R.A did not regard itself as having been defeated and believed that surrendering its weapons would be interpreted by some as the act of a defeated army.

CHAPTER 30

1798 Rebellion. "Who fears to speak of '98

Commandant Conor Maguire of the Irish Army piloted a helicopter carrying Canadian General John De Chastelain on a courtesy sightseeing flight over the northwest of Ireland. De Chastelain had the task of overseeing the disarming of the paramilitaries in the peace process that had become known as the "Good Friday" peace agreement. The Canadian had time on his hands for sightseeing, as so far no weapons had been turned over. Maguire was both pilot and guide. With left hand on the collective and right on the cyclic, he motioned with his head to indicate the hydroelectric dam below them at the town of Ballyshannon.

"The Erne was dammed in the '50s to create a hydro-electrical plant. The old river gorge of the Erne is now buried ninety feet below the surface of the artificial lake down there. In his poem "The Winding Banks of Erne," Allingham spoke of "the thrush that sings through Camlin's groves the livelong summer day." Well, Camlin's groves, since the 50s, are at the bottom of a lake and no thrush sings there now. In earlier times that stretch of the Erne between Belleek and Ballyshannon was a gateway into Ulster and the scene of many battles. Can you imagine the amazement of those buried down there when they awaken on Judgment Day to find themselves arising from the mud at the bottom of a lake?"

De Chastelain looked at Maguire and hoped that the Irishman's sense of whimsy did not extend to his flying.

"There used to be falls down there called the Falls of Assaroe. I saw recently on the Internet that there's a group calling for its restoration by getting rid of the dam and the hydro-electric plant. Good luck to them. They've got their work cut out for them, I'd say. Back in 1969 a Loyalist paramilitary almost granted their wish when he tried to blow up the hydro-electric plant at Ballyshannon."

"Is there some kind of fortification on that mountain top to the south?" asked De Chastelain.

"Where, General? Ah yes, over there beyond Sligo? That mountain is Knocknarea, in Irish "the hill of the king," although the structure on top of it is the reputed grave of a queen. Maeve was a queen of Connacht in ancient times and legend says she's buried beneath that cairn on Knocknarea. We'll fly over there if you wish, sir."

Maguire banked the helicopter and flew south along the coast toward Sligo. On the way he pointed out the small fishing pier at Mullaghmore where Earl Mountbatten had been killed when the I.R.A. blew up his boat. They flew over the cairn atop Knocknarae, but something else had now attracted the attention of De Chastelain.

"What's going on by that small town down there?"

Maguire looked out his window, manoeuvring the helicopter for a better look. "Looks as if we're being invaded, sir. Those are English and French uniforms of the late 1700s. I remember hearing the Sligo Historical Society was to stage a re-enactment of a battle fought in the rebellion of '98 on this its two hundredth anniversary. I'll take her down for a closer look."

Maguire "took her down" all the way and landed in an adjacent field. He reached across and released the general's door. "You go ahead. They probably won't shoot a Canadian if you tell them you're on a peacekeeping mission, but I'd still be careful. Some of those ragged rebels seem to have entered into the spirit of the thing and look to be, as you Amer – as you Canadians say, 'quite riled up.' They may not understand English." Maguire grinned. "I'll join you in a minute or so after I shut her down. You're aware that you must please stay up ahead and within my line of vision and away from the tail rotor."

De Chastelain's curt nod conveyed a slight annoyance and Maguire added apologetically, "You'll excuse the warning, sir, which is merely routine as I'm sure you're quite familiar with helicopters."

A few moments later Maguire joined the general, who had found a vantage point on a small knoll from which he had a view of the strange events unfolding in the adjacent meadow. The French General, Humbert, a large man astride a large black horse, cut a heroic figure as he directed his French troops and Irish irregulars. His counterpart, Colonel Vereker, commander of the English forces, directed his troops in an ordered retreat pursued by the French and Irish. Watching the non-lethal battle, one could easily understand how war could be regarded as gallant and glorious high endeavour. The blue of the French and the scarlet of the English uniforms created patches of brilliant colour across the green meadow. Horsemen dashed about at full gallop with colourful cloaks fluttering. The cry "Cuimhnígí ar Luimneach" (Remember Limerick) floated across the meadow as a squadron of French cavalry thundered across the field in pursuit of Vereker's men. Many members of the French force had returned home so to speak, as Humbert's Seventieth Demi Brigade contained many descendants of Wild Geese Regiments.

"Look there, Commandant. Is that some authentic historical touch?"

Maguire followed the direction of De Chastelain's outstretched hand, and saw that among the French cavalry galloped a woman with a plumed hat, a brace of pistols in her belt and a cavalry sword in her hand.

"Could be, sir. Can't say for certain. May just be some high-spirited lady from the local hunt club out to prove that women, too, can fight for the cause. She's certainly a daring rider."

The blue-clad French foot soldiers plodded methodically forward, long, wicked-looking bayonets thrust forward on the barrels of their muskets. The Irish, a ragged army, some barefoot, armed with pikes, and some with pitchforks, advanced to right and left of the French, their leaders shouting orders in Irish. De Chastelaine turning to Maguire, enquired with some disbelief. "Did the Irish really fight the British army with pitchforks?"

"They did. The world of the Irish of those days would have had more in common with the world of Abraham than with modern Ireland."

Here and there a man groaned, sagged, and fell. One theatrical "Frenchman", with an eye more to his audience than the enemy, gave up his life with somewhat more drama than the others. He threw wide his arms, the bayonet of his musket narrowly missing his alarmed neighbour, who spoke succinctly in Anglo-Saxon. The Frenchman fell forward on the grass with the words "Cochon anglais"[1] torn from his dying lips. The resurrection came almost immediately. He was on his feet again, and still in character, with now the word "Merde!"[2] on his lips, and a liquidly black substance splattering the breast of his blue uniform. He glared with malevolence at some cattle watching the progress of the battle with indifference, and from a safe distance.

A field piece strategically placed on a small hill took its toll on Humbert's men. An officer galloped up to Humbert and, after a short conversation with the general, turned his horse and galloped straight up the hill into the fire of the cannon. A cheer erupted from the French and Irish as the officer shot the gunners and silenced the gun. Humbert lifted his hat and waved it in the air, shouting "Bravo, Teeling."

This event seemed to signal the end of the pageant. Spectators around the field applauded and the dead and wounded arose and walked off, chatting and laughing. Friend and foe happy with the outcome of their battle, moved across the field toward each other to shake hands. The finer points of the battle would be re-fought later on in Sligo's pubs.

---

1 English pig.
2 Shit!

"That is how all wars should end," Maguire informed the general.

"Tell me something of that period. I was not aware the French actually fought the English on Irish soil," De Chastelain said.

"The French were not the only foreign army. Spanish and Scottish also — the Spanish at Kinsale and the Scottish King James against William of Orange, King of England, at the Boyne. Also in the thirteen hundreds Edward, brother of Robert the Bruce of Scotland brought an army to Ireland and was proclaimed king, but he died in battle shortly afterwards.

As they walked toward the helicopter, Maguire gave a brief summary of the events of the 1798 Rebellion.

"The ideals of the French Revolution of nine years earlier inspired the United Irishmen Rebellion of 1798. Wolfe Tone, a Protestant and one of the founders of the United Irishmen, sought French aid. He himself was captured up by Tory Island aboard the French frigate, 'La Hoche', which attempted to make a landing in Lough Swilly. Tone was taken to Dublin and sentenced to be hanged. However he died, supposedly by his own hand, before the sentence could be carried out. A French force landed at Killala in Mayo not far to the west of here, but by that time the main rising in Wexford had been quelled. The Irish peasants, in the initial heat of their successes in Wexford, committed atrocities. General Lake, commanding English regulars and local yeomen, showed what a real army could accomplish in the way of atrocities. Thirty thousand Irish were killed in the '98 rebellion. The French and Irish won initial victories, including the one here at Carricknagat, but Lord Cornwallis finally defeated them, the same Cornwallis, who had been defeated by Washington's "rebels" seventeen years earlier at Yorktown. Cornwallis, credited with the loss of the American colonies retained no love for rebels. He provided ships for the French to return to France and hanged the Irish.

Maguire paused, and then concluded with a sardonic smile, "It was the manner of the times."

"I have never heard of the poet Allingham that you mentioned earlier but isn't Sligo the county of Yeats, or was it Galway?" asked De Chastelain when they were once again airborne.

"Both. He lived and worked in both counties as well as in Dublin," Maguire replied. "He's buried below to your right in that little churchyard at Drumcliff under a tombstone bearing the cryptic inscription, 'Cast a cold eye on life, on death. Horseman, pass by.'

"While he's usually associated with Sligo, he's also associated with Galway and Lady Gregory. The Anglo-Irish Ascendancy had long been accustomed to looking to England as the font of their nurture and culture, but in the late nineteenth century many of them awakened to Ireland's own hidden literary heritage. Lady Augusta Gregory, an Anglo-Irish aristocrat, founded the Abbey Theatre with Yeats. Anglo-Irish poets and playwrights, such as Yeats, Shaw, Synge, and Wilde, found inspiration in Ireland's present and past and built on and enriched the culture they unearthed. Up that valley to the south of Ben Bulben is Glencar, and Yeats's 'pools among the rushes that scarce could bathe a star', but the pools among the rushes are too small to be seen from this height. We'd better head back to Finner, sir, as we're getting low on fuel and I don't want to have to put her down among the rushes."

"It's not something I'd care for either," the general replied coolly.

Later, De Chastelain and his pilot sat under an awning outside the officers' mess at Finner army camp in County Donegal and looked out over the Atlantic.

"Thank you, Commandant, for the interesting tour and for the history lesson."

"You're very welcome, sir. Can I offer you a drink? Have you tried the Guinness over here?"

In response to De Chastalain's laconic "When in Rome!" Maguire, resisting the temptation to respond, "Right then, Chianti it is", went over to the bar and ordered two pints.

De Chastelain pointed to Maguire's shoulder insignia. "In Canada we don't have the rank of Commandant. In the Canadian Forces a Commandant is a position rather than a rank. For instance we have the Commandant of the Military College who is usually a General, and the Americans have a Commandant of the Marine Corps, also a General. I understand that in the Irish Army the rank of Commandant is the equivalent to Major."

"That's correct, sir. On the formation of the Army of the Irish Free State in 1922 it was decided to substitute the rank of Major with that of Commandant. This was mostly for sentimental reasons, as in the preceding war of Independence the guerrilla units that fought the British were led by a Commandant. It may be a throwback to the Boer war where the Boers also used guerilla tactics and each guerilla unit, called a Commando, was led by a Kommandant. It can, though, cause confusion, when we interact with the armed forces of other nations, as can happen in peace-keeping missions. Many of these may not be familiar with the rank of Commandant and would be uncertain as to where it stands in the military hierarchy." Maguire continued with a barely perceptible grin, "Personally I don't mind being confused with a General, but I'd prefer not to be mistaken for a Captain".

Their conversation was interrupted by the bar-steward's arrival with two Guinness.

"Will it be the usual for Bran, sir?'

Maguire nodded and the steward returned with a pint of Guinness in one hand and a large bowl in the other. He emptied the pint into the bowl which he placed on the floor in front of a large aristocratic looking wolfhound.

De Chastelain looked quite taken aback. He looked from the wolfhound lapping Guinness from the bowl on the floor to the pint of Guinness in his own hand and then with raised eyebrows to his host.

"It's good for his coat. Bran has eclectic tastes. Thank God he hasn't developed a taste for Bailey's Irish Cream or Tullamore Dew. He's a large dog and Guinness is expensive enough these days."

De Chastelain seemed actually relieved by this explanation and took a tentative sip of his drink. Maguire continued,

"The wolfhound, as you may know, General, was the symbol of Ireland of old. In more recent centuries our detractors have tried to replace that symbol with 'Paddy's Pig.' The wolfhound features prominently in our mythology. Bran was the great hound of Finn of the Fianna, and now of course, every second dog in Ireland is called Bran, even some that bear more resemblance to a rodent than to a great wolfhound!

"These dogs were highly prized in ancient Ireland and noted for their hunting skills. They were also called gazehounds as they hunted by sight rather than by smell. In medieval times they were used to hunt the red stag. They may even have been used in prehistoric times to hunt the Irish elk, a huge deer that stood seven feet at the shoulder and had antlers with a span of thirteen feet. I'd imagine a gazehound would have little difficulty seeing such a creature! These huge elk are called Irish elk because the best-preserved specimen of this long extinct species was found in an Irish bog, but actually they roamed all over Europe in early times."

The wolfhound looked up with sad eyes as Maguire fondled its noble head.

"Many of our myths and legends also speak of the wolfhound's faithfulness. Although I have not seen the monument to the Irish Brigade at Gettysburg, I understand it depicts a faithful wolfhound keeping a mournful vigil at the foot of a Celtic cross."

"I have, in fact, toured Gettysburg Battlefield," De Chastelain remarked, "and it is indeed a life-sized wolfhound that's depicted on the Irish monument there. It was pointed out to me by an American officer of Irish descent. However, it seems to me that he referred to the Irish wolfhound as being extinct."

"You're correct General. The breed was in danger of becoming extinct, but in the 1800's an admirer of the breed preserved it at the expense of some cross breeding – an Englishman actually."

General De Chastelain was interested in all things related to Ireland, North, or South. "I have read that casualties to date on all sides are over three thousand and that the cost to Britain of holding on to Northern Ireland is one billion annually. If the British withdrew from Northern Ireland and let the paramilitaries fight it out, would the Irish Army in the Republic become involved?"

"We have only a small army in the south, and we are stretched to the limit, as I understand you are in Canada, with peace-keeping duties abroad. The scenario you mention, sir, would be a nightmare none of us cares to contemplate. The Unionist paramilitaries would have around seventeen thousand well-armed men, which is several times the strength of the Irish Army here in the south. The I.R.A. would gain recruits overnight, and we'd have a bloody civil war. If, in the scenario you mention, the Unionists were defeated, they would then fight on as an underground army. Eventually, General, we could have Canadian peacekeepers being diverted from Bosnia to Belfast to keep Trimble and Adams apart. Actually, most men of reason know there is no alternative but to accept the peace proposals. Politicians, however, must also appease the more radical elements among their followers. While there's a lot of political posturing going on right now, there's also, as you know, many initiatives for peace. Tony Blair ordered another inquiry under Lord Saville to review the events of Bloody Sunday that took place in Derry, and many Nationalists feel this shows an open-minded attitude and a willingness to address their grievances. The earlier inquiry chaired by an ex British Army officer was widely regarded as a whitewash job, and reflected poorly on British justice. There is a general consensus that the time has come when peace may at last break out in Ireland. It's what everyone now wants. Any lasting peace will have to recognise the aspirations of all the people of Ireland, and in Northern Ireland that will have to include the aspirations of Unionists and Nationalists. Perhaps one day north and south will stage a pageant of the Battle of the Boyne. Perhaps one day north and south will stand together as they did in 1798 one hundred years after the Battle of the Boyne."

De Chastelain smiled. "If I may quote an Englishman, 'Twere a consummation devoutly to be wished.' As a soldier, I often think perhaps no one hates war more than the soldier who has had first-hand experience of war. Despite what the movies would have us believe there aren't all that many General Pattons in the world. With our present-day weapons of mass destruction, we had better evolve other methods of solving disputes. Perhaps, before we succeed in destroying ourselves, the imperative of survival of the fittest will discard the warrior model and evolve us as a species that is fit to survive. Maybe with women taking an increasingly prominent role in government this evolutionary process is already happening, although the example of some recent warrior maidens makes one think the female of the species is at least as deadly as the male! Failing some such change to a saner and gentler humanity, perhaps our technology will uncage us from our planet, a predatory species loosed among the stars, leaving behind us a blackened and poisoned earth."

"Your own country, General, is a peaceful one?"

"By and large. But we are in a long drawn out process regarding a just settlement of land claims with our native population, and there is concern our French Canadians in Quebec could separate from Canada. We did have a rebellion once in Canada called the Riel Rebellion. Louis Riel, a Metis[1], led a rebellion of some of the Metis people."

"Only one", Maguire laughed, "Ireland has averaged one rebellion every fifty years or so, about two per century.

"Give us a chance, Commandant; we're a relatively new country. Before accepting this assignment, I acquainted myself with some of Ireland's chequered history. England, that brought many things that were good to the world, seems to have had an appalling record in Ireland, and present-day England is stuck with the consequences of that past."

Maguire nodded in acquiescence. "To quote your Englishman, who did bring much to the world, 'The evil that men do lives after them,' and with a straight face Maguire continued 'The good is oft a tax deductible benefit.'

"Kipling, the Poet of Empire, would be proud to know that the grandsons of Empire still shoulder 'the white man's burden.' Forgive me, General, I do not mean to be cynical. It doesn't need to be said that the majority of English people of today are decent and kind people. Kind anyhow to animals, if one does not include foxes! Even among politicians there are men of good faith on both sides, but I'm sure you are familiar with the saying, 'the first casualty of war is the truth.' When the victors write the history, the vanquished suffer their final defeat. The usual propaganda is that the problem in Northern Ireland is a religious war, and seldom is the root cause of the conflict explained."

"There seems to have been inevitability about the ultimate domination of Ireland by England," De Chastelain mused. "After the defeat of the Old Irish chieftains, Ireland never again won a battle of consequence."

"We survived, in itself a battle, and actually we did win one more. Owen Roe O'Neill, nephew of Hugh, the victor of the Yellow Ford, won at Benburb in the 1641 Rebellion. Benburb would have been our last victory in the field.

---

[1] Mixed French-Canadian and native-American ancestry

"A large number of Irish emigrated to Canada at the time of the famine," Maguire remarked, changing the subject.

"Yes and one Irishman played a prominent part in Canada's history. On Parliament Hill in Ottawa there's a statue to Thomas D'Arcy McGee, who was one of the fathers of Canadian Confederation. Had he lived he would probably have succeeded Sir John A. MacDonald as Prime Minister of Canada."

"McGee had an interesting life." Maguire nodded. "One of the leaders of the abortive rebellion of 1848 in Ireland, he made his way to America and eventually settled in Canada. Many Irish in America sympathised with the revolutionary Fenian movement in Ireland, and after the American Civil War, many of those Irish who had fought in that war sought to strike against England by invading Canada. Magee was by now a staunch defender of English Canada, which he regarded, and apparently with justification, as more hospitable to Irish immigrants than America. He spoke out with equal impartiality against both the bigotry of the Orange Order in Canada and against his erstwhile Fenian comrades. One or other of these organizations was responsible for his assassination in 1868.

"Some of McGee's fellow rebels of 1848 also had interesting lives. Thomas Francis Meagher was sentenced to be hanged, drawn, and quartered for his part in the rebellion, but had his sentence commuted to transportation to the penal colony of Australia. He escaped from Australia to America where he became a Union Army general, leading the Irish Brigade in the American Civil War, and later became Secretary of the Territory of Montana. He drowned in the Missouri River, a long way from his native Tipperary. Gavan Duffy, too, was involved in the 1848 Rebellion as the publisher of a radical Irish Nationalist newspaper, 'The Nation'. He however went to Australia of his own volition and eventually became Premier of the State of Victoria and was knighted by Queen Victoria. The queen, enquiring into the history of the man on whom she was conferring a knighthood, learned that earlier in her reign he had been convicted of 'seditious conspiracy' against the Crown.

"These were educated Irishmen, unlike the masses of uneducated Irish who fled the famine of 1845-1848. Most of the famine emigration was to America, where these Irish, disease-ridden, illiterate, and starving, staggered ashore to find the old enemy waiting for them, the old enemy, now the new aristocracy in the new land. The new life offered by the new land would not be offered on a silver platter. One of those who stepped ashore in 1848 was a Patrick Kennedy, whose great-grandson became the thirty-fifth President of the United States. Many of those destitute Irish, who found a refuge in America from famine at home, were later caught up in the holocaust of the American

Civil War. These new 'wild geese' fought in the Irish Brigade, and in other units both for the Union and Confederacy. These immigrants marching through the leaden hail of the blood-drenched fields of Antietam, Fredericksburg, Gettysburg, and many another civil war conflict, by the sacrifice of their blood, gained acceptance for their countrymen in America."

Maguire emptied his drink.

"In the 1500s we had the Tudors; in the 1600s, Cromwell; in the 1700s, the Penal Laws; in the 1800s, famine; and for close on four hundred years, domination by England, which seemed intent on extinguishing us as a people. Despite these ravages to our race we have survived, and today there are seventy million people around the world who claim Irish descent."

CHAPTER 31

A devastated land

October winds soughed and moaned through the bleak Moyry Pass as Lord Mountjoy regrouped his men for a third attempt in as many weeks at forcing his way into Ulster. In both earlier attempts the Lord Deputy's cavalry had become mired in swamps and bogs, and O'Neill's men, who fought from behind well-constructed defence works, had thrown back his army. Lethal volleys of musket fire first disrupted the orderly, close- packed, enemy ranks, then the Irish rushed forward for the brutal face-to-face work of pike and sword.

The bone-chilling damp was a remorseless enemy of both armies. Men huddled and slept in wet clothing on wet ground, arising in the cold dawn, shivering and dispirited, to struggle through another day of death and terror. Separated from each other at either end of the pass, the two commanders were little more comfortable than their men.

The wind drifted dark grey clouds through the crags of the surrounding hills as Colonel Wingfield again advanced into the pass at the head of the cavalry vanguard, his military cloak billowing out behind him. Behind him rode Captain Williams. Both men, survivors of the Yellow Ford, had reason to respect O'Neill's ability as a battle commander. The cold wind sheeted stinging hail into Wingfield's face as he glanced at the woods to either side, awaiting the more lethal hail of lead, which had greeted each earlier advance. Wingfield's cavalry, taut and alert, advanced into the pass, their passage contested by nothing more than the biting lash of the hail.

The well-prepared defences were unmanned and deserted. Ulster lay open before Mountjoy. For the rest of the day, the English Army marched through the Moyry Pass. No enemy barred their way. No thudding leaden hail rent human flesh and splintered human bone. No wailing skirl of war pipes presaged the fierce, headlong charge of savage violent men. No chieftains led their clansmen swarming down the hillsides, wild war cries echoing among the crags. No clang of steel on steel, no raging battle clamour, no shrieked blaspheming curses, no muttered desperate prayers. There was only the dismal howl of the banshee wind.

Docwra, isolated at Derry, had persevered for months against starvation, foe, and weather. Now, with the help of the perfidious Niall Garve O'Donnell, he had broken out of his confines on the shore of the Foyle and rampaged almost at will into Donegal and Northern Tyrone. O'Neill, to face this foe at his rear and in answer to the plight of O'Donnell, had abandoned his defences at the Moyry Pass, and left open the front door to Ulster.

The Lord Deputy stepped up his highly effective scorched earth policy and urged Docwra to follow suit. In the winter of 1600, raiding parties went throughout Ulster burning dwellings, destroying food stores, and slaughtering cattle. An English captain, Blaney, destroyed one of O'Neill's largest storehouses of food and powder, the crannog fortress of Lough Lurcan. The English captain shot flaming arrows from the shore and the wooden buildings on the crannog caught fire. The crannog garrison, under constant bombardment from the shore, was unable to quench the fire, which soon engulfed the storehouses.

Docwra, re-supplied by sea, had penetrated even the remote peninsula of Fanad and forced MacSweeney of Fanad to submit and surrender pledges, but the O'Dohertys of Inishowen followed Niall Garve's example and defected to Docwra. O'Donnell found he was unable to oust Niall Garve from Lifford. Niall Garve and Docwra now boldly made forays to the south and west of Donegal and exacted vengeance on those loyal to Red Hugh. O'Neill and O'Donnell knew they must at all costs preserve and enforce the alliance even if it meant leaving the Moyry Pass open to Mountjoy. O'Neill turned his back on one enemy to face another.

MacRory's sadness deepened the closer he came to the castle at Fanad. It looked as if an avenging angel had swept over the well-remembered land. Blackened stubble stood where fields of corn had grown. The stench of unburied death arose from carcasses of cattle and sheep lying scattered and bloated in the fields. Here and there faces of children and adults, hollow-eyed and frightened, peered from makeshift shelters beside the rubble of what had been their homes. Bird and animal scavengers, unafraid, surfeited but still greedy, scarcely looked up as the horseman passed. Gaunt human scavengers vied with the vultures for the decomposing meat. Is this the glory of war, thought the gallowglass, but what is the price of peace?

The hamlet of Rathmullan, close to the castle, had not escaped, and MacRory's thoughts went back to his boyhood in Sheephaven and visits to Fanad by the side of Lough Swilly, thoughts now saddened and soured by seeing the proud MacSweeney brought to his knees. He thought also of the small hamlet of Cavan and Sheila's mother and father.

Accustomed to war and destruction, of late he found himself thinking back to the few interludes of peace his life had allowed him. His early life at Sheephaven and the times spent with Sheila, his wife, came to mind. Sheila was expecting another child in a few months and now nothing in life seemed more important than to be beside her again. She and his baby, Kathleen, were his only anchors in this churning sea of violence. From that day when the beautiful young woman had first spoken to him in Cavan, he had felt his life changed, as when, too, he had first held their baby and looked in awe at the new life in his hands.

But had his life changed? Was it only in his mind? He still pursued a soldier's life as before. He still destroyed men's lives in battle, looked callously into their dying eyes without thought of what else might die with them. But surely he was not the same person as before. In the past he had never been much given to morbid thoughts, but occasionally of late a terror would engulf him, thinking of his family's vulnerability. Prior to meeting Sheila, he'd had the soldier's fatalistic attitude toward death, and indeed expected to one day die in some battle, but now he could not bear to think of how his death would leave his family unprotected and helpless. If it were not for his loyalty to O'Donnell and his memory of O'Donnell's words in the Curlews, "the only peace they'll allow us will be the peace of the grave", he would have forsaken the life of a gallowglass. He had heard of the newly discovered land across the ocean to the west and wondered if he could take his family there and find peace. But would the perilous ocean crossing and the unknown hazards of an unknown land perhaps put them at still greater risk? Would the new land be any more peaceful than the old?

What hand guides our destinies? We have our victories and our defeats and in our arrogance, we think we forge our own paths. The mighty decay in the earth, as do the humblest. We live our lives in fear of death, but death like birth is another painful portal through which we must pass on our everlasting journey down eternity. Rarely, in a moment of heightened perception, we may peer dimly through the veil into that void of eternity, and with fumbling finite mind reach out to sense some echo of the mystery of creation; sense, too, how sublime must be man's destiny to be an undying part of that creation. Even the dimmest perception of the glory of that destiny must make the agonies of existence pale into nothingness. But what if, as some believed, that the agony of existence was ordained to be reincarnated in forms without end, forever and forever in a world without end! Can a finite mind ever truly grasp the terrifying concept of eternity?

He could remember a hint of one such moment when he had stood alone as darkness crept over the fresh mound of his mother's grave; and an awareness had crept into the hungering soul of a grieving child that his mother had now crossed an abyss that he could not. Faith tells us we belong as much to the heavens above us as we do to the earth on which we walk, but our mortal flesh, cloying the spirit, makes us as incapable of understanding our ultimate destiny as are cattle of understanding the intricacies of the Brehon Law.

"Docwra's men camped before the castle and starved us out." Donal MacSweeney looked sadly around. "Docwra's men together with Con O'Donnell and his Queen's O'Donnells. Niall Garve has rebuilt the castle at Lifford and from there he makes war on those of us loyal to Red Hugh. Without Niall Garve's assistance, Docwra would never have been able to march an army into Donegal. He would have starved at Derry. Red Hugh, however, will see his cousin to hell, and Docwra with him."

"I pray to God that with your help, Red Hugh will send those two to sit out all their future winters in that warmer place," MacRory agreed. "It's for that reason he has sent me to Fanad. He asks that you and your gallowglass join him at Lifford, where he besieges Niall Garve. O'Neill also has come north and I expect he and his English friends will no longer stray far from their fortresses. I am sad to see what they have done to your land and our people, but it is no different than what they have done elsewhere. They employ famine as a tactic of war."

"My people have suffered, and continue to suffer and die of starvation. Tell O'Donnell I will bring my gallowglass to Lifford. Docwra holds my pledges and I fear I send them to the gallows, but I cannot refuse my chieftain."

MacRory nodded, knowing MacSweeney's decision would certainly seal the fate of his pledges. MacSweeney took most of his gallowglass with him, there being little left to guard at Fanad, and he and MacRory rode south through the devastated land. MacSweeney rode dejectedly through the country he had failed to protect. The eyes that followed him, peering around hovels could never have exceeded in reproach the blame he heaped on himself. No excuse was acceptable, and he would not allow his mind to entertain any. He had failed his people, and both he and they knew it.

As they passed not far from Lifford, a group of about twenty horsemen galloped fast toward Niall Garve's stronghold. Presently it became apparent they fled for the protection of the castle at Lifford, pursued by another and larger group of horsemen. MacSweeney realized the men fleeing toward Lifford must be Niall Garve O'Donnell's men and raced forward to intercept them. He and MacRory, together with some thirty mounted gallowglass, galloped ahead and placed themselves across the path of the fleeing horsemen. Niall Garve's men wheeled around a copse of trees and found themselves cut off from the castle by this new group of horsemen. There was little they could do except rein in their horses and await their fate as their pursuers thundered down upon them while MacSweeney and his men closed in from the other side. The leader of Niall Garve's horsemen sat his horse with a contemptuous nonchalance as his pursuers swarmed around him.

"It would not seem to be my lucky day," he drawled, letting the reins fall on his horse's neck and folding his arms insolently.

"Indeed not yours, but certainly mine." MacSweeney rode up, his right hand reaching down for his sword.

MacRory kicked his horse between the two men.

"No, Donal. Wait! This is Con O'Donnell, Niall Garve's brother. He can be useful to us alive. What can you gain by his death?"

"I know well who he is. He can be no use to me alive, and what I gain by his death is revenge, revenge for my people at Fanad."

"Then dig graves for your pledges as well, Donal, for if you kill Con O'Donnell, Niall Garve and Docwra will surely hang up your three nephews. We can hold Con O'Donnell hostage against the lives of your pledges, but your vengeance now will assure their deaths."

MacSweeney reluctantly replaced his sword, while Con O'Donnell sat looking at the two men with the air of a bored bystander at a debate.

MacSweeney turned to one of Con O'Donnell's men. "Ride to Lifford and tell Niall Garve that if Docwra harms my pledges, we'll hang Con O'Donnell within sight of the walls of Lifford. Tell him, too, that when we take Lifford, Niall Garve himself will hang from its walls."

"I doubt my brother will be the one hanging from Lifford's walls," Con O'Donnell retorted. "Red Hugh and his army have not been able to dislodge us, and soon Niall Garve and Docwra will keep Red Hugh's army busy defending Donegal Castle itself. Niall Garve is rightful chieftain and will hang those of you who do not recognize him as such."

"He will hang most of Donegal then. Niall Garve can never be the rightful chieftain of the O'Donnells." MacSweeney had again unsheathed his sword and was in danger of using it. "Red Hugh was inaugurated The O'Donnell at Carraig an Dun. When your brother betrayed his chieftain and crawled to the English, only a handful of faithless O'Donnells followed. Since when does an English captain elect the chieftain of the O'Donnells? Since when does an Englishman hold up the hand of a traitor – the left hand – and declare him an O'Donnell chieftain. Niall Garve will never rule in Donegal except as a puppet for his English masters. How do you think future generations of O'Donnells will regard your brother, if because of his perfidy, the English rule *Tir Conaill*, the land of your fathers? How will future generations look on the man who brought rule by an alien prince to his people? How will your brother compare with the victors of the Yellow Ford and the Curlews, with the man who united the O'Donnells and drove the English from Connacht? Will the bard in the hall sing the praises of Niall Garve, a traitor to his sept, or those of Red Hugh a hero throughout

Donegal and throughout all Ireland? How will future generations look on the man who betrayed Ireland to the English?"

MacSweeney's angry torrent of words had more of an effect on Con O'Donnell than did the sword in his huge right hand. O'Donnell's face reddened with shame. "We will make whatever accommodation with the English that suits us and still be masters of our own house. And as for the rest of Ireland, of what concern is that to us?"

MacSweeney ordered the captive be bound and guarded overnight in a tent before being taken the next day to Donegal Castle.

In the morning their captive was gone. The man assigned to stand guard outside the prisoner's tent was found garrotted. When found, the guard's body was cold, and it seemed likely the prisoner had escaped some time before. It also seemed likely more than one accomplice had engineered the escape. Red Hugh and MacSweeney consulted, and although the chances of recapturing the fugitive were slim, they sent out scouts in the direction of Lifford.

Some hours later, one of the scouting parties galloped into the camp with much tumult and a hooded prisoner in their midst. One of the horsemen shouted they had apprehended Con O'Donnell just before he reached the safety of Lifford. The prisoner was led away from among his captors. Red Hugh then had the whole army assembled and informed them that if the men who had assisted in Con O'Donnell's escape were to step forward neither they nor the prisoner would be shot. Also, since presumably these men would no longer be welcome in his army, he would ensure they were sent back to Lifford. After a pause first one, then two others stepped forward. Two of the men were nephews of Con O'Donnell.

The hooded prisoner was again brought forward and the hood removed. The face that blinked and smiled in the bright sunlight was not that of Con O'Donnell.

Red Hugh addressed the three men who had stepped forward. "I promised you would not be shot nor will you be; I also promised you would be returned to Lifford. For the present only one of you will return to bear this message. If any harm comes to MacSweeney's pledges the remaining two of you will be hanged and your bodies delivered to Lifford."

CHAPTER 32

A Spanish army in Ireland

"Isn't he beautiful?" Sheila's exclamation was far more a statement than a question.

The midwife held up the baby boy for the perusal of mother and father. The baby's mother gazed at her newborn with love and happiness. The father, too, gazed at his offspring with love and happiness, but he would not have described as beautiful the damp, squirming, red-faced, angry-looking mite. Its body was covered with a whitish-grey waxy substance, and its face and mouth contorted as it built up air for a first verbal blast of disapproval of this new world. The baby was large; the midwife estimated it to be all of seven pounds, and Sheila was exhausted after a long labour. MacRory leaned over and gently kissed his wife's pale, tired face.

Quite quickly the room filled with people as Fiona O'Reilly and Sheila's two sisters all crowded around the newborn baby boy. The small, pink face with closed eyes now appeared more accepting of its lot and the baby's initial displeasure at its new surroundings seemed to have abated, at least for the present, as it lay swaddled in a warm blanket in its mother's arms.

Looking at the face of his small, helpless child, MacRory thought how the young of the species always seemed to bring forth a protective instinct in adults. This was probably nature's way of insuring the defenceless young would be cared for until able to fend for themselves. The thought also came to him that it was almost sinful to thus rationalize the sacred love of a parent for a child. But could a mere soldier protect his child, in the midst of this war, no matter how great the love?

Nine-year-old Eamonn MacGowan dodged around, attempting to gain a vantage point between the adults as he struggled to lift two-year-old Kathleen MacRory as high as possible in order that she, too, might see the object of all the fuss. Kathleen MacRory had not as yet many words in her vocabulary, but she already sensed that certain words were stronger and more powerful than others. She had taken note that some words seemed to be used to convey special emphasis on occasions of importance. The little girl had spent her two years of life in a military garrison, and had always been the focus of much attention.

She gazed on her baby brother, and sensing the importance of the occasion, articulated with clarity and emphasis her strong word, "Shit."

Fiona O'Reilly, feeling that some order had to be imposed, now shooed all from the room so the mother could rest and the new parents could be alone with the baby.

Fiona herself was now married, having finally selected a brother of Brian Óg O'Rourke to be her husband. Phelim O'Rourke never knew how little of a conscious choice he himself had had in the affair. Once Fiona O'Reilly decided he was to be her husband, events had proceeded with the relentless inevitability of the Drowes flowing to the sea. By conscious choice or otherwise, Phelim O'Rourke had entered into a marriage that was a happy one. When happily warring far south in Connacht, Phelim often thought fondly of Fiona and Cavan, and at times when the O'Connors would not come forth to fight, he even wished he were back there. The proud Fiona, the product of generations of warrior O'Reillys and with a warrior heart as redoubtable as that of her husband, encouraged him in his manly pursuits, and in any event would not have tolerated a husband who was not gainfully employed. Fiona O'Reilly was as direct and uncompromising as a sword blade, but was kind and generous to her friends. When her brother had sent her off to the relative safety of Ballyshannon, she had insisted on taking with her the MacGowan children.

An unaccountable melancholia took hold of Sheila within days of the birth. She looked at the world with no joy and the world gave her back no happiness. Guilt and despair became her daily companions. At times guilt overwhelmed her. What had become of her! Friends surrounded her, a loving husband was by her side, and she had her children. Yet conscious thought could not lift her out of her dark mood. She scarcely cared for the baby and indeed at times seemed to lack any motivation to do so. The world, that a few weeks ago had been so full of promise, was now a frightening, grim, and dreary place.

Her husband, confused and bewildered, sat beside her and when he found conversation not helpful, he relapsed into helpless silence. The wide innocent eyes that had always reflected love now reflected only emptiness and desolation. His happy, vital wife was gone, and in her place, a lifeless shell. Sheila's sisters, Eileen and Bridie, frightened by Sheila's unusual behaviour, exhibited the same helplessness as the gallowglass.

Helplessness, however, was a condition unknown to Fiona O'Reilly. While she did not know exactly what could be done, she certainly was going to do something. Firstly, she arranged for a wet nurse to care for the baby. Then she insisted Sheila get outside daily and walk and spend as much time outdoors as possible. She felt intuitively that strenuous exercise would combat morbid introspection. She dispatched the husband to fetch the physician. She called the midwife into her presence and asked if she had ever seen any similar occurrence.

The gallowglass was vastly relieved when O'Cassidy took him aside and said with an admirable economy of words, "This time prayer is optional."

The physician looked around.

"Am I to stand here all day with my throat parched from talking?" When he had relieved his parched throat with a draught of *Uisce Beatha*, he continued:

"The condition is temporary, but could last for several weeks. The midwife and I are familiar with this melancholia that sometimes follows childbirth and the midwife has a potion she says sometimes helps, or at least does no harm. *Primum non nocere*"[1] is as good a motto for the midwife as for the doctor. Fiona's remedy of walking is probably as effective as anything else. Getting out in the countryside under God's broad sky is good for the soul, and this melancholia that takes hold of some people seems to be an affliction of the soul. When it happens after childbirth, it passes off eventually, but there is a melancholia that can occur in others and it can be a living death. Indeed some do seek escape in death. When she begins to recover is a dangerous time and she should not be left alone. Let her know frequently that the condition will soon pass, and give her hope by telling her that O'Cassidy himself has said so."

While he spoke, the old man had taken frequent draughts to prevent his throat from becoming parched, and now he looked

---

[1] "First, do no harm."

around for a servant to refill his tankard. He placed a hand on the gallowglass's shoulder.

"When she recovers, Turlough, and she will, enjoy this time together. It's possible Red Hugh will soon again be calling on your services. There's a rumour a Spanish fleet is being outfitted in Cadiz and will soon sail for Ireland. The Maguires are split in their allegiance. The Enniskillen branch will follow Red Hugh, while Conor Roe at Lisnaskea will be with the English. Conor Roe's nephew, Rory, asked me to convey to you that your family will be under his protection should O'Neill and O'Donnell be defeated."

The awful melancholia gradually passed off, but the memory of those dreadful days did not so quickly fade from Sheila's mind. The spectre of a recurrence of that dread melancholia haunted her. She felt vulnerable and afraid. She had never before suspected what nightmarish realms of darkness could lie hidden in the mind, down what dark chasms of despair the mind could make one wander. Now that she was well again, she found it impossible to understand the uncontrollable gloom that like a shroud had engulfed her spirit. An evil presence had taken control of her soul. All joy was erased from life and replaced by a morbid foreboding horror. It seemed as if she had been made to wander, severed from humanity and without hope, in a dark unholy place and that her very soul had been extinguished.

While Sheila recovered, Fiona had taken over with a fierce sense of purpose and marshalled and directed the efforts of all. Even now, with Sheila herself again, Fiona insisted wife and husband spend long hours walking the cliffs and beaches of Rossnowlagh and Bundoran close to Ballyshannon. Fiona was kind enough to allow Sheila visiting privileges with her children, but insisted that until such time as she was assured Sheila was totally recovered, someone else would look after the children. A wet nurse cared for the baby boy, who had been christened Rory, after his father's father and little Kathleen spent much time walking around in the wake of her adored nine-year-old uncle, Eamonn MacGowan.

As Sheila and her husband walked along the windswept cliffs, the vast vista of blue sparkling sea and dark blue distant headlands brought back to the gallowglass childhood memories of the Western Isles. The sight, the smell, and the sounds of the sea were the same, and the same salt taste was borne on the wind. Even the same quality of light and cloud seemed to pervade this part of northwest Ireland as it did the Hebrides.

He and his wife sat on high grassy cliffs, buffeted by warm western winds, and watched seagulls wheel and cry over the heaving sea beneath. They marvelled at the fishing prowess of the gannet, cruising high over the ocean, and then folding its wings to plummet down like a javelin into the wave tops. As they stared toward the far western horizon did the ghosts of their Celtic ancestors whisper to them that somewhere beyond that horizon lay Hy-Brasil[1] the mystical isle of eternal youth?

Sometimes they descended to walk for miles along the wet yellow sand of the curving beaches, shouting to each other above the wind and the ceaseless roar of Atlantic breakers. At others they walked carefully among the wet, barnacled rocks, slippery with seaweed. They bathed in the clean, deep little seawater pools left among the rocks by the ebbing tide.

When Sheila pointed out the antics of the little grey and white sanderlings endlessly racing after the receding surf only to flee back shoreward before the next line of advancing water, MacRory's heart thrilled with gladness to hear again her delighted laugh. They stood with upturned faces, laughing a welcome to the frequent warm rain showers, knowing the summer wind would soon dry their light, linen clothing. He knew her spirit was healed.

Wailing seagulls, banking and wheeling were their constant companions, but occasionally, too, they shared this lonely world on the ocean's edge with an elegant grey heron stalking through the frothing surf, long curved neck tensed to strike, or some red-billed sea pies pecking their course along the beach. Listening to the oystercatcher's call, MacRory related to Sheila a Hebrides legend about the bird.

"Saint Bridget was fleeing from pirates and hid herself in a cave by the seashore. The oystercatcher, or the sea pie as it is sometimes called, collected seaweed and covered the cave's entrance to conceal the saint's hiding place. Ever after, its call proclaimed the bird to be the servant of Bridget. Listen, Sheila." He

---

[1] Another Celtic myth of *Tir na n-Óg*.

imitated the bird's call: "Gillabreech, Gillabreech. Doesn't it sound like *Gille Bridhge, Gille Bridhge?*"[1]

Sheila stopped and listened. "So it does, indeed. Imagine the Hebrides having a legend of Bridget of Kildare, who was an Irish Saint!"

"We have many of the same legends. But perhaps St. Bridget of Kildare is more an Irish legend than an Irish saint. Hugh Maguire once told me there may never have been a Saint Bridget, but that Brigit, the Celtic goddess of the Sun, daughter of Dagda, was reincarnated in Irish Christian legend as Saint Bridget of Kildare."

"St. Bridget not a saint! Oh, Turlough, that's sacrilegious. One of our most revered saints a pagan goddess!"

"There are, indeed, many instances both here and in the Hebrides of the persistence of pagan influence and custom in our Christian religion. In both countries you'll find Christian churches built on the sites of earlier pagan worship. The holy wells of our pagan ancestors are still our holy wells in Christian Ireland.

Ona, the Arch Druid offered Saint Patrick land for the building of a Christian church, and the Christian descendants of Ona became hereditary *eranachts* of that same church in subsequent centuries. Saint Patrick himself sometimes referred to Our Saviour as "My Druid."

"I have heard these Holy Wells were often sacred to our pagan ancestors, too. O'Cassidy feels the water from the holy well at Ballyshannon cures war fever," Sheila said seriously.

On one occasion they returned to Ballyshannon exhausted, having trudged miles of sandy beaches and scrambled around rocky promontories south to where the Drowes flowed into the sea. The wild loneliness of the place and the sense of immensity of ocean and sky were indeed as O'Cassidy had said "good for the soul."

Sheila huddled closer as they sat on a cliff top looking toward the haze shrouded north shore of Donegal bay. September had brought a chill to the west wind blowing in from the sea, but the sun still shone brightly from the blue vault of the sky. Below them in the sand two sets of footprints stretched back along the beach, the symmetry of their trail broken in one spot where they had

---

[1] "Servant of Bridget".

stopped to embrace, the intimate moment mutely betrayed in the sand beneath them. The incoming tide would soon obliterate their footprints and the evidence of their intimacy.

"O'Cassidy mentioned that a Spanish army may soon be landing in Ireland."

They both sat on in silence, both knowing the significance to the other of the words.

Sheila lived these moments they had together with a deep quiet relish, extracting what comfort she could from what she knew would be a transitory happiness. A kind of fatalism dictated she not look too far into the future, but enjoy now whatever happiness was afforded her. Her husband dared not think of what the callous cruelty of war could do to the lives he loved. He was a soldier who was familiar with, but not inured to, the horrors of war. Daily, stories and evidence of the brutality of this war numbed the senses. Atrocities like those of Rathlin and Smerwick had become so commonplace as to be scarcely worthy of mention. He knew his own wife and children were no more exempt from this brutality than were the countless other wives and children throughout Ireland. His mind refused to accept that those he achingly loved could be subject to the dreadful horrors his mind also knew were possible. The thought of Niall Grave's ominous threat was a recurring stab wound to his heart, and a guilt in his conscience. Why had he not killed the man who was a danger to his family and an enemy to his friend? He had derived great comfort from Rory Maguire's promise, and now he mentioned this to Sheila. She did not reply, but merely moved closer to him. They sat thus for half an hour.

A horseman rounded the point in the distance and galloped along the beach, following the tracks in the sand to the foot of the cliff. Here he left the beach and urged his horse up a sandy gully to the cliff top above. The warden of Ballyshannon Castle dismounted and bowed to Sheila. He turned to MacRory.

"A message from Red Hugh. Maol Mhuire MacSweeney of Doe will arrive at Ballyshannon tomorrow. You are both to join O'Donnell at Ballymote."

The man's face broke into a wide grin. "A Spanish army has landed at Kinsale."

CHAPTER 33

March to the final battle

A Spanish army in Ireland! At last! But why Kinsale, which was at Ireland's southern tip and as far away from O'Neill and O'Donnell as it was possible to get in Ireland? Perhaps, MacRory thought, it would divide the Lord Deputy's forces having to turn south to meet the Spanish, but would it not have been better had the Spanish landed in Donegal and joined up with O'Donnell and O'Neill to present a formidable united front in the north? Carew's brutal campaigns in Munster had largely re-established English control in the south. When the northern chieftains marched south to join with the Spanish who would protect the North? Well, it was not for him to question the strategy. This was the long-awaited moment and would probably be the turning point in the war. Perhaps this would even mean a quick end to the war.

Busy with Docwra in the north, O'Donnell did not immediately try to link up with the Spanish at Kinsale, but over the next few weeks messengers arrived from the Spanish to say Carew and Mountjoy had them hemmed in and they frantically called for help from the north.

Before MacRory left Ballyshannon, O'Cassidy visited him. "I am instructed to give you a message from Rory Maguire. His uncle Conor Roe wishes to repay a favour. He bade me tell you that if O'Donnell marches south to Kinsale, the castle at Ballyshannon will fall to Docwra. He is an honourable man but may not be able to ensure the safety of your wife and family. Conor Roe offers to take them under his protection at Lisnaskea."

The gallowglass told O'Cassidy to express to Rory Maguire and Conor Roe Maguire his profound gratitude for this offer of protection for his family. He, too, felt sure that Docwra and Neil Garve would control Donegal if Red Hugh marched south.

"Would his hospitality extend also to Fiona, as she, being an O'Reilly and the wife of an O'Rourke, would also be in danger? Sheila would also ask for sanctuary for her sisters and brother."

"I'm sure Lisnaskea can accommodate a few more souls, but I'm afraid Conor Roe's castle will have a stormy guest in Fiona O'Reilly-O'Rourke. I think it is a wise precaution. Conor Roe will arrange it."

The gallowglass, accompanied by Maol Mhuire MacSweeney and his men, rode south toward Ballymote. The route brought back many memories. Like echoing voices from the shadows of the past borne on the whispering winds, the memories sighed around him. Beyond Ballyshannon he looked off to his left where some miles inland lay Lough Melge and his uncle's grave. On his right the seagulls screamed and swooped above the rolling waves. Out there in her lonely sea grave lay the mortal remains of Maeve O'Rourke. Her essence, her spirit and her joy were elsewhere. What primeval terror as the salt sea fills the lungs and convulsing in death the body sinks down into those silent, never-seen dark depths!

Surely we are truly alone at the time of our death, that moment when the body and all its mortal memories is torn from the immortal soul and alone the naked soul passes through the dread portal to eternity. How unfathomable the chain of fate! A king of one land sends his ships to conquer the queen of another. A chieftain in a remote part of a remote land rescues some shipwrecked men of that armada. The sea claims the chieftain's daughter, links irrevocably forging the past to the present. And for every forged link in that chain of fate, other severed ghostly links, infinite in number, branching off to spectral futures that would never be.

How strange the events that govern our lives and how interwoven are those events in the lives of others.

Would Maeve O'Rourke still be alive had he not rescued her? Would Sheila MacGowan be his wife and would his children have ever come into existence had the flight of a musket ball not been deflected by a matter of inches? How many links in the chain of fate had his own actions forged, and how many had they broken? Was it not strange in itself the fate that had placed him here in a country not his own, a country he now knew better than his own, a country he now regarded as his own? What other paths might other fates have opened? What other fates might this his present path have closed?

He crossed the Drowes close to where it met the ocean. Its waters churned with salmon thrashing upstream, urged on by their blind imperative to renew the cycle of propagation, death spawning life. Beyond the Drowes he rode along beneath the steep face of Ben Bulben. To the south of Ben Bulben opened up the valley of Glencar. Ten years had now passed since he had rescued Maeve O'Rourke in Glencar.

"How is it, MacSweeney, that something as ephemeral as a thought, born in the mind, changes our lives and changes the world?"

"I have no answer for you. My uncle, Eoghan, who was your mentor at Sheephaven might have had an answer for you, were he still alive. I am a simple soldier and no philosopher, MacSweeney the gallowglass, not a Thomas Aquinas, but it is true we live our lives in our mind." After a pause MacSweeney, quoting a line from the song of Amergen,[1] intoned: 'I am the God that creates in the head of man the fire of thought'."

On past Sligo and Knocknarea, past Collooney and the Curlews, the names and the places and the memories passing behind him as he rode.

At Ballymote Red Hugh assembled an army to march to Kinsale, but O'Neill, while assembling his own army in Cavan, still questioned the wisdom of marching his army south in winter. When the gallowglass reached Ballymote, an envoy from O'Neill was conferring with Red Hugh. O'Donnell passionately advocated an immediate joining up with the Spanish at Kinsale.

"We have pleaded for Spanish aid for decades and are we now to leave the Spaniards besieged and short of food at Kinsale? We must march south to aid them."

The envoy, O'Neill's brother Cormac, replied, "The Spanish have drawn Mountjoy away from us. They will keep him and Carew busy while we deal with Docwra and consolidate our position here in the north. We cannot march our armies hundreds of miles south in the winter. What are we to feed them? What of shelter? How well

---

[1] Warrior poet of those Celts who invaded Ireland around B.C. 500.

will they fight at the end of an exhausting winter march? Will we leave defenceless our territories here in the North?

O'Donnell, impatient with this talk of difficulties interrupted him. "Del Aguila and his men have come to our aid as our allies. Mountjoy has encircled them and they are starving. Whatever the difficulties we cannot abandon them. One bold stroke now may win us the final victory."

"One rash and foolhardy move now and we could lose all that O'Neill has fought for over the past five years,"

"I would remind you that Hugh Maguire and myself have also been involved in this fight and for longer than has your brother. Perhaps O'Neill still harbours thoughts of making peace with the English. I will listen to no more of your circumspect reasoning. I have given my word to the Spanish, and I will take my army south. Honour demands it."

"Honour demands that you do what is prudent and in the interest of the alliance."

"You presume to instruct me as to where my honour lies?"

Red Hugh spoke quietly, but the other now realized the ominous turn the conversation had taken. He also realized that Hugh O'Neill would not forgive him for having antagonized O'Donnell.

"I ask your pardon. In pressing my argument, I forget my manners. I meant no offence. You will of course do as your honour dictates, and I will convey your decision to O'Neill."

O'Donnell, too, had no wish to cause a rift in the alliance at this critical juncture. "Tell O'Neill that I myself will visit him at Lough Ramor if he wishes. Unity now is paramount, and no one can doubt how O'Neill has united the country. When he marches south, he will draw to him more chieftains from all over Ireland. I feel strongly that it would be disastrous to abandon the Spanish at Kinsale. Mountjoy has wasted the country to deprive the Spanish of food, but it may be his own men who will starve if we can trap his army between the Spanish and ourselves. If we leave the Spanish to starve, we can never again look to Spain for help, and even now further help from Spain may be on its way."

O'Neill's envoy rose and bowed.

"These are decisions for yourself and O'Neill. He asked that I point out some other aspects, which I have done. I thank you for the courtesy with which you have listened to them."

The difficulty, alluded to by O'Neill's envoy of marching an army several hundred miles in winter, became apparent as O'Donnell set out from Ballymote on 2 November in the year 1601. A week later O'Neill with his southern commander Richard Tyrell set out from his rallying point at Lough Ramor in Cavan, harassing the Pale as he passed south, his army swelling daily as chieftains along his route rode in with their forces to join him.

Years later the gallowglass would remember the privations of that march down the length of Ireland. He would feel again the icy chill as he and his gallowglass forded chest-deep winter rivers. He would live again the shivering sleepless nights in damp tents, the exhausting days of trudging with frozen feet and empty belly over mountain passes. He would hear again O'Donnell's vibrant voice exhorting and encouraging as the red-haired chieftain galloped along the long lines of weary men. He would see again the dawn of hope in Irish faces as they told each other, "The Spanish have landed." That at last the Spanish had come; that they marched south to the last great battle. Above all MacRory would relive something of the exhilaration of those days of hope and gallant endeavour that led O'Donnell's army south to that last battle. Mountjoy sent some of his army north under the command of Carew to intercept O'Donnell, but Red Hugh, who had many times outmanoeuvred England's generals, was not to be diverted from his purpose of reaching Kinsale. He turned his army aside and crossed the snow covered Slieve Felim Mountains, a feat deemed impossible by the enemy. Carew hastened back to Kinsale in O'Donnell's wake. On 16 November, fourteen days after leaving Ballymote, Red Hugh, at the head of a weary and exultant army sat his horse on a hill top and looked down on the walled town of Kinsale.

Hugh O'Neill had raided along the borders of the Pale as he made his way south to join O'Donnell. As O'Donnell had predicted, the English were trapped between the forces of the northern chieftains and the Spanish and commenced to starve.

CHAPTER 34

Nial Garve's revenge

Rory Maguire arrived at Ballyshannon to escort Sheila and her children and Fiona O'Reilly to the safety of Lisnaskea. He told them that those allied against O'Neill and O'Donnell – and that included Conor Roe Maguire, his uncle – were now, in those chieftains' absence, making inroads into their territories, and would soon appear before Ballyshannon castle.

"My uncle Conor Roe has guaranteed your safety. You have a few days to prepare for the journey before we set out."

Sheila had apprehensions about taking her baby, Turlough, who was only a few months old on a trip which could be hazardous given the present state of unrest in the area, but she had a trusting nature and accepted the judgement of her friends. She and Fiona started getting ready for their journey.

A day before their departure a shout from a sentry brought the castle warden hurrying up to the battlements, from which he looked down on Neill Garve O'Donnell mounted and at the head of a large contingent of soldiers. Neill Garve addressed the castle warden on the battlements above him

"I am Neill Garve O'Donnell, your chieftain. Open the gates. I have business with you"

The warden's response was immediate and unequivocal.

"I was present at Carraig an Dun at the inauguration of the chieftain of the O'Donnells and you, sir, are not that man. The gates remain closed."

"I have enough men here with me to lay siege to this castle and starve you out, and for your insolence you could hang. However our taking of this castle in not my immediate concern today. You are harbouring a woman and her children and I have come at the request of Conor Óg Maguire to escort them to his castle at Lisnaskea."

Rory Maguire who had joined the warden on the battlements pushed forward and shouted down.

"With a one hundred man escort! You are a liar. Conor Roe knows nothing of this."

Seeing Rory Maguire on the battlements, Niall Garve knew that any further pretence was useless.

"My one hundred man escort will soon be joined by others with the equipment to storm this castle and I will have that woman and her children. Tell her from Neill Garve O'Donnell that there is no safety for her and her breed anywhere in Ireland. Hand her over and I will deal leniently with you and your men. Resist and you will soon be hanging from the castle walls. I have nothing further to say to you."

The warden, a gallowglass named Owen Crawford who had come to Ireland as part of Ineen Duive's retinue when she married Hugh O'Donnell, paused, and stroked his beard.

"Please give us a few moments to consider your offer."

He turned and nodded to a sentry who primed his Spanish musket and then took careful aim. Niall Garve saw the musket that was aimed at him and jerked his horse aside. The ball missed him but a horseman behind him, less lucky, groaned, and slumped in his saddle.

The warden having ensured that the walls were well patrolled with watchful sentries accompanied by his lieutenant sat in the hall of Ballyshannon Castle with Rory Maguire, Fiona O'Reilly, and Sheila MacRory.

"We'll have to get you to a place of safety. With Red Hugh gone south to link up with the Spaniard I have been expecting an attempt to take this castle. I will hold out for as long as I can but I am certain it will fall if they bring siege engines against us, which they can easily do by sea.

"I could possibly get you to Abbey Assaroe and the monks there would hide you for a time but it would also be one of the first places that Niall Garve would look."

Rory Maguire looked from the warden to his lieutenant.

"If we could get to Belleek I have a friend there who would help us. He knows of a route over the Bar of Whealt. I have hunted feral goats and the red stag with him in the region. It is a wild and remote area with many hiding places. The ford at Belleek will be well guarded and we wouldn't be able to cross there but we could cross by boat above Belleek. But how would Sheila fare with such a young baby and how would we get through Niall Garve's men who surround the castle?"

The warden turned to Sheila as he spoke.

"Getting past Niall Garve might not be such a problem, but how would you feel about taking along such a young baby."

"If there's any chance, it's a chance I must take. Turlough has never spoken to me of Niall Garve's threat, but I have heard of it from others. I fear the man and what he might do to our children. If you think that it's the better course I'll go."

But it was Fiona O'Reilly who answered her.

"It is the better course. Better to accept the risks whatever they may be than to stay here cowering in fear of that traitor Niall Garve.

The warden reached a decision.

"Alright, then. I can probably get you through Niall Garve's men but it will not be without some risk. There is a tunnel that leads from beneath the castle to a ledge behind the falls. There will probably be some of his men guarding the ford by the falls but the tunnel exit is well hidden. A dense stand of trees grows down to the river there and these will conceal you. Once out of the tunnel stay hidden in the trees and make your way up along the north bank of the river towards Belleek."

The Warden looked towards Rory Maguire.

"From Belleek it's up to you. Be ready to leave tomorrow. If it works, Niall Garve will never know that you are no longer in the castle."

The warden's lieutenant spoke for the first time.

"It's a risky plan but it might work. Anyhow what other choice do we have? I'll go down the tunnel tonight to ensure that it's safe. If there's danger I'll return to warn you, otherwise I'll keep watch and await you at the falls in the morning."

The warden agreed that this would be a wise precaution.

"Get ready to leave in the morning then and God be with you on your perilous journey."

With Rory Maguire holding a smoking torch in the lead and Fiona taking up the rear the fugitives crept down a dank tunnel. Five months old Rory was securely wrapped in a blanket fastened across Sheila's chest as bent over she led two year old Kathleen by the hand. Sheila's twin sisters and her brother followed her. Shelia's eyes widened and she stifled a scream as a large well fed rat, fearless, sat in a crevice level with her eyes and looked at the passing procession. When a faint glimmer of light showed the tunnel's exit Rory Maguire extinguished the torch, plunging the tunnel into darkness except for a small oval of light up ahead. As they neared the exit they waded through almost knee-deep water. A whispered voice, and the deputy warden reached out a hand to help each of them out by the side of a veil of water which poured down over an overhang concealing the tunnel's exit. Sheila straightened up gratefully and became aware of the full roar of the falls. She also became aware of a man on horseback emerging from the trees with a group of men behind him.

Niall Garve O'Donnell dismounted dropping his horse's reins and came forward with a grim smile and addressed Sheila. "If you do not know me, you will. Be assured you will. I am Niall Garve O'Donnell and I intend to repay a debt I owe your husband"

He turned to the deputy warden. "I repay all my debts. You will be rewarded for your services. When I take Ballyshannon and hang Crawford, you will be the new warden".

The man bowed his thanks and as his head came up it was to see Rory Maguire's sword lunging at his throat.

"And accept also my reward for your services." Before anyone could intervene the sword was impaled in the man's neck.

Maguire made no resistance as Niall Garve's men swarmed over him and disarmed him. He merely stared with contempt at the dying man who was gasping and clawing at his throat.

Niall Garve did not seem unduly disturbed at the loss of his informant. "Well, we'll just have to find another ward ... STOP THAT WOMAN!"

Taking advantage of the commotion Fiona had rushed for Niall Garve's horse and leaping astride kicked the animal vigorously with her heels. At the same time, leaning low on the horse's neck, she secured the reins and rode straight at Niall Garve, who unable to avoid the charging horse was knocked violently to the ground. A superb rider she galloped expertly through the trees and was gone. Niall Garve, an intemperate man at the best of times, was for moments speechless with rage. Rising to his knees, he pointed in the direction of the departed rider with chopping movements of his hand until he could find his voice.

"Damn, Damn y-you. Get back and get the horses and follow her. Do whatever you must to stop her. She must not be allowed to escape."

He turned to his men: "Guard these others – with your lives – with your lives! The sweet taste of revenge somewhat soured, he strode off towards his encampment.

The captives were escorted to Abbey Assaroe by Niall Garve and held there under guard. The twins and Eamonn MacGowan together with Rory Maguire were held in a tent at Ballyhannon. Before he rode off Niall Garve posted guards at the Abbey and had a conversation with the Abbot to inform him of the consequences if Sheila and her children escaped. Then he had a brief and chilling visit with Sheila.

"You and your children are nothing to me. You are tools that I will use to revenge myself on your husband. I will get word to him of your fate and that you and your children will be kept alive long enough for him to be aware that I hold the power of life and death over his family He will live each day never knowing when you are to die. However, you will know. You are not the targets of my revenge, you are merely the instruments of it, and I will arrange that your deaths are quick and merciful."

In the ensuing days the elderly Abbot visited Sheila frequently. "What has become of us? That an O'Donnell should descend to these depths! Niall Garve is possessed of a vengeful soul. Some madness grows within him. This lust for vengeance brings a madness that pollutes the mind. It dims the soul until no light of humanity shines through. God help us all for such are the men who now hold power over us."

The Abbot choose not to further discourage Sheila by telling her that one of his monks who had been dispatched to reach the Maguires in Lisnaskea had been intercepted crossing the Erne by Neill Garve's men.

"Have courage, Sheila; trust in God and be brave."

But Sheila was no Fiona O'Reilly. Instead of steel there was softness and kindness. Instead of resolve, trust and innocence. Frightful night followed frightful day. Every time she looked at her children a wave of fear swept over her as she realized anew the malevolence that threatened them. A sickening dread enveloped her like a shroud. Knowing that she was powerless to help them took its toll. She could not comprehend a nature that was so different to her own She felt herself sliding into madness.

"You and your children are nothing to me. You will be kept alive only long enough …" The words reverberated. Kathleen sensing her mother's anguish had become unusually silent and would often cry unexpectedly. Had he known it, Niall Garve's cup of vengeance was overflowing.

Sheila and her children had been at Abbey Assaroe for four days when one evening the old Abbot entered their room and sat by her silently. Eventually he spoke.

"We are powerless to help. His men surround us." He stopped and looked at the ground. "He has sent a message that one of his men will come for you tomorrow."

The Abbot sat again in silence by the trembling woman. He took Sheila's hand in his. "Whenever you are ready I will hear your confession."

In the early morning Sheila, who had not slept throughout the night, was sitting with Rory in her lap and Kathleen sleeping on the bed beside her when she heard loud voices without. The Abbot burst in without knocking. The sudden entrance set her heart racing and she reached for Kathleen and placed a protective arm over her.

A stocky man with a moustache and a pointed neatly trimmed beard strode into the room behind the Abbot. The man looked for a moment at the woman holding her two children.

"You have nothing to fear. I am Henry Docwra. You are safe now. I understand from the Abbot that my arrival is timely. This lady", he stood aside as Fiona O'Reilly entered the room," informed me of your plight." His look held a soldier's admiration for bravery as he looked at Fiona

"She crossed one of the most dangerous fords on the Erne to throw off her pursuers who were still scouring the wrong bank of the river in search of her. The ford was unguarded, and for good reason. Few are brave enough to attempt it. She was on her way to Lisnaskea on a very tired horse seeking help when we met her. I will escort you in person to safety at Lisnaskea. Your sisters and brother will join you shortly, as will Rory Maguire. I am an English knight who serves his queen as I see my duty. I have not always agreed with the conduct of this war in Ireland nor do I wage war on women and children. I will not allow any further harm to come to you. Niall Garve O'Donnell is becoming increasingly irrational but I still control him."

Uncontrollable tears rolled down Sheila's cheeks as she held her two children to her.

CHAPTER 35

Famine

"Eileen, take off those shoes, you're limping. They're far too big for you."

"No, Sheila, no. I'm fine." The younger child valiantly strove to walk without a limp, but was only successful in walking a few steps before again favouring her right foot.

"Sit down." The younger Eileen was too accustomed to doing as she was told by her ten year old sister to disobey.

"Ah, Eileen, why did you let it go this far without telling me. Look at your feet. Both of your heels are blistered. You're better off barefooted. I'll carry the shoes for you".

Seeing the look of disappointment on the child's face she added: *"You can wear them on the ship, when you won't be walking all day."*

Seven year old Eileen had outgrown her other shoes. She had been promised a new pair for her First Communion but other events had intervened. For the past eight miles she had walked with frequent downward glances at the novelty of her new shoes. She assumed that the painfully forming blisters were a necessary price to be paid for being grown up enough to wear shoes in summer. She now sat looking at her bare feet and then no longer distracted by her painful feet and her new shoes, a memory surfaced and she began to cry.

One of her earliest memories was of her twin brothers and Sheila kneeling on the cement floor of the kitchen each with hands outstretched towards her and each laughingly pleading *"To me, To me"* as she tried to decide to whose arms she should crawl. Another memory arose of a brother holding her up to the window to watch the never before seen magic of a skyful of fluffy snowflakes that gently curled downwards to transform the small green field in front of their house into a white expanse of wonderment. Yet another memory and another brother, tiptoeing to the ivy-covered wall of the shed, small grubby finger on lips enjoining silence as he parted the leaves that hid a robin's nest with four blue eggs. Daily, they crept to their secret in the ivy. One day her brother tearfully led her to a ravaged nest with a few fragments of blue shells scattered on the ground, their marvellous treasure desecrated and empty.

Another memory arose of the bed in an annex where the twins had slept, now also empty and bare.

Sheila stood helplessly looking down at her younger sister.

"Eileen, don't be sad. Be brave, Eileen. You know what I'll do for you. I'll sing a song for you. I'll sing 'The Bard of Armagh'".

Not knowing what else to do, she commenced singing in Irish the song she had heard since childhood. With it came a host of memories — of wading barefoot in the flagstone bed of the Aghinrawn, the dark-watered mountain stream that flowed by their house - of the well-remembered calamity of a large rip in her only dress while scrambling for hazel nuts in the trees by the riverbank - of her first day at Master Leonard's school in Killesher and how he had made such a fuss of his new four and a half year-old pupil, making her stand up on a bench in front of the entire class of twelve scholars and sing the very song that she now sang - of racing home across the mountain slope to relate to her mother how her fame and news of her talent had spread all around the parish of Killesher - of when she and Eileen had the measles, and how she worried about what her revered Master Leonard would think of them missing school - of the only other occasion when she had missed school - of all four of them standing on the banks of the swollen Aghinrawn unable to cross. In desperation they had attempted to walk downstream along the river bank to reach a point below Monastir Cliff where the swollen river had become a deep swirling pool as it was sucked underground into a sinkhole. However, here again their path was blocked. McCauley's bull, well known to be "cross", was out, and could be heard bellowing on the hillside below the sinkhole. She recalled each evening's proud duty rounding up the six ducks and two geese and herding them homeward to the safety of their shed, which the ducks and geese shared with two cows and a donkey; of the white-washed, thatch-roofed cottage in the shelter of a grove of tall poplars on the dun slopes of Cuilcagh; of warmth and security akin to what fledglings in a hidden nest must feel; of the blinds pulled down and the warm kitchen in the soft yellow light of the oil lamp; of the large oval serving plate so treasured by her mother, placed centrally among the delph on the dresser, its vivid blue and white willow-plate pattern strangely lush and exotic; of the murmuring voices around the turf fire; of a neighbour's knock on the door and Ivan Armstrong lifting the latch to come in out of the darkness to ceidhle and play a few hands of twenty-five; of listening sleepily from their beds to the muted voices of the card players in the kitchen, as they replayed each hand.

"You should have played the Ace of Hearts and kept him from getting out"

"Sure you couldn't have stopped me. I held the Knave as well, and the Fingers was played."

Memories of Christmastime and a hammering on the door and a straw clad figure leaping into the centre of the kitchen, conical straw hat reaching to the ceiling as he chanted:

Here comes I Jack Straw, the funniest man you ever saw

> *Me father was straw me mother was straw,*
> *So why shouldn't I be straw too.*

And then the kitchen is filled with wildly garbed figures cavorting and rhyming, the older children reassuring the wide-eyed younger ones: "It's the Mummers. It's the Armstrong and the Keown boys. Jack Straw! – sure that's only Ivan Armstrong."

The nights when the firelight gleamed on the rich wood of the fiddle as their father sat in the chimney nook, gnarled and nimble fingers playing the beloved old ballads, his eyes encouraging his two youngest children to sing with him, his favourite, "Phelim Brady, the Bard of Armagh."

Another memory now was of those eyes closed for ever, her father lying on the bed in his Sunday suit, large work-worn hands, strangely white and waxen, folded on his chest.

Irish history, lore, and legend were very much a part of the countryside where Sheila lived. King Brian Boru, Red Hugh, Eoghan Roe, Patrick Sarsfield, Wolfe Tone, and Robert Emmet were names, hallowed with a mystical aura, names evocative of a brave glory. The mythic legends of the Fianna, the sorrowful plight of the Children of Lir, the epic Táin that told of Cuchulainn's heroic battle against the forces of Queen Maeve, burned as real in the mind of a child as King Brian's victory over the Danes at Clontarf in 1014, or Eoghan Roe's victory over Monro at Benburb in 1646. Sheila had several times heard that a distant ancestor of her own family had fought alongside Red Hugh and had saved his life at a battle in Kinsale. Hidden up in the rafters beneath the thatch and wrapped in a blanket was the family's most prized possession, a sword with a silver knob on the hilt. On the knob, embossed in ivory, were a star and a crescent moon. It was said to have been given to that ancestor by the great Red Hugh himself, although it was always spoken of, as "The O'Reilly's sword." "Perhaps it did once belong to some famous chieftain", her father had once said. "How would people such as us ever come by such a thing otherwise, for it's not something would belong to any ordinary man?"

She had also heard many times the story attached to the old ballad "The Bard of Armagh". The story of the song dated back to the late 1600s and related to a Patrick Donnelly, Bishop of Dromore. In those days of the Penal Laws under the "Suppression of Popery" act, Catholic bishops were banned from Ireland on pain of death. To avoid detection Bishop Donnelly, then the only remaining bishop in Ireland, travelled around his diocese under the guise of a travelling harper by the name of Phelim Brady. This subterfuge was no idle precaution. The man, who had earlier ordained Patrick Donnelly a priest, Oliver Plunkett, Archbishop of Armagh, was hanged, drawn and quartered at

Tyburn in 1681 because he was a Catholic Bishop who remained in Ireland in defiance of the law.

What the young girl did not know was that the lilting old Irish melody had become beloved in another land, crossing the ocean with Irish emigrants to far away Texas. There, the melody became the iconic "Streets of Laredo".

Her once beautiful voice, now weak and breathless, faltered as her memories, too, overwhelmed her and she, too, began to cry.

It was now the younger child who tried to console her sister. "Don't cry Sheila," she wailed. "It would make them sad."

Two months ago in April the scythe of the reaper had found their nest. The mother and father were first to go, tormented in death, knowing that they were leaving four defenceless children behind. For two of those children the agony of grief was soon over, for within days, and within hours of each other, the twins followed their parents. The two youngest, their innocence profaned, walked now in an alien world of anguished loss. The deaths were due to the famine and resultant fever that swept Ireland in 1845.

Since the deaths, Eileen and Sheila Magrory had been cared for in the Enniskillen Workhouse. The area of South Fermanagh close to the Cavan and Leitrim border had suffered most in the famine. The Barony of Clanawley was an area of craggy limestone hills and lowland moors and lakes, a land of lonely haunting beauty, backward even by Irish standards. In this remote part of Ireland where the people walked daily among an unusually large number of Neolithic monuments they still clung to the old Irish customs and still spoke the old language. The children's townland of Legnabrocky, stretched for four miles, from the top of the Cladagh Glen to the top of Cuilcagh Mountain. Generations of a resilient stoical people had farmed the lower reaches, where the land was poor, and sparsely populated. A heathery bog, unsuitable for any kind of farming, carpeted the upper slopes of the mountain. With the famine, names that had been known for generations in the area disappeared as whole families disappeared from the land.

The workhouse diet of stirabout (porridge) at ten in the morning and soup and occasionally rice at three in the afternoon, while not enough for growing bodies to thrive, was enough to prevent starvation. One evening following the three o'clock meal the two children were called from their work in the kitchen to the administration office where they met their uncle, Patt, their father's brother and their only surviving relative who walked the eight miles from Killesher to Enniskillen to visit them as often as he could.

The tall man who embraced his brother's children was gaunt and hollow-eyed and when he spoke he seemed to be short of breath.

"Listen to me now children. I'm glad to see you being taken care of. But you can't stay here. There an outbreak of fever here in the workhouse. It kills as surely as starvation."

He paused for breath.

"Ireland has become a land of death. The famine is only getting worse. You have to leave this place, leave this country. Whole families, your own and mine are dead and gone."

He reeled and looked around for a place to sit down and finding none leaned against a wall before resuming.

"I have money here for your passage to Quebec in Canada. I've sold everything we ever owned. It's money I was saving to take my own family." He shook his head to rid it of some unwanted thought, "but now it's not needed."

He looked down at a cloth purse that he held in both hands.

"You'll have to try and make your own way to Rathmullan on the Swilly, up at the top of Donegal. There's a man there, a friend of our family, Owen Sweeney, who'll take you to Liverpool. He has a boat that brings back coal. There's enough money here for your passage from Liverpool to Canada. He'll put you on a ship for Quebec. He has relations there. There's ships out of Sligo, which is closer, but I hear they're coffin ships." He was gasping for breath and again had to pause. When he was able to resume he looked at Sheila.

"The journey to Rathmullan is over fifty miles, Sheila. It's a long way for two children in your condition, but it's your only hope. It's better than remaining and dying of the fever. There's a coach going to Ballyshannon workhouse the day after the morrow and the matron says they'll give you a ride that far, but you'll have to walk the rest. Remember these towns. You'll go from Ballyshannon to Ballintra to Donegal Town to Ballybofey to Letterkenny to Rathmullan. You can always ask someone if you get lost. As your father, Donagh, God rest him, used to say, "You have a tongue in your head", but if you have to ask, try to ask a priest or a policeman." When he smiled down at the younger child, his wasted face looked cadaveric. "You'll help her if she forgets won't you, Eileen?"

Without hesitation the younger child repeated: "Ballyshannon, Ballintra, Donegal Town, Bally-Bally- Ballybofey, Let-ter-kenny, Rathmullan."

"Well, and 'deed you were always a smart one, Eileen."

He continued to gaze fondly on the younger child.

"You know 'twas me and Kathleen – God have mercy on her – that stood for you on the day of your christening."

As he spoke his wife's name he had to drop his head low on his chest to bless himself. He seemed to be too weak to raise his arm to do so.

He handed the purse to Sheila.

"Be careful of this. Keep it hidden. I hate to have to say this to you but trust no one. Not everyone is a good person, and starving people are desperate. I'd take you there myself but I – I cannot. It was all I could do to make it here from Killesher."

He again reached down and put an arm around each of them.

"God be with you forever."

He picked up a bag from the floor and handed it to Sheila, then turned suddenly and stumbled from the room. The bag fashioned from burlap contained one whole loaf and one quarter of another of homemade bread, two small last year's apples and a pair of shoes which had belonged to his dead nine year-old child.

Three days after leaving Enniskillen, Sheila and Eileen were climbing upwards towards Barnesmore Gap, a pass in the Bluestack Mountains between the towns of Donegal and Ballybofey. They were both close to exhaustion. Eileen was barefooted as her feet were not yet healed. Sheila carried Eileen's shoes strung around her neck but was herself barefooted. On hearing of their proposed journey, the matron at the workhouse, though thinking it a desperate endeavour, could only concur that it might be the wisest course. She had seen well over one hundred uncoffined bodies buried in a field behind the workhouse in the past month, more than half of them children. Overwhelmed by daily sights of suffering and death she had not the time to focus on their plight. She had asked them if they had enough food for the journey and distractedly accepted their answer that they had food in their bag. She had given the two Magrory children a blanket each and a small piece of towelling about nine inches square.

Outside the village of Ballintra they had found a cow byre where they had slept on their first night, lying on one blanket and covered by another. Since infancy they had shared a bed and now they slept clutching each other, sharing a grief that neither could articulate, as to do so was to reopen a wound, each to the other all that was left of a world that was now only a memory, and as always that grief was harder to bear in the quiet and darkness of night. Before lying down they had knelt to say their prayers. In the morning they had washed by a stream and dried themselves with their fragments of towelling. From early childhood they had become accustomed to this night and morning ritual, kneeling to say their prayers at night and in the morning going down to the river that flowed by their house, carrying a bar of shared soap and a towel. On the second night they had slept in the open, sheltered under a large rhododendron bush, many of which grew by the roadside in this part of Donegal. So far the early June weather had been warm and kind with only an occasional shower, but now approaching the Barnesmore Gap grey clouds swirled in the surrounding hills *and a chilling North East wind blew in their faces. When it began to drizzle rain they looked for shelter but there was none in the treeless landscape. They trudged on cold and wet. They tried sheltering behind a large rock but while they were sheltered from the wind the inactivity made them colder still and when they both began to shiver Sheila thought it best that they keep moving. Eventually they tried to run to keep warm, but in their weakened state soon stopped, gasping for breath. They resumed their resigned gait in the wind and rain. While both children were underweight and undernourished, Sheila was more emaciated and showed more the effects of starvation. In her weakened state she felt the cold more. For all of their time in the Enniskillen Workhouse she had used the pretence of a poor appetite to share a portion of her own food to augment that of her younger sister. This had brought her close to death from starvation.*

Now she frequently felt dizzy, her feet were swollen and her gums bleeding. Swallowing was difficult, and walking painful. Any movement was painful. The thought of what lay ahead each day was almost unbearable; The agonizingly slow progress, the exhausting miles that stretched ahead, as they struggled onward towards the sea to leave their own land, their beautiful land, now a land of poisoned fields and poisoned memories. She fell each night into an exhausted sleep and did not want to arise to the torment of another day. For Eileen's sake, she tried to keep up a brave front but had to fight against an increasing apathy. The younger child trudged doggedly on in grim silence, looking down at her bare feet as if willing each step forward. An uncomplaining acceptance of hardship, a trait absorbed from their parents, was a characteristic of both children. The physical strain was in one way a mercy in that it gave them little time to dwell on all that was now lost to them. The passage of a few months had only slightly blunted their sorrow. Grief and reality still came in waves. They had three-quarters of one loaf left. These home-baked loaves were called "fadges", and despite the fact that now in famine times the white flour was bulked up by the addition of unpalatable India meal, each morsel was manna to the starving children. The apples were being saved for some special occasion.

Descending down from Barnesmore, the rain continued but the cold wind lessened. The countryside was now less stark with occasional trees. Sheila had commenced sneezing and still shivered intermittently. Since leaving Enniskillen they had seemed to travel through an unpeopled land. Even farm animals were scarce. People weakened by starvation were no longer tending crops; indeed there were few crops to tend. Whole families stayed indoors, weak and listless from malnutrition, dying slowly of starvation or disease resultant on starvation.

It was somewhat of a surprise to come on a man sheltering beneath a tree by the roadside. A cheerful voice greeted them in English and the man looked at them expectantly awaiting an answer. Neither Sheila nor Eileen could carry on a conversation in English. The comprehensive national school system that was introduced into Ireland in 1831 had resulted in a national school at Mullanavehy in the lowlands down by Arney Bridge which was too far away for the "mountain children". Their school was a small thatch-roofed, whitewashed building up on the Marlbank at the top of the Claddagh Glen. It had a packed mud floor and a fireplace built into one wall. In wintertime each child was expected to bring one sod of turf each day to provide fuel for the fire. On either side of the fireplace were hooks for the children's extra items of clothing. On one wall was a map of Ireland showing all thirty two counties. Four rows of seating benches took up most of the room. Each bench had four evenly spaced ink-wells, and between each ink-well was a groove to hold a nib pen and a slate stylus. The children were provided with a slate board for doing sums and practicing writing. Each bench shared a sheet of blotting paper. Exercise books were kept in individual school bags at their feet. To one side of the fireplace stood the blackboard on an easel. The local children were taught by Theobald Emmet Leonard, who though not a qualified teacher, was awarded the title of "Master" and received a salary of two pounds a year per scholar from the children's parents, Master Leonard taught through Irish. His own English was limited. What little of the language he was able to teach was by way of having the children recite poetry in English, his favourites being Moore's Melodies, and two poems, by Scottish poets – "Lord Ullen's Daughter", and "Young Lochinvar". As a result the children's manner of speech in their limited English, sounded almost Elizabethan, sprinkled with "thee" and "thou" and poetic contractions that in conversation sounded quaint and archaic. They were conscious of the mild amusement that often greeted their efforts, and hence were reluctant to attempt a conversation in English. Master Leonard taught his twelve scholars reading writing and arithmetic and he taught of the Firbolgs, early inhabitants of Ireland, of the early Celtic invasions of Ireland, and King Conor MacNessa, a pre-Christian Irish king. The children learned modern history also. They learned of St. Patrick's coming to Ireland in 432, St. Columcille's founding of the monastery of Iona in 563, and King Brian Boru's defeat of the Danes at The Battle of Clontarf in 1014. They learned of another Irish victory in 1594 at the Ford of the Biscuits, so called because of the provisions scattered around after Hugh Maguire defeated an English force at a ford on the Arney River. That battle, he told them, was fought, not far from where Mullanavehy School now stood, and no more than three and a half miles from their own school. The site of the bloody battle was still known locally as "The Red Meadows". He taught them some Latin which he himself had learned in a "hedge" school. It was said of him that he could recite the Greek alphabet. He put much of his soul into his teaching. Importantly, and by example, he also instilled in his few and small charges honourable behaviour, good manners, and a love of the country of their birth.

Sheila replied in Irish explaining that they did not understand much English and only spoke Irish. Eileen quietly tugged at her sister's dress urging her to keep walking.

"For heaven's sake take shelter here. Look at you. You're soaked to the skin. You'll catch your death out in this weather."

Strangely his Irish did not have the clipped Donegal accent.

Eileen looked up at her older sister for guidance, and when Sheila slowly moved off the road to the shelter of the tree followed her.

"Your Irish isn't from Donegal. And where are you both from that you wouldn't be speaking English in this day and age and where are you going?"

Sheila was startled by the directness of the question which approached rudeness, but feeling that it would be equally rude not to reply and wrong to lie, Sheila replied truthfully to half of the question. Besides she felt ashamed to mention the workhouse and ashamed that she couldn't speak English.

"We are going to Rathmullan."

"Rathmullan you say. Why would you be going there? Sure that's more than two days walking from here. There's nothing at Rathmullan save a few houses and a pier".

"Well that's where we're going anyways." It was Eileen who replied with a finality that intimated "Let that be an end to your questions."

The man laughed and held out his hand: "Dominic Harvey, I'm from Letterkenny direction and heading back that way as soon as this rain is over".

They had been warned to be cautious of strangers but the man's forthright friendliness was disarming and soon he knew both their names but after Eileen's "take it or leave it" response he expressed no further interest in where they came from. It was getting dark when all three of them approached Ballybofey. When Sheila continued to sneeze he expressed concern.

"You poor child, be careful you don't catch pneumonia. I know a place where you'll both be warm and safe for the night.

He led them to a church and opened the door.

"You won't find any bed in there but try and make yourselves as comfortable as you can on the floor. At least it's dry and you'll be in out of the rain. It's a Protestant church, and the door is always unlocked." He then added with a smile, looking down on them: "Even though it's not of your faith, it's still a house of God." The two children tiptoed in bare feet and in awed shyness into a church quite different from their church in Killesher. This church had a vaulted roof and a bell tower, a wooden floor, and rows of seats facing a raised marble altar. Their chapel at Wheathill in Killesher parish had a thatched roof, an earthen floor and the only seat had been a stool for Father Mason to one side of a wooden altar.

"Sheila, I don't think I like him. I don't think he's a good person," Eileen whispered when he had gone.

"It's alright. Why wouldn't you like him? He has found us a good place to sleep. He offered to share some of his food with us on the road here and never asked us for any of ours. He wouldn't do that if he wasn't a good person."

"I dunno. He didn't look like he was starving, himself, and he didn't actually give us any food. He said, 'If we needed it', and how could we ask a stranger for food? He knew we hadn't much because I saw him once looking into our bag. That showed bad manners. I think he saw the purse with our money. It was bad mannered of him, too, the way he made us feel about not knowing English. Mammy always said that good manners were more important than good clothes. He noticed that our Irish was not from Donegal, but neither was his, yet he said he was from Letterkenny."

"You're a tough wee nut Eileen. Lie down and we'll go to sleep."

"Alright, but he had bad manners and I don't like him."

They lay on the wooden floor at the back of the church, lying on one blanket and covered by another. After some minutes of silence Eileen murmured: "Listen to this Sheila: Ballyshannon, Ballintra, Donegal Town, Ballybofey, Letterkenny, Rathmullan. Did I get it right?"

But Sheila only moved restlessly in her sleep.

During the night something creaked. Eileen, awake beneath her blanket, clutched the burlap bag closer to her, and wrapped her arms around it. She spoke tearfully into the darkness: "It's our food an' our money, an' you yourself said that this is still a house of God." The wind gusted and the flagpole on the bell-tower creaked again ... Sheila slept on in an exhausted sleep.

The "Sarah" lay anchored off Grosse Ile in the Gulf of St. Lawrence. A seven-year-old girl standing on the deck of the ship wondered which of the shrouded bundles being lowered to a barge for burial on the island was that of her sister. She stood in her dead cousin's ill-fitting shoes. The shoes, while still too big, now fitted better because the child's thin bare legs ended in feet and ankles that were swollen due to chronic starvation. Her clothes, a petticoat that reached below her knees, and a grey linen smock over a brown home-knitted wool sweater, looked too large for her emaciated body. Her green eyes, looking startlingly large in a face that was no longer that of a child, were dulled with misery. The eyes mirrored a haunted soul. Auburn hair, lusterless and matted, fell almost to her waist. Her only possession was an empty burlap bag. She did not understand any of the languages spoken around her. She was quite alone, more alone than she knew. The man who had stood for her at her christening, who had paid her fare to Canada and had given her and her sister the last of his food, had died by the roadside returning to Killesher. She herself was now the last of her name.

She was unaware of another child on a nearby ship, "The Prince of Orange" which carried Dutch and German immigrants, staring at her. The other child wore a colourful frock and had white stockings and buckled shoes. Her blond hair was neatly braided. She stared with open curiosity before turning and saying something in a strange language to her mother. The mother too turned to gaze with curiosity before taking her child's hand and leading her away from the rail as if away from something unclean.

Ireland had suffered many famines in the 1800s as had Scotland and parts of England, but never such a famine as devastated the country between the years 1845 to 1848. The Great Famine of these years, which reached its peak in 1847, ploughed a swathe through Ireland's memory that left a livid scar that would never be erased. The Irish died of starvation, and starvation induced disease. They died in their tens of thousands. They died in their hundreds of thousands. The eventual death toll was more than a million, and over the succeeding decades Ireland's population fell from eight million to four and a half million due to death, disease, and emigration.

They died in Ireland in hovels, in fields, and in ditches as they attempted to feed their hunger by eating grass. They died in coffin ships, carrying them away from their devastated land. They died of lingering disease in the cities, towns, and countryside of England, Australia, New Zealand, America, and Canada. Over five thousand found their eventual resting place in a mass grave in a one-acre cemetery on Grosse Ile.

The union of England and Ireland had always been an uneasy one. Continuous smouldering discontent erupting in a rebellion about every second or third generation marked the centuries of English rule, but the famine of those years sundered forever any bonds that might conceivably have held the two countries together in any kind of acceptable union. Two centuries, during which a people were progressively ground into the meanest poverty of any country in Europe in order to glut the wealth of their rulers, culminated in widespread famine and the deaths of millions – two centuries during which the many lived in squalor and misery so that the few might live in ease and elegance; two centuries during which a materially impoverished people, were ruled by morally impoverished lords.

Sir Charles Trevelyan, a Victorian Englishman, was the man responsible for instituting measures to alleviate the famine in Ireland, and many Englishmen of the time would have agreed with Sir Charles' uncompromising statement: "The great evil with which we have to contend is not the physical evil of famine, but the moral evil of the selfish, perverse and turbulent character of the people."

Many a titled head would have nodded in languid agreement with this sagacious utterance.

But was Ireland's selfishness the demand to be granted a measure of human dignity that most would regard as the birthright of all people? Was Ireland's perversity her unwillingness to tug the forelock to a foreign lord? Was Ireland's turbulent character the unbreakable spirit of a people, defeated in battle, but never conquered in spirit? To the ruling English, turbulence was not a quality to be tolerated. It disturbed equanimity and could negatively affect revenue.

Sir Charles would have preferred that those starving Irish go to their mass graves quietly and without any unseemly fuss that might offend the moral sensitivity of Victorian England. Many, too, may have agreed with his fatalistic comment that also seemed to convey the idea that the Irish famine was God's retribution on a perverse people.

"The problem of Ireland being altogether beyond the power of man, the cure has been applied by an all-wise Providence." – An opportunistic indifference on the part of government would aide in bringing a convenient solution to the "Irish question". Victorian England, that gave to the world such politicians as Wilberforce, such poets as Tennyson and Browning, such humanitarians as Florence Nightingale and Elizabeth Fry, and such natural philosophers as Charles Darwin, could find in its heart no generosity towards her sister island. The Janus countenance that was turned towards Ireland was severe, intolerant and uncompromising.

The Victorians looked on unruly Ireland with distaste, feeling that Ireland was unworthy of England's enlightened dominance. To the Victorians, their superior culture was self-evident. But to Ireland with her differing Celtic culture it was not so evident. An unwashed Irish peasant could still find offensive the stench of hypocrisy that emanated from a perfumed English lord. The English, now rulers of an empire, saw themselves as enlightened rulers, but they were at all times prepared to act sternly in response to any nonsense from those whom they ruled. In the aftermath of the Indian Mutiny sepoys were strapped across the mouths of cannon and thus duly dispatched. The cost of the powder and shot was levied on their relatives. The mutinous Sepoys had committed many horrible atrocities – and now it was the turn of the British.

A little over half a century later, at Amritsar, also in India, General Dyer had his men pour bullets for ten to fifteen minutes into a peaceful crowd that had gathered in disobedience to his orders, He coolly directed his men's fire towards the few crowded exits through which the people were attempting to escape, slaying, in some estimates, as many as one thousand men, women, and children. Many of the Indians who had gathered in the walled compound were unaware that the assembly had been banned. A Court of Inquiry under a British Lord admonished Dyer for "continuing to fire for as long as he did."! Most of the British in India, with the memory of the mutiny embedded in their genes, and many in England, approved of Dyer's actions. Some, including Winston Churchill, did not. Dyer decreed that any Indian entering the street where an English woman had been assaulted must do so by crawling on their bellies. This order also applied to the Indians who lived there and who had intervened in the assault to save the woman's life. To the end of his days this product of a Victorian education failed to see anything immoral in his actions. Blandly unaware of any hypocrisy or irony, he proclaimed "The British Raj must continue firm and unshaken in its administration of justice to all men." For his demonstration of stern will, Rudyard Kipling described Dyer as "The man who saved India" and the House of Lords presented him with a jewelled sword. This, from the poet of empire, and this, from an assembly of lords!

At the height of the famine, cartoonists for "Punch", the English satirical magazine, could so insulate themselves from Ireland's agony and the plight of her starving children as to depict the Irishman as a fat spoiled child. Nearly twenty years earlier Daniel O'Connell had obtained for his country Catholic Emancipation, by which Catholics, who accounted for 80% of Ireland's population, were allowed to sit in Parliament. He continued to advocate, by non-violent means, for the dissolution of the Act of Union whereby Mother England held Ireland in an unwholesome embrace.

O'Connell, beloved by the Irish, reviled by the English, was the object of particularly creative caricatures in "Punch". Later, after his death in Genoa in 1847, the Young Irelanders and the Fenians took over O'Connell's organization and advocated armed revolt against England. The depictions of the Irishman then became those of a simian, brute-like creature. Charles Kingsley, a historian, and a devotee of the new "science" of physiognomy, was of the opinion that the Irish looked like "white chimpanzees." It's possible that a starving people did not have the same aesthetically pleasing physique and countenance as a well-fed one. With him, the Celts, the Gauls, and all the numerous Slavic races fared poorly in comparison with the nobler Teutonic race. A century later when Hitler became a proponent of this same theory of eugenics, the concept was not looked on with the same enthusiasm in England. When Hitler planned to make of the Slavic races what England had for centuries made of the Irish race, England's voice was foremost in condemnation of such a vile concept. It must have been gratifying to Queen Victoria, and to Prince Albert, her husband, when the historian reminded them of the heroism of their Teutonic ancestors beneath the walls of Jerusalem. Lest, however, he appear too fulsome in his praise of Teutonic virtue and in order to maintain the semblance of historical objectivity, Kingsley did daub in a wart here and there on the ancestral visage, ever careful not to be carried away by objectivity, lest Her Majesty be not amused. Literary frankness was as perilous for the scribe in the Victorian era as it had been for the file in Gaelic Ireland.

In an earlier century a file, having satirized his O'Donnell chieftain, had fled far south to Limerick, feeling that he had little future in his profession in Tir Conaill. O'Donnell called a hosting and raged south where he invested the castle in which the poet had sought refuge. The poet fled eastward toward Dublin, an infuriated O'Donnell in pursuit, but from Dublin the man managed to reach Scotland and safety. O'Donnell was forced to reluctantly give up the chase and take his army back home. A Celtic compromise was eventually reached and the repentant rhymer, having promised to compose, not one but two poems in praise of O'Donnell, was allowed to return to Donegal. It would be difficult to conceive of Victoria expressing her displeasure with the same full-blooded outrage as had O'Donnell. A frigid reserve would have conveyed to the "cad" that never again in his lifetime would he bask in the tepid glow of his monarch's affection.

Perhaps it was in deference to their majesties' sensibilities that Kingsley refrained from any mention of how those righteous Teutonic knights, hell-bent on doing God's work and assured by the Pope of forgiveness for all sins, had slaughtered, en route to Jerusalem, as well as beneath its walls, Muslims, Jews, and other Christians whose physiognomy did not conform to the Teutonic concept of what a Christian should look like. Victorians would have reacted with bored disinterest had they been reminded that five hundred years before the Crusaders had cut their swathe across Europe, monks from Ireland had trudged the same land to spread the faith that the Crusaders so brutally tarnished.

Queen Victoria was known as the "Grandmother of Europe," as many of her offspring, from her consanguineous union with her first cousin, Prince Albert, had married into Europe's royal families. Had Kingsley lived for a further few years he would have had further cause to be reticent. In the early 1900s grandson Kaiser Wilhelm of Germany unleashed his general, Von Trotha in an unabashed extermination of the Hereros in his South West African empire. The body count there was around 100,000. After 100,000 years of evolution the product of that evolution was returning to ancestral Africa.

Meanwhile, cousin Leopold of the Belgians, was harvesting baskets of severed hands from his Congo domain. Workers in Leopold's private empire of the Congo who failed to meet their quota of harvested rubber and ivory had a hand chopped off. As with the English rulers of Ireland, King Leopold of the Belgians felt that Belgium and the Belgian people were unworthy of him. When foisted on that country he had sniffed: "Small country, small people." He set about ruling something more substantial. Under the pretence of bringing civilization to Africa he acquired the Congo, an area nearly eighty times the size of Belgium, as his own private fiefdom.

Another grandson, Prince Albert Victor, Duke of Clarence, brother to the future King Edward VII was rumoured to be Jack the Ripper. Although it was later proved that he could not have been present at one of the murders, the fact that a grandson of Victoria, and a man who was second in line to the throne of England was at all in the running surely hinted that the crème de la crème of English nobility was not all it might be.

But the obscenities of South West Africa and the Congo were only a prelude to the unleashing of the beast that would occur in 1914 when some of the offspring of the "Grandmother of Europe" had a falling out among themselves that would engulf the world in an apocalyptic orgy of killing. King George of England, Kaiser Wilhelm of Germany, and Tsar Nicholas of Russia were all descended from Queen Victoria, as were many of the other European monarchs who cheerfully sacrificed their subjects in that noble family dispute. The Horsemen rode for four years, and the "butcher's bill" rose to around twenty million dead. What agonies of death for those millions! What agonies of mourning and sorrow for millions more!

Ireland's conquerors, immersed in their own dreams of glory and empire treated with derision any claims to past glory of the vanquished. The pagan splendour of Tara, the heroic tales of the Fianna, the three centuries during which the fugitive remnants of western civilization had looked to a small island on Europe's western fringe as do Muslims to Mecca, were so relegated to a contemptuous obscurity that Benjamin Disraeli, a future Prime Minister of England, could taunt O'Connell:

"When the ancestors of the right honourable gentleman were brutal savages in an unknown land, mine were priests in the temple of Solomon."

At the time he spoke those words, Disraeli had forsaken his own ancient faith, which had proved a hindrance in his climb to the top of the greasy pole of British politics. But after two centuries of brutal domination by an alien and unsympathetic race, the light of other days burned on in the memory of Ireland's wounded and savaged people. The faith that Saint Patrick had brought to their shores burned on in their hearts.

Sir Charles Trevelyan voiced what many of the English ruling class felt that it was the structure of Irish society itself that brought about the famine. Indeed it contributed hugely, but the structure of Irish society of the 1840s was the direct result of centuries of English rule. The shackles of the Penal Laws of the sixteenth, seventeenth and eighteenth centuries – laws that had relegated the Irish to a nation of slaves – had left their scars and were not easily cast off. The mass of Irish people lived primitive lives on small patches of land, growing potatoes for their family's subsistence, and grain and other produce to pay the landlord's rent. The native Irish, comprising more than eighty percent of the population, owned less than five percent of the land. Supporting the grandeur and extravagance of the rich and the powerful in their mansions were the bent backs of those living in hovels, a situation not unique to Ireland, but in Ireland the burden borne for an alien and arrogant master made the load the heavier.

The defeated Irish walked among the relics of a bygone glory. Myth and legend, story and song, surrounded each hilltop fort, each ruined castle wall, each mountain, valley, lake, and river, and spoke to them of that bygone glory, spoke of a past that was far different to their present squalor. While the lights blazed and music and laughter drifted forth from the "Great House," the ghosts of the cairns and raths whispered around the cabins a memory of other days. The Homeric deeds of Cuchulainn and of Finn and his Fianna were recited in smoky hovels to solemn-eyed children clad in rags. Like a phoenix arising from the ashes, the shield-hung halls of Tara of the kings rose again from the glowing embers of the turf fires. Perhaps an escape to a past world of glory and feasts and all-powerful heroes did something to assuage the squalor and the hunger and the helplessness of this.

An illiterate, barefoot peasant shearing corn with a sickle in some remote glen in County Leitrim, might well know each exquisite nuance of "The Táin," an early Irish epic of a cattle raid, which has been compared to Homer's "Iliad". What, however, would such a man, now imbued with the puritanical morals of Victoria's time, think of the lusty ways of another queen, Maeve, wife of Ailill, who bargaining for a prize bull with the Ulster prince Daire, offered him half her kingdom, and then threw in as an afterthought, "and my own friendly thighs?" Despite the more than generous inducements, the cattle deal fell through and Maeve led the men of Connacht through slaughter on an epic scale.

Many absentee landlords continued to demand rent despite the famine, and in many cases, if the rent was not paid, had their agents tear down the cabins and evict the occupants. In the three years of the famine, landlords evicted an estimated 90,000 families amounting to about 500,000 people. These homeless men women and children were turned out into the countryside to starve or to be fed in soup kitchens.

Trevelyan followed the laissez-faire policy of the government that reflected the ideology of the times and felt that the Government should interfere as little as possible in matters of economic trade. England's ship of commerce sailed serenely on bringing home to the motherland the wealth of empire, while in Ireland starving children looked in vain to their starving parents for help. Dying parents, looking at the wasted bodies of their dying children, could only silently mouth a prayer that the pleading eyes would soon close in death. The result of non interference with trade and commerce was that while the Irish people starved in Ireland, shiploads of grain, meat, butter and other produce, more than ample to alleviate the famine in Ireland, continued to be exported from Irish ports. The starving Irish, leaving those same ports, carried with them across the seas a bitterness long to be remembered.

> Our whitening bones against ye will rise as witnesses,
> From the cabins and the ditches in their charred, uncoffin'd masses,
> For the Angel of the Trumpet will know them as he passes.
> A ghastly, spectral army, before the great God we'll stand,
> And arraign ye as our murderers, the spoilers of our land.

The Irish felt that the blight caused the potato crop to fail, but the policies of the English government caused the famine. The English reacted with indignation, pointing out that England contributed money and resources to Ireland's relief – much more indeed than the Irish landlords were willing to contribute. A story circulated in Ireland that Queen Victoria had donated a miserly and contemptuous five pounds towards famine relief. In fact, not only had Queen Victoria made a personal donation of two thousand pounds but she had also written a letter to the Archbishop of Canterbury urging that he get the Church of England involved in famine relief in Ireland. The English government instituted relief measures but the grim statistics showed how ineffective these measures were. Ships carrying relief stores of Indian meal to Ireland met ships carrying sheep, cattle, grain, and food products away from Ireland. In the west of Ireland massive stone piers constructed by gaunt, starving men jut into the Atlantic, present-day reminders of those famine relief work projects. The Quakers, living the tenets of their religion, worked quietly among the starving populace. The Choctaw Indians, remembering their own Trail of Tears eight years earlier, sent relief. The Choctaw, to make way for white settlers, had been evicted from their homeland in the south eastern United States, and when they looked back in longing toward the land of their fathers, they counted four of their people dead for each mile of sorrow along the thousand mile trek to Oklahoma. As commented by Mary Robinson, Ireland's President in an address to the

United Nations, the Choctaw when hearing of another people's sufferings were able to perceive the real link between a Native American tribe and the inhabitants of a small island thousands of miles away. No more and no less than a shared humanity.

If General Sheridan, a Union Army General of Irish descent did indeed say what he was reputed to have said. "The only good Indian is a dead Indian" then he, too, failed to make that connection.

The "Ghastly spectral army" marches on, its ranks swollen since 1847 with men, women and children of many lands — and we are all arraigned.

As the Canadian Forces helicopter approached Grosse Ile, Mary McAleese looked down on a huge Celtic cross, which dominated a rocky promontory on the western tip of the island. The island lay in the mouth of the Saint Lawrence, thirty miles down river from Quebec City and had been used as a quarantine station for immigrants arriving in Canada between the years 1832 and 1937. In a cemetery close by the cross, over five thousand Irish, who had died on Grosse Ile fleeing the Irish famine of 1845-'48, were buried in a mass grave.

Ireland's President, Mary McAleese, accompanied by Liz O'Donnell, Ireland's Minister of State, and by Sheila Copps, Minister of Canadian Heritage, walked up a gravel pathway and stood beneath the Celtic cross, before descending by another pathway to the small green acre of Canadian soil shared by so many souls. Here at the Irish cemetery Mary McAleese unveiled a memorial to those buried there.

Since the Canadian government had designated Grosse Ile a National Historic site in 1984, many visited the island, some as casual tourists and some as pilgrims. An Irish-American group had erected on the island a large Celtic cross to the memory of the Irish dead. On its base were inscriptions in Irish, French, and English. The inscriptions in French and English read:

Sacred to the memory of thousands of Irish immigrants, who to preserve their faith suffered hunger and exile in 1847-1848, and stricken with typhus, ended their sorrowful pilgrimage here, comforted and strengthened by the Canadian priests. Those who sow in sorrow reap in joy.

The inscription in Irish translated somewhat differently:

Children of the Gael died in their thousands on this island, having fled from the laws of foreign tyrants and artificial famine in the years 1847-1848. God's blessing on them. Let this monument be a token to their name and honor from the Gaels of America.

God save Ireland.

From the base of the cross a path led down to a cemetery.

An ocean away from the green and quiet valleys of the land that held the graves of their fathers, the tormented children of the Gael slept heaped in their common grave on this small island lapped by the waters of the great Saint Lawrence. Within mocking sight of the land that had promised a new life of freedom, their weary bodies had surrendered to their final conqueror.

Whatever agonies the dead, now lying beneath the still discernible, symmetrical heaves of green earth, had once suffered; there was now only a sense of profound peace about the place. Close by the cemetery a memorial had been erected to the doctors, nurses, and others who, while caring for the destitute multitudes that had swamped the quarantine facilities of the island, had themselves died of the diseases carried by the immigrants. In 1847, fifteen workers on the island, eight of them nurses, were laid to rest beside those they had cared for.

In nearby Quebec City there were imposing monuments to Generals Wolfe and Montcalm, who had battled for empires. The simple monument to those who died here caring for others was smaller, but surely their glory was greater.

A memorial to the dead, a circle of stone thirty feet in diameter and four feet high, was dissected by crossed pathways and fronted by an interlocking arc of glass panels. The panels bore the names of those who had died on the island since 1832. The vast majority of the names were for the year 1847. At the bottom of each panel a number of small ships were etched into the glass, each small etching commemorating one of fifteen hundred nameless dead.

CHAPTER 36
Preparation for battle

The English force had initially been eleven thousand foot and close to nine hundred horse, but their numbers had dwindled due to desertion, disease, and loss in skirmishes with the Spanish by the time the northern chieftains arrived at Kinsale. O'Neill's strategy was to cut off their supplies and starve the English into surrender. The Spanish commander, Don Juan del Aguila, held the walled town of Kinsale with his force of thirty-five hundred Spaniards, but his men too were starving. Del Aguila sent frequent messengers to O'Neill and O'Donnell, appealing to them to attack and raise the siege. As Christmas approached, the appeals from the Spanish became frantic. Ammunition was running low and the Spaniards were starving.

Hugh O'Neill was not in favour of a pitched battle with the English and his moral authority among the chieftains would have precluded any such attack. A cautious, patient leader, he had for six years worn down successive English armies by drawing them into the intractable bogs and forests of Ulster, wearing down their numbers and morale by sniping on the flanks, never offering the pitched battle the enemy almost frantically craved. After months of futile pursuit, the English staggered back again through the bogs and forests to some coastal town, their once proud army decimated, dispirited, and starving. With each O'Neill success, Elizabeth's epithets became more strident – "Base bush-kern," "Arch traitor," "Running beast".

By slow incremental steps he had eroded English power and prestige and made it increasingly difficult for the invader to govern. He knew one wild Celtic charge would not topple the edifice of English power in Ireland, built up over centuries. He knew and respected the prowess in war of these soldiers of Elizabeth. He himself had lived and fought among them. He would have to contend with the impetuous Red Hugh and the appeals from the Spaniards for immediate action to lift the siege. He also would have to restrain the natural instinct of his chieftains for action. He knew he could prevail and impose his will.

A council of war was called. O'Neill, knowing when to seek consensus and when to impose his will, now felt it safe to seek consensus, as he was sure the decision reached would be the one he himself advocated. O'Neill addressed the council first.

"There is much at stake here. We have much to lose if we do not consider well our decision. We have won many battles, Clontibret, Monaghan, the Yellow Ford, and the Curlews. All these hard-won victories will be as nothing if we are defeated here at Kinsale. All we have strived for, all our people and our land have suffered in these last eight years will be as nothing; for nothing the devastation of your lands; for nothing the deaths of your women and children; for nothing the humiliations imposed by an arrogant and brutal foe."

Some of the listening chieftains remembered the speaker himself as the "arrogant and brutal foe" of the Desmond wars.

"This is a battle we must win. This is a battle we are already winning by turning the enemy's own tactics against himself. When he came to Kinsale, Mountjoy's army numbered almost twelve thousand. It now numbers less than seven thousand. Why should we risk our men and our cause when hunger and disease fight our battles for us? We have only to hold our positions across Mountjoy's supply lines, denying food and provisions to his army, and he is defeated. Time is our ally, and we will let time fight this battle for us. Mountjoy would wish us to offer a pitched battle. His only hope against the certainty of defeat is the gamble of a battle. Why should we oblige him?"

Looking around the assembled chieftains, O'Neill sensed most of them were in agreement with his tactics and he felt it was unnecessary to continue further. He concluded by saying, "I have been in this war for the last six years and some of you for as long as eight. It has been a long and a bitter struggle. The end is in sight. You, who for year after weary year have shown the virtue of fortitude in battle, must now show the virtue of patience, patience for a few short weeks. United we have defeated the English in battle after battle. We will remain united and the victory will be ours. When Mountjoy and his army are starved into submission, all of Ireland will unite behind us. Decide wisely, and once we are decided, we will all of us abide by whatever conclusion we come to here in this tent tonight."

O'Neill sat and Red Hugh O'Donnell rose to speak. In his right hand he held the *Cathach*. This was a one thousand year old manuscript, a vellum Psalter, supposedly handed down to the O'Donnells by Saint Columcille. For centuries it had been carried into battle by the O'Donnells as a talisman for victory. The young northern chieftain was known in person to some in the assembly. His reputation was known to all.

"O'Neill has told you there is much at stake here, and much to lose for all of you and for Ireland. O'Neill is right. You stand to lose all you have fought for in the past eight years of bitter fighting, all that your people, by their suffering, have bought for you, all that you have hoped for, all that you have prayed for, all that your kin have died for. Perhaps none of us truly knows how much we stand to lose here before the walls of Kinsale, and if we do not act now, we will indeed lose all.

"We must fight and we must fight now. We must with boldness follow the course that destiny demands, and we win a country. We are united as never before. We have marched two great armies the length of Ireland to trap our enemy between the Spanish and us. We stand here before the enemy with an assembly of warrior chieftains, who are the pride of our country. Let that same army that showed no mercy when they heard the piteous cries of our women and children now hear the war cries of our avenging army. Give those who came to take our land a grave in our land."

O'Donnell stood silent for long moments. He looked around the assembled men, his eyes seeking those of each chieftain.

"We outnumber our enemy two to one. Our enemy is starving. Ireland's fateful hour has come, and Ireland's destiny demands we act now. Our dead comrades from their graves demand it. If we make the wrong decision now, Ireland and Ireland's future generations will not forgive us. Will we sit and lose this opportunity while England lands another army to our rear at Cork, or Limerick, or Waterford? Will England, with control of the seas, allow the army of the Lord Deputy to slowly starve? Will we waste this fateful moment for a final victory that will unite all of Ireland behind us? If we do, we will be forever shamed before our Spanish allies whom we have so long awaited. We will be forever shamed before our own dead generations. We will be forever shamed before our own as yet unborn generations. Our Spanish allies have held out with four thousand men against Mountjoy's twelve thousand. What manner of men would turn a deaf ear to pleas for help from the very men who have themselves crossed the seas to help us? What manner of men would sit with a superior army and allow that vile breed that ravaged Munster to go unpunished? If you before me are such men, Ireland is already lost."

O'Donnell finished and stood awaiting an answer. The chieftains arose and the roar of acclaim that greeted O'Donnell gave the answer. O'Neill sat in silence.

CHAPTER 37

A new life in Old Quebec

"*Thar isteach Aileen, s'il vous plait*".[1] The old lady pronounced Eileen as Aileen. She sat erect in a throne like chair in a large high-ceilinged room furnished with dark massive furniture. Warm sunlight slanted through the tall windows and mellowed the room with soft yellow light. The lady sitting behind a polished desk turned sideways to hold out both hands to the young girl who entered the room. "How is my Irish, my dear? Not as good as your French but the young mind is more — here she made an encompassing gesture with her hands — adaptable than that of an eighty year old woman. In something less than two years you are speaking French like a Quebecois."

The young girl took the proffered hands. "Merci, Mere superieur."

"Non! Non! Non!" The old lady wagged a long forefinger. "You must learn to speak English. Here in Lower Canada we may speak French but an educated young woman must also speak English. God may one day call you to become an Ursuline Religiouse like us whose mission it is to educate, but whether you become one of us or not all knowledge is useful. Your young friend has taught you some Cree I understand, and you have taught her and us some of your own beautiful old language. She smiled. "We are a multilingual school, are we not, Aileen?"

"Mais Oui, - I mean 'But Yes', Mother Superior."

The nun gazed for some moments at the nine year old girl. "Ah, well, let us now then get down to the matter. I am told that you still are hoarding food. We are sympathetic to the cause of your behaviour, but it is not normal. We will work with you to help. Can you help us in this, Aileen? What together can we do?"

The child's eyes for an instant reflected something like terror before her gaze fell to the floor, and the face that a moment before had been frank and open became pinched with misery. Her hands clenched in a spasm holding her dress on either side.

"We do not accuse you child. You are not stealing. You hoard a portion of your own meals. Sister Therese speaks highly of you. Your character is sterling".

---

[1] "Come in, Aileen, if you please."

She looked with compassion at the child whose shoulders had become hunched with tension.

"Please, please child be at ease. Sr. Therese and I have thought of something that may help. You will assist Marie Tremblay in the kitchen and perhaps preparing meals will help your mind understand that there is no shortage, no necessity to hoard your food. Your mind will come to understand that God — that God is good."

She had been about to say that God provides when it occurred to her that this might not be apparent to a child who had witnessed her family die of starvation and had herself come close to it.

"Me an' you Magrory. We're best friends, always?" Aileen had come to recognize the phrase posed as a question but very much a statement, as a sure prelude to a secret to be shared, but only between best friends.

The friendship had begun two years earlier on Aileen's second day in the Ursuline Convent School in Quebec City. Aileen, on all fours, had retrieved a burlap bag from beneath her bed and was adding half of a stewed carrot to an assortment of food already in the bag. A brown-skinned, brown-eyed, black-haired child who seemed to have materialized from nowhere stood silently watching her. The child waited until the bag was safely stowed back beneath the bed and then took Aileen by the hand and led her over to her own bed and kneeling down beckoned her to look beneath. Squashed between the mattress and the spring was a small doll. It was constructed of pieces of cloth, pieces of animal hide and sewn with sinew. On its feet were mini moccasins. Later, Aileen learned that Millie called this hidden treasure a "Tea Doll". The child continued holding Aileen's hand and looking up into her face spoke some words in a strange language. Aileen did not understand the language but she sensed the wonderment in the other child's voice. Later when she understood Cree she knew that Millie's first words to her new friend had been. "You have green eyes." Mille had no last name, was a pure bred Cree and an orphan. She had an appealing undershot lower jaw which gave her the appearance of being in a perpetual state of wonderment. Her only possession was the doll, which had been with her "always".

Today she placed herself in front of Aileen Magrory stared intently into her face and spoke her secret.

"I have found out who I am. Sister Therese tracked me down for me. Now I know my people. Isn't it great for me, Magrory? Now I too know where I come from." She paused before breathlessly announcing. *"Magrory, I'm a Montagnais Cree". Sister told me that my people live down the river hundreds of*

miles away towards the ocean, in a place called Uashat. That's Cree for big bay. One day when I'm grown up I'll go visit them.

"Hundreds of miles! How did you ever get here Millie? When you go to see your people we'll go together. I'm a good walker too, but the farthest I ever walked was from Ballyshannon to Rathmullan and that was fifty miles.

Millie's "Of course you'll come with me" was so off hand as to infer that anything else was out of the question.

"I didn't walk here Magrory. I've always been here. I don't know how I came to be here and I don't remember much of those times but the nuns told me that the language I spoke was Cree. They said that my father had died and someone took me to the nuns, and here I am."

"Maybe Millie it was a bishop!"

Aileen's conspiratorial tone indicated that now it was her turn to share important information.

"It was a bishop placed me with the nuns. I was what they called "dissolute" and a bishop placed me with the nuns. The man who put me and my sister on the ship in Liverpool said we'd be met at the pier in Quebec but no one was there. I'll bet it was a bishop who placed you too."

Aileen had always felt that being placed by a bishop conferred a level of importance that she now wanted bestowed also on her friend. The non-committal response, "'Spose so, could ha' been." was deflating; so much so that there was a certain annoyance in Aileen"s "Anything 'could ha' been', Millie".

The Ursuline convent and school for girls in old Quebec City had been established in the 1600s. The school was a polyglot of French Canadian society. Daughters of wealthy benefactors of the school, daughters of Indian trappers, of Indian Chiefs, of Montreal merchants, of lumberjacks and sailors, mingled with the few children, who abandoned on the streets of Quebec, were as yet unaware of their luck in finding such a refuge. The girls studied the arts, music, and languages as well as being taught such traditional skills as needlework and embroidery.

The nuns were autocratic most times and kind whenever they could afford to be. They made no distinction between their richest and their poorest charges and the younger children all looked on each other as equals. However, as if in preparation for later life some of the older children had developed the taint of social bigotry.

"Here she comes."

A group of girls commenced their routine of mimicking a war dance, whooping, and ululating with their hands over their mouths. Aileen initially thought their antics amusing and joined in until she saw that Millie did not find it amusing. When she saw tears in her friend's eyes, she approached the group and solemnly asked them to stop as they were hurting her Indian friend's feelings.

She was unprepared for the response of one of the older girls.

"Oh, a little Irish savage tells us we are hurting the feelings of a little Indian savage." They continued their cavorting unaware that their war dance had become a declaration of war.

"O-o-uch! Oh! Oh, you little Irish bitch. I'll wring your neck".

The girl hopped around on one leg holding her shin where Aileen had aimed an accurate kick. A second kick aimed at the other shin struck only a glancing blow. The other two girls were in the process of grappling with the assailant when a whirlwind struck as Millie leaped wildly into the fray. Millie kicked only empty air as she was lifted bodily back by the timely intervention of a large angry nun.

"All of you, Follow me. At once! To Sister Therese". She strode off without a backward glance expecting, and getting, implicit compliance.

Sister Therese was a sergeant-major's sergeant-major. She was a feared disciplinarian, an all seeing eye, a ubiquitous presence, and on occasion a tender nurse to a sick child and a surprisingly consoling presence to a sad one. It was widely known that she would forgive most things except the telling of a deliberate lie.

"Now Celestine D'Iberville you are the oldest. What caused this disgraceful performance?"

"I'm afraid I did, Sister, I ridiculed Millie and called her and the Irish girl savages"

"You others, have you anything to say?"

"I lost my temper and kicked her"

Sister Therese noted the cloud that marred the child's face. Was it fear? She had noticed this before whenever Aileen felt that she was accused of doing something wrong. Millie, despite whatever dire consequences might descend on her head, wanted it noted that she had supported her friend

"I tried to kick her too, but Sister Boniface grabbed me."

Sister Therese choked to suppress a smile as she looked at what was meant to be fierceness on a face that was the essence of innocence. It occurred to her that there was no worry about prevarication here.

"Very well then. The rest of you may leave. I'll consider your punishment later. Celestine D'Iberville remain here."

When they were alone Sister Therese nodded to a chair.

"Please sit. Ma'moiselle D'Iberville, when our young women leave this school we hope that they will take with them as the most important part of their education worthwhile values. Those comments were unworthy of you and I know that when you reflect on it that you too will see them as such. You come from a family of wealth and privilege here in Lower Canada. Those two younger girls do not. They are bereft of any family. I know you as a decent and intelligent young woman and I know that to you I need say no more. Think on this." Sister Therese stood to signify that the conversation was over.

"Please ask Aileen Magrory to see me."

It was more than a buoyant spirit and the resilience of a child that made the Aileen Magrory who entered Sister Therese's office unrecognizable from the grieving waif who almost two years earlier had stood on the deck of a ship anchored off Grosse Ile. The restoration of a sense of again belonging, of having a home and security, these things that had been brutally torn from her, had been to some extent restored. She was now nearing nine years of age and due to a native intelligence and a natural social adaptability she had fitted easily into the life of the convent school. In her daily routine the eyes that looked out from a face of open childlike honesty gave no hint of a scar of the spirit that remained hidden behind them. What had been taken from her once could be taken again. She could again lose her new-found family, her security, her best friend, Millie. As she stood before Sister Therese, the nun again saw the distress which surfaced on the child's face and she made an intuitive and accurate diagnosis.

"Listen carefully to me and believe what I tell you. If we have to chastise our girls it is to guide and direct. It is done to help as a mother or a father would. This is your home here with us and you will always have a home with us. If you wish to spend the remainder of your life here you can. God may call you to join us, or when you graduate from our school you may continue to work in the kitchen. Truthfully, this latter would be a great waste of your talents but I say this so you may know that you can always be a part of our institution – our family."

She rose put both hands on Aileen's shoulders and looked down into her eyes.

"Do you believe me, Aileen Magrory?"

The haunted fear seeped away from the child's face. "I do, Sister."

"Now you must make amends for your actions. I want you and Millie to go to Celestine D'Iberville and apologize for your behaviour. The young can be cruel but I think you will find she has a generous spirit. You may leave now."

As the child turned to leave, the nun smiled at her. "Accept your punishment as a case of Noblesse Oblige."

When Aileen and Millie approached their erstwhile adversary with trepidation but some lack of contriteness, their apology had had a certain strangeness. Aileen spoke first.

"Ma'moiselle D'Iberville. This is a case of noblesse oblige. I apologize for kicking you in the shin."

"What! Do you even know the meaning of that?"

"We do. We looked it up in the library".

Millie who had not as yet fully mastered the nuances of the English language made her apology next. "And I apologize for only trying to."

The niece of Quebec's most eminent citizen and a descendant of Quebec's oldest family stared at the younger girls and then burst into laughter.

"Well, as I've heard my uncle say, 'I'll be damned', and if either of you repeat that to Sister Therese I really will wring your neck. I accept your quaint apology if you'll accept mine."

Aileen did not mention the other girl's familiarity with swear words to Sister Therese and did not get her neck wrung, but she and Millie did acquire a new friend. The twosome, with the addition of the formidable Celestine D'Iberville, became a threesome.

A schooner-rigged craft of about seventy feet called the "Louisiana" was moored alongside the pier at Levis across from Old Quebec City. A large funnel projected through the deck aft and it was this funnel that was causing some discussion among a group of onlookers on the pier. One man spoke with an air of authority on marine matters.

"It can't be the galley because there's the galley stack for'ard."

There had been purposeful activity on deck for some time and then two men disappeared down a hatch. Shortly thereafter there was a belch of steam from the funnel. On shore a horse between the shafts of a buggy reared and the driver of the buggy swore. There was a communal murmur of amazement from the onlookers as water churned astern of the boat which strained against its manila mooring ropes. The man of authority spoke triumphantly. "She's a steam yacht, with one of them new screw propellers."

Pierre D'Iberville was a vigorous and a restless man whose wealth allowed him to indulge his often quixotic interests. His current interest was the steam engine and currently he was stripped to the waist, sweaty and sooty, stoking a boiler in the "steam room" of his yacht.

He frequently delved with enthusiasm into various aspects of the family business. Two days earlier he had appeared at the D'Iberville office buildings in the city and spent eleven hours immersing himself in each minute detail of the construction of a saw mill at the remote settlement of Sept Iles. It was his opinion that the expanding railroads in the United States would result in a demand for Canadian timber, and he had also developed a theory that a pulping mill for the manufacture of paper products might be established there to take advantage of the vast forest resources on the uninhabited north shore of the St. Lawrence. Such interferences were not always welcomed by the professional army of bankers, accountants, and secretaries who ran the family's diverse interests in shipping, banking, brewing and the lumber industry. To their dismay he had recently taken an interest in railways and had been heard to express an interest in a mad-cap scheme involving a railway across North America linking the Atlantic to the Pacific. A week earlier he had attended a function at Bois-de-Coulonge where he had raised the concept with the Governor of the newly formed Province of Canada. He'd found the man surprisingly receptive to the idea but he had had to made his apologies and excuse himself early to attend another function, this one for his niece at the school of the Ursulines.

In the play, Millie was an Indian Princess. She surprised everyone – including her two best friends – by appearing in a beautifully embroidered native Cree buckskin dress. She and Sr. Boniface, who taught needlework and embroidery, had devoted secret hours each day to perfecting the creation. Her tea doll had come out of hiding and was hung from a broad waist-band by a beaded thong. The attire was authentic but the gentle and diffident Millie was more comical than convincing in the role of haughty princess.

At one part in the play the audience was rocked with laughter. Millie had ingenuously deviated from her script and rather than saying "The Shaman had learned that when performing a rain dance, rhythm was very important", recited instead "The Shaman had learned that when performing a rain dance timing was very important". Learning her lines, Millie had enquired of Sr. Boniface as to the meaning of the word "rhythm" and was told that in the context of a dance it was the same as "timing."

Initially bewildered and crestfallen by the laughter she was reassured when the laughter ended in applause, and she reverted to her persona of "haughty princess". Sister Boniface later told her she had been "very creative" in the role.

"Come on you Irish savage. We're about to get going here?"

It was six years since the "Irish savage" had left Ireland and the young girl climbing up a boarding ladder, despite a disarray of auburn hair blowing around her face, did not at all look "savage".

"Hold your horses, Celestine, or your mooring rope or your anchor chain, or something. I can't even see where I'm going here, but I can see that you're in mortal danger. There's a redskin savage standing behind you. They'll creep up on you and all of a sudden there they are, and your hair is lifted".

Millie, wearing her buckskin finery, peered around Celestine D'Iberville's shoulder, gave her endearing upper-toothed smile, and did not look savage either.

Pierre D'Iberville emerged from a hatch donning a rough woollen smock and took his place by the boat's helm. He shouted "cast off" to a man ashore and said to no one in particular: "Alright then, let's see how long it will take us to reach Sept Ile on steam alone."

The "Louisana" churned out an average speed of seven knots assisted by the current moving downriver and close to the south shore of the large Ile d'Orleans. Pierre D'Iberville at intervals surrendered the helm and disappeared down a hatch. He was elated with the performance of his new source of propulsion, and already concocting new applications for the use of this new power source. A steam powered saw mill with an inexhaustible supply of wood to stoke the furnace! Steam powered barges laden with timber plying the St. Lawrence!

They approached a channel between two islands. A line of anchored ships stretched down river from one of the islands, and with shock Aileen recognized Grosse Ile as the island on their right. Six years ago she had had no concept of where the island lay and until now had not realized that their present route would take them so close to the island.

As the boat approached the island she had the feeling of being drawn inexorably into a vortex. The boat passed between the two islands and within a half mile of where her sister lay. A choking sadness filled her, but not sadness alone. Now there was also an overwhelming guilt. She had a new life, new friends. Now when she was hungry there was always food, and even a choice of foods. The barefooted ten year old who six years ago had died of starvation and who had been both sister and mother to her would now never grow older. She herself at thirteen was now the elder sister. She wore stockings and well-fitting shoes, had, as well as a school uniform, another dress, was being educated, and could speak English, French and Cree as well as Irish. She had so many things, even on a boat she had a bed of her own, and her sister on the island didn't have a grave of her own. She lived in a school with many other girls, a school with kitchen, chapel, dormitories, study hall, music room, and many rooms that she had never even seen. It was a world away, indeed, from Legnabrocky's single-room school-house on the Marlbank, with its smell of turf smoke, chalk, and wet clothing, where the four MacRory children had comprised one third of the scholars under Master Leonard's guidance. She lived in a large sophisticated city. With a jolt to her heart she thought of the time that she and her sister had walked the four and a half miles to Blacklion, their nearest village. It had been her first time to Blacklion but Sheila had been to the village once before with their father, who called it by its old name of Largay. Shelia had proudly shown her younger sister the wonderful sights of the village, the grocery shop, the shoe repair shop, the forge and the public house. She had told Aileen with awe that Master Leonard had once said that as many as forty eight people lived in the village. In her short life her sister had known little beyond her own small world. But she had known courage and compassion. Aileen's guilt was such that she felt an urge to cross to the island and there remain with the sister whose unselfishness had probably caused her own death and who did not deserve to lie alone among strangers, so far from her home with its childhood memories. That world, with its deep stamp on childhood memory, could never now come back to either of them. Gone the ceaseless voice of the Aghinrawn, the river's muted cadence as familiar as a mother's whisper; its mountain waters surging down through rocky shale gullies; the ribbon of green bushy banks meandering through the brown heather; the dark storm clouds flanked by stray wispy outriders sweeping down over rock escarpment and upland moor to swell the flood of the river; the fresh, wet wind from the mountain that carried the smell of whins and heather; the rippling breeze through the trembling leaves of the poplars; the lively twittering of the neighborly swallows gliding to their mud nests in the rafters of the barn: the raspy cheep of a corncrake on a summer's evening in an upland meadow; the feel of bare earth on bare feet. Of all who had shared those memories only she alone lived to remember. Only in that one heart, in fading echoes, did the memories live, of a tender touch, of kindly hearts, of loving eyes, of the dear soft voices around a glowing hearth. Do the ghosts of her family, who had lived there with love, return to steal around the now silent house on the Aghinrawn? Do they whisper "Where are Sheila and Eileen?" Is the sudden rustling of leaves that stirs the stillness of the poplar grove, the whisper of ghosts?

  As the island fell astern she experienced again that same desperate need to cling to her sister that she had felt on the night when Sheila died. As the "Sarah" approached the Canadian coast Sheila's health had worsened. She had developed a fever, headache, joint pains and a dark red rash was spreading all over her emaciated body. That last night she and Sheila were sleeping together in their blankets in a corner of the steerage compartment. Eileen dreamed that her sister had stood apart looking down on them both. She awoke from her dream with a sense that a hand had caressed her face. But the hand that lay by her face on the bare wooden bunk was lifeless.

They crossed over to the north shore, the mighty river now about ten miles wide. The prevailing winds were from the south-west which would have been ideal for sailing but Pierre D'Iberville wanted to assess how long it would take to cover the more than three hundred miles from Quebec city to Sept Ile cruising day and night under steam.

As darkness fell, running lights were arranged on the mast heads and look-outs posted.

Aileen lay awake throughout most of the night haunted by a sense of guilt. She slept for a few hours before dawn.

Celestine D'Iberville, as Sr. Therese had predicted, did have a generous nature and her friends were frequently the benefactors of it. In the spirited and accomplished Celestine the two younger girls had found a friend and a staunch ally. It would be many years before Aileen would come to know that Sr. Therese, the rival of any Machiavelli, had taken the opportunity of a kick to the shin to secure for two orphan girls an able protector and patron in the person of her niece. In all their time at the school Celestine D'Iberville never let it be known, even to her two best friends, that Sr. Therese was her aunt and a sister of Pierre D'Iberville. When the opportunity came for a summer cruise down the St. Lawrence, Celestine had demanded of her uncle that Aileen and Millie join her. But Aileen had not known that the island of memories lay in their path.

By the next morning the shoreline was already almost devoid of signs of habitation. Occasionally they passed a makeshift wharf on the river that often accessed a raw-looking clearing in the forest. Eventually there were only endless green forests stretching into the distance as they rounded each point of land. About midday they passed the mouth of a large river flowing in from the north. There were some wooden buildings close to the mouth of the river and an Indian settlement farther upstream on its eastern bank. The St Lawrence widened and the effects of the ocean tides became more apparent. On a flowing tide the passage of the wooded green banks slowed, to speed up hours later as the ebbing tide carried them with increased speed seaward. The boat steamed along the north shore of the gulf. The far south shore which had been progressively falling lower on the horizon disappeared. The air had the tang of salt sea and the boat lifted and rolled on ocean waves.

On the third day the boat approached a group of islands scattered across the opening of a bay. The boat altered course to enter the bay and Aileen standing beside Millie on deck became aware of something agitated in her friend's behaviour. As they progressed farther into the bay Millie became progressively more excited. She was staring ahead, her usual composure markedly altered.

The full extent of the circular bay opened up and Millie ran from one side of the boat to the other. She stopped and grasped Aileen's arm and the girl who would not willingly hurt any living thing was now hurting her friend by the fierceness of her grasp.

"Magrory, I've been here before. I know this place, Sept Ile is Uashat. It's my people's place. I have come back to the big bay of my people and you have come with me, and you promised you would. Oh Magrory, be happy with me".

Aileen had often noticed that when Millie was happy her trusting nature assumed that everyone she knew rejoiced with her. They had been the closest of friends for six years but it was only now that Aileen was beginning to realize what a deep-seated hunger to belong, to be like others, with bonds to the past, had been in her friend's gentle soul, to find again her home and her people. This had been her home but where were her people? Would they, a semi-nomadic people, still be here? Who among them would know her and would she know them? Would the longed-for homecoming to her people be only a sad disappointment?

There was a small pier at the head of the bay and situated on a bank above was a cluster of wooden buildings belonging to the Hudson's Bay Company, who had established a post at Sept Ile fifteen years earlier. There were two canoes alongside the pier, and others upturned on the bank above. They approached the pier and a man walked down the steps and unmoored the two canoes to make room for the large yacht.

"I'm Ian Sinclair, Chief Trader here, and who may ye be? I've seen some of those large steam vessels in the gulf without, but never a yacht sail into the bay without a sail on her masts."

"I'm Pierre D'Iberville." He nodded to the three girls standing by the rail, "my niece and her friends."

"You'll come ashore then, sir?" The tentative note in the man's voice indicated that he was not unfamiliar with the name D'Iberville.

"Thank you."

D'Iberville leaped the eight feet from his deck to the small pier which tilted alarmingly. He reached for and shook the factor's hand. He noticed that the man's face bore the scars of smallpox.

"Imagine a Scotsman chief trader of a Hudson's Bay post! Maybe even an Orkney Island man? You'd be the best man anyway then to answer some questions about this bay."

He looked around the bay and then walked to the end of the pier looking down into the water.

"First, why is this place called Sept Isle when I count only six islands in the bay? What depth water do you have here? How far out till you get a depth of sixty feet? I assume that the two rivers coming into the bay are year-round?"

"Aye, I can answer all'a that. There are indeed seven islands out there, but come'n in from th'east ye could be deceived inte thinking there were less. An, aye, I'd be an Orkney man. It 'id be fifteen years ago now that I left Stromness. But would ye nae come up to the office sir, and have a wee dram while we talk. I'd be glad'a the company."

"That I will. After cruising for three days and three nights it's a pleasure to be greeted by a hospitable Scot. You girls come ashore and stretch your legs whenever you're ready". He looked at the two canoes. "Or would it be alright if they used one of the canoes to explore the bay while we talk over that wee drahm? It's boring for young ones to be confined on a small craft for three days, and even more boring to have to sit politely listening to adults talk.

Sinclair, with a glance at the seventy-foot yacht described as "a small craft" nodded ascent. Walking up the pier Pierre asked a question that had been in his mind since first seeing the trading post.

Where is everyone Sinclair, the Indians, your helpers, the traders? The post is deserted. Wouldn't this be a busy time of year for you? Are you all alone here?

"We have a calamity on our hands; an outbreak of smallpox among the Indians, another one that is, the last one was only ten years ago. As ye know they have nae immunity to many of these diseases that we have brought among them. The death count in the last one was one in every three"

"Have any medical authorities been notified?

"We are a long way from any medical help. The nearest is Quebec City up river, which as ye know is over three hundred miles away. We have contacted a ship head'n up river. In emergencies a canoe will be paddled out beyond the islands in the hope of getting the attention of any ship headed up river tae Quebec. It was after I established the post here some years ago that the prior outbreak occurred. Most likely it was our come'n here that caused it. In a howling north easterly a chief of the Montagnais took a canoe out inte the gulf there in the hope of attracting a passing ship. All of his family had contacted smallpox, except for his three year old bairn that he took with him, feeling that to get her away was her only hope. He was successful, for help did come but I have heard that he himself, and presumably the wee bairn, died on the ship head'n up tae Quebec".

"I have some emergency supplies on my boat. Perhaps I can do something to help. Where is the Montagnais village?"

"The disease is quite contagious,"

"Take me there." The "wee drahm" was forgotten.

"The Montagnais' summer camp is on the west side of the bay two miles away. In the winter they move inland. There's a pathway through the woods to it, or we can take a canoe."

The smell of wood smoke warned of their approach to the Montagnais village. Dome-shaped wigwams of varying sizes covered with birch bark were scattered on both sides of a stream that flowed through a clearing in the forest. Wisps of blue smoke from the wigwams rose into the trees. The stream was forded in a few places by large flat stones. The unnatural stillness of the camp was broken only by the chattering of a squirrel and the flute-like notes of chickadees looping their swift undulating flight through the trees. Generations of mocassined feet had pounded the ground in the encampment smooth and bare, but now there was only the stillness of death in the clearing. No children played, no dogs barked, no voices spoke, a silent unpeopled village, except for a black robed priest who stooped to enter a wigwam on the far side of the stream.

There were a few hide-covered tepees interspersed among the birch bark wigwams, and from one of these a woman emerged. She was tall for an Indian, with high cheek bones and clad in a dress of embroidered tanned deer hide. She appeared to be somewhere in her mid thirties. She stood in front of the tepee and waved her arms warning them away. She spoke Cree which Ian Sinclair interpreted.

"She says for the stranger to go back. I am immune, as is she, having survived the last epidemic. I come here daily to do what I can." Pierre noticed that the woman's face, too, was pitted with the marks of prior smallpox.

"Most of the village has moved to their main summer camp on the Sainte Marguerite River a few miles west of here, but daily new cases arrive from there. It was thought best to isolate the infected here. As a result of the prior outbreak some are immune and these remain here together with this woman and the priest to care for the stricken."

Pierre continued to approach and the woman came forward in some agitation again waving him away. Suddenly she ceased waving and stood staring as if in a trance. The woman's whole body trembled as if she were about to have a seizure. She uttered the word "Mati" and her knees seemed to give way and she sat on the ground. Pierre heard footsteps behind him and turned to see his niece and her two friends who had crossed the bay in a canoe.

The woman sitting on the ground staring at Millie, first at her face and then at the doll dangling from her waist whispered: "Who are you?"

Millie, puzzled, replied simply," I'm Millie."

"You're Mati, my daughter." The words were spoken in an amazed whisper.

"Clothing, blankets, food, any medicines you have available. I will reimburse the company. When do you expect medical help from Quebec?"

"It may be as long as a week. Even then there is little can be done, for these epidemics seem to run their course. These natives have no immunity to smallpox. All we can really do is nurse the sick and comfort the dying in whatever way we can. The disease incubates for about ten days and then appears as a rash. Some die, some survive. You yourself are susceptible."

"I have no fear of contacting the disease", D'Iberville spoke as if that in itself conferred immunity.

"But my niece and her friends must not go near the village. Thank you for your kindness is accommodating them here at the post. The Cree girl especially must not go near the village while the epidemic lasts. Her mother could visit her here at the post. There's an amazing story for you, Sinclair. A dying mother sends her child away with its father as its only hope of survival. The mother lives and the father dies. Years later the child is reunited with her mother."

"Aye, a happy ending if you don't take into account all the others who died."

Each morning, D'Iberville and the Hudson Bay factor paddled over to the village and together with a Jesuit priest and others of the Cree did what they could for the helpless community. Some of the Indians came each morning from the Sainte Margarite River camp and brought with them white willow bark from which they prepared a potion effective for pain relief. They also applied a poultice made from juniper bark to the smallpox lesions. They prepared food over a fire in the clearing. Millie's mother, Wawaseta, padded among the wigwams carrying bowls of gruel. Each morning she washed the soiled clothing and bedding that each evening had been piled by the stream. She then hung them on a line to dry and to air. The disease played dice with a callous hand. Husbands, wives and children, mothers and daughters, fathers and sons – some crossed over the precipice some clawed back and lived. The shadow of death had again returned to hover over the people pitilessly claiming its one in three. A daily sight was D'Iberville and the priest stooped as they carried a shrouded body from a wigwam. Others spent part of each day constructing wooden coffins. This was done out of hearing of the village. Each day mounds of earth appeared on the hillside beside newly dug graves. Each evening a slow procession ascended the path. The fresh-hewn boxes were carried by any family members who were able to make the sad pilgrimage and others strung out behind. The black figure of the Jesuit trudged at the end of the silent procession. A fresh crop of white crosses sprouted on the hill. Many of the plain wooden boxes carried to the hillside cemetery were small and light.

The only interlude from this routine of sorrow was when each evening Millie's mother, Wawaseta, walked the forest path to the post where Millie stood waiting — every evening another joyous reunion for mother and daughter. Questions bubbled forth. Answers and other questions tumbled back. The physical resemblance between mother and daughter was unmistakable. Like a gust of wind that rushes through the tree tops and then suddenly dies to a whisper, each had the same mannerism of changing from a torrent of animated speech to lapsing back into thoughtful stillness. Their smiles, like a summer sun breaking through the forest, brightened with warmth the habitual composure of their faces. Sometimes they sat merely looking at each other, the mother the gentleness of a deer, the daughter the innocence of a fawn, children of the forest in their interlude of happiness.

As a result of their education at the school of the Ursulines the other two girls were somewhat conversant with Cree. Wawaseta told them of the epidemic of ten years ago which had claimed Millie's sister and come close to claiming her own life. She told of putting the tea doll in Millie's hand as she had sent the child away with her father. She told of the tea doll tradition The Montagnais were a semi-nomadic people and all their belongings travelled with them. Everyone, even the older children, carried their share. A child's doll stuffed with tea leaves would thus become both a plaything for the child and a useful utensil. Each tea doll was distinctive and unique. The doll still served its purpose in the twice yearly trek between the interior winter village and the summer camp on the Gulf.

"The tea doll you took with you, Mati, had belonged to your sister who now lies beneath a white cross on the hill. Your father found a mountain ash in the forest and planted it by her grave."

A week after D'Iberville's arrival a boat from Quebec sailed into Uashat with a doctor and nurse, but by then the epidemic was waning.

A small figure crept stealthily through the village casting a dim moonlit shadow. A woman pushed aside the flap of a wigwam and leaned out retching and the furtive figure ducked under a heap of blankets by the stream. The intruder lay quietly beneath the blankets until again all was quiet and then re-emerged to ascend a well trodden path beyond the village. Soon afterwards the silent shadow returned and passed noiselessly through the village to a canoe on the beach.

Ten days after the arrival of medical help D'Iberville sailed back upriver towards Quebec. Millie remained behind with her people. When the rash appeared no one doubted its ominous significance. Her mother had taken her back to the village and nursed her there, but after four days the doctor from Quebec had pronounced, "Hemorrhagic smallpox". When she was carried to a far corner of the cemetery to be buried alongside her sister beneath a mountain ash they found Millie's tea doll hanging from the faded cross on her sister's grave. The blistered face with swollen lips had been difficult to recognize as the eager and guileless face of her friend.

"Don't be sad for me, Magrory, but remember me, for I'll remember you. Tell Sister Therese that I found my people. She'll be so happy. Remember when I played the part of the Chief's daughter in our play and she told me I played the part so well. She said I was a 'natural' Won't they all be so happy for me, Magrory, to know that I really was the daughter of a chief!"

Mati's last words to her friend had not been phrased as a question: "Me an' you Magrory, we're friends for ever."

CHAPTER 38

Kinsale and the Final Battle

Thunder growled and lightning fitfully lit the sky as the Irish Army formed up in the pre-dawn hours of Christmas Eve. The thunder that crashed overhead in a lowering sky sounded a rolling drumbeat to the coming battle. Irish foot-soldiers glanced around in superstitious awe as flashes of lightning danced in the sky. The chieftains of the Gael had come together, united, to defend the land of the Gael. Not since King Brian had united Ireland against the Norse had such an army of Ireland assembled – O'Neills, O'Donnells, O'Reillys, O'Connors, O'Briens, O'Byrnes, O'Rourkes, MacSweeneys, O'Sullivans, MacCarthys, Maguires – Irish names that echoed Ireland's honour back to the whispered dawn of Ireland's memory. Ireland united, her ancient nobility gathered in from her far fields and forests, her hills and plains, to stand at last side by side in a common cause.

MacRory stood with the other captains, eight hundred gallowglass forming a dark, silent mass of men in the gloom behind him. The final battle of the bitter war was at hand. In the pre-dawn darkness of that December morning in 1601, O'Neill and O'Donnell led the army of the Gael to its rendezvous with fate.

The pale winter sun of a grey dawn shone out over the rain-sodden corpses of Ireland's Army. In one brief hour the battle was lost; the battle was won. In one brief hour a country was lost, a country was won. Ireland's hopes lay strewn with Ireland's dead on the field of Kinsale. Ireland's fateful moment had come – and gone. The Celtic impetuosity of a Celtic hero had extinguished forever the light of Celtic Ireland. The grim dawn of that winter day presaged three cruel centuries of long dark night for Ireland.

Red Hugh O'Donnell gazed back to the land astern. The sun shone a farewell light on the hills of Kerry. Long after the sun disappeared beneath the western horizon and the rounded hills of Ireland became one with the darkness, the chieftain's face remained turned toward the land behind. His thoughts remained with the land that had now sunk in darkness. The ship bore him on toward Spain.

Long centuries before Christ had walked the earth, before Roman legions had marched to conquest, before Alexander had turned eastward to conquer Persia, a prince from the land now know as Spain had sailed to conquer the land that would be known as Ireland. It was from this distant forbear that O'Donnell and the ruling families of Ireland claimed descent. It was from this distant forebear that the gallowglass, standing beside O'Donnell, could also claim descent – descent from the pagan Celtic horde that had stormed the infant Rome, descent from the once numerous Celtic people, who had been driven to the far western fringes of Europe, descent from those Celts who had settled on a small island and lived there their of lives of freedom and turbulent passion for another fifteen hundred years after Caesar subjugated their race at Alesia, descent from the pagan Irish King Niall who, four hundred years after his ancestors sacked Rome, had attacked Rome's outposts in Britain and watched Londinium[1] burn, the same king of whom the Roman poet Claudian wrote: "When Scots came thundering from the Irish shores, and oceans trembled, struck by hostile oars."

In the intervening centuries, the life of an Irish chieftain had in some ways changed little from that time when the Roman Caesar had led the last great leader of the Celts of Gaul in chains to Rome.

What were the thoughts of the man who looked back to the land of his ancient race? Celtic boldness so often his ally, had led him to total defeat. His army lost, his reputation lost, *Tir Conaill* lost, Ireland lost. No, not lost. He, too, would sail from Spain with a conquering army and reclaim his country some day. Defeat he could not, he would not, contemplate. His spirit would not accept it; his mind could not endure it. But his mind also knew that fate could inflict what the mind could not endure.

What were the thoughts of Mountjoy, a looming defeat converted into a total and staggering victory? What titles and rewards might he expect from his grateful country? What pride would glow in his breast when he knelt before his queen and delivered to her a country?

---

[1] Roman name for London.

What were O'Neill's thoughts as he staggered back to the north with the remnants of his defeated army, now indeed no more than a bush-kerne in a country he might have ruled? What would he not have given to go back in time to two weeks earlier, when, leading an army of Ireland, he had tightened the noose on Mountjoy!

Too much of the pragmatist to dwell for long on what might have been, O'Neill must yet have bitterly thought of his own failure. Why had he allowed impetuosity to rule when caution had always served him well? He must have known that only he alone had possessed the patience and foresight to defeat Mountjoy. He must now know that his alone was the failure.

Had he felt a first glow of victory as Richard Tyrell in the Irish vanguard repulsed the initial English cavalry charge? Did he feel unease as cannon and musket fire winnowed the closely packed Irish ranks? When he saw the gradual falling back of his men before the repeated English onslaughts had a sickening doubt entered? Did he see again the slowly dwindling ranks of the brave gallowglass as they fought and died, fighting their last battle on Irish soil? Did he see again Red Hugh, reddened sword aloft, intent on leaving his own body among the dead of Kinsale, gallop madly into the advancing enemy army to rally his own retreating army? Did he hear again the war cry of the O'Donnells, defiant in defeat, float over the field of Kinsale? Did he hear again the triumphant shouts of the victors and the defeated groans of the dying as the Irish fled the field, pursued north for miles before the English finally tired of the hacking slaughter? What were his thoughts as he looked back at the trail of dead, the strewn remnants of Ireland's proud army pointing a bloody accusing finger back toward Kinsale?

The two men on the ship's deck still carried the raw wounds of the battle. Red Hugh gently touched the gallowglass's bandaged and bloody right arm, which hung uselessly by his side. "I fear, Turlough that you paid dearly for saving my life. Don't think me ungrateful, dear comrade, but if I cannot get further help from Spain, I would have preferred to lie among the dead at Kinsale. Happy the soul of Maguire that he did not live to see this day."

The enormity of the defeat still dazed both men, but only the backward gaze of history would reveal the true enormity of Ireland's defeat at Kinsale.

Red Hugh, now gazing ahead into the dark sea, seemed also to be gazing into the future as he spoke to his friend.

"We have led our country to defeat. Our sun has set. Another race will walk on that earth that holds our uncountable dead generations. But the centuries will pass; their dust, too, will become Irish earth, and like the Dane and the Norman, the new race will mingle with the old and in time their children, too, will call Ireland their homeland. The soul of our country will live on. The soul does not die. The soul of a country is the soul of its people. Our music, our songs, our language, our legends, are as much Ireland as are the mountains and lakes, the forests, and fields of that loved land of our fathers. Another race will possess the land of our people, but the soul of our land will live in the memory of our people. Memories are not defeated in battle. Memories do not so easily die. True death occurs only when there is no one left to remember. Twenty years ago when we stood as boys on the deck of another ship, our destinies became entwined, and yours entwined with that of Ireland. Brave comrade, dearest friend, you were returning home. It's your country, too. Its memories are yours. Guard them."

EPILOGUE

Five-year-old Rory MacRory sat among a profusion of daisies on a grassy mound on the river bank by a small white wooden cross. He pointed at, and counted aloud, each bubble as it floated by on the water below. On reaching six he started again. Seven-year-old Kathleen MacRory ran down the path and grasped the hand of her brother. Looking back over her shoulder, she hastened back to the safety of the house, shrilling "Daddy! Daddy!" and pulling the younger child behind her. Three horsemen splashed across the Claddagh River and followed her up the path. One of them dismounted and addressed Turlough MacRory, who had come forward around the side of the house with a slight limp and carrying a pitch fork in his left hand.

"Do you speak English?"

"I speak English."

"Can you read English?"

"Yes."

"You live here with your two children and have title here in the Barony of Clanawley to fifty hectares?"

"I do."

"I am the agent of Sir James Balfour, the English undertaker for this part of Fermanagh. You have held your land from Sir Conor Maguire, but this area has been re-assigned to Sir James Balfour. Following the flight of Tyrone, all of Fermanagh has been escheated to the crown and reassigned at His Majesty's pleasure. No Irish are allowed to be tenants of an English undertaker, but as a Scot, you are allowed to hold title to land in Ireland under an English undertaker."

The agent seemed to see no incongruity in his words. He held out a rolled sheet of parchment. MacRory laid the pitchfork against the house and took the rolled sheet in his left hand.

"That is the official deed to your land signed by Sir James' secretary. The cess tax is payable yearly to Sir James Balfour. Your title to the land is now held under English law. Irish Brehon Law no longer exists." The agent remounted and all three men rode off.

Irish Brehon law no longer existed! Since that brief battle at Kinsale, many things Irish had passed out of existence to live only in memory; fond memory for what was, bitter memory for what would be no more, tortured memory for what might have been.

A conquered and crippled country faced an uncertain future, as did he and his children. His friends were no longer men of power, his enemies were. Would O'Donnell's words be prophetic? Would Kathleen and Turlough and their generations of children grow up to be made to know what it was to be a conquered people?

In the nine years of war leading up to Kinsale, thirty thousand Irish, out of a population of slightly over a million, had died, mostly in Ulster and most from famine. But England, too, paid a price in bringing the Ulster Gaelic chieftains to their knees. The cost to England was over a million pounds.

After Kinsale O'Neill fought on in Ulster for another two years in the twilight of Gaelic Ireland. That light dimmed with O'Donnell's death in Spain; the light faded with O'Neill's surrender in 1603; the light died with the Flight of the Earls.

In the dying light of an autumn day in the year 1607 silent ghosts looked down from the Grianan of Aileach as Hugh O'Neill, Earl of Tyrone, Rory O'Donnell, Earl of Tyrconnell, and many other Ulster chieftains boarded a ship at Rathmullan and fled Ireland.

The annalist, who wrote of the departure of these princes of the north, did not know he also described the passing of Gaelic Ireland:

> That was a distinguished company for one ship. For true it is that the sea has not borne, nor the wind wafted from Ireland in modern times a party more eminent, illustrious and noble than they were, in point of genealogy, or more distinguished for deeds of renown, feats of arms, and valorous achievements. Woe to the heart that meditated woe to the mind that planned, woe to the counsel that determined on that project.

The lands of these chieftains, four million acres of Ulster, were settled with English and lowland Scottish planters in what was known as the "Plantation of Ulster." Gaelic Ireland faded into darkness and memory.

The light of the Gael, that light first kindled in the far dim mists of time, flickered on in the Western Isles and Scotland's Highlands for close to another hundred and fifty years before being extinguished there, too, at Culloden.[1]

> *Give me again all that was then, give me the sun that shone.*
> *Give me the eyes, give me the soul, give me the one that's gone.*
> *Billows and breeze, islands and seas, mountains of rain and sun.*
> *All that was good, all that was fair. All that was me is gone.*

---

[1] Battle that saw the defeat of the Highland Scots.

Clachan Publishing Travel books

Antiquarian republications
    Travels In Ireland - *J.G. Kohl* - This is a very readable account by a German visitor of his tour around Ireland immediately before the Great Famine. (1845).
    J.G.Kohl's account has been sub-divided for the convenience of local and family historians.
- **Travels in Ireland – Part 1,** takes us through Edgeworthtown, The Shannon, Limerick, Edenvale, Kilrush and Father Mathew.
- **Travels in Ireland – Part 2,** his journey continues through Tarbet, Tralee, Killarney, Bantry, Cork, Kilkenny and Waterford.
- **Travels in Ireland – Part 3,** this section deals with Wexford, Enniscorthy, Avoca, Glendalough and Dublin.
- **Travels In Ireland - Part 4 –** he goes north for the last part of his journey through Dundalk, Newry, Belfast, The Antrim Coast, Rathlin, The Giant's Causeway.

    A Journey throughout Ireland, During the Spring, Summer and Autumn of 1834 - *Henry D. Inglis* - Inglis travels Ireland attempting to answer the question, 'is Ireland and improving country?' using discussion with landlords, manufacturers and tenants plus his own insightful observations.
    Henry D. Inglis' account has also been sub-divided for the convenience of local and family historians.
- A Journey throughout Ireland, During the Spring, Summer and Autumn of 1834, Part 1 takes us from Dublin. Through Wexford, Waterford and Cork.
- **A Journey throughout Ireland, During the Spring, Summer and Autumn of 1834, Part 2** is an account of Kerry, Clare, Limerick and the Shannon and concludes in Athlone.

    Highways and Byways in Donegal and Antrim - *Stephen Gwynn* - Take this book with you as you travel around Donegal and the Glens of Antrim and you will find that you journey not only over land, but also over time, (1901).
    Stephen Gwynn's account has also been sub-divided for the convenience of local and family historians.
- Highways and Byways in Donegal and Antrim Part One: Donegal
- Highways and Byways in Donegal and Antrim Part: Two - Derry & Co. Antrim.
-
- **Ulster and the City of Belfast** - *Richard Hayward* - This is Hayward's most significant piece of travel writing and is republished in response to the considerable interest in Hayward on the 50th anniversary of his death. This quality paperback edition has a new foreword by Paul Clements and includes all Raymond Piper's original illustrations

Recent travel books

Valhalla and the Fjörd: A Spiritual Motorcycle Journey through the History of Strangford Lough - *Peter Moore* - As former Director of archaeological excavations, the author has researched the sites and monuments with professional care, going beyond archaeology, the spirituality and aura the sites exude.

Aghaidh Achadh Mór, The Face of Aghamore – edited by Joe Byrne. This is a reproduction of a title originally published in 1991 and is of enduring interest to local historians and to those with ancestral roots in East Mayo. It covers such topics as Stone Age archaeology, family history, local hedge schools, O'Carolan's connection with the parish, the Civil War and townland surveys.

Ballads and Songs

Songs of the Glens of Antrim by Moiré O'Neill
These Songs of the Glens of Antrim were written by a Glenswoman in the dialect of the Glens, and chiefly for the pleasure of other Glens-people.

Away with Words - by Michael Sands
A book of poems of family, home, place and music in North Antrim.
"What a joy it has been to have discovered this marvellous collection. It represents a bright shaft of welcome sunlight in a wearying world. It is full of joy, hope, intellect and a deep understanding of who we are and the unquestioned importance of hearth, home and music." - Mickey MacConnell,- songwriter and journalist

A Moment's Notice by Michael Sands
"This collection, Michael's second, is rooted in his environment: family, society, music, the natural world outside his window. Michael's poetry at times sparkles with wit and clever rhymes, and at others it is earnest in its tenderness and humanity. Underlying the verse is an encompassing love for his world and its people – turn the page, and step inside." - Jason O'Rourke – writer and musician.

Walking on Water by Maire Liberace
This is a collection of poems celebrating Ireland, especially North Antrim. Maire has grown up with a love and regard for its history, its legends, literature and poetry. All have been embedded in the marrow of her bones and this is reflected in a deep love for the country she grew up in.

Onr Man's Poison by Sarah Fox
An extraordinary collection of poems wrought through pain that leads to hope and love by a young woman who has used her experience of illness to find a distinctive voice and wisdom beyond her years.

clachanpublishing.com

Clachan Publishing, Ballycastle, Glens of Antrim.

www.ingramcontent.com/pod-product-compliance
Lightning Source LLC
Chambersburg PA
CBHW050833230426
43667CB00012B/1976